GOVERNMENT AND CHANGE IN LESOTHO, 1800–1966

Government and Change in Lesotho, 1800–1966
A Study of Political Institutions

L. B. B. J. Machobane

MACMILLAN

First published 1990

Published by
THE MACMILLAN PRESS LTD
Houndmills, Basingstoke, Hampshire RG21 2XS
and London
Companies and representatives
throughout the world

British Library Cataloguing in Publication Data
Machobane, L. B. B. J. *1941–*
Government and Change in Lesotho, 1800–1966: A
Study of Political Institutions.
1. Lesotho. Politics, history
I. Title
320.9681′6

ISBN 978-0-333-51570-9   ISBN 978-1-349-20906-4 (eBook)
DOI 10.1007/978-1-349-20906-4

To My Wife
'Mats'epo 'Malillo Evodia Morolong Machobane
for her inspiration, support and sacrifice

Contents

List of Tables

Preface

This book is a revised version of a doctoral thesis that I submitted to the Faculty of Law at the University of Edinburgh, for which the degree was awarded in 1986. Whilst some chapters have been condensed, the original study has otherwise been extended in scope, and a chapter has been added.

The general purpose of the book has been to study the institutions of government from the year 1800 – about the time the process of state formation became evident – to 1966, when Lesotho, having become a British dependency in 1868, became independent. An effort has been made to depict indigenous institutions: the chieftaincy as an institution of political leadership; the traditional counsellors according to their various functions; the *pitso* (the all-male public assembly; and the *makhotla* (courts or councils) and their functions in the formulation of policy, law-making, and dispute settlement. An attempt has been made, first, to analyse their character and appraise, from a historical viewpoint, their competence in the pre-colonial era; second, to appraise their continuing use and competence during the period from 1868 to 1966, when a Legislative Council began to operate.

By the 1830s, when Lesotho had been consolidated into a state, its founder, *Morena e Moholo* (or King) Moshoeshoe I, effectively adapted the pre-*lifaqane* institutions of government to cement his political achievement. Inspired by his political tutor, Mohlomi, the son of Monyane, he made peace and justice the foundations of his kingdom.

He made use of a hierarchy of chiefs, all of whom had their *makhotla* (courts or councils) and settled his subjects' disputes under their respective territorial jurisdictions according to the laws and customs of the land. These chiefs were under obligation to attend Moshoeshoe's *pitso* and *makhotla*, and to fight in his wars. In turn he held himself accountable to these chiefs for his public actions and policies. He was subject to customary law and custom. He was sensitive to the popular will. And he made the *pitso* the hallmark of freedom of speech.

Lesotho became a British dependency in 1868 amidst confusion from the point of view of the Imperial Government as to the purpose for extending jurisdiction over it. It was not clear as to whether the aim was to colonise or whether it was to protect it. Although the British authorities of Commonwealth Constitutional Law later asserted that it was a crown colony, the High Commissioner Sir Philip Wodehouse, who had originally negotiated the relationship with *Morena e Moholo* Moshoeshoe I, had accepted the kingdom's request that land should not be alienated. That understanding had been interpreted by the Basotho and some colonial administrators to mean that land had not been ceded to the British Crown and hence Lesotho was only a protectorate. In Lesotho that distinction was of political significance. It meant that the indigenous government would continue to *rule* and the colonial administration would take charge of external affairs. The latter was expected to protect and not control.

The confusion over the Territory's constitutional status thus led, haphazardly and without clear consideration of policy, to 'Parallel Rule'. The *Morena e Moholo* and the Resident Commissioner (who was termed Governor's Agent until 1884) governed as virtual equals. It was a relationship of convenience whereby constitutional questions were interpreted by each in a manner that suited the occasion, and often inconsistently.

During the period from 1868 to 1871, when the colonial administration had not yet established itself and even the constitutionality of proclaiming Lesotho a British Territory was being questioned by the British Crown Law Officers, the indigenous government governed as though the kingdom was still independent. Institutions of government worked without marked deterioration from the way they worked in the past.

The period during which Lesotho was under the Cape of Good Hope rule, 1871 to 1884 (the so-called 'Government by Proxy') was significant in two respects. First the Cape of Good Hope bore down hard on the indigenous government. Bent on destroying the chieftaincy, it sought to disrupt Sesotho customary law and custom, with some assistance from the Paris Evangelical Missionary Society. Colonial officers turned the all-male public assembly, the *pitso*, into a forum for declaring unpopular regulations and decisions. That led to a deterioration of the *pitso* as an institution for policy formulation and the expression of popular opinion. Then, too, put under allowances, in lieu of collecting taxes for the colonial administration, the chieftaincy generally turned its sense of accountability upwards, from their subjects to the colonial officers. The agrarian boom of the 1870s, and its corollary factor, migrant labour into the white settler colonies of the South, generally eroded communal bonds: to a significant degree, fathers lost grip over their sons, husbands over wives, and chiefs over commoners. Social institutions loosened and began to break down.

Second, Cape rule led to a rebellion, or more popularly-speaking, the Gun War. In the main it seemed that the Basotho questioned the entire constitutional arrangement between their Territory and the Cape of Good Hope Colony. The question of whether Lesotho was a crown colony or a protectorate was brought to the surface. The Imperial Government, following consultations with chiefs, resumed its rule through the South African High Commission; but that war also unleashed the heretofore masked factionalism within the chieftaincy.

In 1903 a colonial institution called the 'Basutoland National Council' was established. From the point of view of the Imperial Government and the colonial administration, the National Council was established initially to take the place of the Basotho *pitso*. It was hoped that it would facilitate the formulation of policy pertaining to the internal affairs of the Territory: to effect a two-way communication between the colonial staff and the people and generally to provide a forum where the Resident Commissioner and the *Morena e Moholo* and his chiefs could exchange views and share the responsibility for decision-making. Although initially there was no stated aim to use the National Council as a prototype of a Legislative Council, its conduct betrayed that aim. By the early 1920s, at least, the South African High Commission had begun to concede, however cautiously, that it saw the Council as a midwife of new ideas and a school for preparing the Basotho for self-government along parliamentary lines.

Generally speaking, the colonial administration failed to attain the major professed objectives regarding the functions of the National Council, which never took the place of the *pitso*, as envisaged. The one major characteristic of a *pitso*, namely, the chieftaincy's responsiveness and accountability to the commoners, was virtually non-existent in the National Council. Chiefs attended the National Council mainly to further their own interests and to pander to the interests of the colonial administration. The interests of the nation at large concerned them mostly when there was a crisis, and where, therefore, the position of the chieftaincy was under threat.

As the National Council began, at its First Session in 1903, to draft or re-state customary law, and periodically thereafter to amend it and to add to it, its constitutional status became anomalous. There was no doubt in the minds of the members of the Council that in drafting, amending and adding to those 'Laws' they were legislating; while the colonial administration was split in its opinion: a Resident Commissioner and a Legal Adviser saying in one instance that the Council had merely declared customary law, another Resident Commissioner and another Legal Adviser saying at another instance that it had merely legislated 'informally'. The constitutional status of the National Council was thus paradoxical to its members, while the 'Laws' issuing from it were a legal travesty, which culminated in a High Court judgement four decades later that declared that they had no force of law.

The Parallel Rule of the colonial administration and the chiefs, which was arrived at accidentally and was implemented haphazardly, militated against the consideration of an early increased involvement of the *bahlalefi* (the educated), who as a rule were commoners, in the National Council. Yet a need for that development had become evident by 1917, and urgent by 1922. Consequently the introduction of the elective principle, which was more of an issue to the *bahlalefi* than to the chiefs, had to be postponed until the 1940s, when it was accepted in the form of an indirect election. Parallel Rule did not produce an efficient and responsible chieftaincy. The chieftaincy continued to degenerate in qualities of leadership. The system led neither to an improvement nor a rebuilding, as the case might be, of indigenous institutions. The effort to redress the degeneration of the indigenous leadership through reforms in 1938 came too late. The Reforms were applied precipitately, thus producing a shock effect among the chieftaincy which led to a bout of ritual murders.

Just as crucial as the policy of Parallel Rule in retarding constitutional developments in Lesotho was the question that the Territory be incorporated into the Union of South Africa. From the beginning, when the National Council was established in 1903, the Imperial Government felt the need to reconcile any constitutional developments that might be contemplated for Lesotho with the sensitivities of the white British settler colonies of South Africa. Beginning in 1908, when the idea of establishing a union of those colonies began to take a concrete form, the Imperial Government had the greatest difficulty in conceptualising the contrary of incorporating the High Commission Territories (Lesotho, Botswana and Swaziland) into such a Union. The political folly of the Boer settlers in denying the African franchise, which heralded the policy of racial segregation, so frightened the Basotho as to cause them to protest vehemently against incorporation; but the net effect of their protests was only to defer discussions on the question, and not to persuade the British Government to abandon it altogether. From 1910 up until 1960, when a Legislative Council sat in Lesotho for the first time, the colonial administration felt the need to retard any constitutional progress in the Territory which might be viewed by the Union of South Africa as pre-empting the question.

When, in any event, the colonial administration considered it convenient to concede to internal pressures for constitutional advance, its conceived view of a type of government that was desirable for the future was always clear; it was a parliamentary type of government. In such instances its wishes were invariably explicit, in confidential memoranda at least, that constitutional monarchy would be preferred to executive monarchy.

Initiatives for constitutional development in the Territory were undertaken initially by the Basutoland Progressive Association, which began from 1908 onward to fight for increased commoner representation in the National Council. The *Lekhotla la Bafo*, a grass-roots commoners' movement, began from the date of its founding in 1919 to share this aim, but its primary concern was that a separate 'Council of Commoners' should be formed. That approach failed utterly.

Both the Progressive Association and the *Lekhotla la Bafo* were critical of the abuses of chiefs; but they differed in that, while the *Lekhotla la Bafo* expected the chieftaincy to reform itself, the Progressive Association began – in 1922 – to urge the colonial administration to take the initiative. The timing for the Reforms of 1938 was decided by the colonial administration, which had simply waited until the chieftancy had lost its momentum of resistance; but the initiative came from the Progressive Association.

The last heave of constitutional advance, which began in the early 1950s, owed a great deal to the founding by Clement Ntsu Mokhehle in 1952 of the Basutoland African Congress (BAC). The aims and objectives of the BAC were forcefully promoted, beginning in 1954 with the political paper *Mohlabani*, an independent paper founded that year and edited by B. M. Khaketla. The BAC called for 'self-government Now!' It was uncompromising on the question of incorporation, which still loomed over the country. Equally, it was uncompromising in its fight against racial discrimination, which had gradually been introduced into the country.

As early as 1907 the members of the Progressive Association were clear that education, not 'birth' ought to be the major qualification for participation in public affairs. By 1917 they were calling for an elective National Council. By 1926 they felt that they were ready for a Legislative Council. As already pointed out, from its founding in 1919 the *Lekhotla la Bafo* fought for the establishment of a Council of Commoners. Generally speaking, politically active commoners felt that chiefs were 'an iron bar' to progress. And while willing to retain them out of a sense of history, they were in favour of constitutional monarchy – British style.

While on the whole chiefs dreaded the prospect of a parliamentary form of government, whereby they might ultimately be dominated by commoners, certain leading individuals among them wanted to be seen as being in its favour. Those, in the main, were the chiefs who served in the various committees of the National Council – the Standing Committee, the Constitutional Reforms Committee (1958), the Constitutional Discussions Delegation (London, 1959), the Constitutional Commission (1962), and so on. But whether these chiefs were really committed to a parliamentary type of government or not is doubtful.

From 1960, when the Legislative Council was established, to 1966, when Lesotho was granted Independence, an attempt was made to cram a number of major stages of constitutional development, that needed at least a generation to mature, into a political culture. By 4 August 1966, when the country became independent, it was evident that the Independence Constitution, so hurriedly put together, and which ignored political sensitivities, had little or no basis for success.

The book is aimed particularly at students of Constitutional Law and History, Politics and Government, and generally at readers interested in studies of political institutions and in the history of Lesotho. It is, moreover, the most comprehensive scholarly work on the history of the Lesotho ever written.

L. B. B. J. Machobane
Maseru, Lesotho

Acknowledgements

Many people have given their support, encouragement, and inspiration to this academic endeavour. I would have liked to thank each one of them individually, were it practical to do so. The following, however, were singularly helpful, and deserve a mention.

During the three years that I spent at the University of Edinburgh, where the basic work for the study was undertaken, I received help from several members of the Faculty of Law, the Centre of African Studies, and the Department of History; but the most helpful of these, on whom I depended for guidance, where Mr C. M. G. Himsworth, in Constitutional and Administrative Law, and Professor S. A. Shepperson, in the Department of History. When the basic work was completed, I benefited immensely from Professor Christopher Fyfe of the Centre of African Studies, and from Professor James Read of the School of Oriental and African Studies, who also supported my confidence in the view that the book would make a valuable contribution to scholarship.

I am proud to be able to say that my father, James Jacob Machobane, a historical novelist, early in life provided me with the necessary foundation for history and studies of social institutions. I am fortunate to have had the inspiration dedication and sacrifices of 'Mats'epo 'Malillo Evodia Morolong Machobane, my wife, who read through the first chapters of the book, and lent me the benefit of her knowledge of linguistics where relevant.

It was my good fortune, that during my stay at Edinburgh, I established contact with Mr Gordon Matthews Hector, Lesotho's last British Government Secretary, who made his papers available to me, filled in on the missing gaps with his infallible memory; he also arranged for me to meet the last Resident Commissioner, Sir Alexander Giles, and other former colonial officials to Lesotho.

Mrs Lorna Paterson, secretary, in the Faculty of Law at the University of Edinburgh, Mrs Ntsoaki Motemekoane, my secretary in the Ministry of Education, and the various members of staff in the typing pool of the Lesotho Distance Teaching Centre of the Ministry of Education all worked assiduously to see the book through its six phases of typing. And my brother-in-law, Mr Bangani Tsotsi, spent many a sleepless night editing the final draft and supervising its typing.

All members of my family, especially my mother, 'Malehlohonolo 'Mamotsoahae Rahaba Kou Machobane, gave me their moral support. My son, Ts'epo Mrayisa Machobane, was exceedingly understanding and tolerant of my excuses for not being with him when he needed me. And my daughters, Noliwe Busisiwe Machobane and Nandi Themba Machobane also provided their moral support and love.

I am grateful to the Faculty of Law at the University of Edinburgh for financing my air travel to Lesotho for further work in the summer of 1985, and to my friends Dr Michael Sefali and Dr N. S. Ndebele and their families, for offering me their hospitality during that hectic summer.

The study was made possible by the Commonwealth Scholarship Commission in the United Kingdom, to which I hold myself immensely in debt. Finally I wish to express my gratitude to the National University of Lesotho, who granted me three years' study leave to complete the basic work.

Notes on the Use of Terms

Lesotho, Basotho, Sesotho
When the first members of the Paris Evangelical Missionary Society arrived in the country of this study in 1833, as the first Europeans ever to settle therein, they found that the country was already called 'Lesotho', the inhabitants called themselves the 'Basotho', and they referred to their language as 'Sesotho'. As the Basotho had then not yet learned how 'to make the paper speak' (that is, to read and write), and the French Missionaries were the first to initiate them into that mystery, the nineteenth century orthography of these three terms varied. The terms appear in contemporary sources variously as 'Lesuto', 'Lesouto'; 'Basuto', 'Basouto'; 'Sesuto', 'Sesouto'. For purposes of this study I have used the modern spelling of the terms, Lesotho, Basotho (sing. Mosotho), Sesotho, except where contemporary spellings are in quotations.

Lesotho and Basutoland
The term 'Lesotho' means 'the land of the Basotho'; but, from the instant that the English-speaking people first established a meaningful relationship with the Basotho, notably in the late 1830s, they named Lesotho 'Basutoland'. In turn the Basotho, obviously presuming that Basutoland was merely the English translation for Lesotho, accepted the use of the anglicised term whenever English was employed, while invariably retaining the proper term, Lesotho, in spoken as well as written Sesotho. Upon Lesotho becoming a British dependency in 1868, this linguistic problem was formalised. Lesotho came to be known to the outside world as Basutoland, while to its inhabitants it remained as Lesotho, the former being adopted for the convenience of the English-speaking public. Eventually this confusion led to the acceptance among some scholars that Basutoland was the 'official' name of the country and that in historical writing that is the term that ought to be used, additionally in the interests of historical perspective.

For purposes of this study I have elected to use the term Lesotho. It seems to be historically the more appropriate term to use. The term 'Basutoland' will be used only in quotations, or where it was part of a specific name, for instance, the Basutoland Progressive Association.

King, Morena e Moholo, Paramount Chief, Motlotlehi

Having established in Chapter 1 that Lesotho was a kingdom, I have occasionally in that chapter, as well as in Chapter 2, referred to the Head of State as the King. The preferred title, however, has been that of *Morena e Moholo*, by which the Basotho called their monarchs. The use of the title *Morena e Moholo* has the additional advantage, in reference to the colonial era, of avoiding the terminological confusion which might arise through use of the title 'king', for it distinguishes between the dominant British and the subordinated Basotho monarchs.

I have avoided the use of the title 'Paramount Chief' in this study for the same reason that I have avoided the use of 'Basutoland', except where it is used in quotations. The title 'Paramount Chief' was applied generally to African monarchs, even before the colonial era, not so much because it was linguistically accurate, because it did not seem to English speaking observers proper to refer to them as kings. In short, it was an expression of cultural arrogance. While it may be of academic value to examine the term more closely on linguistic grounds, I have found it profitable for the time being to avoid using it.

The last King of Lesotho was installed in 1960 under the new title of *Motlotlehi*. The constitutional value of this new title is quite vague. The purpose seems to have been to get away from the use of *Morena e Moholo*, which had depreciated in political connotation, in preparation for styling the incumbent as King at Independence. The English title was His Highness.

Sesotho customary law; Basotho customary law

An examination of archival materials reveals the fact that the Basotho referred to their laws as the 'Basotho customary law' rather than as 'Sesotho customary law'. Legal scholars on Lesotho, however, use the latter expression. Why this is so is not clear; but, as this is not a problem that I have had the time to study, and as my study is not otherwise on customary law, I hesitate to argue the point and settle for the use of the expression 'Sesotho customary law' as currently accepted.

Councillor and Counsellor

The term preferred by most scholars to refer to the courtiers of African rulers, at least in the Southern African context, is 'councillors'. This reference acknowledges the fact that these courtiers belong to the ruler's councils, or the councils of his subordinates. While accepting fully the propriety of using the term, in this study

I have tended to use the term 'counsellors', in order generally to distinguish the 'councillors' of the indigenous institutions from the councillors of the Basutoland National Council. The term 'counsellors' is otherwise not inappropriate, on its own value, in that the various officers in the indigenous institutions who are generally called 'councillors' are invariably also 'counsellors'.

1 Institutions of Government and Control of Power

AMONG THE BASOTHO OF THE MOHOKARE VALLEY (c. 1750–1870)

The process of state formation among the Basotho of the Mohokare Valley (the Caledon) in Southern Africa was a slow, unpredictable and, in the end, a jolting experience. Up through the seventeenth century the south and south-westerly migrations of the Basotho and other southern 'Bantu' (Abantu) language communities from the north of the River Lekoa (the Vaal)[1] did not render that process possible. Although in the eighteenth century these communities were more or less settled and a strong economic base of mixed farming was giving rise to an increasingly complex division of labour, their fissiparous nature, itself encouraged by the abundance of land still under the less restrictive political right of 'the sphere of influence', inhibited the development of nationhood and the establishment of territorial sovereignty. 'The tribe', J. D. Omer-Cooper states, 'the unit of political life, though larger than that of the Hottentots, still usually consisted of only a few thousand members. From other points of view, however, it had developed beyond the state of a kinship group and must be regarded as a simple type of state.'[2]

Yet instances of political consolidation were even as then evident. Prototypes were the AbakaMtetwa under Dingiswayo, AbakaNdwandewe under Zwide and AbakaNgwane under Sobhuza from the north of the River Tugela to the north of the River Pongola; and south in the region of the Mohokare valley were the Basotho under Mohlomi, the son of Monyane. This process of political consolidation among the Basotho would be completed during that eventful decade that marked the formative years of Moshoeshoe's accession to power, the period which coincides with the event and consequences of *lifaqane* – the military upheaval unleashed and sustained by Shaka, King of the AmaZulu between 1818 and 1828. To this upheaval also, Moshoeshoe owed the moment for the realisation of his ambition, an ambition jointly espoused with 'Nau Makoanyane, an *mphato*

1

(initiation-age-mate), to whom he had recently vouched: 'Thou art my right hand . . . Together we will found a new empire.'[3]

The history of the Basotho during this period up to Moshoeshoe's death in 1870 (two years after his kingdom, escaping military destruction from the Orange Free State, became a British Colony) has authoritatively been written.[4] I have no cause at the moment to reappraise it. My concern here is with the system of government that had developed during that period – 'the sort of organisation', as Sidney Hartland cogently defined a similar task in his early study of the constitution of the non-literate polities, 'which provides for the seat of authority, the method and extent of its exercise, and the internal arrangements governing the relations of its various parts'.[5]

As part of this task, I hope, as far as it will be practicable, to make a distinction between, on the one hand, the more pervasive and enduring traditional system and institutions of society, which predated both Moshoeshoe and Mohlomi, the most illustrious of its princes, and, on the other hand, the adaptations and innovations of these two men. This is a necessary distinction to attempt to make in a society in which historical writing has unduly, albeit understandably, leaned in favour of the elevation of heroes over the social institutions upon which they rested. For the failure at least to keep in mind this distinction might deceptively lead to the folly of attributing to our heroes the general outcome of generations of evolutionary processes. Indeed in so far as the development of principles of government is concerned, in the Southern Africa of the post-*lifaqane* period it is more the case that 'traditional methods of political organisation were employed and simply used to cover wider areas and larger numbers',[6] than it is that individual rulers prescribed new rules or promulgated epoch-making codes.

THE EARLIEST-KNOWN POLITICAL STRUCTURE OF THE BASOTHO

The Basotho of the Mohokare Valley under Monaheng Alias Kali, – the patriarch of the royal line – and his grandson Mohlomi (c. 1750–1815) were divided into a number of small chiefdoms. Eugene Casalis, the most prolific writer of the three ministers of the Paris Evangelical Missionary Society to join Basotho in 1833, and on whom we rely as much without choice for this period of Basotho history as we do on Livy for the early history of Rome, gathered the impression on his arrival that:

At the time of [Moshoeshoe]'s birth [*c.* 1786] the country of the Basutos was very populous. The tribe presented, on a small scale, the aspect of France in the feudal times. The supremacy of the house of Monaheng was acknowledged, of which Moshoeshoe is a representative, but the chief of each town was continually striving to gain as much independence as possible.[7]

However, his fellow minister, the Reverend Thomas Arbousset, on the basis of the information supplied by the Basotho elders of that period, asserted that in pre-Moshoeshoe days they had 'divided themselves into ten small independent states, although acknowledging one principal chief of the country, called Mothume (sic).'[8]

From the names of the locations that Arbousset was given, these 'small independent states' would appear to have covered generally the area on both sides of the Mohokare Valley which under Moshoeshoe came to be known as Lesotho – the land of the Basotho. Except for the 'Nguni' (Abakuni) polity of the Baphuthi (then called Bamaru – people of the clouds),[9] they were Sesotho-speaking chiefdoms. All of them 'had the same form of government', D. F. Ellenberger and J. C. MacGregor later concluded, 'differing, perhaps, in detail here and there, but identical in fundamental principles'.[10] Taking a cue from Ellenberger and MacGregor's population estimates at the beginning of the nineteenth century, of two of the more cohesive of the polities – the Baphuthi at 3000 and the Makhoakhoa, somewhat suspiciously high at 15 000[11] – we can at least say each comprised only a few thousand people. The Sesotho speakers appear at that earlier period not to have been known by the name of Basotho; they called themselves the Batebang, which, as Arbousset found out, signified 'those from the lower parts, or from the north-east, whence they believe they have all come'.[12]

Each of these chiefdoms was under a ruler styled a *morena* – a term with a functional meaning, as we are bound to agree with Casalis' linguistic interpretation that 'it is formed of the verb *rena*: to be prosperous, to be tranquil'. *Morena*, therefore, signifies: 'He who watches over the public safety and welfare.'[13] Each *morena* had under him a hierarchy of administrative officials. He was normally expected to govern in accordance with established traditional institutions and principles, which might not have been intricate and strict, but were practical. He often settled disputes in a predetermined way. Depending on the degree of his independence from any superior, a *morena* might also forge alliances; and he was expected to honour certain rules in his relations with other independent rulers.

Beginning perhaps in the eighteenth century, a cluster of these *marena* (plural) began also to have what the Basotho styled a *Morena e Moholo* – the Great *Morena* – King.[14] Such, at that time, was the office held by Mohlomi, the son of Monyane, over the ten Basotho polities; except we are forced to conclude that under the son of Monyane the office had not yet become politically functional. For while he was recognised by the *marena* as grand or supreme, he nevertheless exercised no monopoly of coercion over them. Rather he is said to have made it a practice to 'settle the differences of the people' and to have 'entered into treaties of alliance with the chiefs, recommending them to cultivate peace: a subject on which he would say with great glee, "It pays better to fight the corn, than to whet the spear!" ' Basotho of the early nineteenth century assured Arbousset, moreover, that 'He loved them all indiscriminately . . . and he judged according to the rules of equity. He was gentle, affable, and easy to access.'[15]

This is, however, as vivid or as vague a picture as we have of political organisation under this particular prince. Mohlomi's rule, if it can be called that, was one of teaching and moral persuasion; and this was only partially because of his commitment to peace among men. In the main, the fame of Monyane's son stemmed from his practice as a doctor and the rainmaker. In both the functions of healing and precipitation he was far-famed and greatly in demand all over the Southern Africa of his day from the Mohokare Valley and up to the lower fringes of present day Zimbabwe. He had acquired enough wealth to permit him to bequeath *lobola* (the head of cattle given as a marriage guarantee) for a new wife in virtually every polity where he stayed long enough to cure a patient; he would then leave her with any lover who consented to beget royal seed in his name. Through these marriages he formed political alliances, the first Mosotho to use, systematically, the institution of polygamy as an instrument of government.[16]

A paternal great-uncle of Mohlomi named Ratlali, who was otherwise the greatest poet and innovator of the curriculum of initiation schools Basotho had ever known, had only stopped at practising a peculiar, if fatal, hobby of raiding neighbouring rulers' queens, whom he delighted in parading before him in seasons of relaxation. As fate would have it, Ratlali, who was also commander-in-chief of his father Monaheng's armed forces, died in battle in pursuit of this passion, sacrificing thereby to the spear his brothers Motloheloa and Motloang, the latter being Moshoeshoe's great-grandfather. Ratlali was dismembered, his covetous eyes gouged out and the combined enemy of Makhoakhoa, whose queen was to have been the prize, and their Basia allies denied the bereaved Monaheng the international right to bury his son. The aged patriarch died of a broken heart soon after the tragedy.

Mohlomi was a philosopher and a mystic. While he was at the *mophato* (school) for his *lebollo* (initiation), we are informed, he was transported one auspicious night to heaven, 'where he saw many different people and nations' and where he was instructed: 'Go govern with love; see always in thy subjects men and brethren'; and when he was a certain age, he began to observe total continence toward all his wives, including the stateswoman 'Maliepollo', his first and favourite wife, 'in accordance with the religious usage of the wisest of their chiefs'.[17] The doctor's disposition ill-fitted him for the hustling and jostling of the real political life of his times, and indeed he had no taste for it. He thus created no strong and enduring bonds between his chiefdoms. The title of *Morena e Moholo* for him was more honorific than functional. When he died in or about 1815 his experiment went with him.

GOVERNMENT IN THE POST-LIFAQANE PERIOD

Under Moshoeshoe, the son of Mokhachane, Basotho realised a genuine state of nationhood. For the first time, at the end of *lifaqane*, they recognised themselves as one nation of Basotho, of the polity of Lesotho,[18] owing allegiance to one *Morena e Moholo*, Moshoeshoe, on whom they had conferred sovereignty and who, within the framework of commonly accepted traditional institutions and principles reserved the powers of life and death over them. The *marena* were still in existence but they were not sovereign and their authority was subject to Moshoeshoe's commands, while their functions and activities were generally defined by traditional guidelines, which in practice could be enforced or varied at his pleasure.

Succession to the Office of Morena

Exactly when and how Moshoeshoe assumed the office initially of *morena* (as distinct from *morena e moholo*) over his little chiefdom of Bakwena of Mokoteli (a fragment of Monaheng's dynasty) before *lifaqane*, is something we can no longer establish with certainty. He would appear, however, to have assumed greater responsibilities than was usual for a youth of his age shortly after his *lebollo* (initiation), which would have been about the age of eighteen years, presumably just a few years before Mohlomi's demise in 1815. It was around this time that he enlisted the support of 'Nau Makoanyane, the son of a 'Nguni' subject named Ntseke, in the mission to 'found a new empire'.

By 1833, when the French missionaries of the Paris Evangelical Missionary Society arrived in Lesotho, Moshoeshoe was the acknowledged *Morena e Moholo* of a new kingdom forged during the *lifaqane* turbulence. He probably received this recognition as *Morena e Moholo*, at the latest in 1824, when the Basotho were harried by the lady-warrior 'Manthatisi of Batlokoa from Buthe Buthe in the north to Thaba-Bosiu in the centre of the country. For it is settled that the son was in full authority of the affairs of state then, and the father, Mokhachane, who does not even get a mention in connection with the great migration, had been overshadowed.[19]

Yet one thing still leaves us with a puzzle: whenever literary sources have permitted Mokhachane to speak to his own cause, we find that even after *lifaqane* he regarded himself as the *Morena e Moholo* and saw Moshoeshoe only as his 'eyes, ears and arms' in the running of the state. So, had Moshoeshoe acceded to office by sheer power of resolve and his accomplishments on the battleground, thereby relegating a disenchanted old Mokhachane to the background? Or had he initially been installed in an office of *morena* but was fated to rule under the eye of a father who awkwardly demanded filial piety? We cannot say.

Nevertheless in former days some procedure of succession to the office of *morena* had been observed. In principle the heir, in the polygamous Basotho society, was the eldest son of a *morena*'s 'great wife'. The great wife was not necessarily a *morena*'s first wife, although she often was. She might have been anywhere in the number of his wives, provided the royal house had so designated her and, ideally, if her *lobola* had been commissioned in the form of *sethaba-batha* – a cattle levy on the subjects – and not, as otherwise it would have been, from a ruler's father and uncles. Through *sethaba-thaba* the great wife was symbolically made the mother of a nationality and ties of obligation between herself and the subjects were forged;[20] but, as Ashton points out, 'the law [of succession] was sometimes modified by extraneous considerations, such as the popularity or ability of the claimants'.[21]

The Club of the Rhinoceros Horn

However it was that Moshoeshoe acceded to the office of an ordinary *morena*, he and his contemporary *marena* of Basotho, as well as his successors to the high rank of *morena e moholo* under the kingdom, carried the staff of office called *molamu oa tŝukulu* – 'the rod of the rhinoceros horn'. F. Laydevant, to whom we are indebted for notes on this subject, informs us:

> The rhinoceros rod or sceptre is, as the name indicates, a sort of rod or club carved out of a rhinoceros horn. It is generally black or dark brown in colour . . . To-day no-one knows where the sceptre which Moshesh possessed came from. We only know that all young Basuto receive at the end of the initiation ceremonies a rod which is similar to that one and which is called a 'rhinoceros rod or horn' even if it is made from a piece of hardwood. . . . It is therefore possible that Moshesh's rhinoceros horn is the one which his father Mokhachene provided him with at the end of the initiation ceremonies; but it is also very probable that this horn or sceptre was bought by Moshesh himself when his power was beginning to be consolidated.[22]

As we can see from this quotation, the origins, and implicity the universality of the possession of a *real* rhinoceros sceptre among Basotho have become a matter of pure speculation. From the information that the initiation school was, at least symbolically, associated with a horn from the ferocious beast, and considering the apparent static nature of the latter institution, we may surmise that the association goes at least as far back as the late 17th or early 18th century, a period during which the institution was given a firm base by a warrior-poet named Ratlali.

Then comes the problem of the procurement of the article. According to oral evidence,[23] a prince's sceptre was hewn by warriors from a live rhinoceros. The warriors wrestled with the beast, as a doctor procured the horn and subsequently speedily fashioned it in the form of a club, fortified with potent herbal medicines. The procedure was all to take place and be completed before life completely departed from the animal.

Oral evidence thus recognises the rhinoceros horn as the symbol of power: not only had the sceptre to be associated with a beast universally known for power and ferocity, but it had to seem that warriors sacrificed their lives in its procurement for their ruler. And so their bravery and the animal's well-known properties were bound together by medicine and the final product entrusted to a *morena*.

Viewed from the point of view of detached reasoning, however, this method of procurement seems a trifle outside the realm of reality. First, as Laydevant has also pointed out, by 1833 'the rhinoceros had long since disappeared from Lesotho'. The closest that they might have been found was in Natal, and the breed that was in that area was much known for its ferocity, speed and thickness of skin.[24] Second, in that age, when cattle-raiding and defence of country were the two essential preoccupations for warriors, wrestling with any, much less with the Natal, breed of rhinoceros, might always have led to excessive human sacrifice. It is more probable that at some time immemorial a rhinoceros was killed in adversity, its horn used as a sceptre, and a custom thereby established; and then, later, rhinoceros horns could have been procured through trade.

According to Laydevant, Moshoeshoe's rhinoceros club was handed down through all his successors – Letsie, Lerotholi, Letsie II, Griffith – up at least to Seeiso Griffith, the present King's father.[25] There is every reason to believe that the rest of the principal *marena* of Basotho had their rhinoceros clubs similarly handed down from heir to heir, assuming, that is, that Laydevant's submission was universal, that 'the sceptres of the chiefs, instead of being made of precious wood, as is the case with those given to the children of ordinary people, are always, when it is a question of chiefs' sons and of an heir to the royal power, carved out of a rhinoceros horn.'[26] For this information may need to be handled with caution, as it does not permit a distinction (in the custom of keeping a sceptre) between the dominant royal line of Monaheng-Moshoeshoe on the one hand, and on the other hand, the various other subordinate clans and chiefdoms in Lesotho such as, in particular, those of Baphuthi and Bataung, who had slightly different histories and customs.

Eugene Casalis noted that the *marena* generally carried the sceptre 'as a mark of their rank'. In the event that a *morena* lost patience with unruly subjects, it was sufficient for him to throw the sceptre at some distance saying: 'It is enough! There is my rhinoceros: let us see who will pick it up'. Terrified by the club the subjects would take off helter-skelter: 'if any one were bold enough to pick it up, he would be guilty of a crime which would expose him to capital punishment'.[27]

The Installation of a Morena

It does appear that, when things went normally, it was customary for a *morena* to be formally installed. The Sesotho term for the custom was *ho bea* – literally, to place. The formality, which has up to today been adhered to, took place at a *pitso* (a public assembly of all adult males) where, as Ashton noted, 'the senior authority's representative or the person who has been acting in the deceased place presents the heir to the people. He calls upon him to rule wisely, firmly and fairly, and to heed the advice of his kinsmen and councillors'.[28] The custom of installation among the Bantu polities of South Africa was, as Professor Schapera's study revealed, the same and the attributes expected of a good ruler were commonly assumed.[29] Hence, in the absence of any surviving Basotho text of the *bolao ba puso* (the exhortation of government, as it was called), the following, from the neighbouring AmaXhosa, is a safe borrowing. The exhortation was made at the installation ceremony of the AmaXhosa *Nkosi* Ngqika about 1797:

> Son of Mlawu, grandson of Rarabe, this day you are invested with the Chieftainship of your countrymen. May your conduct be reputable. Let worthiness become you, and may you be just. These are your people, be a father to them, and rule them with wisdom. May your hand be beautiful (literally be generous) and not seek out a person's body (literally, lift up the hand against another), for as your country's proverb has it, 'The stick has no kraal' (i.e. misuse of power destroys the home).[30]

There would, of course, have been no fixed text as such of the *bolao ba puso*. Although the theme would have been maintained, the wording would have depended much on the inclination of a chosen speaker and his powers of oratory.

As it may be inferred from the way he acceded to power, Moshoeshoe is likely not to have been formally installed. However he had, at an earlier special and seemingly equally political occasion, received his *bolao ba puso*. Apparently when he was only a *lekoloane* (a young man fresh from the initiation school), his grandfather Motŝoane, alias Peete, who doted on him, had taken him to the aged Mohlomi to be taught principles of government. (Peete and the seer were grandchildren of the same patriarch, Kali Monaheng, through different grandmothers duly married to him. See genealogical table). The point has elsewhere been argued that the young initiate would have paid his tutor in government several visits before the seer awarded him symbols of graduation.[31] Sources, literary and oral alike, deny us the benefit of details as to the lessons received. The most that we are told is that Moshoeshoe was instructed on the effective use of polygamy: for purposes of forging alliances with neighbouring rulers, and for fostering the loyalty of clients (*bahlanka*); and the superiority of peace to the wielding of the spear was impressed upon him.

A Zulu written traditional account, *Umhlomi* (1938) by N. S. Luthango, according to which Moshoeshoe 'stayed a number of nights conversing' with his tutor, has Mohlomi giving the following words of admonishment to his young student at the end of their 'conversations':

> My child, you will be a king and govern people with ideas and wishes like your own – you should govern them well. When you have begun to rule, you should remember all my words and remember also that it is better to thrash the corn than to sharpen the spear.[32]

According to Arbousset's much earlier version (1936) the seer had admonished the ambitious young prince: 'when thou shalt sit in judgement, let thy decisions be just. The law knows no one as a poor man.'[33] While George Tlali, one of Moshoeshoe's educated sons, gave us the version in 1858:

> You should govern only by peace; and the one who will govern in your stead [your successor] should continue to rule by peace only. This is the command that I give you. Now, return to your brethren and govern them by peace. It is for this that I had called you, to give you this commandment of peace.[34]

Moshoeshoe's tutelage was concluded with a ceremony in which 'the errant king' did something quite formal, and, upon closer examination, probably also quite as customary:

> The famous son of Monyane received him [Moshoeshoe] with benevolence, blessed him after their manner by brushing his forehead against his own *ho iphahloetsa*, and, detaching one of his own long earrings, fastened it in the ear of the youth, saying, 'Ke

Lasale (sic) la 'muso (sic)' [It is the earring of governance]. He also presented him with an ox, a shield, and a spear, and even had a beast slaughtered for him.[35]

The ritual of the brushing of the forehead, called *ho iphahloetsa*, achieved the same purpose among the Basotho of the Mohokare Valley as the Roman *augurum*: the transformation of supernatural powers.[36] In living memory it seems to have still been performed by those men in society who were presumed, as with the Roman *augur*, to embody supernatural power in its plenitude. However, even without this conceivably hazardous analogy, a guess can safely be made that following the entire ceremony as above described, the son of Mokhachane perhaps needed no installation or inauguration. Both had been carried out, but by 'the wisest' of the princes of his people.

Divine Right of Chiefs: Indigenous, or Borrowed?

One decade after Moshoeshoe's death, in 1880, a literary source suggests a notion on the imperium of the *marena* of Basotho which immediately strikes one as very fascinating. In the wake of the Gun War, which Basotho had had to wage against the Cape Colony Disarmament Act during the period that the British Crown was administering over Lesotho through that colony, a tense *pitso* (public assembly of all adult males) was held in August that year to review the development. It was at that *pitso* that, probably for the first time on record, a Mosotho alluded to the notion of the divine right of Basotho rulers. Seoehla Jonathan Molapo, the Chief of the District of Leribe and nephew to the then *Morena e Moholo*, Mohato Letsie, Moshoeshoe's son and heir, stated:

> Mogato (Letsie) is the only one who has the right to speak; he is Moshesh's son; what he will do will be truth for me, because he is Moshesh. Even if he wants us to do what is painful for us we will follow him, because *his will is the will of God*.[my italic][37]

A while later, a commoner named Ramatŝeatsana, 'favourite councillor' of *Morena* David Masopha, Moshoeshoe's third son by his great wife, seeking to support his own splinter of an argument interjected: 'All chiefs are from God'.[38] In both instances the speakers made their interjections as to the divine right of *morena* axiomatically, seeking only to give authority to their arguments. How old was this notion among the Basotho?

Aside from what may be inferred from Mohlomi's apparent powers of auguration, there seems to be no firm basis for any speculation that the *marena* of Basotho and their *morena e moholo* made claims to the right of divine imperium before Christian intrusion in 1833. Indeed, judging from the relations between the rulers and their subjects at that time, as well as generally after, it would seem that there were no social circumstances to nurture such an idea. The *marena* generally approached their subjects with deference. 'The chiefs', Ellenberger and MacGregor point out, 'often addressed their subjects as *marena* ('chiefs'), *benghali* ('my masters').[39] As one *morena* put it at one *pitso*, in the years preceding 1860.

After all, we are but your servants; men are born and die in the same manner, be they high or low; if there are some who are entitled to obedience, they derive this right from their fellows, who wield it thus for the welfare of all.[40]

One episode involving the *Morena e Moholo* Moshoeshoe graphically illustrates the point. The drama was witnessed by Eugene Casalis presumably some time in the 1830s. At some time in the past the monarch 'had allowed an officer, distinguished for his valour', to keep some cattle for use under a custom called *mafisa:* a loan of stock to a subject or vassal, the service and produce of which he received the benefit of, except the stock might not be slaughtered. Moshoeshoe had then later seen fit to recall his *mafisa* from the 'officer' for the purpose of passing it on 'as a present to Lephoi, chief of the Bahlaping.' It was a form of political aid. The valorous officer was furious and, 'in his public confrontation' told the King:

Is it thus that a just man must behave? You deprive me of all my food, of all the sustenance of my wives and children to send it to strangers? Have you no other cattle to give, and must you leave those to whom you owe your salvation to want? Behold my body, it is covered with wounds. I have fought against the Batlokoa, the Zulus, and the Korannas, let the enemy come again, we shall see whether Moshoeshoe will expose himself to his assegais. No, he will remain on his mountain [fort] with his wives, and will not dare follow me. It is I who will fight, who will suffer hunger, thirst, fatigue, while my chief eats, drinks, and slumbers peacefully.[41]

If it may be suggested that this officer was probably sufficiently close to power, by virtue of his office, to take liberties with his king, it needs quickly to be added that his was not an isolated incident.

There were other less highly placed subjects who stood up to the monarch on personal matters and he sought not to throw the rhinoceros club at them.[42] If, as it would be reasonable to deduce, Moshoeshoe's demeanour can be credited to Mohlomi's teachings, that in itself would lead us to the view that his example over the subordinate *marena* might be an inhibiting factor to pretences to the notion of divine right. The claim of divine right for the *marena* of Basotho must therefore be sought elsewhere: the most plausible source is Christianity.

Ever since the arrival in Lesotho of the French missionaries, literary sources reveal the Basotho as being quite fond of quoting the Bible in support of their arguments. Moshoeshoe, as can be seen from his biographies by Leonard Thompson and Peter Sanders had, probably above most others, acquired a penchant in this connection. Further to the point, at the same *pitso* in August 1880 at which Jonathan and Ramatŝeatsana made their striking interjections, one Thomas Sethlaba (probably Sehlabaka), in his appeal that Basotho should be pardoned for taking arms against the Cape Colony, had borrowed from the story of the Prodigal Son, pleading: 'What I ask for is that a fat lamb may be killed.' Jonathan and Ramatŝeatsana might therefore, as others who shared their views, have put great stock in the Bible as an exotic source of legitimation – to wit, Proverbs 9:15, 16:

By me kings reign, and princes decree justice. By me princes rule, and nobles, *even* all the judges of the earth.

This point may be more than simply one of academic interest. As we shall see in subsequent chapters, the *marena* of Basotho after Moshoeshoe's death became generally and increasingly heavy-handed on their subjects. They demanded more services from them, while giving hardly anything back in return. A point was finally reached when some subjects complained that the *marena* had turned subjects into 'slaves'. The reasons for this development were many and varied. And it is conceivable that as a *post facto* justification the *marena* also cultivated the view of themselves, supported by selective passages from the Bible, that they owed their disproportionate reserves of power of God.

Responsibilities of a Morena

Before, as after, *lifaqane*, the responsibilities of a *morena* were established and they were well understood by subjects.[43] He provided justice for the injured and the oppressed, punished wrongdoers and generally protected the rights of his subjects. As a rule the royal village had *lekhotla* – the court – where public affairs were discussed and settled, disputes were resolved, and when there were no problems, men's public works – softening cowhides for blankets and dresses, sandal-making and so on – were undertaken. A *morena* exercised the executive, administrative and judicial functions of his domain, yet, as it will be shown later, that did not mean that he was dictatorial in his relationship with his subjects. He fulfilled his responsibilities within guidelines provided by custom, a fact which struck the observant Eugene Casalis who said in 1838:

> Whatever reproach one may level against the ancient social system of the natives, it was nevertheless an order of real value. It was the product of that instinct of preservation which is found among nations and individuals alike and which prompts them to adopt, quite naturally, the customs, the laws, the institutions most conformable with their genius, and therefore the best calculated to perpetuate the national life, and to shelter it against the injurious influences to which it may be exposed.[44]

A *morena*, in the final analysis, assured the economic survival of his society. On him and him alone fell the responsibility of organising the national hunt – *letsolo*. When necessary and prudent he organised cattle raids (*ho hapa likhomo*). The captured cattle were redistributed to the needy or deserving of society in the form of *mafisa*. In times of drought subjects looked up to their ruler to ensure precipitation. It thus made sense for him to keep a rainmaker at his *lekhotla*. Among Moshoeshoe's rainmakers, for instance, was Makara, who had inherited the art from his mother, the great wife of *Morena* 'Mope of a political segment of Bafokeng. A *morena* regulated the use of natural products – raw materials for fire, building, and pasturage, to name a few. He held all land in trust for his subjects and controlled its distribution and use. The health of his people was also in the final analysis, albeit indirectly, his responsibility: Ellenberger and MacGregor inform us that 'accredited doctors were under his special protection, in the event of the death of a patient . . . or any . . . mishap which might occur to them in the exercise of their profession'.[45] This meant at least that no healer (doctor) might walk into a *morena*'s jurisdiction and begin his practice without first reporting to the *lekhotla* to present his credentials. For in the event of a dispute arising between a patient and a healer, the credentials of the latter ought to be known. There was a *molao* [law], according to Jobo Mokhachane, one of Moshoeshoe's half-brothers, to the effect that 'except a cure is effected [a healer] is not entitled to his fees.'[46]

An independent *morena* was the principal spokesman and representative of his people in external relations. However, he delegated his authority to his counsellors and to his *maqosa* (messengers/ambassadors). At the same time he ensured the preservation of certain commonly-observed inter-polity rules. According to Casalis there were 'general principles which should form the foundation of intercourse with other nations': in war, women, children and travellers were respected. Those who surrendered had their lives spared and they might be ransomed. A warrior was deprived of instruments of combat but generally allowed to keep his shield. In keeping with the code that *legosa ha le na molato* (a messenger/ambassador is blameless), the person of a messenger/ambassador was inviolable.[47] The person of a stranger was under the protection of his host.[48] Mohato Letsie, Moshoeshoe's heir and successor further informed us, on the occasion of his brother *Morena* Jeremiah Molapo's betrayal of the AmaHlubi potentate to British colonial officers in 1873 that 'a chief must be killed out in the country and not in a village . . . it would be wrong to kill him after calling him home [that is, inviting him on the pretence that he was granted asylum].[49] An independent *morena* waged war and concluded agreements with other rulers on behalf of his polity.

A *Morena* saw to it that boys were formally initiated into adulthood and joined the affairs of men. (The corresponding role over girls fell on the great wife.) The institution through which the initiation was undertaken was called *lebollo*, often misleadingly called circumcision in literary sources: true enough, the boys were circumcised, but this was only a small part, of the institution, albeit a symbolic one. Generally in the months of February and March a *morena* authorised the erection of a *mophato* (initiation lodge). This *mophato*, as a rule, was secluded from the rest of the community. There, for a period ideally of six months, a son or sons of a *morena* remained with their age-mates. The ruler provided the doctor to consecrate the *mophato*. Medicine for the purpose came from the royal medicine horn. The initiation was superintended by men called *mesue* ('those who render supple').

Under the *mesue* the initiates were given the lore of their people. Instruction was in part carried through the medium of chanted poems called *likoma*, characteristically preserved in an archaic language. These poems are generally said to be the genius of Ratlali, our Mosotho poet with a mixed legacy, although it is doubtful that he was responsible for all of them. The institution is otherwise named after him as *ha Ratlali* – That is, at Ratlali's place.

The initiates or *bashemane* received daily instructions on warfare: learning to throw the traditional javelin (*lerumo*) with swiftness and precision, 'to whirl round in the air a formidable club, and to ward off,' by means of the Basotho shield, 'the blows of the enemy, from whichever side they may proceed'. Corporal punishment was frequently and liberally administered to produce Spartan discipline. The *bashemane* were forced to march long distances at a time throughout their country, to familiarise them with its topography, as well as 'to drive vice from their hearts'. They were frequently admonished: 'Amend your ways! Be men! Fear theft! Fear adultery! Honour your parents! *Obey your chiefs!*. (My italic.) When the training had come to an end the initiates shed their attire of boyhood for that of adulthood, got annointed, and, as their *mophato* was set in flames, ran back to society without ever once looking back.[50]

None might convene a *mophato* within a *morena*'s jurisdiction without his express permission. Even in Moshoeshoe's new kingdom, with several *marena* still administering their people under himself, permission to convene a *mophato* had to be secured from the *Morena e Moholo*, who then supplied medicine from the royal horn. Convening a *mophato* without this permission was tantamount to a declaration of independence.

To receive the loyalty and love of his people a ruler made hospitality a virtue. He used his milk cows to provide food for the poor and for visitors. Subjects were required to give service three times a year in the breaking of the soil, the cultivation and harvest of a ruler's principal field called *tšimo ea lira* and in the fields of his first three high-ranking wives, including the great wife; but they were also to be abundantly fed as they did so. Whenever they were at the royal court for business they expected to be shown an open hand. It was in part to this end that the institution of polygamy was geared. As explained by one of its greatest practitioners, Moshoeshoe, aside from its function as 'a means of contracting alliance with the heads of other nations, which helps to preserve peace':

> [W]e receive many travellers and strangers; how could we lodge them and what could we feed them on, if we did not have several wives? . . . I have warriors not servants. These men, these youths whom you see around me, acknowledge my right to punish them in the event of their refusing to obey me when I order them to watch over my herds, to deliver a message, or to take up arms, but there is not one among them who would not laugh me to scorn if I sought to compel him to draw water for me, to grind corn, to sweep my huts.

To Eugene Casalis, who on that occasion was attacking polygamy, Moshoeshoe added:

> Oh! polygamy, that is a proud rock which you are challenging there; I am very much afraid that you will not succeed in shaking it, at least not in our time. Perhaps our children will be more favourably situated.[51]

Territorial Sovereignty

As Professor Schapera has shown in his comparative study, the political communities of pre-colonial South Africa might have had vaguely defined boundaries, but that does not mean that they did not subscribe to the notion of 'our country'. On the contrary, each political community claimed 'exclusive rights to the land' that it occupied. Everyone living on that patch of land was subject to its ruler, allegiance to whom could be rendered nugatory only by banishment or voluntary removal.[52] Hartland, in his work on 'primitive law' was indeed the wiser for admitting that, generally speaking, in non-literate societies 'each tribe occupies and hunts over a certain territory whose limits, however ill-defined they may seem to us, are well understood by the natives'.[53] For, as history repeatedly demonstrated in the case of the Bantu societies of South Africa, each political community knew where its territorial jurisdiction stopped and that of its neighbour began. The spoor law, universal among the Bantu of South Africa, was enforced in recognition of this territorial principle. As the Reverend Mr Mackenzie, a Wesleyan missionary with a lot of experience working among the Batswana, stated in an interview in 1881:

> When the spoor of stolen cattle crosses a boundary line between two tribes, or reaches the grazing ground of their first cattle post, the men on the spoor return and inform the chief: Then it is either a simple theft, or it is a declaration of war, on the part of the chief into whose country the cattle have gone.[54]

That these political communities had a functional notion of the territorial jurisdiction of their polities explains why the AmaMpondomis counsellors – Gagelizwe, Nyanga, Sangoni and twelve others – in their own comments at the selfsame interview as the Reverend Mackenzie's advised:

> any magistrate coming into this country [of theirs] is supposed to act according to the law of the country, and the chief and the councillors let the magistrate know the boundaries.[55]

In short, if magistrates could not identify boundaries, it might have been to a large measure because they did not know how the Africans understood their boundaries, and not because boundaries did not exist. Although, of course, I should not wish to suggest another extreme, namely, that the boundaries were *never* in dispute.

It was that sense of territoriality, no matter how precariously defined, which prompted Casalis to state:

> The obstinate resistance which the [AmaXhosa] the [AbaThembu], and the Basutos made to the encroachments of the colonists, proves how strong is the attachment of these tribes to the countries they inhabit. In speaking of them they use expressions which touch the heart and waken enthusiasm; 'Home', 'our', 'the land of our fathers'. Something like superstitious respect for the soil has even been observed among them.[56]

Among the Basotho in times of war, a *morena*'s official doctors charmed major paths and passes 'to peg down the country' and keep the enemy outside its boundaries. Before the *Morena e Moholo* Moshoeshoe released his warriors for combat, we are informed, he always concluded with the exhortation: 'Let us die for our country!'; and on that call, 'The whole assembly was electrified; and nothing was heard but the words repeated a thousand times, – 'Let us die for our country!'[57]

If we adhere to Sir Henry Sumner Maine's definition of territorial sovereignty, namely, that the notion is 'associated with the proprietorship of a limited portion of the earth's surface' and that that proprietorship ought to be '*inter se* . . . not paramount, but absol-ute', we are bound to conclude, on the foregoing examination, that Lesotho under Moshoeshoe was a state with the full enjoyment of territorial sovereignty.[58] However, the ruler was called the *Morena e Moholo* of the Basotho (the people) and not of Lesotho (their land). The situation may be said to have been analogous to that of the kings of the Franks under the Merovingian line of the descendants of Clovis, who were known as the kings of the Franks and not of France. The difference between the two, and this was a major difference, was that, whereas among the Franks the concept of 'individual title to land' was developing, in Lesotho political circumstances militated against that tendency.[59]

The Court of Counsellors

A *morena*, whether as a *morena e moholo* and therefore sovereign, or whether as the latter's dependent, wielded a lot of power within a polity. This power, however, was shared with and controlled by the members of his *lekhotla* (court). These courtiers fell into a number of categories, but for the sake of convenience we can divide them into four groups, albeit not discrete.

First there were, from the pre-*lifaqane* days of small chiefdoms, a ruler's *matona*. T. Arbousset is in agreement with Casalis that they were described as 'the eyes, ears, and arms, of the chief'.[60] As the metaphorical description suggests, the minimum number of these *matona* for each *morena* were two. The numbers increased in relation to the size and complexity of a political community. Ideally these 'eyes and ears' were senior members of the royal family – principally a ruler's maternal uncles (from among whom his deputy was conven-tionally designated),[61] his principal sons (from the first three high-ranking wives) and, in Moshoeshoe's case, his own father.

Merit, however, was also recognised. Moshoeshoe had at his court distinguished *matona* of commoner's origins, such as Ramatŝeatsana, later baptised under the name of Abraham. His principal sons like-wise gave merit a high priority in their choice of courtiers.[62] To these *matona* by merit Leonard Thompson and Peter Sanders have added Eugene Casalis, who, at least up to 1848, advised Moshoeshoe in his relations with white governments as well as by attending to his correspondence. After 1848, Thompson qualifies his point, Moshoe-shoe had gained sufficient experience in this area to assume full responsibility (with the aid, no doubt, of his educated sons).[63]

Second were the military commanders (*balaoli*, sing. *molaoli*) of
the armed forces. In Moshoeshoe's time some stratification of these
officials had developed. The stratification was in relation to the
rank of a ruler's houses (wives), to which they were attached. 'Nau
Makoanyane, for instance, the 'Generalissimo', was attached to the
great house of *Mofumahali* (Queen) 'Mamohato. Thafeng was in the
second house of 'Manneko, called the house of Tlokotsing. Letele,
Mohlomi's son, was of 'Masekhonyana's house – the third ranking,
called the house of Maebeng (of the cattle of dove colours).[64] On
Mokolokolo, commander of the *mollo* (fire) regiment, said by
Thompson to have been second in command to Makoanyane and
also a 'composer of praise songs and an ambassador', we have no
information as to the house of attachment; but it is almost certain
that his illicit and uncondoned affair with one of the King's principal
wives, which almost cost him his life, cost him his rank and house
attachment, at the minimum. Until Thompson rescued him from
historical quarantine Mokolokolo was thus more dubiously known
in oral history as a man who had fallen from grace for having abused
the privileges of his office.[65]

Third were the *maqosa* (sing. leqosa) – probably best translated
into English as diplomatic agents or envoys. These were the men that
an independent *morena* sent to other countries to convey messages,
sometimes with his authority to negotiate and commit his government, most of the time without such an authority. 'To prevent the
endless denials and contradictions which would arise from the
absence of written treaties', Casalis informs us, 'the international
communications are usually entrusted to the same men'.[66] Thus a
man named Seetane was accredited to the AmaZulu kingdom, at
least during Mpande's reign.[67] Nathanael Makotoko, besides being
the chief *letona* (counsellor) to Moshoeshoe's second son *Morena*
Jeremiah Molapo (probably the third most powerful chief) to the
north of the country, was also, at the national level, the primary
leqosa to the British Colony of Natal in the 1860s. Ntho Mokeke,
otherwise *Morena* Letsie's chief counsellor, who was familiar with
the affairs of the British High Commission in Cape Town to the
point of citing old correspondence in that connection from memory,
is likely at the national level to have specialised on the Cape
Colony.[68]

Depending on their reliability and political acumen, some of these
diplomatic agents served as heads of high-powered deputations in
times of national crises. Nathanael Makotoko, for instance, in 1869,

was to have been deputised to London, in the company of the King's educated son Tŝekelo, to attempt to reverse a South African High Commissioner's Lesotho-Orange Free State boundary arrangement made with the Boers that year. That mission, unfortunately, ran into difficulties when the High Commissioner, Sir Philip Wodehouse, threatened to withdraw British protection of Lesotho against Boer military destruction. The more experienced Makotoko then responded quickly to the King's stealthy withdrawal of him, while the adventurist Tŝekelo charged ahead both to London and Paris, where he had hoped to woo the French Emperor's support. At the end of it all the King denied all knowledge of the mission. The High Commissioner then discredited it at the Home Office in London, so that by the time the mission got there it had lost its official standing.[69]

Ntho Mokeke provides another example of a senior ambassador with wide responsibilities. As principal agent under *Morena e Moholo* Letsie, following his accession in 1870, Ntho Mokeke seems to have covered a broad range of assignments. Letsie made this point clear when he said that Mokeke was 'like my own book, and knows about everything belonging to me, and he has always been a man I trusted and sent anywhere to the white people or to others'.[70]

Fourth there was a *morena*'s official doctors. Perhaps the most important of these would have been the war doctor. This official was, according to G. Tylden, 'responsible for intelligence, propaganda, security, and the due performance of ritual'. The war doctor, as it may be guessed, could easily be the single most powerful official in a *morena*'s court, if a motive was supplied and an opportunity was enhanced. In such circumstances he could indeed be more dangerous than helpful to a ruler. A classic case in point is one of a doctor named Tsapi, described by Leonard Thompson as 'Moshoeshoe's favourite diviner'. Obviously fearful (and rightly so) that the French missionaries' continued presence in the country would destroy his career, Tsapi took advantage of an epidemic of measles in 1839 to frighten the *Morena e Moholo* into casting them adrift. It is said that he approached the King's residence with one side of his body painted white, the other black, and, with only a panther skin over his shoulder he shouted and cried before a curious audience:

Son of Mokhachane, your grandfather Peete and the mother of Letsie [both deceased] have appeared to me, I saw them this morning seated before my door. I said, 'Tsapi, your eyes lie,' but to dissipate my doubts Peete threw himself on me and almost crushed me under his weight. I tried ineffectively to disengage myself from him, but he agreed to move away only when he had given me a message for you: 'The children of Thaba Bosiu die because Moshoeshoe is polluted and because the school of the *Moruti* [missionary] and the evening prayers offend the *balimo* [ancestral shades].[71]

All these men were a *morena's* counsellors and members of his court. The regularity with which they convened, as well as the extent of their attendance, was dictated by the cause. For daily, routine matters, relating to the settlement of minor disputes or sorting out harmless administrative responsibilities, only those residing at the royal village met as and when the need arose. We surmise that important personages such as the general commander of the armed forces, the war doctor and, under Moshoeshoe, his father, might not in such routine instances even attend, and a *morena* himself probably deputised.

When momentous issues involving major policy decisions or major judicial matters were at stake, all the men of the court convened as a Grand Council. This Grand Council was called *Lekhotla la Mahosana* (council of princes). Under Moshoeshoe it was on such occasions that the allegiance of his territorial chiefs was also tested. Unexplained failures to attend the King's court constituted an act of disloyalty. Under Moshoeshoe the Grand Council was even attended by ambassadors from other polities. In February 1862, for instance, when 150 Basotho notables assembled to adumbrate a treaty of alliance with Great Britain, ambassadors from Moshoeshoe's AmaZulu overlord, Mpande, and from the AmaMpondo Faku, were in attendance.[72] Again, in July 1866, in the wake of the last Basotho-Boer war, which almost destroyed Lesotho, the same polities had sent their ambassadors to the *Lekhotla la Mahosana* that sat for five days at Thaba Bosiu discussing terms and modalities of getting the British Government to intercede.[73]

Although in theory it convened at a *morena's* pleasure, a council in practice expected a *morena* to consult with it on all major matters affecting the polity. A *morena* depended on it for general advice, and it was the primary institution for the formulation of policy; but it also existed to control his power. As George McCall Theal put it, 'with agreement with [his counsellors] he was strong, in opposition powerless'.[74] A *morena* who habitually overruled or side-stepped his council risked unpopularity and the consequent loss of individual subjects to neighbouring polities, or segmentation by powerful members of the royal family.

The Pitso (Popular Assembly)

A ruler and his council might agree on a major issue of policy, but, ideally, and often in practice, he needed next to put the matter before a *pitso* before implementing it.

The Basotho *pitso* was of pre-*lifaqane* origins.[75] Moshoeshoe continued its use and rather upheld its sanctity. True enough, as Peter Sanders points out, 'there are times when Moshoeshoe, accompanied by some of his councillors, relations and missionaries, travelled away from Thaba Bosiu to meet European officials, and then entered into covenants with them without consulting the people at all'.[76] However, this apparent tendency of arbitrariness needs to be understood in its proper perspective. As Sanders hastily adds, on the authority of Eugene Casalis, 'the Colonial Government seldom gave a chief time to consult his people, and in this way promoted "despotic tendencies" and often involved him in "insurmountable difficulties" '.[77]

The *pitso* in Moshoeshoe's times, according to Casalis, was a remarkably democratic institution. Furthermore it was conducted with a discernible degree of order: a subject of discussion was normally put to the people by one of the King's courtiers, 'taking care to let his own personal opinion appear as little as possible'. That done, the *pitso* was open to any one to speak. Those with the gift of speech aired their views 'with the greatest freedom and plainness of speech'. It was expected on such an occasion that the sovereign 'must bear the most cutting remarks without a frown'. There were always those who were in support of, and others who were against, the government. At the end the King summarised the arguments, presented his own, and then created consensus. If the *pitso* was in agreement with his summary, it signified it with applause.[78] Elsewhere the white *letona* informs us that, indeed:

> Freedom of thought and freedom of speech are the foundations and the guarantee of the national rights of [Moshoeshoe's] subjects. They are allowed to express their opinion on the Chief's conduct quite openly; if they disapprove of it, they say so with a virile and eloquent boldness which the most fiery Roman tribune would have envied.[79]

A comparative examination of the question of freedom of speech in contemporary Southern African governments leads us to the conclusion that Casalis' florid statement was in fact no exaggeration. As, for instance, the Cape Colony 'Commission on Native Laws and Customs' on Batswana, the various branches of the AmaXhosa, AmaZulu and Basotho (in so far as Lesotho's Governor's Agent, Joseph Orpen was also interviewed), in 1881 concluded:

> It seems to be a marked feature in the Kafir [Bantu][80] character that if matters in dispute can only be well 'talked over' (which corresponds with our liberty of debate), changes can be made with much less fear of opposition or of exciting disaffection than if these changes are thrust upon the people. The art of discussion is one which had long been practised in Kaffirland, and the gifts of the people in this respect are beyond the average; indeed, . . . they must be considered as remarkable and unique.[81]

Law, Legislation and Royal Prerogatives

The question of whether or not African political organisations in the pre-colonial period had 'law' is positively settled, albeit that jurisprudentially it has still remained difficult to provide a precise definition. Jurists tend to approach it differently from legal anthropologists. In the main the difficulty is one of distinguishing between 'law' and 'custom'.[82] For the limited purpose, in this section, of alluding to law as an instrument of control in pre-colonial Lesotho, I offer the definition, quoted *mutatis mutandis* from the Gold Coast Native Administration Ordinance 1927, s.2:

> 'Native customary law' means a rule or a body of rules regulating rights and imposing correlative duties, being a rule or a body of rules which obtains and is fortified by established native usage and which is appropriate and applicable to any particular cause, action, suite, matter, dispute, issue, or question, and includes also any customary law recorded as such in a statement which shall have been . . . declared to be a true and accurate statement of such native customary law.[83]

It is quite probable that the Basotho of the Mohokare Valley, like their neighbours, the AbaTembu, referred to their *melao*, that is, laws, not as the laws of the nation, but rather as the laws of a reigning monarch. The AbaTembu counsellors under Gangelizwe, in 1881, spoke of the people as being 'under the laws of Gangelizwe, the chief of the country'. While at the same time pointing out that they, the people, 'put the chief right, if the chief wants any law they do not like'.[84] Although I have found nothing as explicit in connection with Lesotho, the notion can clearly be inferred from some social context. In one of these, for instance, in 1872 when certain distinguished Basotho chiefs and counsellors were first formally interviewed on customary law in their territory, they referred to all laws in existence during Moshoeshoe's reign as his laws. Struck by this point, although evidently not by its real significance, a senior British administrative officer, John Austin, remarked:

[N]o reference was made by the chiefs who gave evidence to chiefs prior to Moshoeshoe's advent, such as Mokhachane . . . Motlomi, Monaheng, and other great hereditary chiefs as to what ancient Basuto customs were in those days. From the evidence it is made to appear that the Basuto . . . had not established laws prior to Moshoeshoe . . . who gave them a code.[85]

The answer to Austin's puzzle, in my view, lay in the tendency for monarchies to identify law during a particular period with a reigning monarch. Indeed, in the same way, when the French Missionaries arrived in Lesotho in 1833 finding Moshoeshoe as the King of a new kingdom, they still spoke of cherished laws and legal maxims in relation to the late philosopher 'king' Mohlomi.

The *marena* of the pre-*lifaqane* days had had 'the right of making laws and publishing regulations required by the necessities of the time'[86]; but those laws and regulations needed the approval, either of a ruler's Grand Council, or the *pitso*, or both. As a rule, it appears, the procedure was for proposed legislation first to be discussed and agreed in the council, and then brought before the *pitso*; but whether or not both the council and the *pitso* were required has been difficult to establish. The following of Moshoeshoe's laws, for instance, were discussed at a *pitso*:

(1) The law removing the customary spoor law, stated by Mohato Letsie as 'a law forbidding any person from being punished simply on the evidence of a spoor or of slaughtered meat being found at a village'.[87] The date is not given.

(2) Moshoeshoe's first law against witchcraft (1843).[88] Both of these were proclaimed orally at the *pitso*, probably but not necessarily following a discussion before council.

Moshoeshoe had at least three laws that have survived for examination which were proclaimed in writing, through the printing facilities of his missionaries. All three reveal the fact that they were the work of the King's Council, but they did not necessarily come before a *pitso*:

(1) The second law against witchcraft (1855) considered by a Council which held a long debate on it, concludes with the statement: 'assented to by Letsie, by all my brothers, and by all the men in the tribe, who spit on the lie of witchcraft, and cover its face with the spittle'. The sanction was that 'when anyone is killed in a case of witchcraft, the murderer will be most severely judged, and sentenced to death'.[89]

(2) The law against spirituous liquor (1854) was 'Given with the advice and concurrence of the great men of our Tribe, by us the Chief of Basutos', in recognition of the fact that 'surely the spirituous liquors of the whites are nothing else but fire'. In punishment: 'provided any person, whether white or coloured, contravenes this order, the spirits shall be taken from him and poured out on the ground, without excuse or indemnification'.[90] The law of trade does not reveal the involvement of the Council, but it has been attested that in fact it was the work of that institution. The law, while permitting trade, stressed the fact 'there is no place belonging to the whites in my land'. 'The trader who fancies that the place he is sojourning in belongs to him, must dismiss the thought, if not, he is to quit'.[91]

Judging from at least one case during Moshoeshoe's reign, one is tempted to conclude that under the Kingdom it had become a requirement that only the King had the power over life and death. Dating to 1847, the case involved Moshoeshoe's heir, Letsie, who had just instructed his court to stone a subject to death for contempt of his court. The subject, a Nguni speaker named Soula, had refused to appear before Letsie's court, where the relatives of the elder of his two wives had entered a case of property settlement against him, arguing that as a Nguni he did not owe allegiance to the Chief, nor to the *Morena e Moholo*. Moshoeshoe, on the other hand, seems to have felt that Letsie had, as Leonard Thompson put it, committed a 'judicial murder'. The heir apparent was accordingly summoned to the King's court to be thoroughly rebuked for exceeding the limits of the law.[92]

The case, nevertheless, needs to be viewed with caution. For, on the other hand, the background to Moshoeshoe's second law against witchcraft reveals that apparently subsequent to his 1847 'judicial murder', Letsie had carried out capital punishment for which he was not called to book. In this latter case, a man named Ramothibela had been killed by another named Mpatsi, on the word of a witch. Subsequently, according to the Reverend T. Arbousset's translation, 'the murderer Mpatsi [was] sentenced to death by Chief Letsie'.[93] The second case may suggest, at least, that the king did not have the exclusive right to try blood cases, although at the same time it seems difficult to say which were and were not reserved for his special attention.

The apparent conflict or confusion in a first generation kingdom such as Lesotho is perhaps understandable. Some pre-*lifaqane* prerogatives of the *marena*, notably, military conscription had effectively been transferred to the *Morena e Moholo* as his exclusive domain: while some others, notably the *letsema* – compulsory labour in the cultivation of the ruler's main field, his *tŝimo ea lira*, as it is called – and the requirement to attend the *pitso*, still remained as shared prerogatives between territorial chiefs and their *Morena e Moholo*. The right to capital punishment probably fell in the second category of royal prerogatives, except, so it appears, the *Morena e Moholo* reserved the right, in this regard, to intervene, and territorial chiefs deferred to him when he did so.

We can therefore say in conclusion to the foregoing discussion:

(1) Pre-colonial Lesotho was a kingdom with fairly defined institutions of government, distribution and control of authority, a legal system and territorial integrity. It was a state, with all the major characteristics of the modern definition of a state – a permanent population, a defined territory (much as this is not an absolute requirement at international law), a Government, and the capacity to enter into relations with other states.

(2) As such, however, it was the first generation kingdom. Its institutions, laws and traditions were a carry-over from the previous, less complex chiefdoms and clans of the eighteenth century. These had yet to be fully adapted and tested under the more complex monarchy: but, quite clearly, such adaptation and testing, that is, the maturation of a political tradition, is something that normally requires more than one generation to be achieved. Moshoeshoe's Lesotho did not have such a breathing space before it became a British Colony.

TABLE I *Genealogy of the Royal Line of Bakoena of Lesotho*

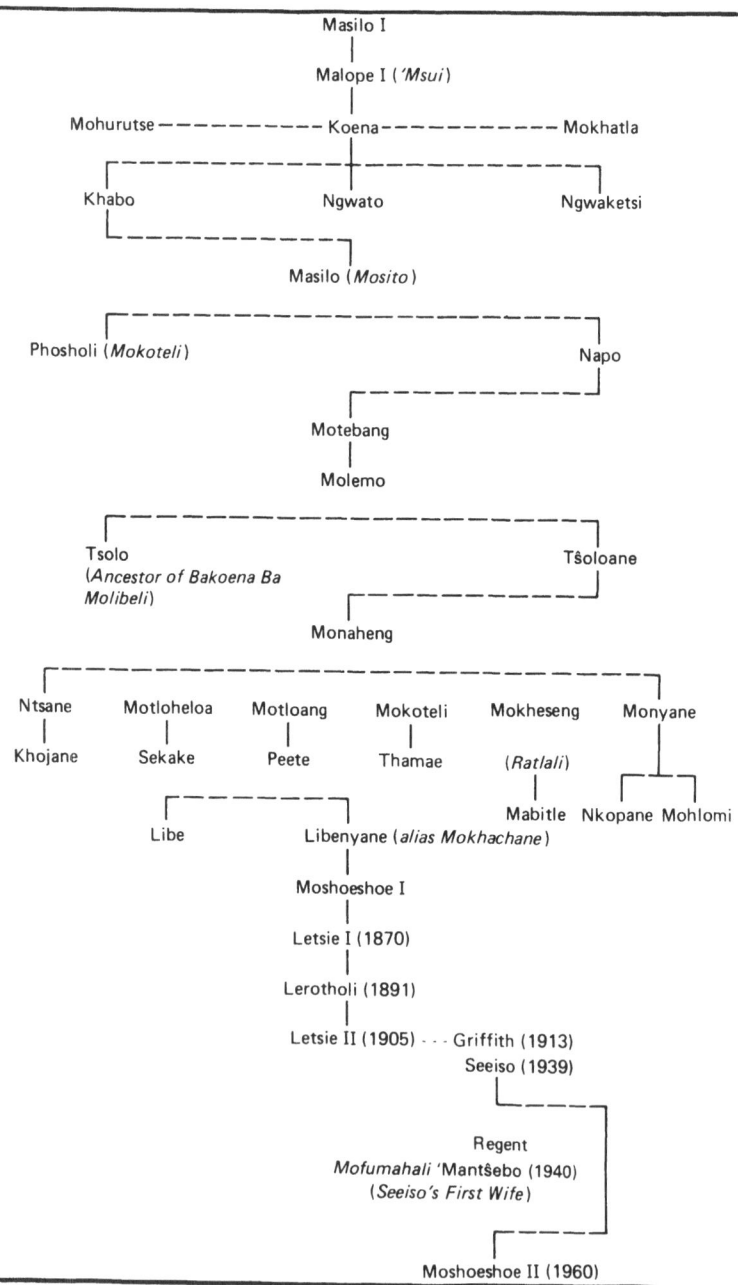

2 The Subjugation of the Kingdom

LESOTHO'S TREATY RELATIONS WITH THE BRITISH GOVERNMENT

Through a Treaty with the British Governor, Sir George Napier, in 1843, The British Government recognised the *Morena e Moholo* Moshoeshoe as the 'faithful ally of the [Cape of Good Hope] Colony'. The *Morena e Moholo* Moshoeshoe was entrusted with the responsibility of guarding the Cape Colony borders against Boer Trekker violations, in the wake of the Great Trek, in lieu of which he received an annual gift of £75, in money or in munitions of war.[1]

Only two years later, in 1845, another treaty was signed between Moshoeshoe and Sir Peregrine Maitland, also British Governor for the Cape Colony. That time the object was to sort out the problems of the strife-torn north-eastern frontier of the Cape Colony and settle the conflicting territorial claims of African sovereigns, one against the other, and with the Boer settlers in that area.[2] As a result of that treaty, Moshoeshoe lost both his annual gift, which Maitland regarded as superfluous, as well as a tract of land. The King of Basotho signed the treaty under protest; and subsequently the London Missionary Society, lobbied by the Lesotho-based Paris Evangelical Missionary Society on the King's behalf, petitioned the Secretary of State in the Home Government in London for the return of the lost tract of land, but without success.[3]

Then in 1848, Sir Harry Smith, the second Governor of the Cape of Good Hope to get the joint appointment with that of High Commissioner for South Africa,[4] fairly hectored Moshoeshoe into signing an 'agreement' mainly for the purpose of maintaining order and good government in the region generally north of the Orange River.[5] (Sir Harry Smith had a thoroughly disagreeable personality to Africans in the region and carried the odium for having once compelled some AmaXhosa sovereigns at the conclusion of a war to show their submission to the British Crown by kissing his feet.)[6] The 'agreement' obligated Moshoeshoe to recognise the paramount authority of the British Crown in the region, while 'at the same time maintaining inviolable' his 'hereditary rights'.[7] It stressed the necessity of keeping him 'in strict alliance with her Majesty of England'; and, notably, as I shall later show, it was textually referred to as 'this day's cemented alliance'.[8] On its basis, and on the basis of similar and similarly-extracted 'agreements' signed by other African sovereigns in the affected area, on 3 February 1848, Sir Harry Smith established a territorial entity called the Orange River Sovereignty.[9]

The Orange River Sovereignty was a constitutional chimera:

> It included, on the one hand, Boer settlers – British subjects, whose allegiance to the British Crown required, in the view of the Crown Law Officers in London, an Act of Parliament to be severed, which had not been done,[10] – while, on the other hand, it included African polities such as Lesotho, whose sovereignty had not clearly been ceded by the Harry Smith 'agreements'. As a contemporary observer later noted: 'Many people found it difficult to understand how the same country could simultaneously obey two Sovereigns'.[11] It was clear from the start that the High Commissioner's creation would not last.

As the most powerful African monarch under the Orange River Sovereignty, Moshoeshoe found his authority constantly challenged by the British Resident, Major Warden, who administered over that creation. Efforts at subjecting the Basotho King to British authority, on the pretext that Basotho had raided cattle belonging to Boer settlers, resulted in an armed conflict with Smith's successor, Sir George Cathcart in 1852, in which Sir George was vanquished. In the end it was concluded that the establishment of the Orange River Sovereignty had been an impractical solution to the problems of that region and accordingly it was abandoned in 1854. On its ruins, through the Bloemfontein Convention, the Boer settler component of the defunct Sovereignty was reconstituted as the Republic of the Orange Free State – once more without an Act of Imperial Parliament to sever the settlers' allegiance to the British Crown;[12] while for his part the Basotho king was informed, clearly as an afterthought, that since 'a war between two persons breaks all pre-existing treaties', his encounter with Cathcart in 1852 had broken his alliance with Queen Victoria.[13]

However assuming, as both the Kingdom of Lesotho and the British Government appear to have done in 1854, that the two states were still in treaty relations and allies with each other at least up to 1852, the Moshoeshoe-Cathcart fracas of that year had not itself broken the alliance, thanks to the political genius of the Mosotho king. For, fearing that he might not withstand the redoubled wrath of Cathcart's forces, which had been certain to descend upon him, the King of Basotho and close men of his Council had, at midnight on 20 December 1852, following the day of the battle, written the High Commissioner a letter which undoubtedly safeguarded his relations with the British Government. Penned by Nehemiah Sekhonyana, one of the King's sons, the letter had stated:

> You have this day fought against my people and taken possession of many cattle. You have thereby achieved the object which you had in view, which was to obtain compensation for the Boers. I pray you to content yourself with what you have taken. I beg peace of you. You have revealed your might. You have chastised. Let it be enough, I pray you, and may I cease to be considered an enemy of the Queen. I will henceforth endeavour to maintain order among my people.[14]

Grateful for the ingenious mending of his prestige, and probably also conscious not to be up-staged in statesmanship by the African monarch, the High Commissioner had in turn, on 21 December, seized the golden opportunity to show his magnanimity. He informed King Moshoeshoe:

> I am a man who never breaks his word, otherwise the Queen would not have sent me here. I have taken the fine by force, and I am satisfied . . . *I am not angry with your people for fighting in defence of their property; . . . I now desire not to consider you, Chief, as an enemy of the Queen* . . . Now therefore, Chief Moshoeshoe, I consider your past obligations fulfilled, and hope that you will take measures for preventing such abuses in future. In the meantime, *as the Queen's representative, I subscribed myself, Your Friend* . . . I shall be glad to see either yourself or your sons, *in the same friendly manner and in the same good faith as before the fight* . . . (My emphasis).

On 3 February the following year, in a letter to King Moshoeshoe by the British Resident of the Orange River Sovereignty, Mr Green, officially approved by Cathcart, the theme was pursued more explicitly: 'You, yourself, Moshoeshoe, now that peace has been made, are . . . an ally of the Queen'; while Sir George Cathcart, personally writing to the Secretary of State for Colonies ten days later, on 13 January, drove the point further home by styling the King of Basotho 'a valuable ally of no small power'.[15]

We can indeed safely assert that on grounds of international law as then understood, neither Lesotho's encounter with Her Majesty's forces in 1852, nor the dissolution of the Orange River Sovereignty and its corollary, the creation of the Orange Free State in 1854, discharged Moshoeshoe's 'agreement' or treaty of alliance of 1848. For that treaty to be discharged and for the parties to it to remit to the *status quo ante foedus*, it ideally required 'a fresh agreement as to the effect of the abrogation upon the position of the parties'.[16] At the least it required mutual consent. Neither ever came under consideration.

The most disconcerting aspect of the 1854 débâcle was the effect of the legal instrument that set up the Orange Free State – the Bloemfontein Convention. The Convention had one article – Article 2 – which had two clauses noxious to the interests of the Kingdom of Lesotho:

(1) The first of these was to the effect that 'no treaty might be signed unilaterally by the British Government, which might be detrimental to the interests and well being of the Orange Free State' with 'natives of surrounding states'.

(2) The second was that British-controlled sources of guns and munitions of war were preferentially closed to those 'natives of surrounding states', in favour of the Boers of the Orange Free State.

Lesotho Attempts to Resuscitate Its Relations with Britain

Following the first major boundary war with the Orange Free State in 1858, from which the British Government, through its High Commissioner for South Africa, had rescued it from potential destruction in the hands of Basotho, Moshoeshoe and his government must have concluded that, given a few more years of preferential access to guns, the new republic would become formidable. Hence, a few days after Marthinus Wessels Pretorius (the son of Andries Pretorius, the voortrekker) of the Transvaal became the President of the Orange Free State in February 1860, thereby uniting the two Boer republics (in a union that lasted but three and a half years), Moshoeshoe had shown great anxiety for a permanent peace with his irksome neighbour. A meeting of the two heads of state had been arranged on 30 March, at which Moshoeshoe spoke for three hours on the need for peace, and Pretorius corroborated that 'I must have security and peace for my people also'.[17] The King of Basotho had spent the night in the President's tent, 'and the next morning he and Mr Pretorius reviewed a portion of the Basuto army, numbering about six thousand cavalry . . . Moshoeshoe danced like mad, and thus the conference broke up'.[18]

Even before the end of the conference, however, it was clear that there could be no peace between the two nations. Supposedly, Moshoeshoe and Pretorius signed a treaty on 30 March. (The treaty remains untraceable, to date.) Supposedly, that treaty 'dealt mainly with the necessity of a border police, but avoided the main issue: the disputed northern frontier'. Moshoeshoe solemnised that day by planting a white flag, saying: 'Let this be a remembrance to all, White and Black, that peace is now for evermore'; but when he proposed the toast, in Dutch, 'alle oude questies tot niet' [let all old questions be forgotten, liquidated]', Pretorius queried:

> Old father Moshoeshoe that won't do. Everlasting friendship if you like, from henceforth, but all the old questions we can't settle in this way[19]

The test of wills and the settlement of old scores between Basotho and the Boers were certain to come, sooner or later.

So, on the occasion of a visit to South Africa of Prince Alfred, in August the same year, 1860, the King of Basotho placed in Alfred's hand a letter to his illustrious mother, Queen Victoria. In that letter he submitted an appeal:

> I am the oldest of the Queen's Ministers in this country from Napier, Maitland, H. Smith, down to Sir George Clarke [who succeeded Cathcart in 1853], and in spite of everything that has happened to me, . . . I have been faithful in my allegiance to Her Majesty. My prayer to-day is that I may be restored to the same position among the Queen's servants that I first held, for I am become as the least of them . . . I have come to have the peace which I enjoy increased and confirmed.[20]

As that letter produced no results, the following year, 1861, the *Morena e Moholo* wrote a detailed and argued letter of application, this time to the British High Commissioner for South Africa in Cape Town.[21] For ease of discussion the letter can be divided into three parts.

In the first part he reviewed the status of his treaty relations with the British Government thus: in 1845, Maitland had 'proposed to me an additional treaty founded on the first' – the Napier Treaty of

1843. As a matter of fact, he pointed out, he had bought the Maitland Treaty with land (in reference to the tract of land that Lesotho had thereby lost), 'and the land has not been returned to me'. Therefore, Moshoeshoe argued, instead of one taking the place of the other, the two treaties of 1843 and 1845 reinforced each other. Following the same line of reasoning, he put it to the High Commissioner that his 'agreement' of 1848 with Sir Harry Smith, the one textually referred to as 'this day's cemented alliance', had not discharged the former two treaties. As he put it: that which had been cemented 'cannot be said to have destroyed that which it had cemented'. With reference to his encounter with Cathcart in 1852, he agreed that, indeed, 'war is a flood which destroys the traces of the past'. Nevertheless he denied that he had been at war with the Governor and cited all the correspondence between the two of them which had a bearing on the question. Finally he referred to the abandonment of the Orange River Sovereignty in 1854 as 'merely the removal of a superstructure' and 'asserted that the old foundation, which were my original treaties, remained firm'.

In the second part, the *Morena e Moholo* registered his protest against the noxious Article 2 of the Bloemfontein Convention of 1854 on the question of guns. The second clause of the Article was to the effect that British-controlled sources of guns and munitions of war were preferentially closed to those 'natives of surrounding states', in favour of the Boers of the Orange Free State. Moshoeshoe's comment was that:

> Though I desire peace and much and above all things, yet, after it, I do desire also that powder and such supplies should be allowed to reach us in such measure as our conduct showed us to be deserving of confidence. I beg this favour, because when these things are prohibited my position is difficult, for it gives power to the arguments of those who say it is the fixed determination of Government to give the native tribes no protection, and to deprive them of the means of self protection. I beg it also because my treaties give it to me.

Moshoeshoe, in the third part of his letter, wished the High Commissioner, the newly-arrived Sir Philip Wodehouse, to support his petition and 'to lay this letter before the Queen', in view of the fact that 'there is still some doubt as to the precise nature of . . . my past relations with Her Majesty's Government and my wishes for the future'.

In response, Sir Philip Wodehouse followed his predecessor's suggestions and sent a commission to Lesotho in 1862. The commission, composed of Messrs Joseph Orpen and John Burnet, was to establish, not the soundness of Moshoeshoe's argument, which the High Commissioner thought to be obscured by the embroidery of his metaphors, but rather, what kind of status 'under the Sovereignty of Her Majesty the Queen' he desired.[22] The net effect would be to detract the *Morena e Moholo* away from holding the British Government to old treaties, into applying for a status that would be negotiated afresh.

At the conclusion of the convention of his Grand Council held at the capital, Thaba Bosiu, in 1862, and which had been attended by a delegation from the King of AmaZulu, his overlord, the *Morena e Moholo* Moshoeshoe then put his application in the following words:

> I am like a man who has a house, the man rules the house and all that is in it, and the Government rules him. My 'house' is Basutoland.[23] So that *the Queen rules my people only through me* . . . I shall be like a blind man, but when [a British Agent] directs me I shall be considered wise . . . *I wish to govern* my own people by native law, *by our own laws*, but if the Queen wishes after this to introduce other laws into *my country*, I would be willing, but I should wish such laws to be submitted to the Council, of the Basutos, and *when they are accepted by my* Council, I will send to the Queen and *inform her* that they have become law. [My italic][24]

Wodehouse grasped the point clearly that Moshoeshoe did not wish to cede his sovereignty. As he pointed out to the Secretary of State: Moshoeshoe did not wish to be 'substantially a British subject'; he was not prepared to submit to British laws.[25] He essentially sought to place himself under the British Government as a vassal – a status which he enjoyed under the King of AmaZulu, and one which the AmaPondo Chief Faku held under him.

Between 1862 and 1863 the High Commissioner was apparently weighing the prospects of honouring Lesotho's application. Unfortunately, however, some time in 1863 the President of the Orange Free State, John Brand, got wind of the development; and, according to the High Commissioner, the President received the news of the pending British offer to his arch-enemy with 'much apprehension'.

As a consequence, in his own words, the High Commissioner 'allowed it to fall to the ground'.[26]

Lesotho Negotiates for British Protection under the Pressure of War

In June 1865 the second war between Lesotho and the Orange Free State broke out. The Boers were far better armed that time than they had been in 1858 and Basotho fared badly. By the end of August 1865 the King of Basotho was pinned to his mountain fortress and capital, Thaba Bosiu. Having asked the Orange Free State for an armistice, the King was faced with demands from its President for 40 000 cattle, 5 000 horses, 60 000 sheep and the submission of two of his sons as hostages until all demands had been met. The Orange Free State demanded also the evacuation of Thaba Bosiu, the handing up of guns, and the kingdom's sovereignty – all in four days.[27] However, as the *Morena e Moholo* felt certain that 'I will never do so', he turned to Philip Wodehouse, 'giving myself and my country up to Her Majesty's Government under certain conditions which we may agree upon.'[28]

The High Commissioner, on the other hand, felt it was 'impracticable' for Her Majesty's Government 'to interpose in any manner' at that juncture. The immediate cause of the war had been an unauthorised raid on Boers by an ungovernable nephew of the *Morena e Moholo* named Lesaoana (alias Ramanehella), and the High Commissioner felt that before that 'troubled spirit' was punished, 'you cannot justly expect me to place faith in your professions of desire to fulfil all *obligations of a faithful ally* of the British Government'. [My emphasis][29] In October 1865 the High Commissioner assured his Secretary of State that he had 'no intention of accepting him and his people as British subjects'.[30] Lesotho was thus left on its own to reverse the tide of the war over the subsequent three years of its duration.

As the war dragged on, however, it became clear to the Colonial Government that, independently of Lesotho's need for protection, a number of factors pointed to the necessity of bringing that kingdom under some type of formal control. In his correspondence with the Imperial Government, the High Commissioner remarked on the embarrassment caused by the protracted war with the Orange Free State – 'a small independent state, peopled by the nearest kinsmen of the Cape Colonists, possessing their warmest sympathies, . . . excessively weak in itself'.[31] In the event that the fortunes of the

Basotho in the battlefield should change for the better, the High Commissioner dreaded the prospect of the Boers' defeat at the hands of their darker adversaries.

At the same time, the prospect of a Boer conquest of Lesotho inspired the fear in him, which fear he shared with the Lieutenant Governor of Natal, Robert W. Keate, that such an outcome might lead to 'important changes in the political position of the several powers' in South Africa which could not be permitted.[32] One of those important changes was, in the High Commissioner's view, that the Orange Free State might gain access to, and control the Indian Ocean port of St John's. Frantically attempting to forestall such a possibility, the High Commissioner had even begun secret negotiations with the AmaMpondo sovereign, *Nkosi* Faku, Moshoeshoe's vassal with jurisdiction in that area, to make 'without any delay, a cession of the navigable part of the St John's river, with a certain portion of land adjoining to the British Government'.[33]

Then, too, there were commercial interests to consider. Lieutenant Governor Keate counselled Wodehouse that the unending border conflicts between the Boers and Basotho would affect immigration from Europe, ruin the Overberg trade, 'which is of such paramount importance to us'. It would freeze the injection of capital for railway construction, affect the exploitation of coalfields and, in general, debilitate 'the development . . . of the latent resources of the colony'. For this and other reasons of a political nature, the Lieutenant Governor favoured a decisive and effective control of the Kingdom of Lesotho.[34] Commercial interests in the Cape of Good Hope were similarly severely affected by the War. The Cape businessmen thus stood ready to support any move, such as that of Robert Keate, to bring the Basotho-Boer hostilities to an end.[35]

Against this background, Lesotho's repeated plea to be placed under 'the power and protection' of Queen Victoria had to be reviewed. Wodehouse forwarded a persuasive despatch to the Secretary of State, Edward Cardwell, on 13 January 1866, vouching for the sincerity of Basotho in their pledges of 'allegiance' to the British Crown. He was convinced, he said, that accepting Basotho as British subjects would be for the good, not only of themselves, but of all of South Africa.[36] He regretted the 'embarrassment' created by the existence in the proximity of British colonies of the 'excessively weak' Orange Free State, unequal to the task of settling its quarrels with 'natives around'. He reviewed the effects of the war on commerce. He registered his view that accepting responsibility over Lesotho had become 'our duty'.[37]

Notwithstanding his sympathies toward the Orange Free State, and also his duty to his own country, the High Commissioner was a great admirer of the King of Basotho. He marvelled at his political dexterity, and also feared it. As he had earlier in 1862 indicated to his Secretary of State: 'Moshoeshoe's great ability and skill in negotiations have never been denied . . . He makes it almost impracticable for me to take extreme steps against [him].'[38] He saw him as a statesman and 'diplomatist' always bent on keeping good relations with the British Government, which often put British functionaries like himself in an ungainly position.

It was due more to this disposition, perhaps, than to other factors that, in the January 1866 despatch to Edward Cardwell, he proposed how Lesotho could be ruled. There should be as little interference as possible, he said, on 'the rights and customs [of the Basotho] now existing'. The Kingdom of Lesotho was to be administered through the indigenous government, with only 'two or three' magistrates. It was to be placed directly under the High Commissioner, who would rule it on behalf of the Crown, and not annexed to either of Her British Majesty's South African colonies. The financial responsibility for administration was to be borne by the Basotho themselves. Finally the chiefs and the people were clearly to understand that British authority was 'for their benefit', so that should they in future fail to provide the necessary financial support for their administration, 'our *protection* would at once be withdrawn [My emphasis]'[39]

In his response to the High Commissioner, 9 March 1866, the Secretary of State, however, expressed his amazement at the latter's apparent volte-face. In his view, British expansion in South Africa could not at that point be contemplated 'without some overriding necessity' and that, as far as he was concerned, had not yet arisen. While appreciating Moshoeshoe's plight, he said, he feared that once the imminent danger was over, especially after Moshoeshoe's death, the kingdom might challenge British sovereignty. Also, in the unwelcome event of British annexation of the kingdom, he disapproved of the High Commissioner's mooted policy of non-interference, charging that some of the customs of the Basotho were 'repugnant to Christianity, and . . . inconsistent with the free institutions of British rule'. The best way of avoiding conflict in this regard was, he felt, abstention, in the first instance, from 'unnecessary extension of sovereignty'. For, once entered into, 'Sovereignty involves correlative obligations under which public and personal rights grow up, such as it is difficult, if not dishonourable, to compromise for the sake of some political convenience arising at the time'.[40]

Meantime, the Lesotho government lost faith in Wodehouse's abilities and *bona fides* and began to look for an alternative 'door to the Queen's Cave'. This other door would be Lieutenant Governor Robert Keate of Natal. In July 1866 the *Morena e Moholo* of Basotho convened a council for five days at Thaba Bosiu to thrash out the modalities of this alternative course of action. The result was that a high-powered delegation, carrying a brief letter penned by one of Moshoeshoe's sons, was dispatched to Natal for negotiations regarding Lesotho's possible annexation to that colony. The delegation was instructed to point out that, while Lesotho was perfectly equal to the task of vanquishing the Orange Free State, the current situation of questionable British neutrality, made worse by the fact that some Cape and Natal levies were busy supporting the enemy, had made the war unfair and a bid for British protection an unavoidable step. In the circumstances, annexation to Natal seemed the more sensible move than going through the High Commissioner, thereby risking annexation to the factious Cape Colony, with its Boer-Briton quarrels. The prospect of being subjected to further Boer harassments under the Cape, the delegation emphasised, was quite disagreeable.[41]

Quickly upon the heels of the first, a second, one-man, delegation was sent to Natal to emphasise that really Lesotho's predicament was essentially one of lack of access to guns. As Lesotho's most trusted ambassador, Nathanael Makotoko, put it:[42]

> The Orange Free State and Basuto nation are both on friendly terms with the British Government . . . Our enemies in time of war are supplied with arms and ammunition to any extent they may require and may be able to purchase any either in time of peace or war; surely this is not neutrality. If the British Government will not receive us and our Country, . . . if it looks upon us and the Orange Free State equally as friends and children, . . . and that therefore we should be left to punish each other, let it not supply arms and ammunition to one side and withhold them from the other, but let both have an equal chance, and if the Basutos[43] must perish let them perish defending themselves with means to procure which they are allowed the same facilities as their enemies from neutral source.

Here the Lesotho Government was going to full lengths to compromise the High Commissioner's role as the chief spokesman in South Africa for the British Government. He was no longer getting Lesotho's thoughts directly; he was having to rely on Lieutenant Keate, whose personal designs on the kingdom were at variance with his own; and through Keate the High Commissioner was tacitly being made a part of Lesotho's problems. The decision to negotiate the reversal of the obnoxious clause of the Bloemfontein Convention, on guns, lay ultimately on him.

Just as the Natal Legislative Council prepared to accept Lesotho's offer made by the first delegation, the High Commissioner moved quickly to salvage his image. On 3 May 1867 he wrote to the new Secretary of State, the Duke of Buckingham and Chandos, a terse letter by which he warned that Lesotho's overture to Natal was an expression of loss of confidence in his own office 'as the paramount British functionary representing Her Majesty in South Africa'. He felt strongly that it was not desirable to encourage this decline in the image of his office. He recommended the acceptance of Lesotho at the earliest convenient moment.[44]

Buckingham and Chandos then responded favourable. He informed the High Commissioner on 9 December 1867 that permission had been granted to receive the Basotho as British subjects for the sake of 'the peace and welfare of Her Majesty's possessions in South Africa'. It stood to reason, Buckingham and Chandos remarked, that this step might 'embarrass our relations' with the Orange Free State, but the step had become necessary.[45]

The Annexation of the Kingdom

As a preliminary step to annexation, therefore, on 13 January 1868 Sir Philip Wodehouse wrote letters to King Moshoeshoe and President Brand on the subject. To Moshoeshoe he indicated his 'satisfaction' that at last Her Majesty's Government had agreed to receive him and his people as British subjects and that the modalities of annexation had been left to the High Commissioner's Office.[46] To Brand, he said he had been authorised to 'take steps' to receive the Basotho under the British Crown and advised him to apply to the Volksraad (parliament), due to convene the following month, for authority to negotiate the boundary question with him.[47] Simultaneously he stationed a Cape police force near Lesotho's capital under Sir Walter Curry, to underline his intention.

This development was evidently seen by the Orange Free State as

Lesotho's diplomatic victory. The Boer Republic was at this point insolvent and on the verge of economic ruin. Public opinion on the continuation of the War was highly divided. The urban and English population for instance, together with a small section of Dutch colonists, had always lamented the abandonment of the Orange River Sovereignty and the subsequent establishment of the Orange Free State. In the meantime, the vicissitudes of the War had seemed to confirm their worst fears. Their reaction to Wodehouse's letters of 13 January was, therefore, one of deep-seated disappointment. The Editor of the Bloemfontein *Friend* lashed out:

> NO: We are to be 'left out' in the cold while the old nigger MOSHESH is to be received into the Colonial family of Great Britain, and taken to the warm embrace of our still beloved QUEEN. MOSHESH . . . is to be petted and pampered, while we are to continue to be treated as castaways.[48]

President Brand expressed his own disappointment from another vantage point. He protested that, after all, 'our armies are, under God's blessing, everywhere successful'. In the circumstances the High Commissioner's intervention snatched from his grasp a well-nigh honestly won prize. Above all, he reminded the High Commissioner, intervention was in breach of Article 2 of the Bloemfontein Convention, in so far as a treaty was about to be entered into with an African state: the first clause of Article 2 referred to provided that 'no treaty might be signed unilaterally by the British Government, which might be detrimental to the interests and well being of the Orange Free State' with 'natives of surrounding states'.[49]

Had President Brand stopped the hostilities upon receipt of the High Commissioner's letter and stuck to his argument that the Bloemfontein Convention was being breached, he might legally have placed the latter in an awkward position. As he did not do so, however, he gave the High Commissioner a badly-needed loophole, albeit a flimsy one. The High Commissioner was then able to write him a letter saying his continued hostilities against the Basotho, a people in principle already accepted as British subjects, constituted 'an unfriendly feeling towards the British Government, quite sufficient to absolve me from all observance of the terms of the Convention of the 23rd February 1854'.[50]

So, on 12 March 1868, Sir Philip Wodehouse proclaimed Lesotho, anglicised as Basutoland, one of Her Majesty's dominions. Crucial in the Proclamation was the clause:

I do hereby proclaim and declare that from and after the publications here of. The said Tribe of the Basuto shall be and shall be taken to be for all intents and purposes, British Subjects; and the Territory of the said Tribe shall be and shall be taken to be British Territory.[51]

However, there was more to the terms of annexation than was reflected in the Proclamation. Evidently because the *Morena e Moholo* Moshoeshoe had still not given up the idea of vassalage, as opposed to ceding his sovereignty to the British Crown, he subsequently wrote to the High Commissioner on 21 April 1868 a letter requesting that Lesotho should be treated as a 'special territory' – 'a Native reserve where natives alone should be allowed to dwell and which would be independent from the High Commissioner'.[52] Moshoeshoe was, after all, conscious of the fact that Wodehouse still held him in high esteem. Besides, he had, up to that point, repeatedly impressed it upon him that his predicament with the Boers had been the British Government's making directly and indirectly he had been indicting the British Government for racial discrimination. Directly and indirectly he had been pointing out the fact that were it not for Article 2 of the Bloemfontein Convention – a British piece of legislation – he could have settled his quarrel with the Orange Free State. In the circumstances, therefore, it seems he was putting the British Government to the test: was its interest the protection of his kingdom, or was it in fact subjugation!

Suffice it to say, Sir Philip Wodehouse granted the King his wish. Although the High Commissioner seems then to have only communicated his agreement verbally, twelve years later when he was called from retirement by the Home Office to say whether or not he had agreed to reserve 'Basutoland for Basutos only' he responded:

I can only reply, that such was the very thing to the attainment of which all my efforts were directed – it was for the purpose of putting an end to Border disputes, and for removing doubts as to the true limits of the Territory to which the claim of that Tribe, and that alone, should be admitted for the future, that these . . . negotiations were carried on . . . The object was to secure peace and comfort for the Basutos in the future.

As we can see, from 1842 to 1868, Lesotho's relationship with the British Government was a progression of treaty relations – never quite clear for legal classification. It is a subject of debate well worth a separate treatment to determine whether or not the status of treaty relations really ended with the Bloemfontein Convention in 1854 or whether British officials in South Africa peremptorily decided, for political convenience and on racial grounds, that the Orange Free State should abandon strict adherence to British legal practices and negate the treaty relations with the Kingdom of Lesotho. The Proclamation of 1868 came as a negotiated settlement in circumstances that were dictated by the British commitment to the continued existence of the Orange Free State, further aggravated by British commercial interests, the balance of power in South Africa, and only marginally the security of the Kingdom of Lesotho. So that, in the final analysis, it was mainly the kingdom's diplomacy that dictated the modality of British intervention and the survival of the Basotho nation.

CONSTITUTIONAL ANOMALIES AND THEIR
CONSEQUENCES

The outcome of this negotiated settlement for the future was that the British Government at home, as well as its officials in South Africa and in Lesotho vacillated in their designation of Lesotho between calling it a crown colony on the one hand, and calling it a protectorate on the other hand. Between 1868 and 1884 Lesotho was variously referred to by the Colonial Office as 'a kind of outlying territory with a High Commission constitution';[54] 'an inchoate Crown colony waiting for annexation to one of its neighbours'; 'the protectorate under Imperial Government'. In 1883, the Secretary of State for Colonies, the Earl of Derby, speaking in the House of Commons, could still state: 'We don't propose to make Basutoland a Crown colony, or introduce the costly machinery of European officers. We wish the Basutos to enjoy Home Rule in the strictest sense of the word.'[55]

To the indigenous government the constitutional status of Lesotho was one of political convenience. In the main, the *Morena e Moholo* and his chiefs regarded their kingdom as having merely entered 'the covenant of the alliance and protection between . . . Moshesh the Wise and Victoria the Good'.[56] The basis of this view, as the *Morena e Moholo* Letsie, Moshoeshoe's successor put it, was that: 'We were told that the Government leaves a man to govern his country, with his sheep, his cattle, and his gun.'[57] In this understanding he was backed by the spokesman of the Paris Evangelical Missionary

Society, who had been with Basotho since 1833, who affirmed that Sir Philip Wodehouse had said that 'the land would be kept for the Basotho, their children and their children's children' and that not even magistrates would be allowed the ownership of land in Lesotho.[58] When there were greater benefits to be reaped by claiming British citizenship, however, with equal facility the Basotho asserted that they were the loyal subjects of the British Empire.

THE HIGH COMMISSIONER'S ARRANGEMENT IS PUT TO THE TEST

The peculiar and confusing constitutional status of Lesotho under Britain allowed the indigenous government constantly to challenge any efforts by the High Commissioner or his officers to take major decisions or assert authority without consultations with it. In fact, it is more to the point to say, Lesotho expected that its consent should be sought, rather than that it should merely be consulted.

The Tsekelo-Buchanan Affair

The first such challenge to the High Commissioner's authority came only a year after his Proclamation. It was over the boundary question: for nine days, between 4 and 12 February 1869, the High Commissioner had alone and on his own authority been negotiating Lesotho's boundary with the Orange Free State with President Brand and his officers. In the process, the Boers had driven such a hard bargain with him that he lost about one third of Lesotho's most valuable agrarian land to the republic. Understandably the Basotho were indignant at this development. As one observer put it, the Basotho came to feel that 'the English have not come here to help them but to take their land and hinder their chiefs from marrying'.[59]

Accordingly when an ambitious Natalian lawyer named D. D. Buchanan offered his services to him,[60] Moshoeshoe seized the opportunity, protesting that he had been 'covered with shame . . . and I feel great grief' at the fact that despite his earlier promise to restore all his country back to him, the High Commissioner had it 'handed to the Free State'. He protested: 'I have no one who will go to the Queen for me and bring her my tears'.[61]

In clear disregard of Wodehouse's authority, Moshoeshoe deputised Tsekelo, a literate junior son of his, to accompany Buchanan to Queen Victoria and duly 'clothed him with all the power to act for me'.[62] From London Tsekelo was to leave for France, in the company of the French missionary, the Reverend Daumas, who, having lost his mission station to the Orange Free State in the War, had his own axe to grind. The King's son, who spoke both English and French fluently, was to represent the grievance to the French Emperor, Napoleon III.

When the High Commissioner was informed of the plan, already in progress, just a few days before the delegation was to board in Cape Town for the high seas, he was furious, and he vowed not 'to give in an inch' to it. He dismissed the scheduled mission to France as 'all rubbish' that had to be put a stop to. He accused the Paris Evangelical Missionary Society of 'trying to create confusion' in Lesotho and threatened to encourage 'the operations of the Catholic mission' against it.[63] The Oblates of Mary Immaculate had just arrived in Lesotho in 1862 from the AmaZulu Kingdom, where they had spent ten unrewarding years. The French missionaries, who had carved their place in the hearts of the Basotho, saw them as intruders and great rivalry raged between the two.

As the stakes got high, Moshoeshoe must have read in Wodehouse the despondency of a man who might throw his kingdom into a worse disaster if he did not abandon his scheme: the High Commissioner might renege on his 'protection'. For he quickly, through his second son, Jeremiah Molapo, whom the colonial administration had already discovered to have had 'a finger in the affair', attempted to recall the delegation. In consequence, Lesotho's most trusted ambassador, Nathanael Makotoko, put the interests of the state above adventure and returned. Tsekelo, Buckanan and Daumas, for their part, ignored the King's messengers and sailed, with their varying motives to London: the centre of power.[64]

Simultaneously all the major actors in the plot on the home front, jointly and severally, washed their hands of the entire affair. Moshoeshoe, Letsie and George Tlali, another literate son of the *Morena e Moholo*, co-signed a letter to Lesotho's High Commissioner's Agent by which Moshoeshoe pointed out: 'I have said that all is right, and still say so, and I am very sorry that such a matter or a thing as this expedition of Tsekelo's should have happened'. So as not to invite reprisals on Tsekelo, however, the *Morena e Moholo* skilfully qualified his statement of disassociation:[65]

I do not forbid anyone to speak as he thinks right, as I myself will speak or write to the Governor or to the Home Government at any time when I find it necessary to do so.

Molapo made a separate letter of denial. Letsie and George Tlali also made additional separate denials to the High Commissioner's Agent;[66] while the Conference of the French Missionaries wrote their own letter, apologising for the Reverend Daumas' participation.

Armed with these letters of denial, the High Commissioner was able to send a lengthy communication to London effectively destroying the delegation's credibility.[67] The delegation had otherwise been given a sympathetic reception. The Permanent Under-Secretary for Colonies had believed that Wodehouse still had the opportunity to armtwist the Boers into disgorging more of Basotho land.[68] In the House of Commons, some fifty MPs supported the delegation's petition that the Convention of Aliwal North, as it was called, on the boundary question had illegally ceded 'British territory', while, significantly, others questioned the very assumption that the Kingdom of Lesotho was British territory.[69] The question, however, had eventually to be dropped because it had no *bona fide* petitioner, either from Thaba Bosiu or Cape Town.

The High Commissioner's Laissez-faire Administration and the Authority of the Chiefs

Sir Philip Wodehouse had drawn up a set of regulations for the governance of Lesotho. These regulations provided, in the extreme, for the division of the territory into three districts, each with a magistrate and a senior chief, as well as arrogating to the High Commissioner the authority for land allocation, heretofore the prerogative of the *Morena e Moholo*. (The Territory would actually be divided into four districts in 1871. By 1900 there were seven districts.) This transfer of authority was, nevertheless, without prejudice to the notion of 'Basutoland for Basutos only'. Magistrates' courts were placed above chiefs' courts, with people having the right of appeal to magistrates. Other than that, the court system remained in the hands of the chiefs.[70]

According to John Allen Benyon, once Sir Philip Wodehouse was back in London in May 1870, having completed his term of office, he further

Significantly recommended that the High Commissioner's competence to govern the Basuto should be based upon the authority which Moshesh, as paramount chief, had ceded, and not upon those legal instruments of royal Prerogative, Letters Patent or Orders-in-Council, by which British 'Colonies of cession' were customarily ruled from the metropolis.[71]

Unfortunately for the High Commissioner, his draft regulations took a considerably long time before they were confirmed and came into force in December 1871;[72] (and that would be in a drastically modified form). In the circumstances he had to be satisfied with asking his Agent, James Henry Bowker, on the spot, to 'make the best of this abominable hash which the Secretary of State is mischievously prolonging'.[73]

The consequences of this delay was that Lesotho remained effectively under the authority of the indigenous government of the chiefs. It was as if the old Kingdom had regained its independence, or that indeed the British Government was only an ally come to assist a friend in time of peril. That spirit of independence would die hard.

At the age of 84, tired, sick and done, Moshoeshoe handed the sceptre to his already 57 years old heir, Letsie, at a *pitso* on 18 January 1870. Significantly the installation was exclusively in the hands of the royal family of Lesotho. The British Government played no part whatsoever to symbolise its authority in the new relationship. On 11 March Moshoeshoe died and was buried at Thaba Bosiu. Wodehouse left South Africa in May, having at least succeeded in appointing two magistrates, John Austen and Inspector Surmon to assist Bowker in his administration of the Territory. There was also a small police force of one hundred officers. On 31 December, Wodehouse's successor, Sir Henry Barkly, arrived in Cape Town. A shift in the already unsteady constitutional position of Lesotho was about to be made.

Lesotho is Annexed to the Cape of Good Hope Colony

For some time before Wodehouse's last return to London, the idea of giving the Cape Colony Responsible Government had been under discussion. In South Africa Wodehouse opposed the idea on the grounds that the Imperial Government would implicitly be abdicating its responsibility as the guardian of the rights of the 'native' population under the colony. This responsibility would devolve upon the cabinet of the Responsible Government, and he feared that, the cabinet being unsympathetic to the rights of the 'coloured race', a lot of mischief and gross injustices were sure to follow.[74] While the Imperial Parliament generally shared this concern, there were those in it who feared that Responsible Government would in fact work to the detriment of the white community. The Marquis of Salisbury, for instance, chief exponent of this view, argued that 'The surrender of all the power, both legislative and administrative, of the Colony into the hands of a majority elected by a coloured race is an experiment that has never been tried yet'.[75]

By the time Sir Henry Barkly arrived in South Africa, however, humanitarian fears regarding the 'native problem' had given way to political realities. A way around 'coloured franchise' had also been found. As the Permanent Under-secretary for Colonies, Robert Herbert said: 'it could be culpable to allow the establishment of Responsible Government without at the same time expressly disfranchising all persons not being three parts, or at least one half, of white blood'.[76] The Cape Colony was certain to get Responsible Government.

In the meantime Sir Henry Barkly, who was less keen on High Commission rule for Lesotho than Wodehouse had been, had decided that the Territory ought to be annexed to the Cape Colony. Hence, as early as May he had visited the *Morena e Moholo* Letsie to broach the subject to him. Yet it does not appear that enough time and effort were taken to allow the *Morena e Moholo* to consult with his council and bring the matter to a *pitso* for full discussion and commitment to the constitutional change.

At the same time, Barkly's rationale and justification for annexation seemed fairly harmless on the surface. For he assured the *Morena e Moholo* that annexation would be without prejudice to the current arrangement under which Lesotho was being administered by the High Commissioner's Agent. The only thing that seemed to necessitate annexation, as Barkly explained to the Secretary of State, was the financial burden currently borne by the Cape toward the Territory. He stated:

> the immediate annexation to the Cape Colony was the only measure which could avert the anarchy which seemed to impend whenever the police force, the return of which to its ordinary duties had been repeatedly demanded by the Cape Parliament, should be withdrawn.[77]

A bill for annexation was hurriedly introduced in the Legislative Assembly. One of its chief critics in the advisory Executive Council, the Attorney General, was pressured by his boss, the High Commissioner to help rush it through. There was a great deal of concern within and outside the Legislative Assembly about the rush; but after the bill had been discussed by a special committee, which reasoned, among other things, that 'Basutoland offers a wide field for commercial enterprise', it was passed on 11 August 1871 and confirmed by an Order-in-Council in November that same year.[78]

DEVELOPMENTS LEADING TO THE GUN WAR AND DISANNEXATION

The Establishment of Responsible Government and Lesotho's Response

The following year, 1872, the Cape Colony was granted Responsible Government; and with this development Lesotho, clearly without appreciating it, underwent a crucial constitutional change. The Governor's prerogative devolved on the Cape Government. As Joseph Orpen, the Cape MP from Aliwal North and a Basotho sympathiser would on a later occasion put it: 'by a mere sidewind, necessarily but disastrously, it transferred legislative power . . . to the ministry of the day'.[80] According to the Reverend Eugene Casalis, who gave his testimony in the wake of the Gun War in 1880, the Basotho were neither consulted on nor advised of this change.[81] Casalis was backed up by Lord Kimberley, Secretary of Colonies at the time, who commented later in 1881 that 'the Basutos received no formal notification of any change in their relations with the Governor'.[82]

In 1872, however, Lesotho had responded to annexation by petitioning to be represented in the Cape Parliament.[83] Both the Governor, Sir Henry Barkly and the Colonial Secretary, Richard Southey, had been disagreeably surprised and embarrassed by this petition. Whether their suspicions were well-founded or not, they blamed it on the tireless Basothophils – Joseph Orpen and D. D. Buchanan. Having successfully circumvented the 'coloured franchise' problem, Cape colonists could ill afford to allow representation to a still stoutly proud and essentially unconquered population of 'natives'. They had to parry the petition.

In parrying the petition, Southey explained to Basotho that representation in the Cape Parliament carried with it, in the main, the obligation fully to accept Cape laws. Whereas non-representation carried the advantage that Lesotho would retain the privileged position as a 'special Territory', that is, it would be governed through Basotho laws and customs. As Basotho feared losing their relative independence under Cape laws, they withdrew their petition.[84]

Between 1872 and 1876 the *Morena e Moholo* and his now 'Governor's Agent', Colonel Griffith, wrestled for authority. In an effort to assert his power and establish British authority, or the Cape's, as it were, Griffith issued a circular on 17 December 1872 to 'chiefs; petty chiefs, headmen' reminding them that 'the Supreme chief in this Territory is the Governor representing the Queen of England'.[85] Apparently the *Morena e Moholo* Letsie challenged the circular, in regard to its implications on the supremacy of magistrates over the Basotho courts, and the right of the Governor's Agent to allocate land. For, two days later, Griffith was at pains to explain, with regard to the judiciary, that the judicial procedure 'is to your interest . . . for the good of the whole country'. He did not, so to speak, assert that he was within his constitutional right; rather he tried to appeal to Letsie's sense of duty. On the question of land allocation, on the other hand, Griffith asked the question, rhetorically: 'If these rights are not to belong to the Government, how can the Government be said to govern you at all?'[86] By October 1874 the question of land allocation had still not been resolved and Griffith had to bring it to the attention of the Governor. The Governor was to hand back the right of land allocation to the *Morena e Moholo* in 'patronage as a privilege' and to emphasise the fact that land was held 'from the Government'.[87]

By the middle of October 1876 the Cape Government was drawing near to a conflict with its appended 'special Territory'. Griffith reported to the Secretary of Native Affairs in the Cape that the situation in Lesotho was deteriorating: The Basotho had come to know that there was a project in the hatching for the establishment of a confederation of white governments in South Africa and that, in the furtherance of its objectives, a part of Lesotho was to be ceded to the Orange Free State. At a recently held *pitso*, a major part of the discussions had been on this subject and the Territory was quite agitated.[88] It was not until the Colonial Government officially denied the existence of such a plan (of ceding their land) that the Basotho regained their composure.[89]

The existence of the project of confederation could not, however, be denied. It was a project to which the new Governor, Sir Bartle

Frere, Barkly's successor, was heavily committed. In his frantic efforts to realise it, the Governor would cause the colony to precipitate an irreconcilable conflict with Lesotho.

The cornerstone of this conflict was first laid in 1878, when the Governor whisked through the Cape Legislative Assembly an Act to disarm the African population under the Cape Colony. Ironically styled the Peace Preservation Act, this piece of legislation passed through Parliament only because it was disguised as an enabling Act, for application in disaffected areas, as and when the situation warranted it. Notwithstanding the fact that Lesotho was an awkward and cantankerous appendage to rule, it was not then disaffected toward the Colonial Government. So there had been no apparent need for the Basotho to be apprehensive about its passage.

A year later, however, the outbreak of a war in Lesotho seemed to have provided the Governor and his cabinet with an opportune moment. An old tributary ruler of Moshoeshoe, *Nkosi* Moorosi of the chiefdom of Baphuthi[90] had, in June 1868, cast his lot with his overlord and thereby retained his ancestral lands in Quthing to the north of the Territory; but, as an old and valiant warrior and head of a people with a strong sense of nationhood, distinct, culturally and linguistically, from the rest of the Basotho, the Baphuthi ruler much preferred the Colonial Government to treat him as a vassal. The thought of being a subject was distinctly distasteful to him. For this reason he utterly and overtly resisted the presence of a magistrate in his jurisdiction. The indigenous government of Lesotho kept its distance from the fermenting trouble, chary of exercising control or exerting influence over the old warrior *Nkosi* (the Baphuthi title for ruler).

In an effort to protect the magistracy in Moorosi's jurisdiction against potential attacks, and obviously also a show of force, a coterie of Lesotho police was established in Quthing at the end of March 1878. Then, in April, Letsie's heir, Chief Lerotholi, was ordered to get 600 of his men ready to discipline the Baphuthi potentate. For a few months these moves had the desired effect of dampening the old warrior's pugnacity.

In the end, however, the magistracy's arrest of Moorosi's heir, Doda, for stealing a horse, precipitated armed conflict. The Cape Premier, Mr Gordon Sprigg, decided that the old warrior must be disarmed. The result was a war between Baphuthi and the colonial forces, sheepishly assisted by the *Morena e Moholo* who, with the Peace Preservation Act in mind, wished to impress the Colonial

Government of his loyalty. After fighting courageously, for several days pinned under siege to his mountain fortress, Mount Moorosi, on 20 November 1879, Moorosi was crushed, and to Letsie's horror and disbelief, decapitated and his head sent to King William's Town in the Cape.[91]

Even before the end of that war, however, Letsie had already been shown the folly of his loyalty. At a *pitso* held on 16 October, Sprigg had announced to The Basotho that the Peace Preservation Act would soon be applied generally to Lesotho. A few days later he would also let them know that Quthing would be confiscated.

Following futile efforts by Lesotho's Governor's Agent, Griffith, and the French missionaries to intercede on their behalf, in June 1880, when the Cape Colony Parliament was to discuss both the disarmament question and the confiscation of Quthing, The Basotho sent a delegation to Cape Town.[92] The delegation, led by Nathaniel Makotoko, Ntho Mokeke (whom Letsie regarded as 'my own book'),[93] and the Reverend Mr Cochet of the French Missionary Society, was armed with two petitions: one was against the confiscation of Quthing, the other against disarmament.

The Quthing petition first recapitulated the Moshoeshoe-Wodehouse agreement that Lesotho was a territory for the Basotho only. Second it maintained that Quthing itself was 'the property of Basuto Nation' on which Moorosi had only been allowed to cohabit with the Basotho. Third it characterised the Moorosi war as not a war but merely an act of disobedience by 'a small band of people' which was crushed by the combined 'large bodies of Basutos' and 'colonial forces'. As such, it legally did not follow that Quthing could be confiscated.[94]

It had been hoped that the delegation would be allowed to participate in the debates in the Cape Parliament, as at a *pitso*; but it was not allowed. As the delegation could not speak to its own cause, that task was undertaken by the MP sympathisers in the House of Assembly. In the vanguard among these was none other than Joseph Orpen, MP from Aliwal North and Wodehouse's member of the 1862 Commission to Thaba Bosiu. Orpen said he knew the exact nature of the understanding reached between Wodehouse and Moshoeshoe on the occasion of the Proclamation of 1868. It had been agreed, he affirmed, that Lesotho would not be Crown land. He is minuted as having said: 'It was the most monstrous doctrine he had ever heard of, that all property of the people of Basutoland was handed over to the Crown'. He was one of the people who had persuaded the Basotho to give themselves up to the British Government, he said; and that was on his understanding that Basotho would be protected, and not that their property would be taken away from them. In the current circumstances, only an Act of the Imperial Parliament could alter the situation. As for the admissibility of the Moorosi rebellion as justification for the confiscation of Quthing, that was 'purely a question for a court of law'.[95]

The Legislative Assembly was far from being in agreement on what, exactly, the constitutional position of Lesotho had been in 1868, and what the current jurisdiction of the Colonial Government was. The Attorney-General, for instance, in his challenge of the notion that Lesotho had been reserved for the Basotho only, said he had searched through all relevant documents and could not 'find one particle of authority for the allegation'.[96] (As it had been shown earlier, such information existed, but it was in the form of oral evidence.)[97] To Mr Vincent, a somewhat uncommitted MP, the debate suggested that: 'If the Annexation Act, as it now stood, was not all that it ought to be, the time had come . . . when it should be revised'.[98] The motion for the confiscation of Quthing had at the end to be dropped.

The petition on disarmament, on the other hand, met with a different fate. The Basotho had grounded the petition on two arguments: first, they had argued that they did not deserve to have their guns taken away from them as they had not, as a nation, rebelled against the Colonial Government; second, while, interestingly, acknowledging 'the right of the Parliament to make laws to preserve the peace', they felt that if it were applied to them they would be 'no longer free men, and we weep to think of being thus reduced to servitude'.[99]

Unfortunately, however, the Legislative Assembly debate on this issue could not be carried to its logical conclusion, which, in the light of a strong opposition against the precipitate action of the Government to it, seemed likely to be decided in favour of the Territory. For, promptly upon the arrival of the Makotoko-Ntho delegation in Cape Town, Sir Bartle Frere had dispatched an urgent message to *Morena e Moholo* Letsie to the effect that he should order his people to hand over their guns immediately. Losing his nerve, the *Morena e Moholo* had sent a circular throughout the Territory for immediate disarmament, even before the return of his delegation from Cape Town. Some sections of the Territory had obeyed the order; but the majority of the population, under the inspiration and leadership of the warrior Chief David Masopha, Letsie's brother, supported by Lerotholi, the heir apparent, and one of Molapo's sons named Joel, had challenged the order. Masopha had charged that Letsie had acted *ultra vires* in issuing his circular before the return of the delegation and the sitting of a *pitso* to discuss the question of disarmament and decide on the proper course of action next to be taken.[100]

The Legislative Assembly debate on disarmament was abruptly interrupted by a report of this turn of events. Using the turn of events to justify the Government's position, the Colonial Secretary pointed to the dangers that lay ahead of the Colonial Government as long as chiefs such as Masopha were 'allowed to possess power which they could use against the Government'. Masopha's disposition was clear evidence, in his view, that the Basotho ought to be disarmed.[101] The Basotho MP supporters on the other hand felt that, to the contrary, the internal opposition to the *Morena e Moholo's* directive illustrated the fact that the Basotho Government rested on the will of the people and not on the dictates of their ruler. The *Morena e Moholo* had acted unconstitutionally and bypassed the decision-making process, while Masopha, in Solomon's words, had 'acted in a more constitutional way than we had ourselves'.[102]

The quickened pace of events in Lesotho, and the posture of defiance to colonial authority, fostered unity within the Cape Legislative Assembly in favour of disarmament, for better or for worse. So in the end the Lesotho delegation had to carry the message home that disarmament had been upheld.

As it might have been expected, when the Makotoko-Ntho delegation formally reported to a *pitso* on 3 July, the more radical Masopha-inspired elements rejected the decision. Disarmament was to them 'a load too heavy to carry'. They preferred war to what they considered as losing their manhood.[103]

Hostilities commenced in September 1880. The colonial officers on the spot were embarrassingly compelled to return guns to the loyals, who had then become the targets of Masopha's front of the rebels, so that they might fight alongside the colonial forces. The *Morena e Moholo* found himself in an awkward position in this war: officially he sought to impress the Colonial Government of his loyalty and obedience to the Peace Preservation Act; but all parties concerned were aware that he was secretly supportive of the rebels: for instance, confiscated property from the loyals, and even a decapitated head (Moorosi's style) of a magistrate, John Austin, were traced to his royal residence.

The Gun War was over in seven months and the rebels had won. All efforts by the Colonial Government such as, at first, a call for the surrender of the leaders of the rebellion and, second, the return of the property of the loyals, 'calculated to make the close of hostilities seem like a negotiated peace', failed. In the end the rebels, who were then seen as the saviours of the nation against disarmament, emerged from the struggle with their guns and personal liberties.

Basotho Views on the Constitutional Position of Lesotho after the Gun War

Throughout the period from 1881 to 1884, in *lipitso* (plural of *pitso*), in interviews with colonial officials, and in correspondence, the indigenous government of Lesotho expressed the view that the Cape Colonial Government had undermined Britain's covenant with the late 'Moshoeshoe the Wise'. *Morena e Moholo* Letsie asked on one occasion 'why Mr Sprigg the Colonial Premier [from the advent of disarmament] was allowed by the Queen to change everything'. He advised the Cape Colony Government that, in the circumstances, his people had lost faith in Britain; they considered its Crown as 'a cave which has fallen upon those who took refuge in it and is full of graves'.[104] Looking back for precedents in Lesotho's history, the monarch cited his father's vassalage under the AmaZulu kings, and briefly under the Batlokoa of Sekonyela, and others, who before British overlordship 'took us, and none of them took our shields' (that is, 'our independence').[105] Indeed, even with Queen Victoria's Government, Letsie maintained: 'We were told that the Government leaves a man to govern his country, with his sheep, his cattle, and his gun.'[106]

The *Morena e Moholo*'s was a moderate voice. He merely queried the apparent change in the constitutional position of his country, but beyond that he was not for change – at least not overtly. There were others in the country who felt that in fact the time was right to fight for complete independence. On 23 June 1881 for instance, a commoner named Ramabilikoe stated at a *pitso*: 'This is what we would like when – if this affair can be arranged amicably and peace restored – the hand of the Queen returns where it came from'.[107] This view would be militantly championed by David Masopha after the war. Masopha became utterly uncooperative with both the Colonial Government as well as with his brother, the *Morena e Moholo*, whose allegiance to the British Crown he read as a sign of weakness.[108]

THE CONSTITUTIONAL POSITION OF LESOTHO GETS REVIEWED

General Gordon's Convention

As a last effort to bring Lesotho under some type of control, the Colonial Office in London appointed a Commandant General C. G. Gordon to come to the Cape in May 1882, specifically to devise a workable plan for the governance of the Territory. It is interesting to note that, after reviewing the Territory's past relations with Britain to date, Gordon came to the conclusion that it was a co-treaty power with the Cape Colony.[109] So that, basing himself on that view, in June 1882 the Commandant General drafted a 'Convention', to be ratified on the one hand by the Colonial Government and on the other by the *Morena e Moholo* Letsie and, in recognition of his independentist position, by Chief Masopha, as high contracting parties.[110] The 'Convention' provided that henceforth Lesotho would be recognised as co-equal with the Cape of Good Hope Colony. Magistrates would accordingly be withdrawn from the Territory. The indigenous government of Lesotho would rule in consultation with a 'Resident' of the Cape Government, assisted by two 'Sub-Residents'. Two consultative councils, one major, the other minor, would serve as administrative bridges between the Resident and the government of Lesotho.[111]

A Draft Constitution Offered

The Colonial Government, however, would hear nothing of Gordon's 'Convention'. It was scrapped even before the Basotho could hear of it. Instead, the Colonial Government sponsored its own plan. Not significantly different from Gordon's 'Convention' in principle, the plan was a 'Draft Constitution' for Lesotho.[112]

Presented at a *pitso* in Lesotho on 2 April 1883, the 'Draft Constitution' provided for the following: Article I recognised the Annexation Act No. 12, 1871, but, significantly, conceded that Lesotho 'shall remain intact for the Basuto people', the District of Quthing inclusive. (This Article was obviously meant to recognise the Basotho claim of the Moshoeshoe-Wodehouse 'Covenant'.) Articles II, III and IV provided for the appointment of a Governor's Agent: the Agent's jurisdiction on judicial matters was to try all civil and criminal cases in the Territory not involving Basotho. Cases where Europeans and Basotho were party to dispute would be tried by the Governor's Agent, or his representative, assisted or advised by a principal chief of a district where an infraction of the law would have taken place, or as the *Morena e Moholo* might decide. Article V provided that cases of treason and sedition would be tried before supreme courts of the Cape Colony.

Articles X, XI and XII provided for the establishment of 'A Council of Advice', to comprise chiefs and headmen – one half of them nominated by the Paramount Chief (*Morena e Moholo*), the other half by the Governor's Agent. The life of the council was to be three years. It was to convene at least once a year on the authority of the Governor to discuss the financial and other matters of public concern and give advice to the Colonial Government. The Council could draw up resolutions suggesting changes in the laws governing the Territory. Article XVI reserved 'the management of the internal affairs' of the Territory to the Paramount Chief. The 'Draft Constitution' had, altogether, twenty Articles.

The Cape Colonial Government clearly saw its scheme as a supreme political gift and accordingly expected the Basotho to show an expression of gratitude. Thus, introducing the 'Draft Constitution' at a national *pitso*, the Secretary for Native Affairs remarked:

> I am sure when you have heard it you will say, what is the fact, that never in South Africa has so liberal and so generous a Constitution been submitted to a native tribe, because it is really governing the Basutos through themselves and by themselves, the same as we white people govern ourselves.[113]

The Basotho response to the 'liberal and . . . generous' document, however, was a complete disappointment to the Colonial Government. In the first place, the *pitso* was poorly attended, especially at the level of the chiefs: only two of the numerous sons of Molapo – Jonathan and Leabua – were present. Chief Lesaoana, the turbulent spirit who triggered the Basotho-Boer war in 1865, still a figure to be reckoned with, was absent. Chief Masopha could logically not be expected to grace the colonial occasion by his presence. Strikingly, the *Morena e Moholo*, who had had some involvement in the preparation of the 'Draft Constitution', albeit without consultation with his Grand Council, was also not at the *pitso*: he had, characteristically, invoked a diplomatic illness. Nor had he sent the experienced and sound ambassador, Ntho Mokeke, in his place. Instead he had sent a messenger named Shoaepane – a novice with a tortuous manner of speech. Although Nathanael Makotoko, the other renowned Mosotho ambassador was there, he had attended the *pitso* in his own right as a representative from the District of Leribe, and not on behalf of the *Morena e Moholo*.

In the second place, the 'Draft Constitution' was seen by the *pitso* as not a 'liberal and generous' gift at all but, rather, as another of the white man's wiles laid for Basotho chiefs. The scheme was technically discredited on grounds of procedure, following Makotoko's delicately posed query:

> It was my duty to ask whether these rules which have been read to us have been fixed or not, so as to be able to let the people know because the chiefs always first commence to speak about things, and after that they lay them before the people for consideration, and in the same way it is the duty of the Chief Letsie to tell his people what is going on.[114]

The response from the Secretary of Native Affairs to the query had not been satisfactory. He pointed out that the Articles of the 'Draft Constitution' had been the subject of discussion in Matsieng, with the *Morena e Moholo* Letsie for two and a half days. Although he sought to establish that Letsie was with 'his sons, some other chiefs, and headmen and people', it turned out that the meeting was neither a Grand Council nor a *pitso* – those in attendance had come mainly from Letsie's District. At the same time, the Colonial Government seemed to have been appropriately represented. Both the Secretary of Native Affairs and his new Premier, Thomas Scanlen were present. Further, had it not been for the insistence on the part of those in attendance that a question of that magnitude ought to be brought before a *pitso*, the Colonial Government would have concluded the matter with the *Morena e Moholo* without reference to public opinion.[115] As Tŝita Mofoka, one of Letsie's counsellors, pointed out, the Matsieng meeting had been disquieting because 'these matters are not [that is, should not be] dealt with by you Ministers and by Letsie as [if] it is a kind of secret meeting'.[116] Finally it appeared clear from the mood of the *pitso* that the *Morena e Moholo* was not committed to the plan and the rumour was rife that he had indicated at Matsieng that 'he does not like to have a chief over him'; a rumour which Shoaepane attempted unsuccessfully to quell.

An unassailable point, however, had been made by one Rampa, who had warned of the dangers attendant on taking any major decisions in a *pitso* where interest groups in the Territory were not all represented:

> I heard one amongst us say that this meeting was good, but I am sorry that all the sons of Molapo are not here. Ramaneella is not here . . . Besides Jonathan other heads of Leribe are absent . . . It won't do any good if we take all the rules which have been said, and tell them. They will say we have nothing to do with that; that belongs to the loyals, and we have nothing to do with the loyals' business.[117]

The Secretary of Native Affairs did not miss the point at that *pitso* that Lesotho was not interested in his Ministry's plan. As the Paris Evangelical Missionary Society had said in an official communication to General Gordon earlier in 1882: 'Basutos have become suspicious, and do not enter readily into plans made for their welfare'.[118]

Disannexation from the Cape and the Return to Crown Rule

The Colonial Government had come to believe at this period that Lesotho was 'a very disagreeably hot potato'. Neither the Colonial nor the Imperial Government was eager to touch it.[119] At the same time, it was a charming potato. As Lord Emily said in the House of Commons on 1 June 1883: 'it would be little short of madness to abandon Basutoland'.[120] He was supported in his view by the Colonial Secretary, Lord Derby, who remarked:

> It holds a central position as regards the British Possessions in South Africa, having the Cape Colony on the West, the Orange Free State on the North, Natal on the East, and a large number of protected semi-independent native chiefs on the South.[121]

Lord Derby felt that, in view of the Colonial Government's late and ardent wish 'to get rid of this dependency, which had cost them so much (over £3 000 000 on the war) without bringing any compensating advantage',[122] the alternative was to '*renew the Protectorate* under Imperial Government'.[123] (My emphasis)

The question of whether to 'renew the Protectorate under the Imperial Government', however, was presented to Basotho in the form of a threat. The task had been given to Captain Blyth, a man who knew, and apparently enjoyed, intimidating Basotho. Captain Blyth, Griffith's successor in the Governor's Agentship of Lesotho, was well-known to the Basotho for his abrasiveness, even before his arrival in the Territory. Letsie had twice unsuccessfully tried to get his appointment nullified, on the grounds both that he had been appointed without his approval, as well as, of course, for his hatred and fear of the Governor's Agent. On the occasion of the presentation of the 'Draft Constitution', where Blyth had chaired the *pitso*, the last unsuccessful effort at his removal had been attempted, by challenging his chairmanship, and Blyth had spent excruciating moments trying to justify his authority.[124] This embarrassing experience probably added to the Governor's Agent's truculence, in particular against the *Morena e Moholo* who, undoubtedly, had engineered the scheme to discredit him.

Blyth had been instructed to ensure that:

(a) Basotho chiefs were united and unequivocal in their expression of consent to the British offer;

(b) in the event of their consent, they had to agree to be taxed, for the purpose of supporting the administration of the Territory; but Blyth added his personality to the offer. When the question was presented to the *pitso* on 29 November 1883 he menacingly warned the *Morena e Moholo* Letsie:

These are the two roads Paramount Chief, the one right and the other wrong; and the queen in her greatness and goodness has at the last moment had pity upon you misguided people – not because she is afraid of you, but because she is good and loves Christianity. . . . It must be a plain answer to a plain question. Remember this – H.M. Govt. come with no cringing to you, they are not afraid of you – They come to you in their greatness and goodness and fullness of heart. . . . May God guide you to a good decision on this matter. . . . No playing around with the Imperial Government.[125]

Repeatedly throughout the *pitso* Blyth rudely interrupted Letsie whenever he spoke, instructing him that he wanted 'straightforward answers – yes or no', 'no ifs, or buts'. Still insisting on a modicum of discussion, the *Morena e Moholo* tried to point out that 'When a person says he wants peace, it is because he wants to live and not die': he wished the entire question of Lesotho's past relations with the British Government to be discussed before the nation was pressured into dealing with one alternative, but Blyth silenced him with the admonishment that 'we are not talking of the past'.

Browbeaten and humiliated in the presence of his juniors, the *Morena e Moholo* broke under Blyth's iron hand and gave him a symbolic, self-effacing submission. Repeatedly he said of himself: 'I am a coward, I am stupid'; 'Don't be deceived when people advise you to throw away the Govt. listen to them (sic) – of all cowards we know a coward breeds a coward'; 'He who is a coward is not left in the chair'. He could not, on the other hand, opt for independence without British protection. The experience of the last war with the Orange Free State was still fresh in his mind. And so were British sympathies for the Boer Republic.

When the *pitso* ended, the *Morena e Moholo* had virtually lost his political image and authority in the eyes of his people. Indeed a little over a month before the *pitso*, when he had felt himself staggering under Blyth's political weight, Letsie had suggested to the Governor's Agent that, owing to his loss of influence in the Territory, he had considered it best to abdicate from the office of *Morena e Moholo*. Perhaps he was only courting a response of reassurance. In turn Blyth, far from placating the monarch, had impetuously told him that it was up to himself to decide the question.[126] Letsie had then remained in office. Yet, symbolically at least, at the end of the November 29th *pitso* he was as good as having abdicated.

THE WANING OF THE MONARCHY

The Introduction of Alien Legal Principles and the Authority of Chiefs

Albeit that the Annexation Act of 1871 had specifically provided that Cape Colony laws would not apply in the Territory (unless where specifically made for that purpose), and the Colonial Secretary, Richard Southey, had, in parrying the Basotho petition for representation in Parliament in 1872, given the assurance that the Territory would be ruled through Basotho laws and customs, the revised version of Wodehouse's Regulations, which came into effect in December 1871, contained a lot in it that was alien and in effect a reflection of Cape laws.[127] The Regulations were calculated to warp

Sesotho customary law and customs considerably, and to whittle away the authority of chiefs in their courts.

The revised Regulations had been the work of Cape Colony officers. They had been, significantly, presented to chiefs and headmen on the occasion of their gathering at Thaba Bosiu where the nation was going to be told formally of Moshoshoe's death. Clearly without giving much thought to their long term effect, *Morena e Moholo* Letsie had quashed his senior chiefs' strong opposition to them and ordered their acceptance.[128] The inspiration and rationale behind the Regulations, however, had come from a member of the French Missionary Society, Emile Rolland. Born and bred in Lesotho, Rolland spoke fluent Sesotho and was well-versed in Sesotho customary law and customs. His authority and *bona fides* to the Cape Colony Government were undoubted.

Hardly two weeks after Philip Wodehouse's proclamation, Emile Rolland had on 30 March 1868 written a thirty-five page memorandum advising Her Majesty's Government on Basotho customs and the powers of chiefs, and recommending ways of pulling down the political scaffolding of the indigenous government. Obviously chary of offending Moshoeshoe so soon after a delicately handled annexation to the British Government, Wodehouse had only modestly tapped Emile Rolland's wisdom; but those whom he left behind when he returned to London later decided that virtually the entire memorandum was good material to ground Regulations on. The memorandum, therefore, deserves our attention here.[129]

Rolland opened his remarks with a shrewd observation. The power of the chiefs, he said, 'was never as systematically or as firmly established . . . as that of the Zulus or AmaXosa'. Moreover 'especially the power of the great chiefs has been considerably weakened by the enormous number of headmen and petty chiefs' who increasingly sought a greater measure of independence from their seniors 'and have acknowledged a merely nominal supremacy on the part of the principal chief'.[130] And so he was correct: the political organisation of the Basotho monarchy was only one generation old; most of the principles and institutions of government borrowed from the old chiefly principalities were still being tested; the kingdom sat on precarious ground.

Even so, Rolland remarked:

It is evident however that notwithstanding this weakening of the power and influence of the great chiefs, that power of chiefs great and small will be the principal obstacle which Her Majesty's Government will have to encounter in ruling the Basutos and rendering them obedient to British law.[131]

It would be necessary, he said, for the British Government 'to supersede and diminish' the authority of the chiefs 'by all the means at its disposal'; but without embittering the people and arousing their jealousy. He then commenced to point out the 'roots' of the chiefs' power – 'the ground and foundation of the power of native chiefs' that ought to be knocked down.

First, he pointed out, aside from his birthright and personal qualities, 'the great secret of his power consists in his wealth', which he uses as the means of patronage to strengthen his ties with those who serve him. That wealth consisted of cattle, part of which is a chief's inheritance, but which, critically, is increased through 'occasional fines, and by bribes' generated by his court. Yet by far the principal source of chiefs' revenue was the payment of *bohali* (marriage cattle) for their daughters – which seldom numbered less than thirty head of cattle per marriage.[132]

Second the power of chiefs rested on the plurality of their wives:

The possession of a large number of women is a great source of wealth and influence to a Basuto chief. Each wife or concubine [ngoetsi – a woman married to serve under a senior wife] has her own hut and establishment, and enriches her husband by the produce of her gardens and labour, and by her children, the boys being servants and cattle herds and the girls being available for sale.[133] A polygamist is thus able, from the abundance of food which he possesses, to exercise hospitality to a great extent, without any expense.[134]

Through polygamy, Rolland theorised, people were bound to a chief in either of two ways: through ties of marriage, or in consequence of the hospitality and material sustenance flowing from his polygamous household.

Third, in which Rolland was conceptually in error: 'The land is the inalienable property of the chief'.[135] (As a matter of fact, the chief, in principle, only holds land *in trust* for the people.) Otherwise correct, he pointed out that a chief's right over land allocation 'is a powerful lever in the hands of an astute man': he in effect determined where subjects could build houses and where they might cultivate their crops. He could either dispossess them of the lands or expel them altogether from his jurisdiction if he grew weary of them.

Emile Rolland therefore sponsored a series of recommendations for dismantling the indigenous government through the law:

(a) All land should belong to the Queen. And (a) 'Private individuals should be encouraged to possess property' and to purchase land, to offset the comparative wealth and power of chiefs. (The introduction of the notion of individual title to land was a direct attack on the religiously held Basotho notion of 'Lesotho for Basotho only'. It could lead to land purchases by Europeans. The Colonial Government therefore thought the wiser about adopting it.)

(b) The individual should be protected from the chief – a practice such as 'eating up', that is, the chief's confiscation of a subject's entire property (for a real or contrived crime), should be forbidden.

(c) Plurality of wives should be abolished, by 'recognising only the great wife as legally such', and depriving all the others of any legal status as wives. The British Government should take every possible means to 'discredit' individuals with more than one wife and 'countenance such as remain faithful to one wife'.

(d) Christian marriages should be protected by legal principles adopted 'in all civilised and Christian countries' and a law against bigamy should be introduced.

(e) Married adult males should be made to pay a 'hut tax', which shall be applied differentially as between Christians (numbering 10 000) and polygamists, 'say 10/- for a single hut and 15/- for every additional wife'.

(f) Contrary to customary law, whereby widows could only resolve their problem of male companionship through levirate, while remaining within the deceased husband's extended family, widows would be allowed 'to marry whom they choose without cattle; – let them be entirely free'.[136]

The last two recommendations were essentially a plea for the British Government to protect missionaries from their rival social practices and institutions. He recommended, in the main, legislation against witchcraft (something which Moshoeshoe had twice attempted to eradicate in his society, but without success), and the demolition of initiation schools.

Emile Rolland's programme was in essence calculated to transform the Basotho society into a Western-oriented entity. The type of legislation that he recommended was culturally biased. And he acknowledged this, stating:

> It may be remarked that all the preceding opinions and suggestions savour of the principle of 'class legislation'. I neither deny nor seek to avoid such a conclusion. Class legislation is not only necessary, but best in the present circumstances of the natives. It would be impossible all at once to introduce colonial law amongst them. All that can be done therefore is to frame temporary regulations, conceived in the spirit of our laws[137]

As already pointed out, Sir Philip Wodehouse had already embodied some of Rolland's ideas in his set of Regulations. For instance, Basotho were already paying a hut tax of ten shillings 'for each hut or wife's residence'; and then, to make the proposition easy to swallow, the principal chiefs were awarded 10 per cent of the net hut tax collected, as inducement for collecting it. According to Sandra Burman, it was the resultant success in the collection of this tax that encouraged the officials (after Wodehouse's departure) to take the more radical step of espousing Rolland's recommendations in their virtual totality. In the new Regulations 'the attack on the chiefs' powers were fully spelt out and various time-honoured customs were challenged'.[138]

The new Regulations introduced the death penalty for certain offences – murder, and arson with intent to kill – for which in customary law punishment was in the form of fines. (Heretofore, the death penalty had been used in Lesotho on a spy, in 1829, on whose information the state had been attacked by the enemy.[139] It could otherwise be imposed on a person guilty of an illicit affair with a chief's great wife.)[140] Three (and later four) principal chiefs, could try minor criminal cases, and of course any civil cases not involving a European; nonetheless disputants could appeal to district magistrates' courts against chiefs' judgements and loopholes were left open to them to evade their fines. The chiefs' customary practice of 'eating up' subjects was construed as theft. All men, including chiefs, were declared equal before the law – a new principle in Sesotho customary law which weighed heavily on the chiefs, especially as the *Morena e Moholo* also came under its general application.

Then there were other alien legal principles, which offended not only the chiefs, but commoners as well: marriage of women without their consent was made illegal. Boys and girls might not be initiated against their consent or that of their parents. Christian marriages were declared valid without *bohali*. Christian as well as customary marriages were to be registered, at two shillings and six pence, or else litigation arising from them could not be heard before magistrates' courts. Widows were given the right the marry; they were given custody of their children until they were of a certain age – fifteen for girls and eighteen for boys; and a widow's eldest son could be recognised as his mother's guardian once he was married. (In Sesotho customary law custody over children always belonged to the extended family that provided the *bohali* and a widow raised them subject to its discretion and on conditions dictated by it. Children born outside marriage belonged to their mother's extended family.) The killing of witches, still practised in society despite Moshoeshoe's early legislation against it, was construed as murder. The practice of flogging – for rape – was introduced.[141]

The Effect of the Regulations on Society

The resultant effect of the application of the new Regulations under Cape rule was a conflict of the juxtaposed legal systems. Yet it was a conflict in which chiefs were to a great measure the losers, commoners trading for advantages between the two. None other than Emile Rolland, who had been favoured with an appointment as a magistrate, found himself presiding over the legal medley. One case from his court serves as a good illustration of the problem:

Motseko v. Adriaan Maphathe and 'Makubutu (8 November 1876) On November 8, 1876, a man named Motseko brought a case before the Resident Assistant Magistrate of Mafeteng, Emile Rolland, against his nephew, Adriaan Maphathe, and the latter's widowed mother, 'Makubutu, Motseko's sister. Motseko claimed the custody of Makubutu's three daughters by an illicit union with one Makolometse, as well as part of the *bohali* cattle, called *litsoa*, entitled to him as the senior *malome* (maternal uncle), which 'Makubutu had already received for the marriage of two of them.

'Makubutu had twice before been married. Her first marriage, to Nganga, had been a Christian marriage; *bohali* had not been issued. Nganga died, leaving a son named Adriaan. Then, subsequently, 'Makubutu got married to Maphathe under customary law, apparently in her own father's life time and, according to Adriaan, not only was *bohali* issued but, 'Maphathe gave cattle for me. So by cattle I am also Maphathe's son'. No children were born of that marriage. Meantime, Maphathe and Makubutu were divorced, and subsequently she lived with Makolometse, who gave her the three daughters, before their relationship went sour and she went to live with her son Adriaan (apparently then married).

In May 1876 'Makubutu went to the Chief Magistrate's Court (Governor's Agent, Griffith's) at the capital, in Maseru, on appeal against the decision of the Assistant Resident Magistrate's Court, in the District of Mafeteng: The President of the Court, Emile Rolland, had upheld Makolometse's claim 'of the cattle for *seholo-holo*' – literally, 'cattle for the pelvis bone' (that is, for the conjugal labours of giving 'Makubutu the three daughters). According to Adriaan's uncontroverted account, 'Mr Griffith decided that the children belonged to my mother alone and that no one else had anything to say to them, because they were children of an illicit connection'. At the same time, the account goes on: 'My Mother introduced me to the Court – she said she pointed me out because the right to the children was disputed by Motseko – and she pointed me out as her heir. She declared that I was her guardian and heir. This is why I say I have a right to these children of my mother's by Makolometse because I have been given them in the Queen's court by my mother'.

In a trenchant onslaught against the Assistant Magistrate, in open court, whereby she 'addressed the Magistrate by name calling him the persecutor of widows etc. – and boasting of her having obtained a reversal of his judgement before', 'Makubutu corroborated her son Adriaan's evidence and went further:

> I refuse to give up my children – Motseko has his own. I am as good as he and have a right to mine. – I also deny that he is the *malome* of these children. I myself am both father and malome to them. *Kia gana* – kia gana [I refuse – I refuse.]

'Makubutu's peppery language incensed the President of the Court who, in his own unmitigated language, in open court, not only threatened to punish her for contempt of court but also harangued her: 'It is highly unbecoming of her to crow in the manner she did at the fact of the decision in a former case being reversed . . . She should remember that she is a miserable harlot and her own acts have in each case brought her into court'. The President's decision followed his mixed emotions (based on a mixed legal system) about the widow:

Certainly as 'between 'Makubutu and Makolometse the children may have been said to belong to 'Makubutu – but only as subject to Motseko's claims. The Court is bound to decide this case according to Sesuto law – and these children have always been acknowledged as belonging to Motseko – not to speak of Motseko's claims as *Malome* . . . The court therefore rules that the plaintiff Motseko on the double ground of his being the heir of 'Makubutu's father – i.e. the father of an unmarried woman – and of 2ndly his being the *Malome* entitled to *ditsuoa* (sic) – is entitled to the father's share of the dowry cattle. The guardianship of the girls remains of course with 'Makubutu and her son Adriaan.[142]

So here was a case in which a Mosotho woman had entered into two marriages: the first, regulated by Western legal principles; the second by Sesotho customary law. The first marriage allowed her, following the death of her husband, to marry again. In the second marriage the law allowed her the application of the customary principle of child adoption by cattle, albeit that the child in question, Adriaan, was a product of a Western type of marriage. The woman's daughters by an illicit union came under her own and that of the son's custody, and not, as it should have been under customary law, under their *malome* as *in loco patris*. When that happened, their biological father, Makolometse had already been compensated for his 'seholo-holo' (that is, hip bone, or conjugal labour) under customary law in the Assistant Magistrates' court, a decision which the Chief Magistrate's court overturned on appeal.

The woman, 'Makubutu, enjoyed more freedom than she ever could have dreamed of under either system of law. By shopping between the chief's court and that of the magistrates she aimed to get the best advantage, and in her case that could be obtained in the latter, where she could even go as far as to give the President of the court a piece of her mind. Her brother, as well as her chief, had definitely no control over her family plans; and she was one of many.

As it gave advantages to some, the juxtaposition of the two legal systems produced convulsions for others. For those men, for instance, who might initially have been lured into Christian marriages and then later wished to have more wives; when they found themselves indicted for bigamy, they felt that the matter was utterly absurd. As George Tlali, one of Moshoeshoe's sons put it to the Cape Premier in 1883:

> According to Basuto customs plurality of wives is not objectionable. . . . The Basuto say, 'But why are Government interfering in such matters? – If they are God's matters God will punish them. People need not fight for God, God will fight for himself.' . . . These laws are just thrown amongst us, we are expected to receive them like the Gospel.[143]

The Disannexation Act and the High Commission Regulations

On 2 February 1884, by an Order in Council,[144] Lesotho was disannexed from the Cape of Good Hope Colony and returned 'under the direct authority of Her Majesty'. As before 1871, the High Commissioner for South Africa was authorised to 'exercise, in the name and on behalf of Her Majesty, all the legislative and executive authority in and over the Territory'. He was empowered 'to make by Proclamation, such laws as may to him appear necessary for peace, order, and good government of the Territory', as well as to appoint all officers to serve in its administration.

The new High Commissioner for South Africa, Sir Hercules George Robert Robinson, then issued a Proclamation on 29 May 1884, embodying a new set of Regulations (under Proclamation 2B, as it famously or infamously came to be known in the Territory). The Regulations were for the most part clearly meant to be conciliatory to the inhabitants. Most of the harsh sections of the Cape Regulations had been removed. Most notable in this regard were sections on bigamy, initiation (circumcision), witchcraft – most likely because it had fallen into disuse – 'eating up', and guardianship over widows and children. Most important for chiefs, the provision vesting 'the right of allocating land' on the Governor was dropped.

What was either retained or added, however, could still have a heavy impact on the reduction of the powers of chiefs and generally on the transformation of social values. Worthy of attention in this respect were the following. The Resident Commissioner (new title for Governor's Agent after 1884) was empowered and authorised to hold a Court with jurisdiction on all civil and criminal cases in the Territory, and, similarly, his assistants, now styled Assistant

Commissioners, in their respective districts. He was empowered *to appoint chiefs*, who could then exercise judicial powers in jurisdictions determined by himself. He was empowered to make rules 'and to amend, alter, or cancel the same as he may think fit'. It was made lawful for any litigant to appeal from the decision of a chief's Court to a Court, in the first instance, 'composed of an Assistant Commissioner and of such Chief and in the event of their disagreeing then the Resident Commissioner shall decide'.

In the area of family law, it remained still unlawful to compel a woman into a contract of marriage. Marriages contracted according to Christian rites, 'or by any civil marriage officer, duly appointed by the High Commissioner' (which might include any minister of the Gospel) were declared ' in all respects as valid and binding, and to have the same effect upon the parties to the same and their issue and property as a marriage contracted under the marriage laws of the Cape Colony'. All marriages, Christian (civil) and customary, were still to be registered. Hut tax, of course, remained in the Regulations. Tax collection was still through the chiefs, on allowance, although the allowance feature was not written into the law.

A general effect of these Regulations was the same as before. Chiefs (and their headmen) gradually lost their grip on the indigenous court system. They lost their grip on commoners, who no longer depended totally on them for justice. Their income, in the form of court fines, was frustrated, and in turn they reacted with more and more acts of intimidation and vindictiveness. By the end of Cape rule they had already grown significantly oppressive. As one headman, Nkau, who, significantly fell under the immediate jurisdiction of the *Morena e Moholo* in Matsieng, put it in 1883:

> among us cattle has (sic) been taken away without any cause by the chiefs, even a garden or field which is under cultivation, or a piece of ground allocated to a headman. If on any occasion a chief's son should be placed alongside a poor man, the chief's son can take away the field or garden. I am talking about property, but even to a man's wife, a chief's son can take her and you have nowhere to go to. The country is in tears.[145]

This style of rule, or misrule, by the chiefs would grow worse as the century progressed, until the 1920s, when commoners would appeal to the colonial administration for intercession. Until then, the colonial administration had been in too weak a position to address itself to the situation. So soon after a war in which the Cape had lost to the Basotho, it had been found imprudent to pull a tight rope on the chiefs. So, the critical provisions in the Regulations – the one on the appointment of chiefs, and the other on the Resident Commissioner's powers of making rules for chief's courts – had not been made use of. They were, in fact, forgotten, until 1928 when they were, as chiefs then said, 'resurrected' as instruments of a drastic reform of the administrative and judicial functions of the indigenous government.

A New Colonial Administration Begins: The Territory Falls into Anarchy

The fact is, the era of direct Crown rule of Lesotho (1884-) began on very shaky ground: the Colonial Office had no clear plans on the Territory. So, it could devise no clear policy. Its policy, therefore, such as it may be called, was 'an experiment'.

The first Resident Commissioner, an Irishman named Marshal James Clarke, arrived in Lesotho on 17 March 1884 armed with the following terms of reference: the financial up-keep of the Territory would comprise tax locally collected, plus a sum of £20 000 contributed by the Cape Colony in lieu of custom duties:

> The expenditure should not be allowed to exceed the revenue. H.M. Government consider that for the present their efforts should be mainly directed to the protection of property and the maintenance of order on the border. The Basutos should be encouraged and assisted as far as practicable, to establish a system of internal government sufficiently stable to enable them to suppress crime and settle intertribal disputes.[146]

Accordingly, therefore, the colonial administration was very skeletal. It comprised thirteen officers and a police force of 159, of whom nineteen were Europeans.[147] (By 1900 the staff comprised the Resident Commissioner, Government Secretary, seven District Assistant Commissioners, each in charge of a District, four medical Officers and a police force of 259 – for a population of about 264 000 inhabitants.) This would hardly be equal to the task at hand. As I shall soon show, the Territory would be riddled with dynastic disputes, most of them culminating in bloodshed. Neither the *Morena e Moholo* Letsie, nor his son and heir Lerotholi (1836–1905) commanded sufficient moral force to bring the country under control.

Troubled by the tentative, or 'experimental nature' of British rule

over the Territory, which neither gave him leave to assert Imperial
control, nor meaningful leverage to give the *Morena e Moholo* a
helping hand in the period of political reconstruction, Sir Marshal
Clarke registered his protest in his annual report on the Territory in
1885, pointing out:

> in justice to the people of this country and those of the neighbour-
> ing territories, it is now most advisable to define a limit to the
> experimental government, and decide as to the future.[148]

However, the Resident Commissioner got nothing more committal
from the Colonial Office than the feeble remark: 'Her Majesty's
Government contemplate no change in their relations with the
Basutos.'[149] The question is: to what end was the experiment?

The first, explicit, answer to the puzzling question was first given
by the South African High Commissioner, Sir Hercules Robinson,
in 1889. Speaking as an echo chamber for the Home Government,
the High Commissioner made it clear that there could be no place
for 'direct Imperial rule on any large scale' in the Southern African
region. The role of the Imperial Government was only:

> by means of spheres of influence, protectorates and Crown Colon-
> ies, to gradually prepare the way for handing native territories
> over to the Cape and Natal as soon as such transfer can be made
> with justice to the natives and advantages to all concerned.[150]

The second answer was in the form of a minute to one other High
Commissioner, Sir (later Lord) Alfred Milner (1898–1902), who had
made it quite awkward for the Colonial Office by insisting, in contrast
to Hercules Robinson, that the Imperial Government should either
exert its authority in Lesotho, or else get out. His strong stand on
Imperial control invited a minute from an officer in the Colonial
Office:

> It seems to me that Sir A. Milner is perhaps a little too anxious
> to attain finality in the Basuto question and chafes at the insolu-
> bility of the problem – 'How to establish the Government of the
> Basutos upon an absolutely secure basis, without having to leave
> a great deal to risk and chance' – The Government is and must
> remain, I feel, a makeshift Government, a Government from hand
> to mouth, for a long time to come.[151]

Meantime Lesotho, under this 'Government from hand to mouth',
had fallen into anarchy.[152] Resulting from the differences of the Gun

War, Chief Masopha had eternally parted ways with his brother, the *Morena e Moholo* Letsie. Until his death in 1891, a decade after the war, Letsie could not bring the war hero under his authority. Masopha was only eventually subdued by Letsie's heir Lerotholi in 1898, just a year before he (Masopha) died at the advanced age of seventy-eight. In his defiant posture to the high office of *Morena e Moholo* he had taken Chief Maama, a pretender to that office, with him. (Chief Maama was twice related to him by marriage: he had married two of Masopha's daughters, and in turn one of Maama's daughters was married to Masopha's heir.)

Chief Lerotholi, Letsie's eldest son and rightful heir to the throne, had also cast his lot with Masopha in the war; but soon afterward he returned to his father's fold – clearly to nurse his fate as his successor. For, although he was Letsie's eldest son, he was twice at a disadvantage as heir apparent: first his grandfather, the late Moshoeshoe, had cast doubt on his birth, subsequently arranging an artificial union (with no marriage) between two of his grandchildren (Letsie's eldest daughter, named Senate, and Molapo's eldest son Josefa) to beget an heir to succeed Letsie. The product of that union, Motsoene Molapo Moshoeshoe, was waiting for the promise to come true. Second his own father Letsie, for no other reason than favouritism, wished his younger son, Chief Maama, to succeed.[153]

Although the Grand Council had followed custom and advanced Lerotholi as the heir and successor at Letsie's death in 1891, that had left the new *Morena e Moholo* with two bitter enemies, in the persons of Chiefs Maama and Motsoene. Far from supporting him, they constantly goaded him into a conflict.[154]

In the house of Molapo (Moshoeshoe's second son), in the largest and most powerful district of Leribe in the north, the situation was worse. The event of the madness of Molapo's heir, Josefa – Senate's suitor – had left the district in the charge of his younger brother, Jonathan, after their father's death in 1880; but one other of Molapo's sons named Joel, older in years than Jonathan, yet from the deceased's second wife, argued, not that he should have been the heir, but that Jonathan was not. Molapo's death coinciding with the outbreak of the Gun War, the two brothers made use of the armed conflict to dignify their family quarrel – Jonathan fighting as a 'loyal' to the Cape Government, and Joel as a 'rebel'. The duel between the two was to be dignified again by the Anglo-Boer War, with Jonathan honouring British orders not to join the Boers, while Joel, 'to promote a tumult in Basutoland by raking up the embers of the old feud between the children of Molapo', joined the enemy. Consequently Joel got tried for treason, by a joint Court of the Resident Commissioner and the *Morena e Moholo* and was fined £2 000 in lieu of 500 head of cattle, on top of a jail sentence of one year.[155] As it was often the case in those days, when a chief got injured, his people bled on his behalf: the £2 000 that Joel paid came from his subjects.

Partly in response to the dynastic feuds, but also due to other factors – the economic and social – the indigenous institutions of government, the Grand Council and the *pitso* were also breaking down. It stands to reason that with so many factions within the 'Sons of Moshoeshoe', the scions of the royal house, there were very few instances when they could all assemble together and agree on matters of policy affecting the welfare of their subjects. Basically, the only issues that forced them to unite were those which constituted a common threat to them as a ruling class. In 1900, for instance, they agreed to the imprisonment of sixteen members of the royal house of the Baphuthi chiefdom because that chiefdom resented the then popular superimposition of Moshoeshoe's lineage over them.[156] The issues in the twentieth century which would unite them would be the question of incorporation of Lesotho into the Union of South Africa, and the commoners' challenge to their rule.

By the year 1900 the national *pitso* had also degenerated considerably. Its degeneration had begun during the Cape Colony rule, and the primary offenders were the colonial officers. They had turned it into a forum for introducing colonial guests, announcing policy matters, and reading unpopular regulations. As they were used to government by consultation and consensus, Basotho began at this period to encounter a type of government whereby the ruled simply had to accept things as they were given. More often than not, it was their understanding that was expected, and not their consent.

They of course resented this type of rule and some of their expressions of resentment are instructive of what was left of their views of an ideal type of government. In 1883, for instance, when the Basothophil Governor's Agent, Joseph Orpen, was replaced with the much hated and feared Captain Blyth, chiefs found it quite odd when the Cape Premier and the Secretary of Native Affairs flatly told them that they were going to have Blyth, whether they liked him or not. They were not being asked, they were being told. Chief Seeiso Maama's reaction, as reported in the third person, was:

When the meeting was called it was not for oxen to come together, but for men. He supposed that on the day of the meeting there would be important matters spoken and these matters would be discussed with them because they were men, and he only asked whether they might not hesitate to come to the meeting when it was fixed upon if they knew that their rulers decided things without letting them know about them . . . According to their custom, when a meeting took place, one matter was spoken of, and when that was a nice matter, then the whole meeting joined together and said that it was a good thing, and when the meeting thought it was a bad matter, then the whole meeting united together and said it was a bad thing . . . It might be difficult for them to receive any communication which came from their rulers, if decided in that way, because a man who was a subject ought to be told in what way he would be ruled.[157]

As a matter of fact, Seeiso Maama's fear that men would be loath to attend meetings if their purpose was merely to announce decisions had already come true. As the Paris Evangelical Missionary Society in Lesotho had pointed out the previous year, 1882: 'The Chiefs have never much liked the yearly meetings held by the Government', and, if they could, they avoided attending them.[158]

We thus conclude that by the end of the Anglo-Boer War in 1902, the indigenous government of Lesotho, never quite on solid ground, had for all intents and purposes broken down. Dramatic changes in society had taken place. Under the impact of Christianity, Western legal principles, the change of economy from subsistence to marketing and, of course, migrant labour, the outlook of commoners to chiefs had changed in proportion to the deteriorating sense of responsibility (and lack of accountability) on the part of the latter. Factionalism among chiefs had virtually reduced the position of the *Morena e Moholo* to one of a *primus inter pares*. In the circumstances, if the colonial administration was going to introduce a new institution that might bind the old order together, this might be the time to do it.

3 The Establishment of the National Council, Its Constitutional Status and Challenges During the First Two Decades of Its Existence (1903–20)

As shown in Chapter 2, the British Government throughout the nineteenth century colonial phase had no fixed plan for governing Lesotho. From Disannexation onward, the Territory was ruled experimentally, if not haphazardly. Always at the back of the High Commission as well as of the Colonial Office mind was the thought that in the final analysis it would have to be attached to one of Her Majesty's European settler colonies in South Africa. Hence the prospect of granting it a Legislative Council, in keeping with the policy that obtained in the crown colony system was, on those grounds of uncertainty alone, out of the question. Meantime, however, in the face of the disintegration of the indigenous government, which in the long run might necessitate a costly expansion of the colonial administration, it was found desirable to create an alternative institution.

NEGOTIATIONS FOR A COUNCIL OF ADVICE

So the idea of a 'Council of Advice' which, as it will be recalled, had been contained in the Cape Colony 'Draft Constitution' of 1883, which the Basotho had rejected, was revived. The history of the negotiations between the colonial administration and Basotho chiefs on that Council is in itself significant. For not only does it reveal the chiefs' fears and suspicions that the Council was aimed at reducing the power of the chieftaincy but, perhaps more significantly, it tells us something about their views on government.

Early upon his appointment in 1884 as the first Resident Commissioner since Disannexation, Sir Marshal Clarke wrote a letter to the High Commissioner on 11 June recommending the establishment of a Council of Advice, 'a proposition to be submitted to a National *Pitso* of Basuto, to be held at Maseru on the 8th of July next'.[1]

If accepted, the Council would be composed of chiefs and headmen, the former to be nominated by the *Morena e Moholo* but approved by the Resident Commissioner, while as to the latter, half would be appointed by the Resident Commissioner and the other half by the *Morena e Moholo*. The proposal stated that: 'Every headman shall hold his position for three years, unless his seat shall become vacant by death, or removed by the joint action of the Resident Commissioner and the Paramount Chief'. The tenure of chiefs, at least by inference from the preceding proviso, was to be on a permanent basis. Sir Marshal Clarke seemed to be under no apprehension whatsoever that the idea of a Council of Advice might be identified with the much hated Cape Colony rule, whence it was conceived, and thereby be rejected on grounds of association solely. On the contrary, he remarked to the High Commissioner in the form of a post-script: 'This is identical with a proposal made by Sir Thomas Scanlen during his visit to Basutoland last year. It appears to me to meet the exigencies of the occasion.'[2]

Subsequent to this proposal, however, we are unable to say what, exactly, happened. The records are silent. We know neither what the High Commissioner's response was, nor whether or not the *Morena e Moholo* was communicated with; but a national *Pitso* was certainly not held.[3]

Be that as it may, the subject next came under discussion on 11 March 1886, at the first national *pitso* held under the new colonial administration, where Sir Marshal Clarke 'invited the views of the people'. Clarke advised the High Commissioner that 'should there be a strong popular desire for it, a definite scheme will be drafted and submitted to the High Commissioner for consideration of Her Majesty's Government'.[4] Consequent upon the *pitso*, the *Morena e Moholo*, who apparently thought he had both the understanding and the mandate of the chiefs, wrote Clarke a letter accepting the idea on behalf of his people.[5] He was mistaken on both counts.

Suspecting, or perhaps having found out, that the monarch and his chiefs were not of one mind on his proposal, the Resident hesitated to take action on the letter and instead, when the next national *pitso* was held on 6 April 1887, for the purpose of announcing the new colonial Regulations, he took the opportunity to refer to it. The upshot of this strategy was two-fold: first, the monarch was tacitly told that by responding to the Resident Commissioner on his own authority he had acted *ultra vires*. Chief Masopha, the monarch's fiery brother was the first to register his protest, stating: 'As for Letsie he last year sent his answer outside of us. Now we wish to go aside with him and talk of these matters.'[6]

Second, when the chiefs returned from their consultations the majority of them seemed to have adopted the view that, as with the Regulations, the Council was aimed at destroying chieftainship. They would not, however, make their charge explicitly; they preferred rather for Marshal Clarke to read their views in the sentiment they held towards his Regulations, concerning which the veteran diplomat, Nathanael Makotoko, rhetorically enquired of Clarke:

> I want to know clearly are the laws to add to his (Letsie) Chieftainship. We will be glad if these laws were to raise him and praise him . . . Truly, you Queen's Government, we love you like a girl chooses a husband. On the other hand we know the law.[7]

The minority view in favour of the Council was nevertheless significantly expressed. It generally portrayed the idea of a Council as a progressive step from indigenous institutions, and the one best suited for the times. Chief Jonathan, the old 'loyalist' of the Gun War stated:

> We want to be advanced. If the chiefs know that the Council is for our good, let them form the Council. I say I also wish for it from my heart. We should be animals without a Council. I with Letsie say so. Bad men work in the dark. The Council the light of the Nations.[8]

One Tšolo Mopeli, apparently a minor chief, or perhaps a headman, expressed a view that: 'This Council will be our eyes. It will provide us with laws to protect us from the Chiefs.'[9] Tšekelo Moshoeshoe, who as it will be recalled had early, in 1869, gone on an adventure to London and Paris, provided what he clearly meant to be an authorative lecture:

> I thank Letsie for the letter he wrote about the Council. I say it will be a good thing to have a Council to be a help and the eyes of the Resident Commissioner and the Chiefs and people. . . . As I know the Basuto don't understand about the Council I will

explain. It is not a new thing. We want a Council in the same way as these laws come to us finished. We have to obey them but they are already written. What can we do if we find any of the laws heavy as regard Sesuto customs. I don't know our own customs. I do not find fault with those who made the laws, but about Sesuto customs I am still learning. I don't know our own customs and much less those who only hear them. Why we wanted the Council is because old men can come in their karosses and help to make laws. . . . At the Council we could all speak and follow enlightened people. Those who are weak could be helped by Council. Sometimes a man is oppressed by chiefs and he could appeal to the Council.[10]

For all his wisdom on the Council, however, Tŝekelo failed to tip the weight in favour of the *Morena e Moholo* and the Resident Commissioner:[11] and that was to be his last speech at a *pitso*. He died on 7 August 1888.

In a letter written to the *Morena e Moholo* two years later, in 1889, the Resident Commissioner made yet another effort to revive discussions on the Council of Advice, but only as 'my own suggestion . . . not from the Government'. Then he provided a kind of constitution for it: the Resident Commissioner and the *Morena e Moholo* would nominate a majority of the membership of the Council, anticipated to have between 60 and 70 men altogether. The Resident Commissioner reserved eight seats for his own nominees, all of whom would be Basotho, 'to give representation in case people are left out or forgotten'. Both he and the *Morena e Moholo* would be members of the Council. The Council would meet once a year, with the Resident Commissioner as its convener, to consider any fresh laws which are submitted to it, in so far as such laws purely affected Basotho In addition, it would consider questions connected with local affairs; receive an account of the hut tax expenditures; and at the discretion of the Resident Commissioner hear 'serious national cases'. In order clearly to make a distinction between the Council of Advice and a Legislative Council, Sir Marshal Clarke underscored the fact that it 'cannot make laws, this can alone be done by the Queen's Government, but it is to give advice and suggestions as to what it thinks best for the nation'.[12]

As in 1886, Letsie responded positively, albeit adhering to procedure on this occasion. Following a meeting 'with my sons and brothers and the men belonging to the country', held in December the same year, Letsie consented to the establishment of the Council, but with two provisos: one, that the 'members of the Council be elected by me together with the Nation' and two, that the councillors 'are to be people with whom we will understand with (sic)'.[13]

It appeared as though on this occasion the Council was certain to be established. In April 1890 the Resident Commissioner refined its constitution, fixing the membership at 40 and extending the tenure of office holders to two years. The Secretary of State gave his approval.[14] However, clearly because of certain critical clauses in the final version of the constitution, the *Morena e Moholo* and, in particular his chiefs, became nervous. The objectionable clauses were: one, the Council was to have a component within it whereby the Resident Commissioner and the *Morena e Moholo*, acting jointly, 'shall have power' to select some members of the Council to form 'a Court of Appeal, to take cognisance of native disputes and question'. Obviously the *Morena e Moholo* did not wish to share his authority on cases of appeal with the Resident Commissioner. For, although Proclamation 2B of 1884 had already given the Resident Commissioner the discretion to decide cases on appeal, that discretion had for the most part not been used. In the circumstances, the envisaged Court of Appeal might serve effectively to bring his own court of appeal under strict scrutiny. Albeit that his chiefs, for their part, had heretofore frustrated all efforts for appeals to senior courts, including that of their monarch. The joint Court of Appeal seemed potentially to be coercive. Two the *Morena e Moholo* had not been granted the unqualified right to appoint people with whom, as he had put it, 'we will understand with'.[15]

Letsie died in 1891 having failed to see the inauguration of the Council of Advice. For the last time in October of that year, he and Lerotholi had attempted to convince the chiefs that the Council had become necessary: 'it is a long time that this matter has been in discussion, and its end has not been seen yet. I say now, let it be worked and let there be no further vacillating';[16] but the majority of the chiefs had baulked. Disgusted by their intransigence, the Paris Evangelical Missionary Society newspaper, *Leselinyana la Lesotho*, issued the censorious statement on 1 January 1982:

> Does the Lesotho Chieftainship not realise that as long the Council is not established it is disgracing itself? . . . This Council would be one of the agencies for progress; without it there will be retro-

gression. And as Lesotho is surrounded by progressive countries, it must go forward with them; otherwise they will destroy it.[17]

The chiefs' resistance to the establishment of the Council had, however, centred around one man – the independentist Chief Masopha. His military subjugation by *Morena e Moholo* Lerotholi in 1898, and subsequent death in 1899, shattered the last ditch resistance. Indeed Masopha's death was symbolic of the passing of an era. And it was of more than passing interest to the colonial administration, whose new Resident Commissioner observed with mixed feelings:

> The Chief Masupha, who had failed to succeed in resisting constitutional orders and defying the Paramount Chief, soon lost the prestige which tradition had associated with his name, and sank into oblivion as a political factor. . . . So mortifying was this to his arrogant nature that he broke down and died in July under humiliating circumstances, no chiefs of consequence being present to witness his last moments. His own children only were present, and the obsequities were performed in a hurried and unceremonious way. . . . With all his faults . . . he had the merit of struggling gamely for independence of control.[18]

The surviving chiefs fell behind their *Morena e Moholo* in most of his efforts to satisfy the colonial administration. Regarding the Council of Advice, the Assistant Resident Commissioner, Herbert Sloley (soon to be confirmed as Resident Commissioner), observed 'the support in the matter of most of the leading chiefs and councillors' and considered it possible in 1902 'to shape definitely the proposals for the constitution and functions of a representative assembly'.[19] In 1902, when the Resident Commissioner did commence the oft-repeated exercise of drafting a constitution for the Council, the *Morena e Moholo* was badly needing it to perform some of the functions of administration that custom bound him to perform. His health had deteriorated and was 'such as to cause considerable anxiety'.[20]

In his son and heir, Letsie II, he had an exceedingly weak successor. Letsie II indulged excessively in brandy.[21] His interest in the affairs of the state was feeble. According to one account, he was 'weak, mentally and physically, mean, cowardly and idle – influential on account of his birth, but not popular. – Drinks heavily.'[22] He could certainly not be counted upon to maintain even a semblance of power over the indigenous government.

Against this immediate background, then, the colonial administration received an unequivocal consent on the part of the chiefs to
establish the Council of Advice. It was established in 1903, under
the name, Basutoland National Council – in Sesotho, *Lekhotla La
Lesotho La Sechaba.*

THE PURPOSE AND CHARACTER OF THE NATIONAL
COUNCIL

The National Council was not established with a 'constitution' as
such. In fact it had no statutory force. It would not be until 1910
that a proclamation establishing it would be promulgated. Until
then it operated under the Resident Commissioner's 'Regulations',
approved by the High Commissioner.[23]

The Regulations provided for an advisory Council of 'not more
than' 100 members, of whom the Resident Commissioner had the
power to appoint five. (In practice these five would all be commoners, appointed on the advice of the Paris Evangelical Missionary
Society.) The names of the rest of the members, 'Chiefs and Headmen' were to be submitted by the *Morena e Moholo* to the Resident
Commissioner, who before confirming the appointments would
satisfy himself that 'all sections' of the Nation received 'their fair
share of representation'. The *Morena e Moholo* and his 'Principal
Chiefs' (then numbering about 20 by my count)[24] were automatically
to be members of the Council.

As a tentative measure, the tenure of councillors would be for one
year. The Resident Commissioner, acting with the *Morena e Moholo*,
could dispense with the services of any councillor, while the High
Commissioner reserved the right on his sole motion to dismiss any
of them. The Resident Commissioner was the President of the Council, but at his direction he might appoint 'an Assistant Commissioner
or other Officer to preside as his substitute at any time'. He was the
Convener of the Council.

The status of the *Morena e Moholo* in the Council was not clearly
defined in the Regulations. However when the Council did convene
for the first time in July, he was styled 'Chief Councillor'.

An account of the Revenue and Expenditures of the previous year
would be submitted to the Council for its scrutiny at each annual
sitting. The Council might be consulted on any proposed laws 'of a
domestic nature' and its expression of opinion thereon be submitted

to the High Commissioner for his consideration. It might, when it deemed fit, propose changes in legislation 'having local application', in which case the Resident Commissioner shall submit to the'High Commissioner, 'who alone has the right to make laws'. Such submissions would be accompanied by the Resident Commissioner's remarks.

The proposal for a Court of Appeal, earlier made in 1890, was carried forward in the formulation:

> The Resident Commissioner acting with the Paramount Chief shall have power to form the Council, or such members of the Council, as may be selected, into a court of Appeal to take cognisance of native disputes and questions.[25]

This provision was essentially meant to handle the increased and bloody conflicts of chiefs over territorial jurisdiction and seniority, which the office of *Morena e Moholo* could no longer handle.

Cases involving Europeans, or Europeans and Basotho, as well as all other cases originating outside the Territory, fell outside the jurisdiction of the 'Court of Appeal'. They would lie in the Resident Commissioner's of Assistant Commissioner's Courts. External affairs, questions relating to extradition, the Crown prerogative, were all specifically stipulated as falling outside the jurisdiction of the Council.

THE CONDUCT OF THE COUNCIL

The Regulations laying out the constitutional features of the Council were accompanied by Regulations for its Conduct.[26] The Council was to commence its annual proceedings with a prayer, to be followed by 'an address' by the President. Once again, the responsibility of the *Morena e Moholo* in the latter regard was not spelled out. However from the commencement of the first session of the Council, a convention was established whereby he would always respond to the President's Address. As they began, the proceedings were to close with a prayer 'read by the Native Secretary'. The attire of the Council was specified as 'European Clothing'.

The proceedings were to be in Sesotho, subject to interpretation 'when desired by the Presiding Officer'. The record of the proceedings would nevertheless be in the English language. Councillors could address the President either from their seats or in the body of the

Council Room'. Should it become necessary, the President could put a question under discussion to a vote, and councillors would signify their view 'by holding up their right hands'. The Council was open to the Public. However if the President deemed it 'desirable' he could 'direct all strangers to leave the meetings'.

In other words the National Council could be viewed as a chrysalis of a parliament. Thus the resident French missionary and historian D. F. Ellenberger characterised it as 'the first attempt . . . at establishing a regime which was like the shapeless embryo of a parliamentary system'.

THE OPENING SESSION: THE PRESIDENT AND THE CHIEF COUNCILLOR EXPRESS CONFLICT IN THE PURPOSE OF THE COUNCIL

The National Council opened on 6 July 1903, in great pomp. The ceremonial opening was fully attended. Full attendance for the rest of the Session was broken only once, significantly by the most powerful Councillor in the land, Chief Jonathan Molapo, the Chief of Leribe.

The High Commissioner's Address, read on his behalf by the President of the Council, was to set the tone. Although brief, it was to the point: he conveyed his wishes to the 'Paramount Chief' and his councillors for the success of 'the scheme' and hoped that it might be useful in the discussion of 'matters of local interest' as well as in advising him. He would be pleased to see the chiefs use the Council as a forum for 'settling on a friendly and enduring basis their local difficulties', while leaving him to deal with 'the greater questions' affecting the Territory.[28]

The responsibility for filling in the critical details was left to the President of Council, Herbert C. Sloley. Also getting straight to the point, the President warned the chiefs that 'the opening of this Council does not mean the alteration of the system of Government and Chieftainship': the High Commissioner, as representative of the British Crown, remained as the sole authority empowered to make the laws of the Territory. The National Council, he said, was only 'a good substitute' for the national *pitso*, which had fallen into disuse. The *pitso* had become unwieldy in numbers and made efficient discussion of issues difficult. Besides in his view too much time was lost travelling to attend it. (As a member of the colonial administration the President could not appreciate, or perhaps admit the responsibility for, the fact that colonial rule *per se* had contributed greatly to the deterioration of the *pitso*.)[29]

The President's last major point before he tabled the account of Revenue and Expenditure was an invitation to the councillors to reappraise Sesotho customary law and reduce it to writing. The point was of course not new: as we shall recall, the late Tsekelo Moshoeshoe had already, in the April 1887 national *pitso*, called for its consideration. Endorsing its need in 1903 the President of the National Council remarked: 'I know you have your own laws. . . . It will be well for you to consider whether these laws are being kept, or whether in some cases, they are not departed from.'[30]

His invitation in this regard was timely. The chiefs were themselves abundantly aware of the fact that their laws were falling into disuse, and much as they benefited from that situation individually, they were generally embarrassed by it. As Chief Jonathan, the Chief of Leribe, would put it a year later, in September 1904: 'Moshesh's laws were good, but after his death his laws were spoilt, because there were too many chiefs, and too many children.'[31]

The statement of Revenue and Expenditures was of more than passing interest: the Revenue was £100 180, of which £62 200 came from Hut Tax, £28 000 from Customs, and only £110 from Court Fees.

Expenditures consisted of Emoluments of £10 254 toward the support of the colonial administration, £5494 for the Allowances of Chiefs (virtually all of which would have been paid to principal chiefs), £15 745 for the payments and clothing of the Mounted Police Force, and £6600 toward Education. There was a sum of £90 000 in the bank. Quite clearly the Territory was solvent; but what was more, it could be deduced that chiefs were frustrating the efforts for appeals to the Resident Commissioner's and Assistant Commissioners' Courts. Most of the money was expended on administration – the European officers, chiefs and law enforcement. Only £4652 had gone for Agriculture. The use of funds underscored the Imperial Government's commitment to the maintenance of law and order, and not so much to the development of a sound economy. It was merely a holding operation.

Be that as it may, the speech by *Morena e Moholo* Lerotholi revealed a divergence of views from the colonial administration on the purpose of the National Council. Having acknowledged the fact that the establishment of the Council had been delayed by the reluctance of his chiefs, the *Morena e Moholo* suggested that the colonial administration had heretofore been deaf to complaints of his Nation, 'for we had no Council nor laws'. Contrary to the High Commissioner's and the Resident Commissioner's declaration, he asked the the National Council be recognised as 'the King's council in reality'. Accordingly he made his own declaration that 'it shall be a Council of Laws as I have already stated'.[32] As if to make it clear that his Opening Speech was not simply a piece of rhetoric, he wrote the Resident Commissioner a letter about two and a half weeks later putting his point succinctly:

> When I asked for this Council, which my late father wanted to have during his lifetime, I wanted it to be a Council which will speak out the Laws of the Government we are under, so that we may be governed by the Laws of that Government which rules us; and then may be released from slavery.[33]

Lerotholi was ready to take a giant leap. He wanted a 'Parliament'; although it was not clear that he was ready for a popular election. He expressed his conviction that the British constitution was more advanced and efficient than indigenous institutions of government, and he wished Lesotho to espouse it all the way. However the colonial administration denied him his wish.

Throughout the first two decades of the establishment of the Council, chiefs held the same vision as Lerotholi in this regard. So convinced were they of the wisdom of adopting a parliamentary form of government that one of them in 1906, upon the visit to Lesotho of the High Commissioner, Lord Selborne, wished the colonial government to accept the fact that the Basotho subscribed equally to the Rule of Law as Britons. As cited in the High Commissioner's report of the visit:

> Chief Maama pointed out that in all civilised countries where they had one King over them, as in England, they had one King above that, and that was the law. They had agreed to be governed by the law.[34]

(Chief Maama, as it will be recalled, is the pretender to the throne who during the reign of Letsie I had sought to wrest the sceptre from his brother Lerotholi.)

Only one of the prominent principal chiefs in this period had attempted to strike a note of discordance on the constitutional status of the National Council; and that was Chief Jonathan Molapo. The Chief's note of discordance had otherwise been a characteristic volte-

face. Like Lerotholi, he had expressed his full support for the establishment of the Council, attesting that 'you have obtained at last what
your grandfather Moshesh had long desired', and what remained was
to revise the laws.[35] Yet, a year later, Chief Jonathan was to write
a letter of recriminations to the High Commissioner, generally criti-
cising the Council's Regulations and accusing the *Morena e Moholo*
of using favouritism in his appointments, the tone and substance of
which the High Commissioner rejected. He concluded his criticisms
with this indicting petition:

> I would humbly pray your Excellency to abolish the Council as
> it is at present constituted and either revert to Government by
> Proclamations or appoint a Council similar to that of the Orange
> River Colony, to consist of Officials of the Government and rep-
> resentatives of Basuto Nation with a casting vote to the Resident
> Commissioner. . . . The present Council is a weapon given to the
> Basutos which they do not understand the use of, and with which
> they will do themselves harm before they have found out the way
> to handle it properly. And I hope your Excellency will take the
> weapon away and teach them the proper way to use it before you
> give it back.[36]

Had Jonathan's sentiments been motivated by altruism, they might
have passed as perceptive and perhaps even noble. As the history
of his political activities will show, however, the contrary was the
case. The Chief was more anxious to gain an advantage for himself
than to consider whether he was trying to get it by means beneficial
to the nation at large: he was motivated by the fear that the *Morena
e Moholo* might use the Council to curb his increasing tendency to
establish himself as an independent monarch. Jonathan was at the
time the most powerful chief in the Territory, heading the second
house in the royal lineage. His relations with the senior house was
far from cordial, and his dealings with Lerotholi were only tenuously
held together by the colonial administration. As the Resident Commissioner's annual report for 1901–1902 put it: affairs in the District
of Leribe were vexatious and yet most difficult to resolve, on account
of 'the jealousy existing between the Paramount Chief and Jonathan
Molapo'. The report expressed regret at the fact that whenever
'arrangement . . . is satisfactory to one does not please the other,
and the intrigues carried on by two such influential Chiefs are the
main factors in perpetuating the unrest among the Leribe people'.[37]
As an afterthought, and with hindsight, the Chief of Leribe must

have decided that his acceptance of the National Council was tanta-mount to signing his own death warrant.

Always loyal to the colonial administration, with which he enjoyed mutual trust, Jonathan had actually confided his fears to the High Commissioner to that effect. In a separate letter bearing the same date, he had disclosed his worry over the fact that 'a number of my brother chiefs hate me . . . they dislike me . . . because I am and have always been loyal to His Majesty's Government'. He believed that the time would eventually come when 'direct rule by chiefs' would have to give way in favour of 'central national rule', but at that juncture chiefs were all too often still guided by 'their private aims and quarrels when making laws for the nation'. In the current situation, therefore, he pleaded with the High Commissioner 'not to ask me to resign power or authority' over to the National Council, 'whose first action will be to punish me' for the unbroken record of loyalty to the British Crown. 'I am no longer a young man'.[38]

The High Commissioner did not, of course, abolish the Council. He simply gave him the assurance that he would be protected from his brother chiefs and that no one would be allowed to deprive him of his 'legitimate position as one of the leading Chiefs of Basutoland, and second only to the Paramount Chief'.[39]

THE LAWS OF LEROTHOLI: HOW THEY WERE MADE
AND THEIR POLITICAL SIGNIFICANCE

If members of the National Council did not generally comprehend its constitutional status, they must be forgiven. In reality it was difficult to understand. This was even more the case as its first major task in 1903 and the most important achievement before its battle against incorporation into the Union of South Africa beginning in 1908, was to draw up and approve a body of customary laws. In so doing, its members considered themselves to be exercising the func-tion of legislation. Each and every President of the Council could never clearly explain why it was that councillors were making laws and yet they were said not to be legislating.

On 8 July 1903, Councillor Dichaba Labane of Mefeteng, one of the Resident Commissioner's appointees,[40] moved 'that the Sons of Moshesh be instructed to write the old laws of Moshesh'. Josias Mopeli, an appointee of the *Morena e Moholo* from the colonial capital, Maseru, suggested that a Committee be formed 'to write these old laws . . . and submit to the council'. A committee was duly formed, consisting of 24 men, some of whom claimed acquaintance with the revered Moshoeshoe and the workings of his councils, to dust off their memories and present the National Council with a version of his laws.[41]

There were no written samples of Sesotho laws to start from. Although in his Address the Resident Commissioner referred to the existence of the Cape Colony Report of the *Commission of Laws and Customs of the Basutos* of 1872, either it was not available or it was discarded as an unhelpful guide. No further reference was made to it, and certainly the Committee's draft of laws does not reflect its use. Otherwise, it was mentioned that there were written laws made by Moshoeshoe which, from Chief Nehemiah Sekhonyana's synopsis, can be surmised to be the published laws on Trade, Brandy, Circumcision and Witchcraft, but even these were not helpful as 'all trace of them was lost during the wars with the Orange Free State'.[42] Nevertheless the drafting Committee sat for three days, from 11 to 13 July – a very brief period; and on the 14th of the month it tabled its report of the full Council.

Areas Covered by the Laws

In all, the Committee had prepared twenty-one Laws. At the end of their discussion by the full Council they had been reduced to eighteen, a reflection of the fact that some had overlapped with others. Briefly, and in their numerical sequence, the Laws covered the following problems: (1) Succession to chieftainship. (2) The supremacy of the *Morena e Moholo* over his territorial chiefs. (3) The right to appeal from chiefs' courts, and the extent of the *Morena e Moholo*'s authority in the process. (4) The chief's rights and limits to subjects' free labour. (5) Appeals from the *Morena e Moholo* to the Assistant Commissioners' and Resident Commissioner's courts. (6) The application of due process of law to the custom of 'eating up'. (7) Debtors' right to due process of law. (8) Just and equitable allocation of land. (9) Grounds for forfeiture of land use. (10) Administrative procedure for summonses in chiefs' courts. (11) The disposal of immovable property upon permanent removal from a chief's jurisdiction. (12) Restating Moshoeshoe's law for theft, 'to wit a beast for a beast, a second beast as compensation and a third as a fine to defray the costs of the court'. (13) Seduction and abduction of unmarried women. (14) Inheritance and the heir's rights, limits and responsibilities. (15) Estates, property and the rights of widows without male children. (16) Compensation for physical injuries. (17) The jurisdiction of the Assistant Commissioner's and Resident Commissioner's courts. (18) Belligerent use of firearms.[43]

Politics, Social Issues and the Problems of Restating the Laws

Quite clearly not all of the eighteen could be said to be the laws of ancient origin. The colonial situation, in no less a manner than change in social values and the impact of South African neighbours on Lesotho, had given rise to new kinds of problems that called for a readjustment of the old laws, and in some instances an introduction of new ones. All the Laws having to do with the jurisdiction of Assistant Commissioners and the Resident Commissioner in the indigenous court system were a reflection of the colonial political order. The Law on the taking up of firearms in the settlement of personal quarrels sought to address the negative aspects of the otherwise patriotic Gun War. The end of the era of wars with external enemies, coupled with the increasingly shrinking arable land created tensions and the subsequent resort to violence, but this time by means of guns and not spears and stones.

Another problem that went hand in hand with the free use of guns, but to meet which no Law was made, was the alarming consumption of whisky. The reason why no Law was made in this connection was not too far to find. As with gun-toting, however, they had lost the will to resist whisky. Letsie I, Lerotholi, Letsie II, Chief Masopha, despite their varying degrees of personal constitution, were so regularly inebriated that they often failed to attend to their responsibilities as a consequence. Letsie I could figuratively describe his brave son and heir Lerotholi in 1880 as having 'gone mad from drinking'.[44] Masopha's heir, Lepogo, by his own father's admission, died in 1886 from the effects of the drink.[45] In the twentieth century, in 1909, an intelligence report by the South African Government, which was preparing for a potential rebellion from Lesotho in the probable event of its incorporation, were confident of a quick military solution on the reasoning that the chiefs' leadership was as divided as it was dipped in whisky: 'Out of the sixteen Chiefs . . . the principal ones are drunkards.'[46] In order more easily to support their habit, as well as also to make a profit, chiefs were in partnership with white traders across the borders pumping liquor into the Territory. In the circumstances, therefore, it would appear that the colonial administration preferred to keep the responsibility for the control of liquor in its own hands.

The National Council had performed a historic task; and it had done so with a clear understanding that it was attempting to give the indigenous government a new lease of life. It had attempted to restore the nation's faith in the indigenous government; and by bringing the chiefs under the law, it had sought to keep that institution in its place of leadership. Even so, in this second objective, of bringing the chiefs under some semblance of order and unity, the Council should have been left in no doubt as to the fact that the battle had been lost from the start. The most powerful chief in the land, Chief Jonathan Molapo of Leribe, had been the most uncooperative. Had he had the capacity to do so, he would have wrecked the entire project.

Chief Jonathan's Role in the Formulation of the Law

When the National Council convened on the agenda of formulating the laws and accordingly set up its drafting Committee on 8 July, Chief Jonathan had asked 'my Chief, Lerotholi' permission to return home to attend to some family business.[47] Permission was denied, 'except with the Resident Commissioner's consent'. Jonathan then defied Lerotholi and left for Leribe anyway. When the National Council reconvened to discuss the Committee's draft Laws on 14 July, and the Chief of Leribe was not in his seat, the rest of the councillors had cause to worry, and they quickly predicted the consequence. As Councillor Setha Matete put it, 'if these laws are passed in Jonathan's absence and were found distasteful to him he will say he had no voice in making them'. In order to avoid such potential embarrassment, therefore, the *Morena e Moholo* personally, supported by the chairman of the drafting Committee, Chief Theko Makhaola, moved that a telegram be sent to Chief Jonathan summoning him back to the Council, and meantime discussions on the Laws be postponed until he arrived. Lerotholi and Theko Makhaola were at one with the President of the National Council, to whom the ugly truth had by then occurred that he could 'not write to the High Commissioner and say that the Nation was unanimous when Jonathan was absent'. Both the President and his Chief Adviser (Lerotholi) were perturbed by Jonathan's 'irregularities'. The Council supported Lerotholi's motion unanimously.[48]

When he did arrive, the Chief of Leribe performed exactly as predicted: he was absent when the Laws were drafted, he protested, and now he returned 'as a man to be tried for some fault'. He wished to know whether the National Council's Laws would not 'clash with those of the Government', to which the President replied that in the event of any such conflict the Government would inform the Council; but Jonathan still pressed ahead. He requested his name to be struck from the record in consequence of having gone home without leave. He complained that his own position in the National Council was not clearly defined, presumably in the same way as the position of the *Morena e Moholo* was. He therefore declined to be recognised as a member of the Council altogether.[49]

Chief Jonathan was overpowered and his filibustering was effectively quashed. Chiefs Leshoboro Majara and Theko Makhaola pointedly counselled him 'to desist' from his obstructionist behaviour; but they could not dissuade him from his sentiments against the Laws, in particular Law 2, 'that the Paramount Chief of Basutoland shall have full power and authority over every Chief in the Territory'. Thus on 26 September 1904, when he was interviewed by the South African Native Affairs Commission to give his account of the nature of the National Council, he responded, in Lerotholi's presence:

> It has to speak on Basutoland matters, and there are certain Native laws which are made in this Council; although I was not asked my opinion about the laws formed by the Council.[50]

Lerotholi was irate, with that as well as with others of Jonathan's disagreeable surprises. As he was still unnerved and could not lucidly put his thoughts together, he asked Philip Molise to respond, and Philip said:

> It was the wish of the nation to ask the Resident Commissioner and the Paramount Chief to draw up some written laws for the guidance of the Basutos, and those laws were discussed and passed in the presence of all these Chiefs, and we, as a nation, were satisfied with those laws, which were passed in this Council, because that was out wish.[51]

Because Chief Jonathan did not wish to be bound by *The Laws of Lerotholi*, he would for the most part ignore them. Until his death in 1929, he would constantly defy the instructions of every *Morena e Moholo*; and when pressure was brought to bear to bring him under control, he would petition the High Commissioner to proclaim his District a separate country, with himself as the *Morena e Moholo*. These developments will be examined later.

THE LEGAL STATUS OF THE *LAWS OF LEROTHOLI* AND THE CONSTITUTIONAL POSITION OF THE NATIONAL COUNCIL

The role of the National Council in the making of *The Laws of Lerotholi* gave it an ambiguous character. The process had involved not merely the reduction of customary laws to writing but, as already illustrated, virtually drawing up new Laws to meet current problems. It was not the first time that the Basotho had sat down to formulate similar rules. They had done the same within the framework of their traditional Grand Council (*Lekhotla la Mahosana*) and the *pitso* in the colonial period. We have established (in Chapter 2) that the process that they had gone through then could properly be described as one of legislation, and that was how they themselves viewed it; but now they were engaged in the same exercise under a colonial institution, the National Council, and within a political order in which only one man was said to be the legislator. In the circumstances, what were they to consider to be the status of the Laws they had just made, and what were they to understand of the constitutional status of the institution under which they had them made? It was difficult for members of the National Council to understand the thinking of the colonial administration on this problem.

Aware of the problem, although not appreciating fully its magnitude, the Resident Commissioner explained to the High Commissioner when he forwarded the Laws to him in 1903 that 'I was careful to point out that the Council was an advisory body', and that legislative authority 'was the sole prerogative of the High Commissioner'.

> I therefore forward these 'Laws' merely as an expression of national opinion in the direction of regulating certain tribal customs, and judgements, and opinions of important and respected Chiefs; such laws are preserved and handed down by oral tradition, and the suggestions made by the Council are not intended to be a complete collection of such Basuto laws.[52]

Indeed he was correct on the former. The latter, however, was a prevarication. He had not explained to the councillors that their

Laws were 'merely . . . an expression of national opinion'. He had not instructed them on the distinction that he made between 'law' and 'custom', so as to convince them that their Laws fell in the latter category. Had he done so, they might well have instructed him on their own distinction between the two, thereby leaving a debate of some academic value; and he most certainly had not given them the impression that they had merely made 'suggestions'. On the contrary, he had acknowledged to them, as earlier cited, that 'You have laws . . .' and consequently exhorted them to reduce them to writing.

The reason why the Resident Commissioner had not disclosed his opinion on the status of the Laws of Lerotholi is not too far to find, and it can be fully appreciated. Had he told the councillors that they had merely made 'suggestions', 'merely . . . an expression of national opinion', they might have formally declared that in that event there was no sense in requiring the indigenous courts to enforce them; and that was something that he could ill afford putting to the test. So he chose to say the councillors had made Laws, but not legislated. They had made Laws, but within the framework of an advisory body. That was ambiguous, and it made the constitutional role of the National Council in the eyes of the councillors paradoxical.

In just a few years' time, this unsatisfactory situation would come back to haunt the Resident Commissioner. At the Third Session of the Council in 1908, there having been no meetings in 1906 and 1907 for no sound reasons, Philip Molise, the spokesman of the *Morena e Moholo*, posed the inevitable question to the President of the Council:

> I wish to draw attention to something that was said in the Resident Commissioner's address – that this Council is not a legislative body, but only an advisory one. Now this Council passed some laws and I would ask whether these are to be considered as really being laws or not.[53]

The President of the Council had his second chance to say the things to the councillors that he had originally said to the High Commissioner; but he did not do so. Instead he dithered and chose the easy way out:

> I wish to remind you in my address that the council had no power to make laws that you speak of, they were only written out by the

Council and your Paramount Chief signed them and they were printed and circulated.[54]

This was a very unhelpful answer, particularly in the circumstances in which the new *Morena e Moholo*, Letsie II, was finding himself since his father's death in 1905. The situation was that the chiefs were generally not obeying these Laws, which after all were made to curb their own abuses of power. They flagrantly disregarded them, and the *Morena e Moholo* was in no position to enforce them. So desperate was the new monarch that the previous day, in the same Session, on 28 January, he had committed the folly, in the eyes of his chiefs in the Council, of pleading with the Resident Commissioner to ask the High Commissioner to confirm the Laws by Proclamation, as it seemed that they were not being obeyed because they were not 'Government laws', having been made by a mere advisory body.[55] The folly had quickly and obliquely to be redressed by his uncle Chief Alexander Maama who, determined to keep Sesotho customary law under Basotho, censoriously remarked that 'it would be very bad if [we] had the Resident Commissioner [here] to listen to what he had nothing to do with'.[56] Subsequently, on 30 January, Letsie II found himself in the unregal position of having to eat his own words:

I wish to apologise for what I said the other day asking that the laws should be confirmed by the High Commissioner. After consulting with the other chiefs I now ask that the Resident Commissioner and the Paramount Chief may be given power by the High Commissioner to carry out these laws.[57]

The person who came to the President's aid by giving Philip Molise a straightforward answer on the status of the Laws, and the only one that the councillors could understand, was the Reverend C. M. Sebeta who said that 'there are two kinds of law in Basutoland, the laws of Moshesh and the High Commissioner'. In his view, if only Letsie II enforced the latter, 'there would be no complaints'.[58]

The confusion over the legal status of *The Laws of Lerotholi* and, consequently, the constitutional status of the National Council, was not simply a product of misunderstandings between the colonial administration and the Basotho councillors, wilful or unintended. A fair measure of it resulted from genuine want of knowledge or sophistication on the part of the colonial officers involved. When faced with technical issues over which they had no expertise, they were loath to admit uncertainty to the 'native', preferring rather to leave him thinking that *he* was the victim of ignorance. The Resident Commissioner, H. C. Sloley, was one such victim of ignorance of constitutional Law. Thus in May of 1910, upon the death of King Edward VII, he had announced the death through a proclamation. The proclamation was a joint piece of legislation with the *Morena e Moholo*, who had not signed it personally – his uncle Chief Maama had signed it on his behalf.[59] In the end, after the Proclamation had attracted the attention of the Legal Advisor, it was concluded to be a legal muddle and dismissed with two embarrassing statements: first the Legal Advisor, Mr A. E. Balfour, pointed out that it 'has no binding force – The king is King over all his dominions (which include Basutoland) and all his subjects (including the Basutos) owe him allegiance independently of the Proclamation. Second the Imperial Secretary in the High Commission observed: 'The proclamation had no legal effect and no harm had been done and nothing need be done.'[60]

It is no mere coincidence that the meeting of minds between the colonial administration and the chiefs of Lesotho on the establishment of the National Council took place in 1902, the year of the conclusion of the Anglo-Boer War. Just as the end of that War meant the beginning of a serious preparation for the forging of a union of the South African settler colonies of Natal and the Cape with the Transvaal and the Orange River Colony, so it also meant that a change of policy on the part of the colonial administration was compelled by developments in the post-war period to define the Territory's place within the context of the pending union, and that possibility was greatly in favour of its incorporation into the union. In the second place, it was found desirable, in the event of incorporation, that the union should inherit a more tractable and orderly chieftaincy. In order to achieve these objectives, a more interventionist policy in the affairs and conduct of chiefs was adopted. The drafting of *The Laws of Lerotholi* can be seen as one illustration of that change in policy. Another was to be a direct intervention in the dynastic disputes of the chiefs, as well as the effort to resolve its succession problem.

In this section we shall examine the problem of dynastic disputes and succession; and in the next, we shall devote a few pages to the issue of the transfer of the Territory to the Union – its effects on the role of the National Council and on the institution of chieftaincy.

The Baphuthi Chiefdom is Dismembered

The first direct, and remarkably ruthless, twentieth-century intervention in the chiefs' dynastic disputes began, significantly, as a joint effort between the colonial administration and Moshoeshoe's royal lineage. It was the passionate effort to strip the Nguni Chiefdom of Baphuthi of its power and political role in Lesotho. The scheme of its destruction had begun in collaboration in 1879, when the *Morena e Moholo* Lerotholi placed his second son, Chief Griffith, at the ancestral home of Baphuthi at Phamong, in the Mohales Hoek District. According to the then Resident Commissioner, Godfrey Y. Lagden, Griffith's placing had followed upon 'the earnest request by the Paramount Chief, extending over several years, that his second son be recognised by Government in a ward appointed for him'.[61] At the placing, the then chief of Baphuthi and grandson of Moorosi, Mocheko Moorosi, had challenged the placing, which was to be at the expense of his own authority, and 'attempted to disorganise the *pitso* by calling upon all Baphuthi (sic) to rise. But Mocheko was promptly suppressed by the Resident Commissioner, who ordered him to sit down.'[62] And so the Chief did.

Before the year was at an end, however, the *Morena e Moholo* sought to test Mocheko's allegiance to him. For no other reason than to see whether or not the Chief would obey, he sent his counsellors to Phamong to summon Mocheko and his principal men to the royal court at Matsieng. According to the leader of the royal counsellors, 'If they do not obey, I was to call them through their goats' – that is, 'eat up' their animal flock.[63] As it was expected, Mocheko defied the summons. In the effort to 'eat up' his flock, an affray ensued. Gun-shots were fired from both sides. One of Mocheko's brothers was killed. Losing his nerve, Mocheko took his principal men and some warriors and fled to the nearby District of Hershel, in the Cape Colony.

This situation was sufficient for the colonial administration to press for the Chief's extradition from the Cape Colony. Mocheko and eighteen of his principal men, all members of the Baphuthi royal lineage, were put in prison without trial for the duration of the Anglo-Boer War, while the *Morena e Moholo* and the colonial administration considered what to do with them. In the meantime, the Resident Commissioner advised the High Commissioner:

[The] location of this troublesome person will have to be defined.

Mocheko claims land rights and chieftainship to a preposterous and inadmissible extent, and in view of his personal character it will be necessary to strictly limit his sphere of influence.[64]

Early in April 1902, a national *pitso* constituted in the form of a supreme court was held at the colonial capital, Maseru, to try Mocheko and his men. The Resident Commissioner presided over the *pitso*. All the principal chiefs of Lesotho were present. Charges were: 'Contempt of Court of the Paramount Chief. Resistance to Lawful Authority. Breach of Peace. Endangering the Peace of the Neighbouring Territories by Entering the Cape Colony with Armed men.'[65]

Chief Mocheko's defence was to be his own undoing. He shifted the focus of the trial from the relatively lighter charges that lay before the *pitso* to the more serious, and potentially treasonable, question of territorial sovereignty: 'I understand, I am in jail for the country', he said. Mocheko renounced, or perhaps denounced, the generally accepted view that he was Lerotholi's vassal and argued, instead, that he was his ally. He premised his argument on the allegation that his grandfather Moorosi had been Moshoeshoe's friend and ally, a position the contrary of which we have already established. Hence he challenged Chief Griffith's placing at Phamong, expressing unhappiness over the fact that Griffith 'was sent to my place without my knowledge'.[66] In his current circumstances that was a fatal form of defence. He had played too daringly into the noose. His liege lord, Lerotholi, pulled it remorselessly:

> I received Mocheko and his wife from Matatiele [after the Moorosi Rebellion] against my father's wish. . . . If Mocheko remains here he will endanger me. Give him a letter chief to remove from this country.[67]

Mocheko was deprived of his chieftaincy, and in order to make sure that his chiefdom remained under Griffith directly, and not through its own head, Mocheko and the eighteen other members of his royal lineage were kept in Maseru for another fourteen years, while alternative plans for their resettlement were being considered. Both the colonial administration and the Sons of Moshoeshoe contended that their presence in Lesotho constituted 'a danger'. Subsequently Mocheko had recanted and begged for pardon from the *Morena e Moholo* and the National Council. But in March 1914 a decision was reached that they should be banished to Matebeleland on the tribalist reasoning that the Matebele of Mzilikazi were their kith and kin and they would be the merrier there. They were to be banished under a Proclamation passed in 1907 for the removal of 'undesirable persons', a piece of legislation which, when it was promulgated, the chiefs had challenged through the National Council, dreading that it might be used against them. Following assurances to the contrary, their fears had been allayed; but now they thought it was appropriate if used against the Baphuthi royal house.[68]

Fortunately for the Baphuthi, however, when the matter was referred to a Legal Adviser, the Resident Commissioner was advised that only an Act of the British Parliament might achieve the objective. So the project as abandoned.[69] The next extreme alternative, proposed by the *Morena e Moholo*, was to settle them on top of the mountain of Qeme, not far from the colonial capital, at which Mocheko rightly complained when he was told of it.

Many chiefs have shed blood and have been imprisoned, but after serving their time they have been allowed to go to their homes. No one has been sent to Qeme, though they had shed blood . . . I do not agree to go to Qeme Mountain.[70]

It was not until 1916 that the saga ended: the Baphuthi royal lineage was permitted to return to its ancestral home, but utterly shorn of power. As a political unit, it would never again be permitted a political role in Lesotho.

In the meantime, Moshoeshoe's royal lineage was engaged in more virulent and politically enervating dynastic disputes. Its factionalism shattered what was left of the commoners' faith in its leadership. It virtually destroyed the indigenous judicial structure. It rendered the office of *Morena e Moholo* politically more vulnerable than it had been in the nineteenth century, and consequently subject to increasing manipulation by the colonial administration.

Colonial Policy and Letsie II's Succession

Morena e Moholo Lerotholi died at his capital at Matsieng early on the morning of 19 August 1905, following a chronic illness that had lasted for six years. He had carried his people through a difficult period and in the course of it proved himself a worthy grandson of Moshoeshoe. Despite their challenges to his authority, his chiefs saw him as a sound ruler, and certainly the last of their great monarchs.

The colonial administration was giving him a fair and just tribute when it said:

> For 14 years he occupied his difficult position, dexterously strengthening himself by playing off one chief against another . . . He knew to an ounce the breaking strain of the bonds which attached the people to the chiefs, and the chiefs to each other and to himself. Though shrewd and highly diplomatic on occasion, he was naturally bold and masterful and completely fearless.[71]

He was succeeded by his eldest son, Letsie II, then a man of about 34 years of age who, in the view of the Resident Commissioner, Herbert Sloley, 'has never displayed any remarkable ability or force of character'. Herbert Sloley was doubtful whether he would receive 'undisputed support of his kinsmen and other Chiefs';[72] but of course, Lerotholi had started out with the same disability: his succession had been disputed. Yet the difference between father and son would be that whereas the father had had the capacity to deal with the consequences of that fact, the son would be a total failure in that regard.

Until Letsie II came to power, the colonial administration had not developed a clear policy on the question of succession to the office of *Morena e Moholo*. As we have already seen, when Letsie I came to power in 1870, it had had no involvement in it. When Lerotholi came to power in 1891, however, the disputed nature of his succession had invited its involvement. As Letsie I had previously sought to appoint Chief Maama as his successor, and meantime had died, leaving the colonial administration uncertain as to whether his Grand Council had subsequently agreed unanimously on Lerotholi as the rightful heir, the then Resident Commissioner, Sir Marshal Clarke, had intervened. As later recounted in the case of *Bereng Griffith. 'Mantšebo Seeiso Griffith*, in 1943,[73] Sir Marshal Clarke had advised 'that the Chiefs-in-Council should send through him *a message* to the High Commissioner giving their views as to who was entitled to succeed, whereupon Her Majesty's Government could say if it agreed or not and the decision could be published to the nation.'[74] Except it must not have been so clear to 'the Chiefs-in-Council' that that procedure was taken as a matter of policy, and indeed, when Lerotholi had challenged the procedure, Sir Marshal Clarke had fallen short of taking a stand on it, stating:

> Your brothers are, I think, wrong in saying that I am inaugurating

a new way of acting in Basutoland. Moshesh introduced Letsie to the Nation during his lifetime as his successor, though no one could question Letsie's birthright. I myself urged Letsie to similarly introduce his successor. Masupha told me he did the same, but Letsie replied that there was time enough, and died before he did so.[75]

In other words, Lerotholi had been made to understand, not that his recognition derived from the High Commissioner's approval, but rather from the fact of an announcement, which in his case had not been carried out, and which was necessitated by the disputed nature of his birthright.

The colonial administration at that point had clearly only manipulated the succession and not asserted constitutional jurisdiction over it. This came out clearly in the High Commissioner's message of congratulations to the Resident Commissioner for his role in influencing the final outcome of the succession:

[It] is greatly due to the tact and judgment with which you have for some time past been preparing the minds of the principal chiefs to accept this result as the best security against intertribal quarrelling and as the most likely course to conduce to the peace of the country.[76]

With Letsie II's succession, however, the colonial administration would take a firmer position and establish a policy.

To begin with, the Resident Commissioner did not permit the nomination of Lerotholi's successor to be made by the chiefs in their customary Council at the royal capital at Matsieng. The nomination was made in the National Council in Maseru. Then, once the chiefs had agreed, in keeping with Law I of *The Laws of Lerotholi* on succession, that Letsie II was the rightful heir, thirty 'Chiefs and Members of the Basutoland National Council', headed by the heir's uncle Chief Theko Makhaola, were required to write a letter to the High Commissioner requesting 'with respect, that His Majesty the King and the High Commissioner, may recognise Letsie as the Paramount Chief of the Basuto.'[77]

Letsie II was nominated on 28 August and appointed 'provisionally' on 18 September 1905, pending the High Commissioner's confirmation. The High Commissioner subsequently had him officially announced at a *pitso* in February 1906. The point was not to be missed that in the final analysis Letsie II owed his legitimacy to office to the High Commissioner, only after whose approval he could consider himself a *Morena e Moholo* of Basotho. His successor would be treated in like manner.

LETSIE II SURRENDERS HIS POWERS TO THE NATIONAL COUNCIL

The new monarch's problems of authority began promptly with his provisional appointment in August 1905. Still determined to reduce the powers of the office of *Morena e Moholo* so as to attain his relative independence in the country, Chief Jonathan proposed that Letsie II should 'sign a document binding himself to respect the rights and property of others'. In order to give that motion the image of constitutional enlightenment, albeit incongruent with his role in the 1903 Session, he additionally suggested that the National Council be broken into two Chambers, one representing Chiefs, the other Commoners. As such he was the first chief to advocate bicameralism in the Council.[78]

Jonathan lost on both points. Chiefs were not prepared to share power with commoners along the lines of a Bicameral House as he proposed. The majority of them opposed the idea. And it can be surmised that the Resident Commissioner was pleased with the outcome. For had the idea enjoyed majority support, the next logical step might have been a request that the Council be given legislative powers, a step which the colonial administration was not, at that point, prepared to entertain. On the question of requiring Letsie II to sign an oath to respect the 'rights and property of others', it turned out that Jonathan was opening a hole in the indigenous form of government bigger than he had intended. For, Councillors Molise and Abiatara, obviously expressing the commoners' sentiments, then went on record as having said:[79]

> If an oath had to be taken, it should not be confined to the Paramount Chief, but that all Chiefs should be pledged to observe justice in dealing with junior chiefs and people.[79]

Finding his proposal thus assuming the character of Basotho Magna Carta, a development that he had not intended, and could ill afford to countenance, Jonathan would not argue it further. It was dropped: but the proposal had been significant. As the Resident Commissioner said to the High Commissioner:

The Clause as suggested, appears innocent enough, but Jonathan's intention is probably to impose limitations upon the Paramount Chief's constitutional power to redress wrongs in, and to listen to complaints from . . . Districts . . . Jonathan's intention in introducing this clause, was to limit the Leribe, and Berea Districts . . . It would reduce the Paramount to the position of a Chief merely 'primus inter pares,' and might lead to an unworkable position.[80]

Actually Letsie II did not require Jonathan's oath to become a *primus inter pares*. His own personal weaknesses were sufficient to reduce him to that position. He neither ruled nor reigned. He was not interested in the affairs of government, leaving those to his uncles, principally Chiefs Alexander Maama and Theko Makhaola.

His chiefs had little respect for him. His full brother, Griffith Lerotholi, who was under his direct control as a territorial chief, would provoke a needless attack on a Chieftainess named 'Masefabatho in December 1907, attempting in arms to denude her of her territorial caretaking. Letsie II was helpless, or uninterested, in the development. Griffith was at the end brought under control by the Resident Commissioner and principal chiefs in the country, who convened a national *pitso* to look into his provocation and to instruct him to desist from his belligerence. The *Morena e Moholo* was present at the *pitso;* but he appears not to have uttered any significant statement to assert his authority; and perhaps it was understandable that he did not. It was privately hinted to the Resident Commissioner 'that Griffith's intention was to provoke a conflict with Letsie himself'. And Letsie II was not one to hold his own in a contest of wills.[81]

Letsie's weaknesses was of course very much to Chief Jonathan's liking. His own district was torn by political conflicts between his sons, Mathealira and Motsarapane, who were fighting for seniority with each other. The situation was made complex by a third party, Chief Tau, whom Jonathan had, in keeping with custom, sired for his mentally-demented brother Josefa. As in Sesotho customary law a child's legitimacy derives from *bohali*, and not paternity, Tau duly considered himself Josefa's heir and thus senior to both Mathealira and Motsarapane. It was made unbearable by Chief Motŝoene, a prodigious man in physique, weighing over 360 pounds.[82] Motŝoene felt that, having lost his place as *Morena e Moholo* to Lerotholi in 1891, to which, contrary to law and custom, his great-grandfather Moshoeshoe had designated him, Jonathan ought at least to yield to him and let him rule Leribe. He was a biological son of Josefa and Princess Senate, Letsie's only child by his great wife, in an arranged union without marriage: the union was King Moshoeshoe's personal innovation. Otherwise it was uncustomary and unpopular. Then, too, there was a grandson of Chief Lesaoana (Ramanehella), Chief Mitchel, who in 1906 burned down a local chief's village, fighting to expand his own caretaking in Mapoteng, to the south of the District.[83]

Just the same, Jonathan seemed contented as long as Matsieng did not interfere. In a despatch to the Colonial Office in June 1911, the High Commissioner, Gladstone, who had just paid a visit to Lesotho, commented warmly on the Chief's status:

> The personality of Jonathan gives him an ascendency over his people which the paramount Chief is unable to claim, and the success of his endeavour to eclipse the latter in the impressiveness of his demonstration of welcome was materially aided by . . . Superior discipline and spontaneity.[84]

It was during the monarch's reign that the office of *Morena e Moholo* first manifested serious signs of inability to cope with the problems of the indigenous court system. Appeal cases from lower courts piled up at Matsieng. The blame was of course placed fully on Letsie II, by the territorial chiefs, in no less a manner than by the colonial administration; but this was only partially correct. There were two other factors that accounted for the situation. The first was that the implementation of *The Laws of Lerotholi*, in so far as the question of appeals was concerned, was yielding some results, unsatisfactory though they still were. Hence Matsieng was handling relatively more cases than it had previously done. The second was that the traditional machinery for clearing such cases, which was basically still the local court serving the immediate jurisdiction around the royal capital, could no longer cope with the new volume of work. The old Grand Council had always been reserved for 'big' cases, and it was impractical to call all its members – the principal chiefs throughout the land – to reside permanently at Matsieng for cases 'big' and 'small', just because they were of the nature of appeals.

Thus, at the Fifth Session of the National Council in 1910, Letsie II made a request that the Council should appoint men to help him try cases at Matsieng so that he may be left only with the responsibility to pronounce judgements. He repeated this request to the Council at its Seventh Session in 1912, through Philip Molise who said: 'On this matter people are speaking badly about him by saying, he delays their cases, and I say he is correct in asking for help because maybe this blight on his person will disappear.' Letsie believed that if at least he was given men to assist him for just two to three months he would be able to clear the cases. His health was failing. He was desperate.[85]

On both occasions the request was met with dismay. The majority of the chiefs in the Council asked: 'why is there a need for people today, whereas cases had always been settled in Moshoeshoe's days' with the same set-up as Letsie II was given; but Philip Molise was perceptive: 'Times have changed';[86] while Chief Motŝoene was outrightly hostile to the *Morena e Moholo*. As he said to Chief Makhaola, who had deputised for him:

> You should look after this seat of Moshoeshoe . . . If you do not hold your blanket firmly, somebody will per chance step on it, and tear it up . . . I will not work for Letsie, nor will I take away his chieftainship from him. I have resolved never to go to Letsie's place.[87]

Motŝoene's hostility toward Letsie II was of course personal: he still believed that he should have been the *Morena e Moholo*, and in Letsie II he saw someone much less worthy of the office. However the hostility was by no means confined to himself: the Council in general was cool toward the monarch; and this was so because of the monarch's own hostility toward it. He seemed to feel that it was replacing his own authority; and he had gone so far on one occasion in 1909 as to swear that he would 'wipe it out' if it did not comply with his wishes.[88]

In the end, however, the National Council was convinced that there was 'undoubtedly a great pressure of work in the Paramount Chief's Court'. Except, ironically, the agreement was reached at a Session held four months after Letsie II died, in 1913.[89] Some members of the Council were appointed to serve at a special Court of Appeals at Matsieng, which convened for periods of a few weeks at a time, on the call of the *Morena e Moholo*. The members of the Court were not paid for their services. In the course of the decade it would gain additional responsibility as a roving Court, settling both the judicial and administrative problems in the several districts, in particular those that were badly hit by internal strife. This role was distinct from the one served by the combined Court of the Resident Commissioner and the *Morena e Moholo*.

Thus a steady shift in authority from Matsieng to the National Council at Maseru began. From that point on, there would be an increasing contest for authority between the two.

GRIFFITH LEROTHOLI COMES TO POWER: A CONTEST FOR AUTHORITY BETWEEN MATSIENG AND LERIBE CONTINUES

As he had lived, a rather unimpressive life, Letsie II met on 28 January 1913 a rather unimpressive death. He had strayed due southwest of the country into the neighbouring Orange Free State in the Union of South Africa, steering a Scotch cart, practically unattended by courtiers. In circumstances heavily shrouded in mystery and unsavoury gossip he took ill. His uncles, chiefs Maama and Mojela were suffered to fetch him at the little farm of Runnymede, where he had wandered. There he died in their hands. He was buried beside his ancestors on Mount Thaba Bosiu, on 31 January, 'with customary ceremonial in the presence of an immense concourse.'[90]

Letsie II had left a complex succession problem behind. He had no heir and this was so because throughout his adulthood he had lived with one of the younger wives of his grandfather Letsie I, Bokholane ('Mamojela), by whom he had even sired a male child, named Mojela. Mojela was 14 years of age, but as his mother was the wife of Letsie I, he was viewed rather as Letsie II's uncle than as his son and heir. Meantime, Letsie II had shunned the company of his own wives, keeping them for the entertainment of important and favoured persons. His father Lerotholi had even tried in 1898 to involve the colonial administration to return him to his first wife, Mahali. 'Letsie however became violent and nothing could be done with him.'[91] Mahali had herself been reduced to begging the High Commissioner, H. C. Gladstone, in 1912 'to grant my case a hearing as the principal wife of Paramount Chief Letsie' who had 'for several years been denied the privileges of my rank . . .' The High Commissioner had been unable to help, as 'the matter is one in which I am unable to interfere'; and she had been referred to the National Council, which recourse she had declined to pursue.[92] Thus, unto the death, Letsie II had remained in the affectionate throes of his grandmother, as it were, thereby frustrating a smooth succession.

The last remaining hope, in the person of a toddler named Tau, by one of the monarch's highly placed wives, was crushed by a mysterious death shortly after the royal burial. True, his paternity was already a subject of debate; but in Sesotho custom he might have been accepted as Letsie's son, in that his mother's *bohali* had been negotiated and Sesotho says 'Ngoana ke oa Likhomo' – 'A child derives its legitimacy from its mother's *bohali* cattle.'

In the bewildering circumstances, Chief Griffith, as the full brother to the deceased *Morena e Moholo*, was approached to fulfil the custom of levirate and raise seed for his brother by his senior wives, and meantime to accept the role of Regent; but Griffith, who was by then a staunch member of the Roman Catholic Church, albeit with 28 wives, declined the invitation. First he argued that his faith did not permit him to raise seed for the deceased. Second, however, he was adamant that the throne had naturally devolved upon him and he meant, in his quotable phrase, 'to sit on the throne with both buttocks'.[93]

The majority of 'the Sons of Moshoeshoe' finally yielded and gave Griffith his wish. Among the opponents to his recognition was none other than the Chief of Leribe. In the main, Chief Jonathan's opposition was based on an understandable, if arguable, point of custom. He believed that Griffith should be required to honour custom and only raise seed for the royal house, failing which he should yield to another member of Moshoeshoe's lineage to do so. Behind his argument, however, another factor was apparent: he probably hoped that the impasse might give him the opportunity to propose Chief Motŝoene as the successor. As Herbert Sloley had pointed out five years earlier in 1908, Motŝoene's presence in Leribe was 'a source of great embarrassment to Jonathan and a great relief to the house of Letsie'.[94] The Resident Commissioner would once more observe at the conclusion of Griffith's appointment in July 1913:

> Motŝoeni (sic) has in addition to his claims in Leribe a very serious claim to the Paramount Chieftainship and were it not for the fact that he has at times displayed a certain mental inability (perhaps inherited from his father) he might have proved a formidable rival claimant to the late Letsie and to Griffith.[95]

It is indeed probable that Chief Motŝoene might have personally tried his luck for the high office in 1913, but the Resident Commissioner promised to better his material condition to offset his political loss. For, as he made the above observation to the High Commissioner, the Resident Commissioner commented with a sense of achievement that 'I have had a private meeting with Motŝoene' at which he had given him 'a substantial increase to his allowance' to the end of taking 'the edge from his discontent for the present'.[96] Against this background then, Griffith Lerotholi was duly recognised as the *Morena e Moholo* of Basotho in April 1913. The High Commissioner came to Lesotho especially to install him, 'In the name of the King.'[97]

The consequence of Jonathan's opposition to Griffith's appointment was an irreconcilable difference between the two members of the royal lineage. Unlike Letsie II, Griffith was determined to bring Jonathan under control. In turn the latter redoubled his efforts to maintain his independence. The general outcome of the struggle for power between the two was that divisions within the royal lineage were intensified, whilst the commoners caught within the conflict, particularly those in Leribe, suffered. The contest of wills began only a few months following Griffith's installation. In December 1913, the Resident Commissioner advised the *Morena e Moholo* to call Chief Jonathan to the royal residence at Matsieng 'to discuss in a friendly way some long outstanding difficulties' in the District of Leribe. Pleading old age and infirmity the Chief, then 61 years of age, offered to meet the *Morena e Moholo* halfway, significantly either at Moshoeshoe's historic mountain fort Thaba Bosiu, or at the colonial capital in Maseru.[98] Unofficially though, the *Cape Times* credibly reported that the Chief had otherwise intended not to honour the call, saying he would not 'talk to a boy'.[99] Following a caucus with his uncles, the *Morena e Moholo* declined the Resident Commissioner's advice that a special Session of the National Council be called to discuss the old Chief's conduct and resorted, instead, to a more direct approach. According to the *Cape Times* he sent 'several Chiefs' to Leribe with a command. 'Their visit was also bootless, the recalcitrant chief again refusing to obey.' It was not until Griffith had personally decided to descend upon old Jonathan, 'riding at the head of a large force', that he went to Maseru and not Matsieng.[100] The Chief, however, denied any allegations that his delay had been actuated by defiance. He was fined 20 head of cattle for contempt. (In March 1914, as it will be recalled, Chief Mocheko L. Moorosi of Baphuthi would tentatively be made an offer to settle on top of Mount Qeme for his own act of defiance.)

His age notwithstanding, in August 1914, Chief Jonathan set out to rake up the embers of the old feud between himself and his half-brother Joel. Employing his sons as commanders for the purpose, he raided Joel's flock, burned his subjects' houses and returned with 1716 cattle, 7942 goats, 5794 sheep and 418 horses, mostly the property of the common people, and three men lost their lives. The attack was totally unprovoked and, except as a retaliation to Joel's offensive during the Anglo-Boer War, unjustifiable. In August 1915, a combined court of the *Morena e Moholo* and the Resident Commissioner tried the Chief of Leribe for manslaughter and disturbing the peace. He was fined £3341, in lieu of 1000 head of cattle. He was the wealthiest Mosotho in hard cash and in cattle, for he had exploited the common people by imposing an extraordinary cattle lavy (*morohane*) on them – then a common practice among chiefs. The *Morena e Maholo* kept £634 of the fine, the rest of it going to the central treasury of the Territory. In addition, Jonathan was required to pay £8000 to Joel in damages; but he also kept all the *morohane* cattle in excess of his fine. So that at the end he came out the richer from it all.[101]

The colonial custom of sharing fines accruing from judgements in chiefs' disputes had the positive effect of motivating the successive holders of the office of *Morena e Moholo* to be active in the joint court system with the Resident Commissioner. However it also had very negative effects: first, it whetted Matsieng's appetite for money. Second it stimulated or, as in the case of Jonathan, reinforced chiefs' resentment of *Morena e Moholo* for his monopoly on the privilege of big fines. Third as commoners in the end paid the fines for their chiefs, it meant that the *Morena e Moholo* and the colonial administration were indirectly bleeding the common man for the aggression of chiefs.

In this regard 1915 was a good year for Griffith. He had sat at three joint Court sessions, got between 18 to 21 per cent of the fines for each, and made a clean £859 for the year, excluding his annual allowance of £1680, thus: he had sat at the judgment of Chief Masopha in April, getting his share of £200 out of a total fine of £1109.16sh.6d. In August he got £25 out of Chief Seeiso Maama's total fine of £110.12d. Then, the same month, it had been Jonathan's case, for which initially he got £334; but he protested to the Resident Commissioner:

> However, Chief, I pray that I may be given a share that becomes me and my chieftainship, and my position in the country and my position as Government servant.[102]

And so the share was raised by another £300.

Jonathan was perceivably as disenchanted with Griffith's assertion of authority as he was with his financial gain. He would not comply with the requirement to pay damages to Joel until 1918, when Joel got the services of a lawyer to recover his losses. Meantime, in September 1915, he tried to smuggle a huge consignment of rifles into the Territory, obviously positioning himself for a last ditch resistance against Griffith. However the plan backfired very badly. He lost £1311 in hard cash to a European smuggler who, he found later, had procured him 'nine large cases' of salt, instead of rifles and ammunition.[103]

The Chief made his last desperate attempt to rule independently of the *Morena e Moholo* in 1916, when he petitioned the High Commissioner to recognise his District as an independent state, to redress the situation that 'Griffith . . . constantly and unlawfully interferes in your Petitioner's inherited rights in Leribe.'[104] To entertain such a petition was, to the High Commissioner, out of the question. Jonathan was thus forced to accept Griffith's authority.

It must be said, in the final analysis, that the new colonial policy toward dynastic disputes achieved its main purpose: it tamed the chiefs and made them more manageable by both the colonial administration as well as by the *Morena e Moholo*. Although imprisonment had been introduced into the Territory since Cape rule, chiefs did not generally serve jail sentences for breaking the law until the start of the century when Joel was incarcerated during the Anglo-Boer War. Thereafter it was used more regularly. Used in combination with the heavy fines imposed by the Joint Court, it had a dampening effect on the chiefs' pugnacity.

To this we may add the fact that by the end of the second decade of the twentieth century most of the veterans of the Gun War were either dead or tired. Chief Maama died in 1916. Joel died in 1919. Both Jonathan and Motšoene survived the decade; but Jonathan was so tired that about March in 1920 he requested Griffith to allow him to abdicate in favour of Montšoene. A *pitso* was duly called at Matsieng at which, on Griffith's evidence, 'The sons of Moshesh have agreed to this matter and I have confirmed.'[105] The Chief later changed his mind, however, apparently because of Griffith's warning that Motšoene was not clearly sound of mind and he just might 'require him to hold the reins of his horse when he rides'.[106]

THE QUESTION OF LESOTHO'S INCORPORATION INTO
THE UNION OF SOUTH AFRICA: BASOTHO'S RESPONSE
TO IT, AND ITS EFFECT ON THE CONSTITUTIONAL
STATUS OF THE NATIONAL COUNCIL

Divided as they were individually, and generally unable to acquit
themselves as effectively as they had done in the pre-colonial period
as an institution, the chiefs were united against the proposal that
their country be incorporated into the Union of South Africa. They
feared the prospect. And they did all in their power to forestall or
delay it.

The basis of their fears, generally speaking, was the memory of
the Basotho-Boer War of 1865–8, which drove them to seek British
protection. They feared that the Boer element of a United South
Africa might be still eager for a conclusive victory over them. They
loathed the idea.

More recently, since the conclusion of the Anglo-Boer War, when
discussion on the unification of South Africa began in earnest, these
fears had been confirmed. European settlers, English and Boer alike,
were making clear in the press and other media that they were
not prepared to share power with Africans. Perhaps expressing a
representative view of Europeans' basic fears in regard to giving
Africans franchise, the Honourable J. G. Fraser, a solicitor and
former member of the Orange River Colony volksraad stated, when
interviewed by the South African Native Affairs Commission on 21
September 1904:

> I should be very chary of giving the Native the franchise in the
> country at all, for the simple reason that numerically it would
> eventually become a black Government. They outnumber, and
> they are so much more prolific than the white populations, that,
> if they got the franchise, it must eventually culminate in the whole
> country being under a black Government.[107]

C. H. Hobson, a merchant resident in Lesotho, echoed a sentiment
to the same Commission which was only a variation of Fraser's
argument, and equally widely shared by the European community:

> I think they are utterly unfit for it, either by education or by public
> spirit. At the present time they are almost in the power of their
> (sic) and would vote as their Chiefs told them. You cannot have

a feudal system and the franchise together: they are diametrically opposed.[108]

Basotho chiefs were certainly aware of these sentiments. Besides, they were participants in, and the focus of, the Commission. Lesotho's response to political developments in South Africa at this point in history took two forms. The first, by the intelligentsia, was the newspaper. The second, by the chiefs, was the National Council.

The Reaction of the Educated Elite

Until 1904 the educated élite, by which I mean teachers, clergymen, writers, and the employees of the colonial administration, had only one local paper through which they expressed their views, and that was the missionary-controlled *Leselinyana la Lesotho*. Coincidentally with the establishment of the National Council, a new and more political weekly newspaper called *Naledi ea Lesotho* or *Basutoland Star* was founded by the family of N. M. Tlale and E. N. Tlale, with Simon Phamotse as its first Editor. Unlike *Leselinyana*, which published in Sesotho only, *Naledi* published both in Sesotho as well as in English. About 1910, apparently marking the event of Halley's Comet, which appeared that year, another activist paper called *Mochochonono* or *The Comet* appeared. Started by E. Monyakoane, by 1920 it had been overtaken by the proprietors of *Naledi*. Both *Naledi* and *Mochochonono* began with a weekly circulation of about 400, and in 1929, when *Naledi* closed down, the weekly circulation was 658 and 800, respectively, compared with *Leselinyana* at 1120 per week.[109]

Early in June 1908, just as the colonial parliaments closed their special sessions devoted to the question of 'a closer union', and a National Convention was to be held in Durban in October, *Naledi* entered the debate with two lengthy articles. Its primary aim was to educate its readers on the issue of unification itself, and then to make its own proposals. First it explained the difference between the two types of constitutions under discussion – one for a federation, the other for a unitary government. The difference between the two, it said, was that under a federation 'each of the colonies is a family, where federal interference is limited'. Whereas under a unitary constitution, the central government gets into the family. Quite clearly, it said, the former was to be preferred because 'little countries such as Lesotho will remain as they are today'. Second, whereas European newspapers were saying that the various South African colonies should first unite, and then deal with 'the Native Question', *Naledi* proposed that the procedure be reversed. As it was, only the Cape Colony was known to have taken a step favourable to the rights of Africans. *Naledi* feared that if the question were addressed later, it would be easy to strip Africans of whatever rights they brought with them from their respective territories.[110]

It was of course clear by the time the white colonies held their parliamentary sessions that they themselves preferred a unified government, and *Naledi* was not in favour of Lesotho's incorporation in that event. On 'the Native Question' also it was clear to *Naledi* that the Orange River Colony, in particular, 'judging from the remarks of several of its members . . . natives must look elsewhere for protection from Colonial tyranny'. The newspaper expressed dismay at the suggestion by the Orange River Colony that under a united South Africa Africans would have to be lumped together in 'Native States' and remarked, ironically:

> The suggestion of establishing Native States in the already crowded Colonies in which Natives will be given local government, and which has been harped on from time to time by the *Bloemfontein Friend*, is utopian. Such a thing can never happen and is impossible of fulfilment. Were (sic) will such a land come from that will be set aside for the segregation of Natives.[111]

The irony lay in the fact that, 'utopian' as it seemed, the Union of South Africa did eventually implement the idea. Unlike their chiefs, however, the educated élite had one point on which they were in perfect agreement with Europeans, and that was the view that franchise and 'civilization' go hand in hand. As *Naledi* said, 'we do not believe in the indiscriminate grant of political right to people most of whom have not as yet any knowledge of how to make use of it'. The paper subscribed to the view that:

> The test of civilization should be a real one, the man who can only sign his name is not civilised [he must not only] have thrown off his native blanket but also the heathen influence of native law and custom, and is leading a truly civilised life. That is the kind of test which ought to be acceptable to all enlightened and intelligent Natives and which we in our humble opinion, accept as a true test.[112]

Needless to say this 'true test' left the majority of the chiefs outside the political calculations of the educated élite. It was a challenge to their authority. And the chiefs viewed it with resentment and hostility.

The Reaction of the Chiefs and the National Council

Alarmed by the increasing tempo of discussions on unification, and dreading its consequences on themselves and their country, chiefs convened their *Lekhotla la Mahosana* (Court of Princes) in May 1908 to decide on a course of action to be taken in the circumstances. Consequent upon the meeting, *Morena e Moholo* Letsie II wrote a letter to the Resident Commissioner seeking further information: he saw in the newspapers 'a scheme' to unify the white South African Governments, he said. 'I do not understand the nature of this matter.' He wished to be advised on the reasons for unification and how it was to be achieved. More specifically, he wished to know just how 'the preservation of us Basuto differs from that of other colonies. Are we of Basutoland also thought of in this unification?'[113]

The Resident Commissioner's response was brief: 'I know nothing beyond what I have seen in the newspapers.' He promised, however, to forward the monarch's letter to the High Commissioner and await further instructions.[114]

The High Commissioner's response was exactly what the chiefs had dreaded: it was desirable in his view, he said, to have 'the control of the Protectorates' (Swaziland, Bechuanaland, and Lesotho inclusive) transferred to the planned union because 'I much fear that, if the Protectorates remained as it were "islands" under the Imperial administration in the midst of a United South Africa there will be friction between the South African and Imperial Governments.' Such friction, he feared, would be bad for all three parties in the long run. Nonetheless as 'an absolute obligation of honour' upon the Imperial Government, specific provisions would be embodied in the South African constitution to guarantee that chiefs and their people in the respective 'Protectorates' could continue with the types of government they already enjoyed.[115]

The Colonial Office was evidently uneasy about the High Commissioner's posture on the question. A minute was penned next to the relevant paragraph on his report:

Lord Selborne is in too great a hurry in this matter. Basutoland is a very prickly hedgehog and it is not at all certain that the S.A. Union when it is made will be anxious to handle it. *The Basutos are already asking questions, they are warlike and armed.*[116] (My emphasis)

On their part, chiefs panicked and decided to take up the matter more actively through the National Council at its Third Session in 1908.

Quite obviously, the chiefs concluded when they were advised of Lord Selborne's response that, not only was he bent on transferring their country to the planned union but, he was actually committed to breaking their power altogether. Just a year preceding the political conflagration of unification, he had passed a Proclamation reserving for the High Commissioner the power to remove what might be deemed 'undesirable persons' from the Territory. This was the infamous Proclamation No. 46 of 1907 under which Chief Mocheko L. Moorosi would be nearly banished to Matebeleland. The chiefs now thought it should be formulated in the form of a Petition to be taken personally to the 'great white father and protector', His Majesty King Edward VII by a high-powered delegation. The Petition, in part, read:

[The removal] may be done summarily and without notice and without fair trial, a fact which . . . [is] like a great sword overhanging us . . . the Proclamation ignores our existing tribunals which are presided over by Your Majesty's representatives . . . We feel that it places us in a position of great degradation and must be looked upon with suspicion and distrust.[112]

The Petition on the question of unification submitted a strong plea that Lesotho should not be incorporated into the planned union of the South African Governments but should remain, 'as far as possible, independent as now'. The Petition expressed the fear that if Lesotho was incorporated, 'Our national existence will cease'. In the unfortunate event that the Imperial Government should insist upon Lesotho's incorporation, the Petition submitted a plea that at least 'our present form of Government, our ancient customs and our ancient laws' should be preserved.[118]

The Lesotho Petitions to King Edward VII were based as much on Basotho disdain and fear of potential Boer domination as on the suspicion that, as they have proved with the Bloemfontein Convention of 1854, the white people of South Africa, including the High

Commissioner, were united in a scheme to sacrifice Basotho to their own political expediency. One unfortunate fact, however, was that in drafting the Petitions, the members of the National Council were as good as making bricks without straw: they were being systematically short-changed of crucial information necessary for them to build a strong case to present to the Imperial Government. The most they could do in the circumstances was to fall back on diplomacy – a legacy that Moshoeshoe had bequeathed them, and one which they sought to turn into a national heritage. They flattered and wooed the British King, addressed him as the 'great white father and protector', and assured him that if he did not intercede on their behalf, 'our whole constitution, as granted us by Your August Mother, Queen Victoria, and continued by your gracious Majesty, will be shattered.'

The Views of the South African Colonies and the High Commissioner on 'The Native Question'

As the chiefs consulted on the Petitions and made preparations during the latter part of 1908 to proceed to London in the new year, across the border a union was being forged. A convention of the white South African colonies, including Rhodesia (which took no part in the discussions or the divisions) was held in Durban from 12 October to 5 November, and at Cape Town from 23 November 1908 until 3 February 1909 when it produced a draft Act of the Union. Of relevance to the South African High Commission Territories (Lesotho, Bechuanaland and Swaziland) were two points. The first was that, right at the start of the proceedings, an agreement was reached, on the motion of the Prime Minister of the Cape Colony, that the debates would be absolutely secret, and that no records of speakers would be made.[119] That meant that the National Council of Lesotho was barred from knowing the facts necessary in the preparation of its own position in relation to the framers of the Union Constitution.

The second fact was that, as a consequence of the secrecy of the debates of Convention, the National Council was denied at least one crucial piece of evidence on the posture of the framers of the Union Constitution, the knowledge of which should greatly have fortified its contention against incorporation. For we now know, from what little came to light from the Conventions's debates, that from the start the Convention did not, generally, intend to come to terms

with the fears and hopes of the African population in the future
Union of South Africa. This view was stated lucidly by the Chairman
of the Convention, Sir Henry de Villiers, in his opening speech when
he remarked:

> There appears to be an impression abroad that this Convention is
> going to lay down the lines to be followed upon such questions as
> the future native policy of South Africa, but I think you will agree
> with me that questions of that nature can only be dealt with by us
> in so far as they bear upon the immediate matters submitted to
> us for consideration.[120]

Indeed such was to be the general posture of the Convention. In a
situation at the time when Africans outnumbered Europeans by a
ratio of five to one, the fathers of the Union Constitution would not
consider it expedient to give Africans franchise. Only the Cape
Colony, whose African population was already enjoying a franchise
(based on property and wage qualification) put up a struggle. The
Transvaal and the Orange River Colony refused to extend African
franchise northward. In the end both the solutions – to adopt the
Cape franchise, and to fix a civilisation test for all electors – were
ruled out.[121] By the time that the draft of the South Africa Bill was
brought to London in the middle of 1909, all that had been agreed
was to vest the administration of 'native affairs' in the Governor-
General.[122]

Lord Selborne, the High Commissioner for South Africa, in whose
care the welfare of Basotho was vested, was not less negative in
his view of the African readiness to participate in parliamentary
institutions. He made this clear to the Colonial Office in February
1909, the very week that the Lesotho Deputation submitted its Petitions at the centre of power in London. On the eve of the delegation's departure for London on 29 January 1909 the Conference
of the Paris Evangelical Missionary Society had submitted a proposal
to the High Commissioner associating themselves with the stand of
the National Council and adding that, in the event of incorporation,
Lesotho should be given 'the right . . . to a large amount of self-
government'. In regard to the National Council they had proposed:

> The continues (sic) existence of that Council should be secured in
> the Charter, and means found to give it a more representative
> character and to gradually increase its powers so as to lead eventu-
> ally to representative institutions.[123]

In his reaction to the proposal the High Commissioner made it clear to the Secretary for Colonies, The Earl of Crewe, that he was totally opposed to the idea.

> H. M. Govt. are the trustees and at all times will be far better judges of what is really to be to the advantage of the Basuto people than the Chiefs and Council ever can be. These uncivilised natives have not the knowledge or the education to form a sound judgement under the complicated conditions of modern civilization and politics.[124]

A Visit to the Centre of Power

Against this background, then, the Lesotho Deputation set out to England to see the white Lord Paramount in person. The Deputation was to have been led by *Morena e Moholo* Letsie II himself.

Indeed his chiefs and headmen did all they could to show him that it was essential and fitting for him to do so; but he pleaded ill-health and could not be moved out of Lesotho. The point of fact was that the *Morena e Moholo* had an almost pathological aversion to official trips outside his country. He had never even as much as taken the opportunity to go to Cape Town, the only Mosotho monarch in Lesotho history to distinguish himself with such a sedentary existence. Nonetheless his representatives were well-picked. They consisted of four chiefs, Seeiso Letsie, Mojela Letsie, Masopha L. Masopha and Leshoboro, representing the families of three of the four prominent sons of the house of Moshoeshoe. Chief Jonathan, the son of Molapo, the second son of Moshoeshoe, declined to complete the dynastic quartet of the Deputation. While in complete agreement with the objects of the Deputation, and while attaching his signature to both of the Petitions to be submitted to King Edward VII, he refused to go himself or to provide a representative, owing to what he claimed to be his grievances against Letsie II – an allusion to a perennial claim for grazing ground for his cattle in the mountain areas. The chiefs were accompanied by two Government Interpreters, Bernard Matete and Manama Molapo, the two Secretaries, Philip Mochekoane and Dyke Mabitso.[125]

The Deputation arrived in London on 6 February 1909, and it was well received. It was housed in a first-class hotel at 29 Inverness Terrace, with a special cook assigned to it. It was clothed with new suits and saturated with activities of pleasure – bus riding, sightseeing and dinners. As for its objects it saw the Secretary for Colonies, the Earl of Crewe, twice, and even got an audience with 'the white father and protector', the King.

The Imperial Response to Petitions

By the time it got to see the Secretary for Colonies and the King, however, one of its objects, the Petition against Proclamation No. 46, 1907, had already been greatly undermined. The High Commissioner had sent a lengthy telegram to the Colonial Office on 11 January, ahead of the Deputation's arrival, justifying the need for the Proclamation, and recommending the nature of the response that the Deputation was to be given. The most immediate cause for the Proclamation, he said, was 'a most undesirable class of white men' resident in Lesotho, living among Basotho, 'conforming to their customs to a large extent, and in some cases intermarrying with them by cattle in native fashion.' This class of low white men was a source of 'considerable embarrassment' to colonial officers in the performance of their duties. He needed the Proclamation to sweep the poor white problem out of the Territory.

In so far as the chiefs feared that the Proclamation might be used against them, he said, their fears were not misplaced. He had intended it to be the Sword of Damocles over their heads. This he found to be necessary all the more as he anticipated a bitter struggle for succession after Letsie II, who had no son. In the event the claimants to the sceptre resorted to arms, all of which was in their tradition; 'it would mean for many years to come a state of unrest and friction, manifesting itself in continuous internal tribal disorder and constant faction fights accompanied by loss of life.' Against that background, therefore, and although he had studiously avoided being explicit to Letsie II, he intended to remove any such belligerent chiefs or confine them to such places in the Territory as might seem convenient. Besides, he said, such action had already recently been taken among the Batswana where, for a similar offence, Chief Sekgome Letsholathebe had been removed from his ancestral place at Tsau and 'detained against his will at Gaberones for two and a half years'. Nonetheless when the Deputation presents the Petition on the matter,

> I suggest . . . that your Lordship [the Secretary for Colonies], in advising His Majesty as to the answer . . . should state quite

clearly that you regard such a power as a justifiable power in the hands of the High Commissioner and necessary for him to fulfil his responsibilities, and that you should express surprise that . . . the paramount chief should not show more confidence in the manner in which such a reserve power is likely to be exercised . . . under the direct supervision of His Majesty's Government.[126]

The High Commissioner concluded his telegram by stressing the point that the Deputation should be told 'quite definitely' that the Proclamation would not be repealed. So that was the response that the Deputation was given.

The Petition against incorporation got a slightly encouraging response, albeit still failing in its ultimate objective. The Delegation was informed, as already suggested by the High Commissioner in his communication of 15 February, that, as it always had, the Imperial Government would safeguard the interests of the Basotho. It could not be guaranteed that Lesotho would not be incorporated into the South African Union; but if and when it happened, it would be under terms favourable to the Territory.[127] Thus the Deputation returned from the centre of power, three weeks later, with an epic of adventure, but intangible political results.

The visit, however, had left an impact in London. The Colonial Office might have dismissed the Deputation with empty gestures, but it did not deceive itself into thinking that it had cleared the road to Lesotho's incorporation. More than anything else, the visit had vindicated its long held view that Lesotho was 'a prickly hedgehog'. It would not be prudent as yet to make plans for its incorporation. It were better to delay such a prospect, and hope that in the course of time the political circumstances of South Africa would accommodate it without spines flying in the face of the Imperial Government.

The National Council Requests Guarantees for the Survival of the Nation and for a Change in Its Own Constitutional Status

Be that as it may, when the National Council met at its Fourth Session in March 1909, the Basotho's attitudes on the home front had taken a new turn. All the while the Deputation was in England, various interest groups in the Territory were making preparations in anticipation of incorporation. The various Church denominations, with the Paris Evangelical Missionary Society at the vanguard, mounted pressure on the colonial administration to give Basotho reasonable guarantees: (1) special treatment in regard to 'a large amount of self-government', in recognition of the fact that the nation was more 'civilized' and politically more sophisticated than the Swazi and the Batswana; (2) the right to exclusive use of the Territory, such as to 'make impossible for any South African Ministry of Parliament to ever confiscate it, or any portion of it, under any pretext whatever or for any pretext whatever or for any reason whatever;' (3) laws governing the Council were to continue to be promulgated by the High Commissioner, on the advice of the National Council; (4) 'No alterations should be made in the Charter granted to Basutoland without the free consent of the Basuto tribe represented by its Chiefs and Council and of the Imperial Parliament'; and (5) appropriate disposal of revenue by the Resident Commissioner, under reserve of the approval of the High Commissioner on the advice of the National Council.[128] The Basutoland Chamber of Commerce, under the chairmanship of George R. Hobson, whose views on African franchise in 1904 were earlier cited, associated itself with the Church denominations, with two major exceptions: it urged for an immediate review of the land tenure of trading stations, residences and buildings of Europeans; and it wished to be represented in the National Council, 'with a vote if possible'.[129] These were to be the major items in the agenda of the Fourth Session. Stakes were high. The High Commissioner had come in person.

The general attitude of the National Council, and likely of the nation at large at that juncture, was that Lesotho was being made a sacrificial lamb to an essentially wicked government, and all that the nation could do was to plead for guarantees. The *Daily Mail* of South Africa cited the view of the *Morena e Moholo* as follows:

> Letsie declared himself afraid of the Union of South Africa Government, which he compared with a snake trying to kill his people. 'If,' he said, 'the snake tries to kill me, others may try to kill the snake. I am frightened of the Union.'[130]

In the event, then, that no one came forth 'to kill the snake', the National Council drew up a list of twenty guarantees, headed by the four crucial questions:

(1) Land should remain inalienable.

(2) 'The Paramount Chief, Chiefs and National Council to be recognised as the mouthpiece of the Basuto Nation. That the

Council be allowed to improve until its members shall be elected by the Nation.'

(3) 'Succession of the Chieftainship of Basutoland to follow the laws and customs of the Basuto, and the rights and privileges of the Basuto people to be respected in accordance with the law.'

(4) Proclamations intended for Basutoland be first laid before the National Council by the Governor-General, before being put for discussion by the Union Parliament.[131]

Virtually all the recommendations of the Church denominations and of the Chamber of Commerce were adopted. Of those that were excluded, the most significant were: (a) the inclusion of Europeans in the National Council; and (b) individual title to land.

By the time in June 1909 that the white colonial governments of South Africa approved the final draft of the Convention's work, they sensed a mood of war from Lesotho. There were rumours in Lesotho, most of them deliberately put into circulation by chiefs themselves, that Lesotho was soon to be seized by the Boers and carved up into farms. As a consequence, the people generally were getting aroused. In preparation for a possible uprising, the General commanding the Forces in South Africa had prepared an intelligence report spotting the weaknesses of the chiefs and assessing the probabilities of a quick military conquest.[132] In a secret memorandum written on 4 June, the Cape Colony Prime Minister, John X. Merriman, recorded his Minister's disappointment at 'the result of a generation of direct Imperial rule' which had erected a system of government through chiefs, instead of breaking down and minimising their power. As a consequence of that policy, the Ministers felt,

Basutoland must be considered the Storm Centre of South Africa, a condition of things which is all the more remarkable from the fact that the position of these people has evolved in less than a hundred years out of the scattered remnants of broken fugitives and some cases of cannibals.[133]

The net gain of all these developments to Lesotho was that the National Council was established on a permanent footing. A special building for the Council was built in 1908 and completed in 1911. A Proclamation was promulgated in 1910 giving the Council statutory force, still as an advisory body,[134] and the councillors began to get a special attendance allowance, initially £10. The Council was allowed to discuss external matters, provided they affected the Territory: and it was written into the Schedule to Section 151 of the Union of South Africa Act that in case of transfer, 'It shall not be lawful to alienate any land in Basutoland'.[135]

LESOTHO'S ROLE IN THE FOUNDING OF THE AFRICAN NATIONAL CONGRESS

The homogeneity of the Basotho, their early exposure to Western civilisation, and the fact that they were an unconquered nation, had always given them a distinctive place in the eyes of the majority of Africans in South Africa. Their persistence against incorporation elevated that image even higher. Lesotho was seen as having a role to play in the politics of a wider South Africa; and, with all its limitations, it responded.

A distinctive illustration of this point was the role that it played in the founding of the African National Congress, then styled the South African Native National Congress, in 1912. It is significant to note that when the idea for the Congress matured in 1911, the *Morena e Moholo* of Basotho was appointed Honorary Vice-President of the Convention that was to be held the following year, in Bloemfontein. It is further significant that when that Convention was held, on January 1912, it was a Mosotho of Lesotho who chaired it. However this was consequent upon a logistical difficulty: the man who had formerly been given the chair, a Mr Mocher, otherwise Chairman of the association's Orange River State Branch, could not keep order and the chair had to be rescued from him. Letsie II had deputised his uncle Chief Alexander Maama to the Convention, who was then given the honour. Although Maama declined it, 'on the grounds that he did not think his Chief would wish him to accept', a member of his entourage, Philip Mochekoane, one of the secretaries to the 1909 Deputation to London, assumed the responsibility 'and kept good order throughout'.[136]

The Chairmanship notwithstanding, Lesotho maintained a sense of political balance and pragmatism in its involvement. Thus, when the Convention called for 'unity' and 'sympathy', Chief Maama was quick to lay down Lesotho's policy: 'he was quite at one with the speaker as long as sympathy meant sympathy, but if by sympathy, rebellion was meant, he on behalf of the Basuto would have none of it.' All assured him that by sympathy they meant sympathy –

'moral support and no more'. Similarly the Basotho representatives would not join in the discussion of 'Union Laws' lest they be accused of 'interfering in another man's house'.[137]

THE QUESTION OF INCORPORATION THREATENS LESOTHO ONCE MORE. MORENA E MOHOLO GRIFFITH GOES TO THE CENTRE OF POWER

The long range effects of the question of incorporation were twofold. First it made the chiefs permanently vulnerable to the colonial administration. Their lifeline from incorporation was the Imperial Government. The Imperial Government got its recommendations from the High Commissioner and the officers on the spot in Lesotho. It became necessary not to ruffle the feathers of these officers without compelling reasons, lest they became unresponsive or negative when and if South Africa should continue to press for the transfer of their country. Second it provided justification for the colonial administration and the Imperial Government to resist constitutional advance. For it appeared antithetical to the prospect of incorporation to do so, especially as the Union of South Africa kept a vigilant eye on any such move.

Meantime, the Union of South Africa intermittently raised the question of having the High Commission Territories, keeping the chiefs constantly on their haunches. The first major such occasion was in June 1919, when the Prime Minister of South Africa, General Botha, expressed his readiness to incorporate Swaziland.[138] However, by the time he came to make so explicit a pronouncement, suspicions in Lesotho had already been aroused when, two years previously, in 1917, the Union of South Africa had proposed the Natives Administration Bill, segregating black people from whites. (The Bill in fact became law in 1920.) *Morena e Moholo* Griffith had then anxiously enquired of his Resident Commissioner, R. T. Coryndon: 'I ask you Chief to explain to me the reference to black people, as to place from which it starts and how far it goes. I ask for an answer by letter.'[139] Although he was answered *by letter* and informed that the Bill would not affect the High Commission Territories, as long as they were not a part of the Union of South Africa, Griffith remained anxious. By early 1918 rumours were rife in Lesotho that the country was about to be seized. One junior chief in particular, a grandson of the late rebel Chief Masopha, himself named Thakampholo Masopha, was on an ingenious, if prophetic, propaganda campaign among Basotho in the Kimberley mines, alerting miners that word was out from Cape Town to the effect that Lesotho 'must come under the Union Government'. He said a part or perhaps the whole of it was due to be appropriated and carved out into farms for white people. Those removed from their land holdings would in exchange be given land strewn all over Southern Africa, from Thaba Nchu and Matatiele in the Orange Free State and the Cape, respectively, to Bechuanaland, Natal, the Transvaal, and even in Rhodesia.[140] Early in 1919, when the *Morena e Moholo* requested a trip to London, to renew his loyalty to His Majesty King George V, and 'to rejoice over this Peace' terminating World War I with him, the National Council thought the primary objects of the trip might as well include another Petition against incorporation. The Fourteenth Session of the Council, held from 12 to 30 May, was hence devoted predominantly to the subject of incorporation and the draft Petition. Time was ripe, the Council generally agreed, to draw the attention of King George V to the fact that, just as it had predicted, the Union of South Africa had begun to deprive Africans of land and to harass them. In a brilliant feat of diplomacy, the Council agreed to commemorate the day on which Lesotho came under Queen Victoria, 12 March 1868, as a holiday marked as Moshoeshoe's Day. And in October *Morena e Moholo* Griffith was in London – the first Mosotho monarch to go to the centre of power.

On that occasion, the response from His Majesty was more explicit, more encouraging, and more flattering than the one given to the 1909 Deputation. Fittingly so, perhaps: this time it was one monarch to another – or liege lord and his vassal, as it seemed. His Majesty King George V expressed the hope that:

> between Britain and Basutoland and between the Basuto nation and the King and his successors there will remain the silken but enduring fetters of today.[141]

4 Commoners' Political Agitation and the Dilemma of the Chieftaincy

By the end of the nineteenth century the structure of the indigenous government had loosened and virtually broken down. Thus, with the collapse, in the main, of the *pitso* and the decline of its traditions, commoners' general criticism of chiefs no longer produced the same salutary effects as they had in Moshoeshoe's times. Commoners' political role in the management of their own affairs diminished. Yet, at the same time, their grievances mounted. They had at the end to find new avenues to redress those grievances.

The establishment of the National Council served to release their frustrations. Initially, the handful of commoners in the National Council seized the opportunity to speak out on behalf of the majority outside; but, simultaneously, they discovered the press as a complementary and, sometimes, a more effective weapon.

As already pointed out in the previous chapter, this role of political agitation was taken up first by the educated élite – persons who had a greater measure of economic and political independence than those who were still tied to the soil or else were finding their escape in migrant labour. In the nineteen-twenties, however, these 'educated' men would enter into competition with a political movement that was more agrarian-based, but less co-ordinated, in organisation as well as in its aims. The combined effect of both was to expose the weaknesses of the chieftaincy, and to ensure its reform. This chapter will examine the activities of these two sectors of commoners, their conflict with chiefs, and how that conflict was resolved.

As the educated élite were the first to get into the political arena and to make the impact fully felt, it will be useful at this juncture to describe just who they were. How educated were they? And what can be said of their numbers?

THE EDUCATED ELITE: THEIR TRAINING AND NUMBERS

Although the Paris Evangelical Missionary Society introduced literacy among the Basotho quite early in 1833, university education in Lesotho did not begin until after World War II. Nor were opportunities provided for Basotho to undertake university education abroad – in Britain, continental Europe and the Americas any time in the nineteenth century – by which opportunities West Africans were so greatly favoured. Thus, at the turn of the century, Lesotho had no medical doctors, lawyers nor journalists, such as were to be found in such significant numbers in the Lagos Colony and the Gold Coast. Such as were styled 'educated' men in Lesotho, however, deemed themselves equal to the political task they had set for themselves, and judging by their activities, it seems fair to conclude that they were.

They were the products, for the most part, of the protestant education introduced by the Paris Evangelical Missionary Society. By 1903 the PEMS had 150 schools in Lesotho providing education for 11 338 pupils in primary education up through Standard VI, and it had a Normal School (for the training of teachers), with an enrolment of 125 pupils.[1] All told, there were 224 primary schools in the Territory in 1906,[2] and in 1907 they were issuing 752 Standard V certificates.[3] In 1906 an Industrial School (Lerotholi Technical School) was opened in Maseru which would soon be competing in enrolment with the Normal School.[4]

In addition to the Normal School at Morija and the Industrial School in Maseru for post-primary education, Basotho youngsters pursued comparable education in South Africa, in Lovedale, Tiger Kloof, Adams College and Ohlange Institute – in the Cape Colony and in Natal. Beginning in February 1916, when Fort Hare University College for 'natives' opened, with an annual contribution from Lesotho of £300, they began for the first time to pursue university education.[5] By 1927 there were even two medical doctors, Calvin Motebang and W. M. T. Sebeta, both graduates of Edinburgh.[6]

The majority of those who went to the Normal School and the South African schools found their professions in teaching and in colonial administration, while a few, but a very influential few, became clergymen. By 1903 the Conference of the Paris Evangelical Missionary Society, under the presidency of the historian D. Fred. Ellenberger, was beginning to complain to the Resident Commissioner that it was losing its teachers to the South African colonies, owing to the teachers' 'natural desire to receive a higher salary', and requesting financial aid to retain them.[7] Altogether there were 900 teachers in the territory in 1925, with the highest-paid – the head teachers, earning £50 per annum, and senior teachers £40.[8] While in the employment of the colonial administration there were 258 Basotho (alongside 50 European counterparts) serving as interpreters, clerks, dispensers, nurses, postal assistants and school supervisors. Those in senior scales of emolument, and the most highly regarded – interpreters, clerks and school supervisors – were earning between £60 and £144 per annum.[9] These were the educated élite of Lesotho during the first forty years of the twentieth century.

Generally speaking, clergymen and writers – most of whom would have been employed at the Morija Printing Depot as editors and interpreters – were the ones who carried the torch for political agitation. Perhaps the most outstanding of these, before as after retirement, were the interpreters. The most influential were Simon M. Phamotse, the Editor of *Naledi* (styled by himself as 'the recognised press organ of the Basuto Nation'),[10] Abimael Tlale, George Masiu, J. Molibeli, Philip Mochekoane, D. Mochochoko, Bernard Matete, and Manama Molapo – the last two despite the fact that they were members of royalty.[11] The most influential among the clergy were the Reverends John Mohapeloa, Edward Motsamai, and Cranmer Sebeta. School Inspectors (or Supervisors, as they were sometimes called, to distinguish them from their European counterparts) were Elias Letele, S. Pinda, A. J. Mofubetsoana, E. B. Ramaqabe, H. Tshiki, C. D. Mokhehle and F. Mapetla ('Senior Clerk', Lerotholi Technical School).[12] The writers were Azariel Sekese, an 'eaten-up' and persecuted former secretary of Chief Jonathan, who in 1928 paid him back with a satire – *Pitso ea Linonyana* (The General Assembly of Birds) – in which the smallest bird (*Motinyane*) accuses the bigger birds, especially the vulture (Jonathan), of tyranny.[13] E. Segoete, the author of *Bophelo ba Basotho ba Khale* (The Life of Ancient Basotho), 1913, and Z. D. Mangoaela, the author, among other books, of *Lithoko tsa Marena a Basuto* (The Praise Poetry of Basotho Chiefs), 1928, while greatly under the influence and control of the Paris Evangelical Missionary Society, by which they were employed, were intolerant of the abuses of chiefs and enlisted their support in all *fora* for the correction of those abuses. Thomas Mofolo, Lesotho's most powerful novelist, the author of *Moeti oa Bochabela*, 1925, and his most famous *Chaka*, was once also an employee of the P.E.M.S. at Morija but he fell out with the missionaries and thereafter combined his writing with business.[14] He was the most political of the writers in the 1920s and 1930s. The rest of the educated élite who carried the political torch in this period were the unflinching Labane F. Chokobane, a pairing front-ox with Simon Phamotse in the National Council, E. N. and N. M. Tlale, James R. Makepe, the two junior sons of the royalty – Josias Mopeli and Abraham Moletsane, and the first proprietor of *Mochochonono*, Mr Monyakoane. (By 1919 the paper had been taken over by 'S. Tlale & Sons'.) Quietly backing up these men with moral support and material assistance were the successful business-men of Mohales' Hoek and Mafeteng – George Kou and his brother Rantsatsaile Serobanyane, and the flamboyant 'Willie' Mafoso, who in the inter-war years already had a fashionable house with a bar counter in it, where the *bahlalefi* (men of learning) converged and conversed.[16]

The Formation of the Progressive Association

These *bahlalefi*, as they saw themselves and their educationally less fortunate commoner brethren called them, felt a closeness and a common destiny in history. They saw themselves as the future leaders of a Nation of 'educated' Basotho – educated in missionary schools and not at the *lebollo* – and they took up the challenge to point the way. In order more effectively to pursue their general goal, there-fore, on 28 November 1907 the *bahlalefi* founded an organisation called the Basutoland Progressive Association (BPA). The Associ-ation was to function under the motto 'Not for us, but for our country and humanity'. Its first President was Reverend Cranmer Sebeta.[17] Cranmer Sebeta was fated not to live long thereafter. He died in 1913.

The stated objectives of the BPA, as reiterated by its new Presi-dent, Abraham Moletsane, in 1914, were 'to pay particular attention to questions relating to the progress of the Basuto, and to work in harmony with the Government, the Chiefs and the Missionaries'. It aimed to do nothing itself 'without being supported by some authoritative body', a path from which it regularly departed, especially in regard to chieftaincy, which it often accused of abuses and sometimes even condemned.[18] Its regard for the chieftaincy would increasingly wear thin, until by the early 1930s the aim was virtually reversed.

Nonetheless, in 1914, before it thus revised its general aim toward chiefs, the BPA was granted the representation of one councillor, in its own right, in the National Council. As the chiefs did not then perceive it to be a real danger, they did not oppose the representation. The Resident Commissioner, Sir Herbert Sloley, however, predicted its political future in the affairs of the Territory:

[The Progressive Association] has not at present a great deal of influence nor does it include among its members many men of importance by reason of their birth or intelligence. However it does represent a section of the people who probably will in the future acquire more influence in tribal affairs. It is regarded with some suspicion by the older and more conservative members of Council who appear to think that the Council itself is quite sufficiently progressive for the present.[19]

In 1914, according to its President, Abraham Moletsane, the BPA had '200 active members' (the total population of Lesotho was 402 434 in 1911); while in 1924, according to the then President, Z. D. Mangoaela, it was 1500 (without any qualification as to the active as differentiated from the non-active members). About 30 of these were women.[20]

Initial Conflict with Chiefs over the Composition of the National Council

The chieftaincy's suspicion of *bahlalefi* (a term used interchangeably with *matsoelopele*, 'progressive persons') was well-founded. Early upon the founding of the National Council these *bahlalefi* had commenced publicly to challenge its place and utility as an institution. The first public criticism came in the middle of 1904 in *Naledi*, when a critic under the *nom de plume*, 'Mohlori' – One-who-feels-persecuted – indicted the National Council as being merely 'a Parliament' of chiefs, without a mandate from the people. 'Mohlori' asked, rhetorically, 'have they been chosen by the Nation by vote?' Further elaborating on his criticism he stated:

Now these men who have not been chosen by the Nation go to Parliament [*Paramente*] at the end of the year, to say what? Only they know, as even in the course of the year they never convene meetings with men of the Districts from which they come(,) so that they may hear what they say and what [those men] wish to be brought to the attention of Parliament. There they go, these men who have been appointed by one person to speak at this Council(,) which is said to be respectable,(.) [A]s some of us know(,) . . . it is the foundation of a strong government, when it is run properly.[21]

The National Council and its composition became a subject of regular editorials in *Naledi* thereafter. The theme was the same: the Chiefs in the National Council represented themselves and not the people. Then in 1907 one of the *bahlalefi* came up with a suggestion for redressing the situation. In an article that appeared in *Naledi* on 4 June that year, F. Seele counselled his readers:

> This is, indeed, a Council of chiefs. It is they who asked for it and it was given to them and it is to be attended by them as also to run it. If the nation wishes that it should hear (be informed) on matters of government it should ask for a council which will be attended by these (who) are called *bahlalefi* who will be chosen (elected) by the nation in the districts of Lesotho.[22]

The elected members of Seele's proposed council would hold meetings in the districts from which they were returned, to get the views of their constituents on issues which they ought to present to the National Council when it meets, to be deliberated on by that body first, and only then be passed on to 'the council of chiefs'.

Even in England, Seele pointed out, 'from where we are governed, there is a council (*lekhotla*) of chiefs and a council (*lekhotla*) of the nation' which stood as he had described, 'in order that the nation too may have a voice in matters of government . . . The nation should think in terms of advancing its own country.' There were issues such as those of the jobs in the country which were given to foreigners whilst qualified Basotho stood by, Seele said. It was doubtful that chiefs could bring such a matter before the National Council, 'they not having this grievance which we poor people have'.

Reading F. Seele's article, one is inclined to conclude that it must have been about this time, May-June 1907, that the *bahlalefi* adumbrated the idea of founding the BPA. Indeed it is tempting to suggest that the Editor of *Naledi*, Simon Majakathata Phamotse, and Seele had put their minds together on the article, intending to use it as a feeler, or perhaps an announcement on the idea. For Seele's entire article seemed in the final analysis to be building an argument primarily to that end. Concluding his argument he stated:

> Now you who are learned, what disables you from having your own meeting (gathering) to discuss a request for that council . . . Ask the Resident Commissioner to ask from *Morena e Moholo* and his council for you. When the council of *Morena e Moholo* agrees it shall instruct the Resident Commissioner to present its deliberations to *Morena* Edward's High Commissioner. Or else we should not keep on speaking contemptuously of the council of chiefs.

The 'meeting (gathering)' referred to here may have meant only that – an assembly of the *bahlalefi* for the sole purpose of discussing the request for a Council of Commoners; but, in view of the fact that the BPA would be founded just six months later, on 28 November, it is reasonable to think that in June it was already under discussion.

Be that as it may, by the time that the BPA was founded, a more urgent matter than that of a Council of Commoners was pressing. It was the matter of Lesotho's incorporation into the mooted Union of South Africa. As it has already been shown, *Naledi* expressed the view in July 1908 that in the event of incorporation, when the question of franchise would need to have been settled, 'the test of civilisation should be a real one' and people (such as the majority of the principal Basotho chiefs) who could only sign their names were not yet fit for franchise. To qualify, a person must not only 'have thrown off his native blanket but also the heathen influence of native law and custom, and [be] leading a civilised life'.[23]

Nevertheless, in 1909 and 1910, when the peril of incorporation was imminent, the *bahlalefi* rallied behind the chiefs in a common cause to make the National Council a legislative body. Although that common aim was not realised, at least the National Council was established on a more regular basis and it was established by a Proclamation.

Only two years later, however, on 23 February 1919, *Naledi* reactivated its criticism of the National Council. In an editorial entitled 'Basutoland Council and Free Speech', *Naledi* referred nostalgically to the old national *pitso*, the place of which had been taken by the Basutoland National Council:

> At this abolished Pitso the people had freedom of speech which they indulged without being interfered. Whatever was passed by this Pitso was in consequence of the nation's opinion. At any rate the Basuto public Pitso resembled the European constitutional meetings in attitude.[24]

The editorial nevertheless acknowledged and accepted the rationale for the establishment of the National Council. The National Council had been 'considered and approved' by the late *Morena e Moholo* Lerotholi as an expedient substitute for the *pitso* because it was regarded as 'a constitutional council where the matters affecting the affairs of Basutoland should be dealt with'. As it had been assumed that it would be a truly representative body, where 'debates and decisions of the representatives were to be based and decided in accordance with the general opinion of the Basuto', it was generally welcomed, and it 'received the sympathy of the people at large'. That much the editorial considered fair to concede.

But at present there is a common but justified cry for justice perpetuated by the gross mistake of overlooking the most import- ant matter which would very well guard the steps of the councillors in their deliberations. The non-ascertainment of the general opinion which all the civilised would do is a gross mistake which should be corrected.

Beyond these representations, the editorial was guarded. It pointed out that it was not its intention to hamstring the machinery of govern- ment in the Territory with 'cumbersome responsibilities . . . but our simple aim is to have things run on proper and stable principles'. For otherwise, if 'the people's cry for justice' on issues affecting their lives is ignored, 'we are sure of trouble'.

The Resident Commissioner, more so than the chiefs, seems to have been the one who was embarrassed by the editorial. The chiefs, at the Seventh Session held in May, showed no specific reaction to its content beyond accepting a proposal by one of the councillors that the names of appointed members should henceforth be published as soon as possible after the first of January each year so that people might know who they should bring their grievances to before the commencement of the session. Such as it was, it was a poor gesture to *bahlalefi*. Nonetheless, when he submitted his report on the Ses- sion to the High Commissioner on 22 May, the Resident Com- missioner took the opportunity to refer to the *Naledi* editorial and to assure his superior that: 'This ought to meet the complaint that is implied in Naledi article, viz: that the mass of the people are unable to have matters affecting their interests discussed in the Council.'[25] Beyond that, the Resident Commissioner put up his defence for keeping the National Council as it was currently constituted. His defence was of course not new; he had offered it to the High Commissioner's predecessor when the National Council opened in 1903: the national *pitso* was superseded because it had become 'a large and unwieldy gathering which lasted only a few hours', besides which, 'very few of the Basuto availed themselves of the privilege and their utterances received little attention'. (He might have added that, that was principally as a consequence of the misuse of the institution by the colonial administration.) His preference for the National Council was that it was small enough to allow the full exercise of freedom of speech: 'I have heard in the Council much bolder criticism of the chiefs than was ever heard in the general pitso.'

The Resident Commissioner's characterisation of the *pitso* was, of course, an exaggeration. For, did not Eugene Casalis observe, in 1934, that under *Morena e Moholo* Moshoeshoe, 'Freedom of thought and freedom of speech are the foundation and the guarantee of the national rights of his subjects . . . if they disapprove . . . they say so with a virile and eloquent boldness which the most fiery Roman tribune would have envied'?;[26] and could not, as late as 1891, when Letsie attempted to bypass Lerotholi as his heir by foisting the younger Maama on the nation, a councillor publicly scold him saying, 'Letsie, *u'a hlanya* – Letsie you are mad!'?[27] For their part colonial officers little tolerated freedom of speech from Basotho to that degree. As shall be shown later in the chapter, they saw such freedom of speech as a manifestation of 'disrespect' and 'insolence' and they suppressed it, with threats or with legislation.

The following year, 1913, the *bahlalefi* resorted to a different strategy. Apparently trying to test the sincerity of the National Council in its recent professions that it did act on the complaints of the public, the BPA presented it with a letter of national grievances at its Ninth Session held in April that year.[28] The 'Parliament of chiefs', as the *bahlalefi* were wont to call it, found itself in a dilemma: if it discussed the contents of the letter, its act would have been tantamount to giving the BPA official recognition. If it rejected the letter, it would have proved the *bahlalefi*'s point that it was a 'mere Parliament of chiefs'. It opted for the latter and decided that '[the BPA] should not be officially recognised'.

However the National Council could not for long have it both ways. So the Resident Commissioner, who must have sensed imminent trouble between chiefs and *bahlalefi* and feared being caught between the two forces, initiated the move in preparation for the Tenth Session (1914) to give the BPA official recognition and one seat in the National Council. The foregoing background, against which the proposal was made, meant that it would be impolitic for the chiefs to do otherwise than to accept. So, following consultations with his principal chiefs, *Morena e Moholo* Griffith Lerotholi, on whose authority the responsibility fell, made his first appointment of a BPA member, who took his seat at the Tenth Session of the National Council.

The BPA councillor increased the membership of *bahlalefi* in the National Council to six, including the five appointed by the Resident Commissioner, and enhanced that group's self-confidence; but, perhaps more importantly, it fostered a sense of collective responsibility to the BPA, of which all the six were members. As such, it meant essentially that the National Council was composed of two formally defined interest groups: chiefs, and *bahlalefi*; two groups with incongruent political outlooks, and with conflicting self-perceptions: chiefs saw themselves as the natural superiors to *bahlalefi* by reason of their birth. *Bahlalefi* saw themselves as the intellectual superiors of chiefs by dint of their education.

It is, indeed, of more than passing interest that, no sooner had the official BPA councillor taken his seat in the National Council, the question of status surfaced. To date, some principal chiefs, on the recommendation of their *Morena e Moholo*, were being paid more than the ten pounds allowance which other members were getting for attending the sessions of the National Council, in recognition of their 'birth'. Several times before, the *bahlalefi* had expressed their displeasure over the arrangement, obviously feeling that to introduce the element of 'birth' in an institution in which all were equally entrusted with the same responsibilities was a superfluous affectation of authority. So, now they banded together and demanded that henceforth the practice should be abolished and all members be given 'equal payments'. As the President of the Council noted: 'Some of the chiefs themselves, either from conviction, or from a wish to be on the popular side, supported this view'. The principle was conceded without having to be pushed to a division.[29] Subsequently payments were set at £15 for each and every councillor.

The BPA was nevertheless not satisfied with the grant of one representative; but for the time being it accepted the outcome. In 1916, when its councillors sponsored a series of motions, it would reopen the issue. Labane F. Chokobane rose on a motion requesting the *Morena e Moholo* to give more than one seat to the BPA. That Session of the National Council, however, turned out to be one of the most humiliating ones for the chiefs: the *bahlalefi* councillors pressed them somewhat hard against the wall, accusing them of a number of abuses of commoners throughout Lesotho. The chiefs were therefore not inclined toward increasing the numbers of an interest group which was increasingly proving to be inimical to their interests. Chokobane's motion for an increase of BPA representatives in the National Council was turned down.[30]

Be that as it may, during the discussion of the motion some of the chiefs began to feel that the chieftaincy's resistence to commoners' greater representation was untenable and in the circumstances they questioned the worth of the National Council as an institution of government. Chief Motŝoene, in particular, whose own sympathies with the point of view of *bahlalefi* probably stemmed from his political frustrations within the royal lineage, recorded his discomfort as follows:

> I should like to know whether this Council is doing any good to the nation – whether it be only a Council for discussing matters or saving people. Do we members of the Council come to express the opinion of the nation in this Council? I shall be glad if this Council is approved by the nation.[31]

Anxious to reproduce themselves, and conceivably also bent on replacing the colonial administration in Lesotho, the *bahlalefi* additionally sponsored a motion on education at the Session which, had it carried, would have had far-reaching implications for its own future in the affairs of the nation. Lebane F. Chockobane rose on a motion that 100 scholarships be provided, from Government funds, to send young Basotho to England for higher education. The children of the *bahlalefi* were then the ones ready for the opportunity. To wit, the first Mosotho medical doctor, Dr W. M. T. Sebeta, who completed his medical studies at Edinburgh in 1921, was the son of Reverend Cranmer Sebeta, the first President of the BPA;[32] while all of the ten Basotho students at Fort Hare University College in 1939 were from this group. One of the ten who completed a BA in English with distinction that year was J. M. Mohapeloa, Reverend John Mohapeloa's son.[33] That motion was defeated, not by the chiefs, but by the President, Sir Herbert Sloley – on his sole discretion. As he explained it to the High Comissioner when he submitted his report on the Session: 'I refused this request owing to the excessive cost involved and because the time was not opportune.'[34]

Sir Herbert Sloley's defence that the scheme would involve 'excessive cost' was, however, a poor excuse. In 1903 Lesotho had a balance in Assets of £90 000.[35] In 1919 the balance in Assets was £131 599, of which £11 000 was on deposit with Crown Agents, £20 000 was invested in Treasury Bills, and £72 500 was on loan to Swaziland.[36] Meantime, by September of 1917, Basotho had raised £52 000, through *sethabathaba* (a national collection), toward the War Fund.[37] As Sir Herbert Sloley's successor, R. T. Coryndon, pointed out that year (1917): 'The tribe (sic) is probably the wealthiest in South Africa.'[38] From this account it can be inferred, therefore, that in 1916 the nation was sufficiently solvent to sponsor a substantial part of the BPA educational training scheme over a short period of time. This would lead to the conclusion that the substantive reason for turning the scheme down was the one that 'the time was not opportune.' For, had the scheme been adopted, it might easily have meant that within a decade the number of *bahlalefi* with degrees would be so high as to make it imperative to grant Lesotho a Legislative Council. The colonial administration was not ready for such a constitutional advance.

Bahlalefi Assail Chiefs on Their Abuses of Commoners

As it was pointed out in the previous chapter, as early as 1908, only five years after the writing of *The Laws of Lerotholi*, chiefs in the National Council were themselves admitting their gross violation of the 'Laws', and their *Morena e Moholo*, Letsie II, was admitting his political impotence in the situation. With time, the situation took a turn for the worse. On his visit to Lesotho in 1911, the new High Commissioner, Lord Gladstone, felt the need to rebuke the chiefs at the Sixth Session of the National Council for a number of transgressions. Chief among these were the flourishing of guns, injustices in the courts, and 'eating-up' commoners' property. In an effort to lend authority to Law 6 (against the practice of 'eating-up') he reminded the chiefs that 'no man should be deprived of his property unless by sentence of the court after a careful trial';[39] but his words of admonishment did not produce desirable effects. Time and time again the subject of these abuses came before the National Council. The responsibility over motions on the subject fell on the *bahlalefi* councillors. They would attempt within the controlled framework of the National Council to make the chiefs responsible. When that attempt failed, the *bahlalefi* would resume the struggle through the newspapers and wage it venomously, to a point of direct confrontation with the chiefs.

In so far as the *bahlalefi*'s efforts within the framework of the National Council were concerned, the year 1916 must be taken as an eventful year. The *bahlalefi*'s criticisms focused on three major areas of chiefly abuses. The first was on the chiefs' misuse of commoners' free labour in agricultural work (*matsema*). They viewed these *matsema* in the chiefs' fields by their numerous wives (without remuneration, and often without food) as exploitative, and they suggested that they should be reduced and kept within customary expectation: that is, commoners should contribute free labour only in the fields of the first wives of the twenty odd principal chiefs (and certainly not the fields of junior sons of these chiefs as well). Further, they suggested a reduction in 'the numerous occasions when work, generally agricultural work, is avoided or postponed for superstitious reasons and upon occasions of the death of chiefs'.[40] The second criticism was that chiefs deliberately delayed in settling land disputes until affected parties were compelled to take the law into their own hands, the final result being that what had begun as civil cases ended as criminal cases, for which chiefs could then exact fines for their own personal enrichment. The criticism attempted to explain at once the primary reason for violence in the Territory – land disputes – as well as the chiefs' contribution to it by way of greed.

The third criticism went to the heart of the chieftaincy abuses in the indigenous court system. It was, in a nutshell, that chiefs blocked the common people from appealing against their judgments: if a chief passed a judgment against a person, and that person appealed and the *Morena e Moholo* overturned the chief's judgment, the chief still went ahead to implement his own judgment as if it had never been appealed. 'The chiefs', so the criticism went, 'make haste to send to collect fines when they have judged common people, they do not do the same in the case of chiefs.'[41] (As it would further be pointed out the following year when the subject came up again in the National Council, a commoner who appealed against a chief's judgment might in the end have his house pulled down, while he himself was ordered away 'without reasonable cause'.[42]

The *bahlalefi*'s view of chiefs at that Session of the National Council was summarised by Councillor Tsoloane Liphoto, not a member of the BPA, who intoned:

> Does the law apply to common people only or does it apply to chiefs as well? I see the sons of Moshoeshoe break the laws, there is not one of them which they observe, I see not respect. The

nation is being ruined through the chiefs. Should we be scattered we will blame the sons of Moshoeshoe, you sons of Moshoeshoe like to rule us common people, and yet you do not like to be ruled by the Paramount Chief . . . The reason why I say the sons of Moshoeshoe wish to rule us common people is because when you judge us you want us to carry out judgments quickly but chiefs do not do the same . . . I say yet you are selfish, you want us to respect you and yet you do not respect your seniors. As you do not respect the Paramount Chief we will not respect you also.[43]

Councillor Tsoloane concluded his scathing statement with the observation that the most lawless and abusive chiefs in Lesotho were Jonathan and his brother Joel in the District of Leribe.

The *Bahlalefi* Fall Out with the *Morena e Moholo* over an Issue of Constitutional Morality

So far the *bahlalefi* were only critical of the abuses of chiefs, but the nature of their criticisms suggested a degree of hope that chiefs could mend their ways on their own initiative. Moreover, explicitly or by inference, they made it clear that their criticisms were not levelled at their *Morena e Moholo*, Griffith Lerotholi, himself. In fact, they sought to establish the point that the chiefs were rendering it impossible for the monarch to govern, hence the *bahlalefi* coming to his rescue. Yet, when the rupture did come, it was with him in particular.

The immediate cause of this rupture, ironically, was the one event on which chiefs and *bahlalefi* had otherwise initially been amicably united. It was Griffith's trip to London in 1919; and the colonial administration was the immediate cause of the misunderstanding that snapped the relations.

On 24 May 1919, four days before the Petition to King George V was to be discussed in the National Council, the High Commissioner, Lord Buxton was in Lesotho and he had arranged a private interview with the *Morena e Moholo*. The latter was already by then in possession of the Petition and, whether in keeping with protocol or simply as a gesture of goodwill, he had given the Resident Commissioner, R. T. Coryndon, a copy, which in turn had been put in the hand of the High Commissioner. The Petition had presumably been drawn up by the members of the BPA. For reasons known to himself, however, Lord Buxton maintained that it was 'evidently the language' and it had been 'drawn up by someone outside Basutoland'; and he was bent on embarrassing the *Morena e Moholo* with that accusation.[44] The primary reason for the private interview, however, was to attempt to browbeat the *Morena e Moholo* into dropping one Section of the Petition in particular, which it was feared could be of great embarrassment to the British King, and one which certainly had serious political consequences. Section 12, as it came to be popularly known, was a request that the Imperial Government should use its power and exercise its political morality to aid Lesotho in recovering the pieces of land since lost to the Orange Free State by use of the Aliwal Convention of 1869 (negotiated by Sir Philip Wodehouse with the Boers). The Section lucidly supplied its own rationale:

Finally(,) we humbly pray and beseech your Majesty to give his gracious and generous consideration to our prayer for the restoration of our rights of which we have been deprived, that is, large tracts of our land which lie to the North-West, West and South-East of Basutoland of to-day. Our reason for submitting this prayer to Your Majesty is on account of the understanding made by Your Majesty's Government and those of Your Majesty's Allies that all nations, great and small, which had had their rights violated by those more powerful than they, are to have those rights restored, and being in the same category we therefore humbly pray that Your Majesty may graciously accord us the same recognition.[45]

Griffith, as much as the *bahlalefi*, was keen on the question. The ultimate cause of land disputes in the Territory was that land had shrunk, in relationship to expansion in population. Meantime, the relative prosperity of the nation had led to a rapid increase in population since Lesotho had become a British dependency. If 'the conquered territory' could be restored, the problem might greatly be alleviated. Then too, Basotho had proved their loyalty to the Imperial Government by contributing liberally to the cause of the war, financially and with manpower.[46] South African newspapers carried the good tidings that Alsace and Lorraine were being returned to France. So there appeared to be no sound moral ground on which Lesotho should not as well be favoured by the general justice of the Western Democracies by presenting its case before the League of Nations.

Lord Buxton, however, thought otherwise. As he told *Morena e Moholo* Griffith, at the private interview:

I can say at once that there is no question of any of the British colonies coming before the League of Nations. This League will not be allowed to deal with any of His Majesty's Colonies, and therefore, whether it be a Nationalist [South African] Petition or a Petition of the Basuto, neither of them will be heard by the League of Nations.[47]

Buxton wished both that Griffith should admit to having been put up to the idea of the Petition by an outsider, as well as that he should drop the embarrassing Section 12 from it. Griffith did neither. Instead he insisted that the Petition was the property of the Drafting Committee of the National Council, to which Committee Buxton was free to make his representation when the Fourteenth Session convened.

His tenacity notwithstanding, the *Morena e Moholo* seems then to have begun to worry that the question of 'the conquered territory' might jeopardise his trip to London, the centre of power, and he began to weigh the merits of the two probable options: to drop Section 12 of the Petition and risk the loss of confidence from his *bahlalefi*, or maintain solidarity with them and risk the journey to the centre of power and forging friendly, personal relations with King George V. By the time the National Council met, he had clearly made up his mind: it was going to be the former.

That the Fourteenth Session of the National Council would be a crucial and delicate one was marked by a proposal by Councillor Bernard Matete, a close courtier of the *Morena e Moholo*, that the Council Room be cleared of visitors and the proceedings be regarded as 'private and only intended to be read to the Councillors alone'.[48] The debate centred on Section 12 of the Petition.

Those, such as Councillor Mokhethi Moshesh, who expressed Griffith's new fears, counselled that, by presenting King George V with two major requests – the one against 'incorporation' and the other on 'the conquered territory' – 'you are shooting this animal before it has shown its whole body because you are tempted by the nice words about the "restoration of Countries!" ' That is, you are likely to miss your main target, the question of incorporation. Additionally, there was the embarrassing issue that kept coming up from some councillors that Lesotho too had robbed other people of their lands, specific reference being made to the dispossessed Chief of Baphuthi chiefdom, Mocheko L. Moorosi. Griffith of course refuted the allegation on the Baphuthi chiefdom stoutly, stating his understanding as the one that:

[Moorosi] brought himself under Moshoeshoe, he was taken after he had fought for his independence, he was taken prisoner together with some of his sons. He came to Thaba Bosiu, following Mohale [Moshoeshoe's half-brother] who had been sent by Moshoeshoe to call him, he was driving an ox.[49]

Except for the fact that it was Moroosi's father, Mokuoane, who had actually given himself up, Moorosi being then in his minority, Griffith's understanding was historically accurate.

Others, such as Councillor Alexander Mopeli, who evidently began to feel that their monarch had abandoned his original stand on the question of 'the conquered territory', and were nauseated by the realisation that he was increasingly more anxious to go to England for adventure than for diplomatic work, insisted that he should make the trip worth the money:

The nation is quite justified in asking him to do something . . . while he is in England. He is going to see 'The Big Doctor' and it is right that he should tell him of our complaints.[50]

Simon Majakathata Phamotse, a member of the Drafting Committee, and the man who was soon to be Griffith's bitter enemy, probably formed his negative view of him at that Session, and on the basis of that question. For Griffith finally made his fear on Section 12 explicit, stating: 'I cannot take it Home [London] with me.' Angered by this attitude, Phamotse then cynically retorted:

I certainly agree with those who say this paragraph should be taken out of this Petition, not because it is an unreasonable request but because the Paramount Chief is afraid, he has told us the truth. I do not agree with those who say it should be brought forward at some future time, those who say this are cowards . . . Let us speak the truth to each other, Chiefs . . . do not deceive us.[51]

The worst thing that the *Morena e Moholo* did in the circumstances was that, although the ayes had had it when the question was eventually put to a vote, and the National Council therefore expected him to take it 'Home' – to England, he undermined the constitutional process and dropped it, on his own authority. In so doing, however, Griffith was responding to the Resident Commissioner's veiled threat in his comments right after the vote[52]:

[T]he council that said that you were hunting two animals and that you would probably lose both is mine. I am interested in this in that I hope to be able to take the Paramount Chief Home, and would be sorry that anything that could spoil the object of the visit should be contained in the Petition.

What the Resident Commissioner had done, in essence, had been to impress the view on the councillors that, although the National Council was as much of a parliamentary institution as the colonial administration deemed fit for Basotho at that stage, and considering the fact that as of 1910 (Proclamation No. 7, 5.8 and 9) *all* questions affecting the Nation were within its jurisdiction, for discussion, suggestions and amendments, in the final analysis the President could use his authority to frustrate its wishes.

To Griffith, at any rate, the message was clear: if he wanted to go London, he had to drop the offensive Section 12 of the Petition. Consequently, he wrote the Resident Commissioner a letter on 13 June stating that since the matter was concluded in the National Council he had come to the conclusion that 'it would not be right' for him to 'take it "Home" with me'. He asked for permission to drop it, as well as two other Sections, in his own name, 'as Paramount and Chief Adviser of the Basuto Nation'.[53]

That the formulation had been suggested to the monarch by the Resident Commissioner, who did not himself want to appear to have violated constitutional morality, was revealed in his (the Resident Commissioner's) own telegram to the High Commissioner: 'I have informed Paramount that I consider alterations desirable but that it must be done on his own responsibility'.[54] And equally anxious as the Resident Commissioner to keep his head above the cloud that they had both made for the monarch, the High Commissioner responded: 'While I feel that it would not be right for me to instruct him to omit them, I think that he would be well advised in leaving them out if he can do so on his own authority'.[55]

Griffith did not have the executive authority to do what he was being pressured to do. Under the indigenous institutions, with regard to both the *pitso* as well as the *Lekhotla la Mohosana* (Grand Council), he was in principle not free to go against a decision once it had been declared. Similarly Proclamation No. 1 of 1910, which gave the National Council statutory force, did not reserve such power to him, either in his capacity as 'Paramount Chief' or as 'Chief Adviser'. Yet in the end he did use his personal authority critically to amend the decision of the National Council, following consultations with councillors who were sympathetic to his point of view.

Although the *bahlalefi* did not make a specific reference to the way the Petition had been handled, they obviously lost hope that anything worthwhile could any longer be achieved by the trip to London.

The *Bahlalefi* Vent Their Frustration Through the Press

The *bahlalefi* then vented their frustration and loss of respect for authority through the press. On 26 November, shortly after Griffith arrived in London, an editorial appeared in *Mochochonono*, with a Parthian shot to the Petition to the effect that the door to 'the "Great White Queen", or King rather, is closed forever and anon'. The editorial accepted the outcome as 'a bitter pill . . . to swallow but, *bon gré mal gré*', one that had to be swallowed. It lamented the fact that:

> From being a Protectorate simply and purely Basutoland had gradually been turned into a subject state which the sovereign of the British Empire can deal with without reference to or consultation with a native Potentate. In other words Basutoland is to-day regarded as private property of the King of England to deal with as he may choose, the same way as the Duke of Westminster is the owner of the Westminster Estates . . . which he can either sell or make over to whoever he pleases.[56]

The general theme begun by the editorial was continued in the *Mochochonono* issue of 3 December, which accused the King of England of having 'departed from the solemn understanding made by his illustrious mother [that is, grandmother] Queen Victoria', and concluded with the comment that Griffith's humble effort to 'remind him of the compact' was futile.[57]

So far the political diatribes were directed overtly at the Imperial Government, and covertly at the colonial administration (which was the one that made recommendations to the Colonial Office and the British King). *Morena e Moholo* Griffith was awaited to return from 'centre of the Empire', as he himself called it,[58] to collect his share.

Meantime, a start was made, by way of scathing criticisms of the administration of justice by chiefs in the Territory. As an alternative to the local press, these were funnelled through the *Cape Times* in South Africa.

On 5 December 1919, *The Times* carried an editorial with the title: 'A serious indictment of the native administration of Justice in Basutoland is made by a prominent native resident.' Just who the 'prominent', but obviously not 'chiefly' Mosotho was, it is difficult to establish and, worthwhile as it might be to know the answer, not crucial to do so in this connection; except, perhaps, to note that textual examination rules out Simon Phamotse as the person in question. Whoever it was, 'the prominent native resident' was purported to have specifically stated that his indictment was not meant to impugn the European Commissioners in Lesotho, whom he described as 'full of justice'. Rather he asserted that the native chiefs have turned Basutoland into 'a nation of slaves'. They compelled the common people 'to work the lands belonging to the many wives of the chiefs'.[59] The common people who had occasion to use courts, he said, were 'kept hanging on for weeks', with the result that by the time they returned to their homes 'their stock and goods have been stolen'. If a complainant were to leave the court to attend to his affairs, as often happened, when his name was called and he was found to be absent, 'judgment is given against him, or he is fined for contempt'. Woe betide a commoner who appealed a chief's judgment 'without the chief's consent, which is seldom given'. The chief sought revenge 'by confiscating his stock'.[60]

The 'prominent' Mosotho, oddly enough, appealed, either to the Union of South Africa, or to the Imperial Government, to appoint a Commission of Enquiry to examine the national complaints on the 'maladministration of justice' in Lesotho and that the Commission should be responsible to the Colonial Office. Why the Union of South Africa was considered to have a role to play in the affairs of Lesotho, especially at a time that Lesotho's monarch was in England to appeal against 'incorporation', is puzzling.

Nevertheless the general theme of the anonymous Mosotho was acknowledged in Lesotho. On 19 December 1919, *The Times* carried an article based on an interview with Simon Majakathata Phamotse entitled: 'The Complaints Against Native Court.' *The Times* cited Phamotse, 'whose knowledge and experience entitles his opinion to respect', as having endorsed the allegations made in its issue of 5 December. Phamotse was confirmed to have said that 'the country is seething with discontent at the want of justice and sympathy shown *both by* the native chiefs and the Government.'[61] (My emphasis) He certainly did not share the 'prominent' Mosotho's view 'that white men are full of justice'. He rather saw the colonial officials in Lesotho as 'individuals under native influence', but his chief complaint was against the system. Additionally he thought it was folly to involve the Union of South Africa, as the matter was 'one for the Imperial authorities'.

Phamotse's focus was on the conduct of chiefs in the courts. He alleged that when a court convened to consider a case, 'the members are already divided according to their likes and dislikes of the accused or disputants'. As such, litigants could not expect justice before the indigenous courts. 'No amount of evidence or argument', he alleged, 'has the slightest influence on the verdict.'

Unlike the 'prominent' Mosotho, who had proposed a Commission of Enquiry, he had a specific solution to the problem:

> Phamotse suggests the establishment of a new Department of Justice, under the direction of a fully qualified and experienced Judge, and staffed by magistrates learned in the law instead of native assessors, chiefs, and police officials.[62]

Morena e Moholo Griffith Lerotholi returned to Lesotho early in December, a few days before *The Times* published Phamotse's views, to be greeted by unfriendly sentiments from the *bahlalefi*; but he did not immediately attend to the newspaper criticisms, understandably because he was anxious initially to give a report of his journey to 'the centre of the Empire'. Obviously anxious to keep the report confidential, as the National Council had set the guidelines when it discussed the Petition in secrecy, he instructed his entourage not to disclose any part of it to the public. Meantime he requested the Resident Commissioner to convene a Special Session of the National Council to report to; but the Resident Commissioner, who conveyed the request to the High Commissioner on 19 December (the date of *The Times'* article on Phamotse), recommended to the latter that, in view of financial constraints, a Special Session could not be arranged. The High Commissioner, in turn, much preferred that, in the circumstances, the report should be put in the agenda for the ordinary meeting of the National Council.[63] That meeting would not be held until July 1920.

Unfortunately for Griffith, as he thus waited for the National Council to convene, South African newspapers leaked the entire report. Picking it up, the Sesotho newspapers opened it to the nation; but then it was with vengeance against the *Morena e Moholo*, who was suspected of having turned the report into personal property. Issuing its version of the report on 14 January *Mochochonono* criticised the entire journey, from the start to the conclusion. The Editor charged that the nation 'did not know what the deputation was out for'. Yet the nation had borne the financial burden for the trip. Although the draft of the Petition had been discussed in the National Council, the Editor queried, the final version had not been published: 'How the members of the deputation knew that they had the confidence of the people they were working for, nobody can say.'[64]

The composition of the Deputation itself came under fire. Griffith had gone to 'the centre of the Empire' with an entourage of fourteen people. Twelve of them were principal chiefs. The Resident Commissioner, E. C. F. Garraway, and his Assistant, F. L. Ford, had escorted them. Obviously with the memory of the sinking of the *Mendi* in February 1917, with 615 Africans, Griffith had dreaded the prospect of braving the Atlantic and so, additionally, he had insisted, against the strong advice of the Resident Commissioner and the High Commissioner, to take his white Catholic priest with him, in case the Sacrament of Absolution was needed.[65] The *bahlalefi* were evidently dismayed by the choice of the entourage, and they were disappointed that none of their number was included in such a mission, where they viewed their sophistication as particularly needed. Yet, in the light of Simon Phamotse's indictment of chiefs as 'cowards', it is fair to assume that Griffith had intended their exclusion as a lesson for them to remember their place.

The chickens now came home to roost. The editor of *Mochochonono* reminded the *Morena e Moholo* of 'our comment on the departure of the deputation' by which 'we pointed out that [the Deputation] was not elected by the Council, *as it is the custom of such institutions*, but it was picked 'solely' by himself 'for reasons known only to himself.' (My emphasis). The outcome was that he had chosen only principal chiefs, 'most of whom were of little use as advisers . . . and left behind men who had all the qualifications so to say, who had confidence of the nation'.

Turning to the question of the secrecy with which the report had so far been handled, the Editor went for the monarch's character:

It should not be wondered (sic) that this has happened, our Paramount Chief is a strict observer of the primitive customs of his predecessors and nothing better could have been expected from a backward and illiterate man like him. He still believes in making public affairs confidential but we hope he has had a lesson today, of the uselessness of keeping private what ought to be published at once.

(Griffith, who was raised by his uncle, Chief Bereng Letsie, had attended an Anglican missionary school for less than a year but found it not be to his liking. So his uncle sent him to *lebollo* (initiation school), which he rather preferred.[66])

Griffith's Response to the Press Attacks

The *Morena e Moholo* did not immediately react against the general press attacks on his journey, his chieftaincy, and his person; but it is apparent that he felt threatened by the ascendancy of the *bahlalefi* in the political affairs of Lesotho and that he thought of a strategy for counteracting its effects by strengthening his own position. That strategy, it appears, comprised an educational scheme for the children of those chiefs whom he perceived as being supportive of his authority. For, on 14 January, and 6 February 1920, he wrote to the Resident Commissioner expressing 'my intention and wish – if means could satisfy the heart – ' that the Government should 'initiate my children'.

His wish was to pick two children of royalty from each of the Southern Districts of Quthing, Qacha's Nek, Mohale's Hoek, Mafeteng, up to Berea in the centre of Lesotho, in addition to four of his own children, to be sent to the best schools that could be found. With the impressions of England still fresh in his mind, he was precise in that he wished his request to be brought to the attention of the High Commissioner, who should 'kindly send *my son* to a school overseas which he knows to be a true good and perfect school.'[67] (My italic.) Notably missing in the choice of the *Morena e Moholo*'s Districts was Leribe, Chief Jonathan's jurisdiction.

Unfortunately for Griffith, the Resident Commissioner and the High Commissioner did not think it was feasible to send his sons to any 'true and perfect school' in England, which is where he obviously preferred. Of his four sons, all of whom were receiving instructions under the Marist Brothers at the spiritual and educational centre of the Catholic Church at Roma, one was 20 and two were 18 years of age, all three reading Standard V. The fourth, 15 years of age, was reading Standard IV. One of these four children was the heir apparent, Seeiso Griffith. The Resident Commissioner advised the High Commissioner that the monarch's sons were, as such, too old to pursue higher education overseas. However, he felt that an effort should be made to find them a place in one of the schools in the Union of South Africa. As to the children of the other chiefs culled from Districts, the Resident Commissioner and the Director of Education in Lesotho were totally negative. They thought that such money as might be spent on them was better spent on the education of commoners' children.[68]

The monarch's scheme thus suffered the same fate as that of the *bahlalefi* in 1916: it was frustrated; except in this instance the motivating factor on the part of the colonial administration was perhaps not that the time was not 'opportune', but rather that the scheme was perceived undesirable – in the short run as well as in the long run. In the short run, it might not only have enhanced the prestige of the chieftaincy and improved its calibre, to the political disadvantage of the *bahlalefi*; it might also have created a core of intellectuals among the royalty less easy for the colonial administration to manipulate. While in the long run, and in the event that Lesotho was granted a legislative Council, that core of intellectuals might be clumsy to fit in: it would, for all intents and purposes, be a part of the *bahlalefi*; at the same time, it would be deriving its political legitimacy from 'birth'. The final outcome, so to speak, to establish a constitutional monarchy – the form of government with which the colonial administration was familiar and to which it was committed – would be problematic. That is, of course, assuming that events took a turn in the direction of self-government.

Beyond that effort, the *Morena e Moholo* did nothing to mend his prestige against the *bahlalefi*. The Fifteenth Session of the National Council (1920), where one would have expected sound and fury between chiefs and *bahlalefi*, was uneventful. Perhaps both sides had had sufficient cooling time; or perhaps some informal discussions had taken place which, if they had, would be proven to have only forged a truce. The *Morena e Moholo*'s report was received passively, as if to say: he has had his trip, and so be it.

The Colonial Administration's Attitude Toward the *Bahlalefi*'s Use of the Press

The *bahlalefi* took to the press, and sustained the momentum of their criticisms through it, not because the colonial administration was favourable to freedom of the press, but in spite of its repression of it. That repression took two forms: one was a 'subtle' tactic of intimidation; the other was legislation. As the *bahlalefi* would, beginning in 1920, employ the press to push their political contest with the chieftaincy to a head-on collision, it will be helpful at this point to give a brief review of those tactics and the piece of legislation under which action could be brought to bear.

When *Naledi* was first published in 1904, and subsequently *Mochochonono* appeared in 1910, the colonial administration was not alarmed; and certainly it was not threatened. In 1916, however, one of the two newspapers put freedom of the press to the test. On 23 August of that year, a few days before the National Council held its Eleventh Session, *Mochochonono* published an editorial in which it criticised the colonial administration generally, and tacitly it accused the new High Commissioner, Lord Buxton (since Lord Gladstone's departure from South Africa in 1914), in particular, of identifying more with the Union of South Africa than he did with Lesotho. The High Commissioner, whose office was combined with that of the Governor-General for South Africa since 1909, was accused of having first visited the Boers of the Orange Free State, the Basotho's traditional enemies, people who had rebelled against the Imperial Government, before he could ever consider visiting the Basotho. Consequently the editorial concluded that to give the Imperial Government loyalty was of no use.[69]

When the National Council convened, the Resident Commissioner tabled the matter for discussion, and he wanted the councillors to take a stand on it. Speaking his own view, he pointed out that, while 'English people as a rule have always been a very free people and as a general rule they let people say what they like and speak what they like', there were things written in *Mochochonono* 'which do a lot of harm'. He was more particularly perturbed in that the long article, 'which I think is very disrespectful', was published in English. The greater harm in that regard was that, although he did not think that *Mochochonono* had such a large circulation, 'at the same time other papers in South Africa look through these papers and take little bits and publish them in their papers, so that a disrespectful or a disloyal and seditious thing published here may be taken over at King William's Town, Durban or Johannesburg'. While he was mindful of the fact that there were several 'disrespectful' comments made about him in *Mochochonono*, he said, he was particularly concerned with remarks made about the High Commissioner, and he wondered if the councillors were aware that 'you can do a man a lot of harm without calling him a thief'.[70]

The *bahlalefi* councillors maintained solidarity against the onslaught, except for one – the Reverend Edward Motsamai. The Reverend Motsamai, who had recently been gored by the paper regarding his being given the Maseru parish, but whose proprietor he nevertheless still affectionately referred to as 'my friend Monyakoane', understandably wished its editor to be held on a leash. He had already spoken with the proprietor and the Editor 'and pointed out to them that I had a right to bring an action against them'. He certainly thought that the issue of *Mochochonono* under discussion trod dangerously on the verge of defamation against the High Commissioner. He could not understand, he said, why *Mochochonono*, and by inference *Naledi*, could not 'be at peace' with authority, which virtue he attributed to his own Missionary Society's paper *Liselinyana*. In his view: 'The native papers are always fighting against people who have positions in the country.'[71]

Aside from being an expression of a personal grievance, the Reverend Motsamai's speech suggested the existence of subtle but real divisions with the *bahlalefi* themselves. Here it probably illustrated the case of a man who was susceptible to missionary control and who, therefore, could ill afford to associate with a cause on which his superiors were not keen. The Paris Evangelical Missionary Society, which Motsamai served, was generally not disposed to risking a confrontation with the colonial administration, except where its own immediate interests were threatened.

Nonetheless, as the discussion had tended quite at length to deal with the two papers, and not on the section of the Basotho whose views they represented, Chief Motsoene, probably mischievously – as sometimes he relished controversy for its own sake – decided to point the finger at the collective culprits:

> We know nothing of these newspapers, it seems as if these newspapers go together with the Basutoland Progressive Association. Some of you members of the Association do not know how to control yourselves . . . I advise the 'Mochochonono' to give the names of the people who write in it.[72]

Chief Motsoene's blunt approach apparently took the *bahlalefi* councillors by surprise, and it almost threw them into disarray. Labane Chokobane, notably, decided to disassociate the BPA as a body from the Editor of *Mochochonono* in his capacity as a journalist. He was sorry that Chief Motsoene had pointed the finger at the BPA 'The Association is of the Basotho', he said. Otherwise:

Every paper does its work, so does the Association. We cannot be wrong because one of our members is wrong; the 'Mochochonono' does not consult the Association in managing its affairs. If 'Mochochonono' is wrong do not blame our Association.[73]

In the interest of the BPA, whose members in the National Council stood much to lose by associating themselves with an issue over which the Resident Commissioner was so cross, Chokobane's response was probably prudent, and politic. Yet it did not address the principle behind the discussion: freedom of the press. That was to be addressed by his political fellow-traveller, Bernard Matete, the interpreter, who said:

How are we to regard a newspaper, as a white man or [as] a native? . . . The Resident Commissioner has said this paper has spoken badly of the High Commissioner and the Assistant Commissioner. Our advice is that the courts are open, this newspaper should be charged. There may be only one word which has offended the Resident Commissioner and about *his government*; if such is the case let the case be tried according to the law. [my italic][74]

That certainly went to the heart of the matter: the Resident Commissioner was being counselled against using his political office, under the cloak of the President of the National Council, to muzzle the press, and shown the proper recourse – the courts. He was accordingly compelled to drop the discussion, which he had pursued passionately; except, he did so only after he had threatened independent action:

The point is not a legal one. I have said if there is anything to do I will do it. I am not asking the chiefs whether they understand our law about newspapers, I am asking them to say whether it is right for a Basuto paper to publish something disrespectful or not . . . I have asked you the question and I have not got an answer.[75]

Here, then, would be one of those instances that illustrated the intolerance of the colonial administration to freedom of speech. There was seemingly nothing in the *Mochochonono* that could readily be construed as a libel against any member of the colonial administration. As the Reverend Motsamai's wound-licking speech revealed, what was objectionable about independent Basotho newspapers was the pluck of their Editors to criticise all authority. The colonial administration could not bear such criticism from 'a Basuto paper'.

Having lost the battle in the National Council, the Resident Commissioner went ahead to carry out his threat. He made a recommendation to the High Commissioner to promulgate a law for dealing with the problem. That law came into force on 23 February 1917, as Proclamation 3, 1917: Newspaper Registration and Regulation Proclamation.[76] The declared purpose of the Proclamation was: 'To regulate the publication of newspapers, and to provide penalties in respect of the publication of seditious libels'.

The Proclamation lent itself to a broad interpretation. It was obviously aimed at instilling more fear than merely caution on all classes of people who had lately come to use the newspaper for political ends. So, introduced in a society that had never formally been given parameters for freedom of speech, beyond which sanctions might be imposed, it was probably hoped that it would have the necessary effect of silencing the Basotho newspapers.

Proclamation 3, 1917, may have temporarily restrained the zeal of the independent Basotho newspapers in their criticisms of the colonial administration, but in the long run it did not achieve its political objective, viz: instilling habitual obedience. As it has been shown, by late 1919 and early 1920, *Mochochonono* was back in its old form, accusing the King of England of having 'departed from the solemn understanding made by his illustrious [grandmother] Queen Victoria', and blasting the Basotho Potentate as 'a backward and illiterate man'. Further, at that juncture the *bahlalefi* forged links with the South African English newspapers, through which they funnelled their truculent criticisms. Within just a matter of months they would launch a political blitz against missionaries, the colonial administration and the chieftaincy, combining the local with the South African press, and introducing pseudonyms as a new feature for frustrating an easy application of the Newspaper Registration and Regulation Proclamation. The blitz, in the case of the chieftaincy, would lead to a head-on collision.

'How Shall We Do Away With the Black Race?' Commoners Cross the Political Rubicon

On 3 September 1920, *Naledi* featured an article that must have mortified missionaries in Lesotho, and which certainly shocked the colonial administration. The article was entitled: 'How Shall We Do Away With The Black Race?' It described the Young Women's Association established for Black people in Johannesburg as an institution created for Christian whores of conquest. The author was Josiel Lefela, one of the members of the National Council appointed by the Resident Commissioner.

Josiel Lefela, who resided in Mapoteng, in the District of Berea, had for some time been a borderline case in the National Council between the *bahlalefi* and the peasant migrant labour sector of commoners. He had not gone beyond Standard IV in education,[77] although he was an avid reader and he could perform incredible stunts with his mind, quoting pages on end from George McCall Theal's documentary history, *Basutoland Records*, from memory. For want of political company he had been consorting with the *bahlalefi*; but he was not of the same ilk. His relationship with them was an uneasy one. He was certainly overshadowed by them, and his contribution in the National Council was meagre. Finally, while not resigning, he had fired his Parthian shot at the closing of the Session in 1919, saying to his fellow councillors: 'This is the fourteenth session of the Council and yet nothing has been done for the nation, . . . why are you Councillors paid £15'.[78] On 27 September the same year, he founded his own association, appropriately named *Lekhotla la Bafo*, literally, 'The Commoner's Council'. His article on the Young Women's Association was essentially his political debut.

Aggressive in its style, the article charged that a number of plans in the Union of South Africa had been devised to do away with the Black race. As one of their contributions, and with a 'deep design', missionaries were encouraging everywhere 'women and girls' to collect money 'for building a home for Christian whores, young and old, to whore in. That is the way that our people will be put an end to'. Life in this 'home' would be 'pleasanter (sic) than in their own homes', from which, purportedly, they were being protected 'against those customs which they say are sinful'. Yet, he said, the ultimate goal was to produce half-castes, 'so that in ten years time the black race would diminish and half-castes increase'. 'Have European whores ever had houses built by them? Why this kindness to our women and girls?' Reflecting on his knowledge of history, Lefela pointed out that, wherever they had been, missionaries had destroyed the 'tribes' among which they had worked; 'many governments in difficulties had had their path made easy by missionaries'.[79]

Following consultations with the Imperial Secretary, the Resident

Commissioner, E. C. F. Garraway, took two courses of action. The most immediate one was to call the Editor of *Naledi*, Edwin Tlale, to be 'brought up with a round turn'.[80] At the 'round turn', in the presence of his own staff of officers and a representative of *Morena e Moholo*, Garraway thoroughly rebuked Edwin Tlale and even threatened that 'I have power to do more than talk to you in this manner . . .'. Tlale kept his composure during the 'round turn'; but once he was back in his office he wrote Garraway a caustic letter. He told him that he resented the way the Resident Commissioner had tried to 'bully' him in the fashion of 'a mining boy compound foreman' in the presence of his staff and Griffith's representative. He was not going to permit freedom of the press to be muzzled, he said, albeit the bullying had given the chiefs the confidence that he could be gagged, and therefore his task as Editor would be difficult in future.[81]

Garraway's second course of action might have been to bring a court case against Josiel Lefela; and, indeed, he discussed this possibility with the Imperial Secretary; but, while he felt that both the Editor as well as the writer of the article deserved a 'telling off', the latter was doubtful 'whether the article could be regarded as a "libel expressive of seditious intention" within the meaning of Section 10(3), (v), of the Newspaper Registration and Regulation Proclamation No. 3 of 1917. He therefore advised him to seek legal advice before taking legal action.[82]

The legal advice that Garraway received was that a libel suit would not stick and that, besides, it might have the effect of turning Lefela into a martyr. The Legal Adviser recommended, instead, that he should use his powers as the President of the National Council (but certainly not as Resident Commissioner) to suspend Lefela from the National Council. The powers conferred on the Resident Commissioner in that office, as provided in Section 14, Proclamation No. 7 of 1910 (establishing the National Council), could only be exercised on the High Commissioner's instructions; whereas, as the President, according to Section 3(3) of the Proclamation, he had 'the power of the Council during such period'. (See Appendix 2). The Legal Adviser further proposed the modality for effecting the suspension: as Lefela's conduct under scrutiny had been manifested in an interval between Sessions, Lefela could not be debarred from attending the next Session of the National Council, 'and would have to be allowed to attend, and then be ejected in accordance with the President's sentence of suspension'. Nonetheless the Legal Adviser felt that that procedure 'would be very inconvenient'. (Presumably that meant that the procedure might result in a hubbub in Council, which would complicate the execution of the suspension.) So Garraway was led to conclude that it would be more efficacious, if constitutionally dubious, to suspend Lefela before the next Session.[83] And he did; with Griffith's unremitting support.

On 9 March 1921, Edwin Tlale gave both Garraway and the chieftaincy a tempestuous review, using Lefela's suspension as his *causus bellum*:

> Be the *arbitrary* powers of the Resident Commissioner what they may in regard to the suspension of councillors, the reasons which have prompted him to take so *drastic* a step against Cr. Lefela are *puerile and unreasonable* as to warrant anyone saying that it is simply *scandalous* . . . I shall not go over the ground that has been gone by other writers in this connection but all I can say is that the impetuosity of the President of the Council in taking action will one day be the cause of his ruing the day on which he took so rash an action. If the President desired to exercise his authority over the Council which has lain dormant for many years why in all goodness did he not start by suspending *thiefs, murderers and law-breakers who constitute a majority of the Council?* He is pleased to listen to the advice of such outcasts and confer with them in matters of theft, murder and lawbreaking, but shuns the society of a man who fights tooth and nail against such barbarities. (My emphasis.)[84]

The editorial ended with a forecast to the effect that, since the Resident Commissioner had commented 'on this game on which angels before him have feared to tread', it was certain that he would go on with it until he had purged the National Council of 'every Councillor who dares to criticise in public doings of those of his "tool" or "master" '.

The High Commissioner Counsels Patience

Quite clearly, the Newspaper Proclamation had not had a deterrent effect on the Basotho newspapers; nor had the Resident Commissioner's resort to intimidation. So, in 1921, the High Commissioner Prince Arthur Frederick, Queen Victoria's grandson, decided to make a personal intervention. He had reason to hope for success: Basotho held his grandmother in great admiration, invariably addressing her as 'Queen Victoria The Good', in contrast to their own 'Moshoeshoe The Wise'. This may explain why the visit, his first to Lesotho, attracted some 60 000 people, who came to receive him at a national *pitso* held on 18 May that year. This was probably the largest *pitso* in the century to date.

As with other parties who wished to impress him with their *bona fides* and accede to his good books, the Basutoland Progressive Association took the opportunity, through its President, Zakea Mangoaela, to introduce itself. The Association, Mangoaela explained, 'was the outcome of a desire on [the] part of a certain section of the commoners' who were convinced that 'the time had come when the masses of the people' ought to be given a say in the administration of the country. Obviously anxious to allay Prince Frederick's understandable fears over the recent press attacks on the Resident Commissioner and the chiefs, Mangoaela pointed out that it was not the intention of the BPA members 'to look down upon, nor to be in conflict with hereditary chieftainship'. On the contrary, they looked upon it with 'great gratitude', mindful of Moshoeshoe's achievements and those of his successors to preserve 'the integrity of this nation through times'. Nonetheless it was their earnest desire that the common people should have 'substantial representation' in the National Council; because they believed that commoners would contribute 'in a great measure' in combating 'the two great evils which are convulsing the country', namely, faction fights between chiefs, and stock theft.[85]

It was in response to this Address that Prince Arthur Federick took the opportunity to address the press question. First of all he was not convinced that there was a need for increased commoners' representation in the National Council. He felt that the number then appointed by the Resident Commissioner served the purpose. Secondly he disagreed with the *bahlalefi*'s methods and questioned their readiness for representative institutions. He admonished them:

> In order to be useful [the BPA] must of course *be reasonable* in the views which it expresses and *considerate on the feelings of others* . . . a tree does not grow in a day, and *wisdom in public affairs cannot be acquired without many years of experience and much patient thought*. A young Association, like a young man, must be prepared to learn from those who have longer and riper experience, and must be respectful to them. It must not be *in too much of a hurry*. [my italic].[86]

The BPA Motion for a Partially Elective Council

On neither of his two points – the one on respect for the feelings of others, the other on patience – was the High Commissioner heeded. The point for increased commoners' representation in the National Council would come up again at the Sixteenth Session on 2 July, only a month and a half after the High Commissioner's *pitso*. It came in two forms. The first was a motion by Simon Majakathata Phamotse that the constitution of the National Council be amended and that the body should become a partially elective Council. The motion stated that with the exception of 24 principal chiefs, all the rest (76 councillors) should be elected by the Nation. The motion was defeated. The second, also a motion by Simon Phamotse, was that BPA should be given ten seats in the National Council. This motion too was defeated.[87]

The *bahlalefi* were understandably frustrated and angered by their general defeat in all their aims that year. The High Commissioner had so much as told them that they were still children – tyros in politics, 'too much in a hurry' for big things. He did not appreciate the magnitude of the problem because of which they felt that increased commoner representation in the National Council had become imperative' namely, the problem of chiefly abuses – faction fights, injustices in the courts, misuse of privileges. The President of the National Council, for his part had come to view the *bahlalefi* with suspicion and distrust, and so he was not ready to throw his weight on their side. In the circumstances, to expect the chiefs in the National Council to cure themselves at that stage, was overly optimistic. They needed someone else to douse them in medicine. The *bahlalefi* then decided to arrogate that role to themselves, once again through the press, but this time it was a blitz.

Josiel Lefela's Attack on Imperialism

As would be the case constantly thereafter, the commoners' voice broke out in two discordant notes – one note by Josiel Lefela, the President of *Lekhotla la Bafo*, the other note by members of the BPA and their sympathisers. The former took the lead.

Between 19 March and 25 November 1921, Josiel Lefela contributed at least half-a-dozen intemperate articles in *Naledi*. They were all on the same theme – an attack on imperialism and its 'sentinel', the missionary. Two of these summarised the author's view of the problem. In the 30 September issue, Lefela attacked the British Government for duplicity on the question of Lesotho's constitutional status. He accused the British Government, inter alia, of breaking the compact between Queen Victoria and *Morena e Moholo* Moshoeshoe, whereby Lesotho was to be given protection, and of doing to Africans the opposite of what it was prepared to do to the Europeans:

> The Government of England only does away with Basutoland. You should remember why the Government of England went out to fight Germany and why Germany had been deprived of her colonies, and what England published as the reason for her fight, or did she fight meaning to take small nations back to bondage and deprive them of its rights? . . . Does the protection of the Government of England mean deprivation of the rights and the swallowing-up of it?[88]

The article concluded by condemning the British Government of conduct in international affairs 'unbecoming of her fame as [a] Christian Government', and of projecting good appearances 'with the tongue', while the deeds betrayed the contrary.

In the 18 November issue of *Naledi* Josiel Lefela particularised his analysis on the role of missionaries to the Paris Evangelical Missionary Society. Describing its members as 'fellowmen of conspirators whose plans congeal . . . blood', he charged that when they came to Lesotho originally (1833), they came with cynical plans, which the chief of Lesotho never became cognisant of, as the missionaries were always giving them the ' "outer part of the hand" '. The PEMS missionaries, he said, 'have been brought here to be used as dynamite so that the Government may complete the career, through them, of 'divide and rule'. He advised Basotho, as an alternative, to accept 'the American Negroes', (who were then making their presence in South Africa felt), 'and let us look forward to His Excellency Marcus Garvey the President of Africa . . . with anticipation'.[89] Josiel Lefela was a great admirer of Marcus Garvey and supporter of his Universal Negro Improvement Association.

Josiel Lefela was quickly and effectively squeezed out of the Lesotho newspapers, however. On 20 December 1921, the High Commissioner, Prince Arthur Frederick, authorised Resident Commissioner Garraway to call Edwin Tlale, the Editor of *Naledi* again 'to warn him against the publication of objectionable letters and articles' of the Josiel Lefela type.[90] This time Edwin Tlale evidently obliged. For thereafter Lefela's publications in Lesotho virtually ceased. He turned to the communist and African controlled South African newspapers, especially *Inkululeko* (Freedom), and *Umsebenzi* (The Worker) – edited by his friend and member of *Lekhotla la Bafo*, the Russian educated Mosotho, Edwin Mofutsanyana.

The reason for Edwin Tlale's change of heart is not far to find. According to the *bahlalefi*, among whom he was in the vanguard, two issues demanded the attention of commoners at that point. The first was the indigenous court system and chieftaincy administration. The second was power-sharing between chiefs and commoners within the framework of the National Council. Josiel Lefela's priorities, on the other hand, were: a) advocacy for the view that Lesotho was a 'Protectorate', and not a 'Crown Colony', and therefore fighting against all tendencies inconsistent with that view as manifestations of imperialism; and b) a relentless fight for the establishment of a House of Commoners, to operate alongside a Council of Chiefs, in the fashion of the Westminster model. Aside from that Lefela seemed to have his irons in too many fires. In addition to his onslaught against missionaries, he had joined hands with South African nationalists. He subscribed to Garveyism. He was forging links with the Communist Party of Russia and the Communist Party International. He was fighting the battles of Indians, in Lesotho as well as abroad. In short the *bahlalefi* would have seen him as someone who had taken too many enemies. He had to be dropped because he was becoming a political liability. By dropping him, however, the *bahlalefi* lost Lefela's respect. As so often afterwards he would say of them:

It is not exaggeration that defective education is worse than illiteracy because of its misleading effects, and diseased knowledge is poison to every healthy mind and brain, that is why our so-called educated in Basutoland are not able to distinguish bread coated with political poison from bread without poison.[91]

Thus, at critical points in their political battles, the *bahlalefi* could often count on Josiel Lefela to take the opposite side.

The Bahlalefi Precipitate a Head-on Collision with the Chieftaincy

At the same time that Josiel Lefela attacked imperialism and missionaries, the *bahlalefi* launched their own onslaught against the abuses of the chieftaincy. On 25 November 1921, *Naledi* published two letters that set the tone and tempo of the onslaught. Two of them came from Basotho then working in Cape Town. One letter, by Sephatsi Marung, began by denouncing the role of chiefs in the National Council, charging that as a consequence of their decisions in the Council the people's eyes 'have been pierced and they are being dragged to ruin'. Sephatsi Marung charged that generally speaking the Basotho 'have been turned into an inheritance of the chiefs and Europeans also harvest from here.' If there could be correspondence with heaven, he said, 'we would write to Chief Moshesh on our cries which fill the country and he would judge for us with justice'. As with Lefela (but not the rest of the chief's critics), Marung saw missionaries as collaborators in a general plot to dispossess Basotho of their political rights in the country. Since Mosheoshoe's death, he said, they had abandoned their originally proclaimed mission of 'salvation' and, instead, 'today they have turned [Lesotho] into trade, they cooperate with our enemies the English in the ill-treatment meted out to us'. Missionaries will 'rob you', he said, and when you tell the truth about their robbery they say, 'my child, the Evil One has entered your heart, let us kneel down and pray for him'; and those who attempted to protest through 'the butchery' called the National Council were rusticated.[92]

The other letter, by James N. Phalatse, was significant in that, while sharing Marung's view of chiefs (but not that of missionaries), it went further to suggest what kind of government Lesotho needed to replace the chieftaincy:

> I shall only speak about the 'iron bar', which is birth chieftainship, which is useless to us people in Africa. I think it is more than hundred years we have been supporting this rock which is useless. Now I advise that we should do away with birth chieftainship, we should set up a Republic and see if we cannot make progress.[93]

The following month, in December, the Bloemfontein *Friend* carried two aggressive articles against the court system. Both articles basically restated charges made in *The Friend* in 1919. One writer, under the pseudonym 'Mosotho' charged in general that chiefs had in effect 'turned the Basotho into a nation of slaves'. They made them work in the fields of their 'several wives without food or payment or even a drink of water'. 'Mosotho' alleged that some people had been killed by frolicking 'young chiefs' in a spate of violence perpetrated by indigenous rulers. As a rule, he said, court cases were awaited to stockpile before trial began. Yet, in the event a litigant lost heart and disappeared from the court, judgment was brought against him and he was fined for contempt of court. People could not even have their cases allowed on appeal to higher courts. When they attempted to appeal, higher chiefs' courts returned them to the courts whose judgment they appealed. 'Mosotho' let it be known that his article was aimed at the white public in general and colonial authorities in Lesotho in particular, as a strategy to expose 'the great misuse of justice carried out' by chiefs in Lesotho, from whom 'we groan under a burden of oppression'; and he hoped that as result of his agitation a Commission of Enquiry into his allegations might be established.[94]

A fortnight later, Simon Majakathata Phamotse followed. He said indeed any Mosotho 'would be wanting in patriotism were he to fail to endorse' the anonymous 'Mosotho' on the question of the 'uneven balance of justice' in the Territory. Chiefs, he said, ran their courts with extreme subjectivity and vindictiveness, and that they each had a 'black list' of commoners in their jurisdictions. In reaction to such a state of affairs, Basotho throughout the Territory were 'clamouring for reform of some kind or other'. He hoped to 'gain the ear of high officials and to draw attention to this woeful state of affairs in this our fair little country'. Finally he reiterated a proposal that he had made back in 1919, namely, that the first step to be taken in dealing with the situation was to establish a Department of Justice, which should be presided over by an 'experienced and qualified judge', and which should 'have nothing to do with political affairs'.[95]

Then a barrage of newspaper charges followed in *Naledi* and *Mochochonono* through February of 1922. At one time it was Simon Phamotse once again, at another, somebody who called himself 'Another Mosotho'. At yet another time it was an anonymous 'Mohlouoa' – 'The-Hated-One'. The punch-line from these critics, following which chiefs felt compelled to fight back, was carried in a leading article in *Naledi* on 24 February:[96]

> I am sure neither of our Paramount Chiefs . . . know anything of the Proclamation No. 28. To their knowledge and belief every male child born of a woman whose dowry was paid with cattle belonging to Moshesh's estate is *ipso facto* a chief with the right to adjudicate upon and try any case, criminal or civil, and to exercise jurisdiction defined by his superior . . . The condition of affairs in the country are (sic) going to the dogs all because the Resident Commissioner will not make use of this power . . . [Yet], in order to save the Basuto chieftainship from sure destruction to

which it is now speeding headlong, and to have freedom in the country, some way must be found out of the deadlock.[96]

As the Resident Commissioner learned when a BPA deputation approached him on the subject on 17 January, the newspaper barrage was a coordinated strategy by the *bahlalefi*. The BPA deputation, said the Resident Commissioner, was 'entirely agreed as to the correctness of the statements'.[97]

Exposed and driven to the wall, chiefs reacted against the newspaper charges with vigour and venom. *Morena e Moholo* Griffith convened a huge *pitso* at the royal capital in Matsieng at which 'the Sons of Moshoeshoe' were practically all present, and he summoned Simon Majakathata Phamotse and his followers to come and speak to their various charges against his government. Probably the longest in the century to date, the *pitso* lasted for eight days, from 18 April to the 25. Plenty of food was provided. The BPA members were given a whole ox to themselves.

According to the Bloemfontein *Friend* which covered the event, the spokesman of the BPA – Simon Phamotse, C. H. Mofokeng, Bernard Matete and the novelist, Thomas Mofolo, and Zakea Mangoaela underwent 'a severe cross-examination as to which Chiefs were accused . . .'. It was a hazardous procedure. The spokesmen declined the bait, saying it would not be prudent to give names as the accused were in the audience (and apparently they feared victimisation). They said they could name names only in a proper trial court, and not at a *pitso*. Meantime they referred their *Morena e Moholo* to the Proceedings of the National Council for the years 1912 to 1921, the relevant parts of which they duly read out to him. Significantly individuals began to approach the BPA spokesman with their personal grievances, and volunteered to give evidence of bad treatment received from the chiefs. 'Some fearless men, not members of the Association, who were present had the temerity to stand up and tell the Chiefs that it was true they ill-treated the nation. Many voices . . . vociferated their support of this.'[98]

Backed up by 150 members of the Association alone, Phamotse and his men were obviously feeling triumphant throughout the duration of the *pitso*. 'The meeting was constantly interrupted by voices from the crowd, which formed a ring supporting the Association's spokesman, and deriding the Chiefs', although the owners of the voices could not be identified. At the end of the *pitso*:

Women of the Paramount Chief's village came to shake hands

with the President of the Association [Simon Phamotse], whom they called their Moses and to whom they turned their eyes for their salvation and the salvation of the country. Many women sat at the approaches of the village, just to see 'the one who had come to deliver them' and newly born infants there were named after him.

Just as the *pitso* concluded, however, that triumph was commingled with trepidation. For, as Simon Phamotse and Thomas Mofolo informed the Resident Commissioner, to whom they repaired for sanctuary soon thereafter, the *Morena e Moholo*, speaking through his chief councillor, Chief Leloko Lerotholi, concluded the *pitso* by warning them 'that we must never organise in the villages of the chiefs and headmen, for we shall meet with accidents which will cause him trouble'.[99]

A threat of that kind made through Chief Leloko Lerotholi, which might very well have come from his own chest, and not that of the *Morena e Moholo*, was very likely to be carried out. Chief Leloko Lerotholi was a volatile personality. By 1928, according to one of the many reports of his conduct made to the Resident Commissioner, he had physically assaulted all members of the royal Court at Matsieng, including the President of the Court, Chief Goliath Mohale, and no one was able to bring him under harness.[100] Hence spokesmen of the BPA had good reason to fear for their lives. The Resident Commissioner moved fast to advise the *Morena e Moholo* that 'such words are dangerous and might be taken as an order to the chiefs who heard them' that they should accordingly arrange accidents for the members of the BPA.[101]

Summarising the views of the Association on the role of chiefs in government in *Naledi* (picked up by *The Times* on 3 May) Simon Phamotse stated, in an evident display of bravado and learning:

To their habitual indifference, born of years of unlimited authority and indulgent luxury, [Chiefs] very soon got over the shock they had received when their incorporation [to the Union of South Africa] . . . was first mooted . . . For over ten years, the Basutoland Chiefs have been callous to the cries and grievances of the people . . . History is truly repeating itself in Basutoland. *All the incidents which happened in the reign of King John and King Charles in connection with the trampling down of people's rights [in England], by both Kings, have taken place in the reign of the present King of Basutoland* . . . Like the English of old, the Basuto love their kings and will think twice before they declare against them. But the love is only on one side. The King and his barons show no reciprocity of that love, all they do is maltreat them, dispense uneven justice and make them slaves for them, without any recompense. (My emphasis)[102]

The Measure of *Morena e Moholo*'s Authority

Morena e Moholo's Griffith's authority in Lesotho in 1922 was at a very low ebb. As proof of the decline in his authority, the Resident Commissioner received confidential information through the Assistant Commissioner of Mafeteng in July that there was 'a scheme afoot' to depose him and put his half-brother, Chief Makhaola Lerotholi, in his place.[103] The Resident Commissioner, apparently, had reason to suspect the involvement of both Chief Maama, who had on more than one occasion accused Griffith of trying to 'kill' him (that is, 'eat him up'), as well as Chief Jonathan, on account of his own long standing feud with the monarch. Nevertheless both chiefs totally denied complicity in the scheme, and the Resident Commissioner was left to believe that it was simply a malicious piece of gossip.

Even so, the gossip (if that is all that it was) seems to have been efficiently put into circulation. For it is significant that at this very time – in July – a 'Criminal Investigation' made in Johannesburg and sent to the Police Headquarters in Lesotho stated that it had been 'ascertained' that all Basotho who had then just completed or were about to complete their contracts in the South African mines were anxious to return home; there was 'the general link . . . of coming trouble between Chief Jonathan and the Paramount Chief Griffith'.[104]

The least that it seems can be drawn from this otherwise confused state of affairs is that some members of the public suspected collusion between Simon Phamotse and Chief Jonathan to depose Griffith. Such a suspicion would have rested on the knowledge that the two were brothers-in-law, having both married two full sisters, significantly high-ranking grand-nieces of Moshoeshoe. It must have seemed a logical thing to those members of the public that if Griffith lost his throne, consequent upon the historic Matsieng *pitso*, Chief Makhaola would be the undisputed candidate for the high office. Chief Makhaola, who together with Jonathan was conspicuously absent from the Matsieng *pitso*, was the most level-headed of 'the Sons of Moshoeshoe' at the time. He was frankly the most critical principal chief of the abuses of the chieftaincy; and it is even plausible that he had absented himself from the *pitso* as an indication of his disagreement with the principle on which it had been convened.

The rumour of his de-stooling notwithstanding, Griffith had two serious political liabilities, one of which set him against a part, while the other set him against practically all, of his subjects. The latter was his half-brother and chief counsellor, Chief Leloko Lerotholi. Besides physically assaulting other chiefs and counsellors of the royal court in Matsieng, the Chief was inflexible to any change in the structure and functions of the chieftancy. Any proposals for change in this connection he described as 'forced progress'.[105] He effectively shielded the *Morena e Moholo* against his own people, while giving him a voice that was at once autocratic as well as belligerent. To wit, at the recent historic *pitso* at Matsieng, it was his voice that created the political climate. Not once did Griffith speak to his people with his own tongue, keeping in-doors or aloof from them for the entire eight days. Even the chairman Chief Sekhonyana's voice (presuming he spoke at all) was drowned under that of Leloko Lerotholi and his threatening gestures against the Progressive Association. The Resident Commissioner was hence accurate when he observed to the High Commissioner on 14 July: '[Griffith] has some very bad advisers, amongst the worst being, in my opinion, his younger half-brother Leloko, whom I distrust greatly and who is detested by the people.'[106]

The other political liability of the *Morena e Moholo* was his faith. Since his conversion in 1912, the Catholic Church wielded immense control over him. From the point of view of the Catholic Church it was the numbers' game against the rival protestant Paris Evangelical Missionary Society. By bringing the monarch under its influence, the Church hoped to create an impact on the rest of the Nation, as a result of which its adherents would increase and overwhelm the PEMS.

As evidence of the techniques used by the Catholic Church to work on his sentiments (and unwittingly perhaps to present an alternative authority in his mind from the colonial administration), His Grace J. Genez, the Bishop of Lesotho, had earlier, on his visit to Rome in 1914, carried a personal letter from the monarch to Pope Pius X. Unfortunately the Pope had died that year before he could respond. Nevertheless it would be one of the monarch's treasured achievements that the Pope's successor, Benedict XV, would respond to the letter, praising him for his gesture, and acknowledging it as 'true evidence of your faith, of your love to the Messenger of Jesus Christ, and your loyalty to the Catholic church, for which it is now four years that you have had the blessing of being its child'.[107]

On the occasion of his visit to London in 1919, Griffith would have received an even greater honour than that one, had the jealousy and fear of the colonial administration not destroyed his hopes. The Fathers of Roma Jesuit Mission, of whom he was an adherent, had apparently urged him to take the opportunity of the trip and visit both the Grotto of Massabielle at Lourdes in the South West of France, where the Blessed Lady appeared to St Bernadette in 1858, as well as the Vatican, to meet the Pope. The visit failed when the High Commissioner had the monarch informed that, so soon after the War, continental Europe was still unsafe to visit. That was not the real reason, however. The real reason, as the High Commissioner's confidential telegram to the Colonial Secretary pointed out, was that:

> I think it undesirable visit should be extended to Rome and Lourdes Griffith might be unduly impressed by pomp and state of reception at Vatican and might form conclusion that Pope was more important than His Majesty the King.[108]

As the colonial administration had feared in 1919 that the *Morena e Moholo*'s loyalty was in danger of diminishing in favour of the Catholic Church, the *bahlalefi* were convinced by the early 1920s that he had already abdicated his responsibilities to the nation in its favour. The impression needed not, of course, be true; but the political core of the *bahlalefi* belonged to the PEMS. While they themselves were critical of their white clergy, in so far as they saw it as monopolising key posts of leadership and occasionally supporting the colonial administration on issues inimical to their vested interests, they were part and parcel of denominational rivalries. Hence they feared the tilt in the balance of numbers, which was moving at a remarkable rate. To illustrate the point, in 1904 there were about 5700 Catholics to 40 000 PEMS members in Lesotho. In 1924, the Catholic congregation was about 50 000;[109] and by 1929 the Colonial Report on Lesotho estimated the numbers at 80 000 PEMS to 60 402 Roman Catholic members, out of a population of approximately half-a-million.[110]

The Resident Commissioner's Initial Response to the *Bahlalefi*'s Call for Reforms

The picture emerges quite clearly that, until the BPA launched its coordinated press attacks calculated to produce action in 1921 and 1922, the colonial administration was aware that something had gone wrong in the indigenous government of Lesotho, but it had no idea as to how to go about putting it right. Indeed it can even be suggested that the colonial adminsitration had no answer to the problem precisely because it had still not conceived a policy for administering the Territory. This much, at least, would tacitly be admitted by one Resident Commissioner, R. C. Sturrock (E. C. F. Garraway's successor) in 1928.

As the colonial administration was not clear on its own policy, therefore, when the BPA press attacks erupted it could not initially do more than be circumspect about the situation and, from the embarrassment of its own helplessness, make a few feeble suggestions. Garraway's initial response, communicated to his High Commissioner on 24 December 1921, was to send the first two aggressive articles by Simon Phamotse and the anonymous 'Mosotho' to the *Morena e Moholo* with a brief, non-committal note: 'I have been asked by R. H. for remarks.' (As a matter of fact, His Royal Highness, the High Commissioner, had given no instruction to that effect.) Beyond that timid step, and while admitting both the accuracy of the newspaper charges as well as the need for reform, Garraway refrained from involvement on the grounds that:

> I am of [the] opinion that such reform can only emanate from the natives themselves, and I have no doubt that this will ultimately eventuate. Every session the subject is vigorously discussed in the council and these grievances openly ventilated there, but so far without result.[111]

Toward the end of January 1922, however, the Resident Commissioner was beginning to see his way through the situation and his communication to the High Commissioner began to reflect a tangible suggestion. He had just received a deputation of 30 BPA members who had come to ask him what positive action he intended to take consequent to its agitation for reform. In the course of the audience, so he admitted to the High Commissioner, the deputation had convinced him that Simon Phamotse's proposal for a Department of Justice, which took the more precise description of 'Special Court of Appeal' at that audience, 'expressed the unanimous feeling of the whole nation'.[112] Hence he recommended the idea to His Royal Highness, having taken the trouble to give it an organisational framework. He recommended the idea of a 'Special Court of Appeal' to deal with 'purely native cases' tried by chiefs' court and from appeals of judgments in those courts.

As the situation then stood, such appeals lay to the Royal Court at Matsieng. The establishment of the 'Special Court of Appeal' would thus critically alter that arrangement. Hence the Resident Commissioner noted that 'strong opposition from the Paramount Chief and his immediate followers may be expected'.[113] Opposition could be expected all the more because of the proposed structure of the Special Court of Appeal, which was as follows: the President was to be the Assistant Commissioner of the District of parties in dispute. He presided over seven members, one from each of the seven Districts in the Territory. The President and three members were to form a quorum. The provision making an Assistant Commissioner the President of the Court was a contribution from the BPA, which had advised the Resident Commissioner that it was the general wish of the nation.

As the BPA pressed him to take a stand on the general question of reforms, and as he was obviously awake to the fact that failure to do so might have immediate political repercussions on him, he opted to offer it his support. So he recounted to His Royal Highness:

> I told them that I considered they were taking the right steps in the right way in beginning to move in the matter, and that any proposed change in the present procedure as regards the chief's courts should come from the nation, and on behalf of the administration I assured them that all such suggestions would receive full and sympathetic consideration.

By 18 February the Resident Commissioner had become creative of his own accord. In a search for a general solution for reforming the indigenous government, he had dug out Proclamation 2B 1884, only to discover, to his amazement, that after all, all chiefs' courts and rules for their guidance in the Territory ought to be laid down by the Resident Commissioner. Yet, as he remarked to the High Commissioner, during the entire 37 years of the existence of the Proclamation, 'in no case have the conditions laid down therein been enforced'. Of the rules mentioned in the Proclamation, 'none appear to have ever been issued from the Resident Commissioner's

Office'.[114] As a step rectifiying the situation, therefore, he asked the High Commissioner 'to instruct me' to write to the *Morena e Moholo* to submit a full list of chiefs who hold courts and explain by whose authority they did so. Although it could be argued that chiefs derived their authority and the right to hold court from the custom of 'placing', the Resident Commissioner felt that, even the custom notwithstanding, 'many of these younger chiefs have never been given authority, and should not be allowed to hold court of any description'. His prescription was that as soon as he received the names, it should be possible to issue 'instructions for a considerable reduction in the number of courts, and to forbid a large number'.

In none of his initiatives did the Resident Commissioner make headway. *Morena e Moholo* Griffith soon found himself so besieged by the press that his mind was apparently not clear enough to give an argued defence to the chieftaincy. The Resident Commissioner was soon also to find out in October 1922, at the Seventeenth Session of the National Council, that the idea of a Special Court of Appeal was as then only an attractive dream in his own mind and in the minds of the *bahlalefi*. The Chiefs in general, and the *Morenea e Moholo* in particular, would hear nothing of it.

A Statement of Policy by the High Commissioner

Between May 1921, when His Royal Highness, Prince Arthur Frederick, tried without success to talk the BPA into being 'considerate on the feelings of others', to September 1924, no policy statement issued from the High Commission in Cape Town, either publicly or confidentially. From the foregoing background it may be assumed that the silence derived more from the lack of clarity on policy, than from judicious reticence in the wake of the bewildering political situation in the Territory. By September 1924, however, when the Earl of Athlone, the successor to Prince Arthur Frederick, paid a visit to Lesotho, he deemed it desirable to break the silence. Nevertheless he spoke as a man who was seeking to use his authority and power to repress the political agitation of the *bahlalefi*, and not as a chief executive simply attempting to provide direction. In this regard his speech bore a striking resemblance, in tone and content, to the one given by the abrasive Governor of Nigeria, Sir Hugh Clifford, against the Nigerian-educated élite in 1920. While it was less acetic, it was nevertheless still overbearing:

[The] Government is patient because it realises that a nation as a whole cannot progress at the same rate as individuals who may happen to be specially gifted or who may have profited by unusual opportunities to achieve a degree of education far in advance of their countrymen. You must remember that the white races have only reached their present state of civilisation after centuries of struggle and unceasing efforts. They know from their own experience that a nation cannot be hurried in its development and although the Government is composed of wiser men than yourselves they are careful to uphold the authority of the chiefs. They have instructed the Basotho with the assistance of, and not in opposition to, the recognised leaders of the people and the established laws of the land. Moshesh has done more for your countrymen than any Mosuto living or dead but he succeeded on account of his wisdom for he was not a learned man. I spoke to you at length because I do not want discontented people in Basutoland.[115]

The High Commissioner's speech must have been particularly disagreeable as it was made in the presence of overseas Parliamentary delegates, including the Secretary of State, Mr J. H Thomas and, worse, the Prime Minister of South Africa, General Hertzog, who had been dragged along. Political realist that he was, the South African Prime Minister had confessed doubt as to whether it would be tactful for him to attend the *pitso*, but the High Commissioner, who needed his presence for its psychological effect on Basotho, had pressured him into coming. As The High Commissioner reported to the Colonial Office:

My opinion is that General Hertzog's visit will have a very good effect. The Basuto are mortally . . . afraid of being taken over by the Union and the presence amongst them of the Prime Minister, who is not only Dutch but 'Free State' Dutch at that, will keep the benefits of British rule fresh in their memories for some time to come. It certainly had a most simulating effect upon their loyalty which on this occasion was professed with more customary emphasis.[116]

As it could have been expected General Hertzog was an object of Basotho scorn and hatred during the entire occasion. The Earl of Athlone remarked, with unmistakable alacrity:

Several of the rank and file appear to have identified General Hertzog, and I am told that some harsh things were said as he left the Pitso. But, fortunately, he is profoundly ignorant of the Sesuto language, and was therefore able to depart without any clear idea of their sentiments. In fact I even heard it alleged that certain most abusive remarks were courteously acknowledged by the General who was under impression that they were bidding him goodbye.[117]

Beneath the apparent self-confidence and bravado in the High Commissioner, however, lurked a deep sense of helplessness regarding the steps to be taken in the current political circumstances. On this he was frank to his superior, the Secretary for Colonies, to whom he confessed:

> One of the worst defects of the present method of governing the country lies in the fact that the Administration has no effective authority over the Paramount Chief or through him over to the subordinate Chiefs. The Resident Commissioner seems powerless to force them to introduce unwelcome reforms or to check . . . abuses in matters which should properly fall within their jurisdiction.[118]

The Stand of the National Council on Reforms from 1922 to 1926

From 1922 to 1926 the question of chieftaincy reforms was a permanent item in the agenda of the National Council; but also permanent was the tension between the *bahlalefi* councillors and the chiefs. From the outset, when the Seventeenth Session of the National Council convened in August 1922, the *bahlalefi* were pilloried by their royal peers.

Worthy of note, when the Seventeenth Session met, was the attendance factor on the part of certain outstanding personalities: *Morena e Moholo* Griffith was absent, allegedly indisposed, probably from a diplomatic illness, and Chief Makhaola Lerotholi – the half-brother rumoured of coveting his sceptre – was acting for him; and Chief Jonathan Molapo, the Chief of Leribe, who had not attended the National Council since 1917, was in attendance, and he remained for a full five days (out of three weeks). He was quiet for practically the entire-period of his stay, having apparently come to witness the cross-fire and get a first-hand knowledge of the outcome, but not to offer any solutions.

Fully three days of the Session were spent discussing the activities of the BPA, which were roundly condemned by the majority of the councillors, who said the BPA was out to undermine the power of the chiefs. Speaking somewhat out of character, but understandably in an effort to shake off rumour and remain in Griffith's good books Chief Makhaola Lerotholi came down hard on Simon Phamotse. While describing the BPA as an essentially wholesome Association, he regretted the fact that its members 'are very bad people'. 'He [Phamotse] says he leads the people to the right way. My views are too strong to be expressed before your Honour [the President].' Chief Makhaola promised to ask the *Morena e Moholo* to confine the activities of the Association to the 'camps' – the six administrative centres presided over by Assitant Commissioners – and not be allowed in the rural areas. (The instruction was subsequently duly given.) Had Chief Leloko Lerotholi, the volatile Matsieng councillor, had his way, the activities of the BPA should have been stopped altogether. Chief Leloko spoke for quite a long time and particularly harassed Simon Phamotse, consistently accusing him of 'untruths'. While, in a bold admission of his advocacy for violence he said: 'With reference to the beating of the people at the "matsema", some of the people smoke "opium" and have to be made to do work.'[119]

The most scathing, if condescending speech from the chieftaincy, however, came from neither the Acting *Morena e Moholo* nor his chief councillor; it came from a minor chief, Makoanyane Seeiso, Chief Maama's grandson, who characterised the *bahlalefi* as the Absaloms of the Territory:

> The sons of Moshoeshoe should be aware of the many Absaloms who wait at the gates asking the people if they have unsettled cases, and promise to give them their assistance. I know for certain that the members of the Progressive Association are not on friendly terms with their Chiefs . . . A councillor once said that it was difficult for educated persons to hold the plate while the Chief eats, it is such 'collar-wearers' who never go to their Chiefs.

The *bahlalefi* councillors were helplessly overpowered. Their defence was spasmotic and feeble; but two of them were worthy of the record. One defence, by Labane Chokobane, was that the *bahlalefi* had resorted to their recent tactics because 'We did not wish to be regarded like little boys playing outside'. While the other, and the more incisive, by the Reverend Bennett Leshota, read:

> If you think that you are looking for justice, be steadfast until the Chiefs accept your motion [for reform]. It appears that the

Councillors who are Courtiers are frightened that they will lose their bread . . . Basutoland is the England of the natives. Whenever they are ill-treated, the natives of South Africa say they will run to Basutoland. They are all grieved when they hear about miscarriage of justice.[120]

The motion of reform that the Reverend Leshota was referring to was the one of Special Court of Appeal, earlier mooted by the Resident Commissioner on the suggestion of the BPA, and which had been broached in the press as a Department of Justice. The intention and the logistics were still the same: the BPA members were still strongly in favour of setting up the Court under the Resident Commissioner, instead of the *Morena e Moholo*. They wanted it as a 'high court' 'whose decisions cannot be interfered with by any individual'. Additionally they wished it to function as a Circuit Court to clear the backlog of cases in the Territory, especially in the badly-hit Districts, such as Leribe. Its members would be selected by and be responsible to the National Council. It was envisaged that its establishment would lead finally to a separation of powers in the indigenous government. One councillor, an educated chief, Libopua Maama, who appreciated the essence of the last point, restated it in a clear political context. He said:

We must consider the future if we are to look after the interests of the future progress and the people are complaining against the present administration of justice. In civilised countries affairs are separated by their departments. The suggested court of appeal will help the Paramount Chief so that he may only deal with politics. Let us not leave problems which are too big for our future children. What is the good of considering our own selves if that will ruin us in the future.[121]

The majority of the chiefs were against the idea of the Court of Appeal. Chief Leloko Lerotholi, who led the opposition, said it was nothing but 'forced progress', acceptance of which would lead the country into 'a peat'. Concluding the subject, for which he received loud 'cheers', was the Acting *Morena e Moholo*, Chief Makhaola Lerotholi, who said: 'That means the Paramount Chief would have no power . . . we submit to you that the Paramount Chief should not be deprived of his powers.'

In the place of reform, the chiefs preferred to amend and to add to *The Laws of Lerotholi*. And in this connection, once more, both the peculiar constitutional nature of the National Council as well as the ambivalent legal status of the 'Laws' came into evidence. For if when the 'laws' were put together in 1903 it was only as an exercise of codifying customary law, or if, as the then Resident Commissioner advised his High Commissioner, the 'laws' were not law at all but only 'custom', 'suggestions', 'merely . . . an expression of national opinion', what was the legal effect of 'amending' and adding to those nebulous concepts? What authority were the councillors exercising?

The problem did not, at this time, preoccupy the councillors. They seemed clearly to labour under the impression that they were exercising the function of legislation; but the colonial administration saw the need, for its own purposes, to be clear as to what transpired. The problem was referred to the legal advisor, Mr Feetman, who gave the following pragmatic opinion:

> It appears that when the Laws of Lerotholi were first submitted to the High Commissioner under cover of Mr Sloley's despatch of 31st August 1903, they were put forward rather as a collection of *existing laws and customs* which it was desirable to formulate in definite terms, than as legislative enactments, but since that date the National Council has tended to assume the functions of a legislature in making from time to time additions and amendments to these native laws. *This informal expansion of the Council may serve a very useful purpose* in securing the gradual revision and development of native law and custom, so that it may be adapted from time to time to the changing needs of the Territory, but there is the obvious danger that the *laws framed of the native law and custom may be found to cover the same ground and to clash with laws made by the High Commissioner.* [My italic][122]

Here then, at last was a straightforward answer to a question put forward to Philip Molise at the Third Session in 1908 (cited in Chapter 4): if the National Council is only an advisory body, what was the legal status of the 'Laws'? The answer was that they were laws, framed by the Council 'in its capacity as interpreter of the native law and custom', on authority derived from its 'informal expansion', by which it had come to 'assume the functions of a legislature'. Thus the Reverend C. M. Sebeta was correct on that occasion to say that 'there are two kinds of law in Basutoland, the laws of Moshesh and the High Commissioner'.

This pragmatic approach to the development of customary law, however, was inherently defective: no legislative authority or official recognition had been extended to the 'Laws'. Under colonial rule such authority derived neither from the *Morena e Moholo* and his customary institutions (the *lekhotla* and the *pitso*) nor from the National Council; it derived from the High Commissioner. The High Commission saw no need to extend official recognition to the Laws. Time would come when the 'unique deficiency' in the Laws, as Sebastian Poulter has characterised it,[123] would be called into question in a court of law.

Be that as it may, the intention of the 'amendments and additions 'to *The Laws of Lerotholi* was to impose more and tougher sanctions. The focus was on two Laws: Law 3, on the right of appeal, imposed £20 on the *Morena e Moholo* and equally on a chief, sub-chief or headmen refusing any person the right to appeal. To date, no specific fine had been stipulated. Law 19, on the lawful conduct of cases in chiefs' courts, imposed a fine of £50 on principal chiefs, who for the first time were numerated and identified by name[124] – £20 for lesser chiefs; £5 for headmen, for unlawful conduct in the courts (for instance, threatening appellants with reprisals). Previously the fine was £10, without regard to the hierarchy of authority. Of the added Laws, Law 21 declared the selling of Sesotho beer (*joala*) to be unlawful.

As in their original form of 1903, the amended Laws, with their additions, were doomed to fail. The reason for failure was the same: lack of enforcement. The *Morena e Moholo* could not control his chiefs. At the same time, the colonial administration did not see the administration of justice in Basotho courts as falling within its juridiction and, indeed, the chiefs were ready to pounce on it if it interfered or intervened.

The direct confrontation between the chiefs and the *bahlalefi* was not, however, without any immediate, positive effect. If nothing else, it convinced the *Morena e Moholo* that he could not totally ignore the *bahlalefi* or 'collar-wearers', as they were jeered. Accordingly he made a political gesture following the Session in 1922, and quite independently, to co-opt four members of the BPA into the Royal Court at Matsieng.[125] For at least two years the outcome was remarkably positive. In the first place the move temporarily dampened criticism against his person. In the second place it produced a net improvement in the running of the Court. As evidence, in a nine month period between 23 May 1922 to 30 January 1923, the Royal Court had settled 168 cases. By contrast over the first four months from 30 January 1923 that the BPA members were co-opted, the Royal Court had cleared 198 cases.[120] However the experiment carried the seeds of its own undoing: intense jealousies developed between the old and the new courtiers, for the *Morena e Moholo*'s patronage. In the ensuing struggle the old courtiers won. By the middle of 1925 the Royal Court was once more fully under the control and caprice of the 'sons of Moshoeshoe'.

In the National Council, as in the Royal Court, the *bahlalefi* were the losers. For the last time in the decade, the BPA tabled a motion at the Twenty-first Session of the National Council in 1926, asking for parity in the Council between chiefs and commoners. Following discussions lasting for a day and a half, the motion was lost.[127]

The Colonial Administration Takes the Initiative for Reforms

Having thus found the chieftaincy to be too cumbersome to take on, the *bahlalefi* changed their focus and declared a press war on the colonial administration. In their most trenchant attack by an anonymous 'Basutolander', which was featured by the Bloemfontein *Friend* on 15 January 1926, they put the blame for the stagnation of the indigenous government on British rule. Praising Moshoeshoe, the founder of the nation, for having made laws that were 'almost Mosaic in their simple justice', 'Basutolander' denounced the colonial administration for its failure to capture the essence of those laws and to get them working. He charged that 'the long list of administrators, O.B.E.'s, C.B.E.'s, C.M.G.'s, K.C.M.G.'s have done next to nothing to help Basutoland along!' He accused them of 'conservatism of the worst type'. He castigated them for 'procrastination' and for 'slackness and funk, or peace at any price'. The basic flaw in the colonial administration, as he saw it, was that the officers on the spot were 'taking their cue from the native [chiefs] they are supposed to rule'.[128] As in 1921–22, a volley of press attacks followed.

The renewed attacks coincided with the appointment of a resourceful Resident Commissioner. Described by the Dominions Secretary as 'a capable and progressive administrator',[129] J. C. R. Sturrock came to Lesotho from Uganda, where he had a great deal of involvement in the organisation of the indigenous court system. It was felt that he could be trusted with the responsibility of shaping up the indigenous government which had become crucial, especially in the phase of renewed South African pressure for incorporation. The Dominions Secretary, Mr Amery, was in communication with General Hertzog on the question of the transfer of the High Commission

Territories in 1927, and although he had informed him that 'there was no hope of Parliament agreeing to any transfer' until his legislation on the 'native question' had proved satisfactory, he was hopeful that it would eventually be achieved. Meantime, he had agreed with him 'to push ahead with development' in the Territories, 'so as to make transfer an easy and natural process when the time for it eventually came'. In Lesotho, as the Dominions Secretary saw it, the problem of development was 'purely one of native administration and education'.[130]

Having studied the situation, J. C. R. Sturrock arrived at the conclusion that the breakdown in the indigenous government was basically of the making of the colonial administration, and that it derived essentially from the virtual lack of policy. As he put it:

> It can, I think, be assumed that the principle of 'Indirect Rule' is one that had been adopted in Basutoland . . . It is clear, however, . . . that the circumstances of various territories . . . differ so greatly as to make it impossible that this principle can be adopted for all with the same details of application . . . I cannot help feeling negative rather than positive – in other words we have not so much made a positive attempt to rule through the chiefs, as allowed conditions to stagnate under the chiefs . . . Has there been any consistent attempt to improve and build upon the organisation – as it was – that we found? Has not the whole tendency been towards the disintegration?[131]

For one such as the Resident Commissioner, who had just emerged from Lord Lugard's second seedbed of the principle of 'Indirect Rule' in Uganda, and who probably saw himself as a chosen disciple, it is perhaps understandable why he was not discouraged by its misapplication in Lesotho, and instead felt it ought to be established properly. As he put it:

> [S]o far am I from any desire to curtial the rights and responsibilities of the Paramount Chief that, in spite of the poorness of the present material, I feel it to be essential to strengthen his position if we are to succeed to any extent in putting more life into the Native Administration.

In the course of attempting to understand the difficulties of the indigenous government, J. C. R. Sturrock took his assignment a step further. He tried to find out how efficiently the colonial administration itself had exercised its judicial functions. His findings were bewildering: the colonial administration had done just about as badly as the chieftaincy. Within its own jurisdication, which in criminal cases encompassed culpable homicide, murder, assault with intent to murder, malicious injury to property, arson, for the most part, and in civil cases mostly of divorces involving civil or Christian marriages, the backlog was an indicting testimony. There were cases, for instance, of people who had spent five months in jail without trial (in a society that was hardly used to imprisonment as punishment), only to find at the end that they merited no more than a fine or a month in jail.[132] The Resident Commissioner's Court, which handled these cases, was presided over by a Deputy Commissioner (at least beginning in 1916).[133] The holders of that office, however, had no more than a smattering of legal training to go by.

Sturrock's approach to reforms in the circumstances was twofold. First he made a recommendation in 1927 for the introduction of the office of Judical Commissioner. A post similar in function to the one that he desired for Lesotho was already in existence as Judge President of the Special Courts of Swaziland and Bechuanaland Protectorates. As of January 1928 that office was held by Patrick Duncan, who was at the same time the Legal Adviser for the South African High Commission. That same year his responsibilities were expanded to include the office of Judicial Commissioner for Lesotho, with the understanding that he would be devoting only a few months of his time in fulfilment of its functions.[134]

Clearing up the backlog of cases under the Resident Commissioner's jurisdiction and keeping the judicial machinery running properly, as it turned out, was not all that easy. Aside from taking up the bulk of cases, there was the problem of distances and transportation to the various districts, where the Court was actually held. From the colonial capital, Maseru, due north by motor car, Patrick Duncan had to drive 29 miles to Berea District for one and a half hours, 60 miles to Leribe for three hours. Due south to Qacha's Nek he had to travel two days via Pietermaritzburg in Natal by train, one and a half hours by motor car, and then had to scale a steep climb, arising some 3000 feet on horseback, to try a few cases at that venue alone.[135] Contrary to his expectation, he found out that the judicial work in Lesotho was more than double that of Bechuanaland and Swaziland combined.[136] There was so much on Patrick Duncan's plate that in 1929 an Assistant Registrar and Assistant Master of the Court had to be appointed to relieve him of the majority of civil cases.[137] In the interim, the legally untrained Resident Commissioner had been compelled by the congestion of cases in 1928 to try fourteen criminal cases, an added responsibility which he thoroughly detested. As he informed the Imperial Secretary, B. E. Clifford: 'I must, however, admit that it is the case that I have had practically no experience of Civil work [trying cases], and do not approach it with anything save the most lively dislike.'[138] By December 1929 Patrick Duncan had himself to complain about his harassing schedule and proposed: 'In my own interests as well as his [party on trial] I should be glad if the amount of travelling could be reduced by the hearing of as many cases as possible in Maseru.'[139]

Sturrock's second, and more difficult task, was the effort to reform the general administration of the indigenous government and its court system. This task would take twelve years before it could be accomplished.

Having gained the impression in 1926 that chiefs had at last accepted their failure to deal with their own administrative and judicial problems and that they would welcome intervention by the colonial administration, the Resident Commissioner set about drafting a lengthy set of Regulations in 1927. The Regulations defined the responsibilities of chiefs, sub-chiefs and headmen, who would be 'recognised as such by the Resident Commissioner of Basutoland'. The Regulations set out specific penalties on chiefs for 'neglect to exercise the powers' to be bestowed by a pending Proclamation. They systematised courts into Class 1, the courts of district chiefs and Class 2, the courts of chiefs and sub-chiefs in general; and they established 'Rules' for the conduct of those courts.

The regulations were modelled after the Uganda Native Administration and Court Regulations. The Resident Commissioner was making them under the authority conferred upon him by Section 4 of the Regulations published under Proclamation No. 2B of 1884. They were subsequently circulated throughout the Territory, as 'only suggestions', bound in the form of a booklet carrying the title: *New Native Court Regulations.*[140]

Sturrock had intended to present the Draft Regulations to the National Council at its 24th Session in 1929, as a last step before passing them to the High Commissioner for proclamation. As he pointed out to the High Commissioner in June 1928, chiefs were ready for reforms: 'Practically all councillors save one, who is closely connected with the Paramount Chief's Court, have admitted it in my hearing in Council.'[141] (It could safely be deduced that the lone objector in the Resident Commissioner's mind was Chief Leloko Lerotholi.)

Just at that point, however, the *Lekhotla la Bafo* reversed the tide. The relations between the *Lekhotla la Bafo* and the Progressive Association had soured and were at their worst in those years. At the same time the latter had gained considerably in numbers, estimated at 1900 in 1929.[142] (As earlier shown, the BPA had been estimated at 1500 in 1924.) In great contrast to the BPA, the *Lekhotla la Bafo* was composed of the disaffected poorer Basotho – the landless, the spasmodic migrant labourers, small shopkeepers, members of independent African Churches, and prophets – who had been generated by the tensions arising from rumours of incorporation into the Union of South Africa, and who generally led the *Lekhotla la Bafo* Presidential Addresses with prayers. There were also disgruntled (mostly uneducated) junior chiefs with an axe to grind with their seniors. There were women, who usually livened major gatherings with Josiel Lefela's self-composed songs of protest.[143] It can even be assumed that Indians, whom Josiel Lefela affectionately referred to as 'our senior brothers the Indians', were warm, if calculating, supporters of the organisation. Numbering then no less than 150 adults, at least 20 of whom were married to Basotho,[144] Indians were getting increasingly bitter with the colonial administration's restriction of their number in Lesotho. Lefela championed their cause on the grounds that they 'have been ousted from their home by hunger and want of clothing which were caused by the English and all white nations of Europe'.[145] *Lekhotla la Bafo*, in short, comprised a broad assortment of disgruntled people of lesser means, less independently critical on issues, but suitably malleable under Lefela's charismatic personality, and his brother Maphutseng Lefela's intellectual prowess.[146] At that juncture, 1927-9, Lefela was prepared to use them against the joint aim of the colonial administration and the BPA's *bahlalefi* – the aim of reforming the chieftaincy.

So, partly to foil the reforms, as a counter political attack on the perceived 'imperialist ploy', and partly, perhaps, from the genuine fear that the Nation was about to be deprived of its natural leadership, the *Lekhotla la Bafo* initiated a campaign a few weeks before the Draft Regulations were to be discussed in the National Council, in defence of the chieftaincy. Going back to the old question of the constitutional status of the Territory, Lefela argued that Lesotho was a Protectorate. The colonial administration, he said, had been sent only to protect his country. In the event, he was appalled in

1929 to find that colonial officers were bent on the 'breaking down of our social fabric to bring about the detribalisation of our political existence as a nation . . . [and] the vilification and pollution of our chiefs by the officers of the Government through enmeshing them in judicial manoeuvres directed against them to prepare for their expulsion from posts of exercising their duties as judges for their people.'[147]

Largely owing to this political ammunition, and to no less a degree because *Lekhotla la Bafo* obviously prepared the strategy for the chiefs to foil the reform, when the Resident Commissioner's Regulations were brought for discussion in the National Council in October 1929, chiefs torpedoed them out. The strategy was to knock down the centre pin of the Draft Regulations, namely, the enabling Proclamation 2B of 1884. In typical Josiel Lefela fashion, which had become a common article in his Presidential Addresses, the chief argued that Proclamation 2B was a Cape Colony law and not one of the Imperial Government, and as such it was null and void. The contrary was the case; but the new Resident Commissioner did not know his facts. Further, again one of Lefela's pet arguments, chiefs asked the Resident Commissioner if he was familiar with what they termed the Treaty of Mokema, by which Moshoeshoe and Wodehouse had agreed that Lesotho would be a protectorate, and they submitted that the Treaty had been reduced to writing. No such a 'Treaty' existed; but, ignorant of the fact, J. C. R. Sturrock admitted confusion and virtually threw in the towel. He did so when he granted the chiefs leave to go and consult the nation. Five days later the chiefs came back to say they had held *pitso*s throughout the country (11 700 sq. miles) and the nation was in agreement with them that it did not want his 'little book' of Regulations.[148]

Yet that grievances existed was admitted by none other than the *Lekhotla la Bafo*, which pointed out just a year later in 1930:

> The treatment of the chiefs upon the people is most vexatious and . . . you all see that our success in repelling the proposed regulations for the abolition of hereditary chieftainship is no better than an ephemeral success.[149]

Indeed the success was ephemeral. Effectively beginning in 1931, the Resident Commissioner established a procedure of consultation between chiefs and commoners: before as after each Session of the National Council, chiefs were to hold meetings with their people in their respective districts, and they were to bring back motions on subjects affecting their welfare. The procedure established a measure of accountability between the rulers and their subjects, but it also placed chiefs in the awkward position of having to introduce to the Council motions from a majority of commoners who indicted them of maladministration and injustices in their courts.

At the same time, as a result of a study in 1934–5 of the financial and economic problems in Lesotho, undertaken for the Imperial Government by Sir Alan Pim, the colonial administration gained more confidence that by introducing a reform it was doing the right thing. Sir Alan Pim's report had pointed out, among other things, that:

> The history of Basutoland presents a very different picture and the *protectorate policy* followed with reference to it has little in common with indirect rule. It has been a policy 'of non-interference, of proffering alliance, of leaving *two parallel Governments* to work in a state of detachment unknown in tropical Africa, while under indirect rule native institutions are incorporated into a single system of government and subjected to the continuous guidance, supervision and stimulus of European officers.'[150] The Nation is ruled by its Chiefs, and the Government can merely proffer advice; this is not asked for nor welcomed when it is a question of how the rule should be administered, but is clamoured for when a difficult position arises. The Basuto received *protection without control*, and not only the Chiefs or the National Council but the mass of the people consider that their obligations are fulfilled by paying taxes. Apart from this they are obsessed by the idea of their absolute independence, except those who have suffered severely under the oppression of their Chiefs. [My italic][51]

From the account of the history of the Territory so far given, it has to be admitted that, except for a touch of exaggeration as to receiving 'protection without control', Sir Alan Pim's perception was quite accurate; and, in essence, his was only a more elaborate, and probably better reasoned, statement than the one given by J. C. R. Sturrock in 1928.

Moreover Sir Alan Pim's thinking had to a great extent been shaped by the views that he had gathered when he interviewed a delegation of the BPA. The delegation had counselled him on 'the need of measures of reform by peaceful methods and persuasion'; but of great significance, while conceding that there were some benefits in 'British indirect rule', the BPA had informed Pim of its view that that type of rule 'hindered or retarded' progress, owing to the fact that 'some of the customs are no more suitable for the changing conditions brought about by European contact through which people are passing and require some re-adjustment'. The BPA summarised its view as follows:[152]

> The British policy of non-interference with the domestic affairs of the Basuto is in our opinion, responsible for the backwardness of the chiefs, for the autocracy of most of them, as they feel secure under this British indirect rule which protects 'Moshesh' and leaves 'the blanket [i.e. the country] and the lice [i.e. the people] thereof at his mercy.'[152]

Beginning in 1936, 'motions' from the districts calling for a major reform of the indigenous government began to filter into the National Council. In 1937, when the National Council held its 22nd Session, these 'motions' came from every major chieftancy jurisdiction in the Territory. All principal chiefs agreed that they had lost control of the reins of government. Chief Leloko Lerotholi could, of course, be counted upon for a solo protest, albeit he had some inconsequential company on that occasion. He still did not see anything wrong in the indigenous government. As he put it:

> It is alleged that the chiefs do not make use of the laws contained in the Lerotholi book. I cannot quite understand what is meant by this, as I have been thinking over it, I feel I will go mad . . . How long will the people expect angels to come down from heaven to see the aim of these people is to try to put a stop to the rights of the Paramount Chief and his junior brothers.[153]

Having now emerged from the political liability of the rumoured de-stooling of the *Morena e Moholo* to which his name had been drafted, Chief Theko Makhaola fairly much set the tone of reason for the majority of the chiefs as to what, in his own view, had gone wrong in the indigenous government:

> I find that some people are afraid of advising their chiefs because they think if they advise them the Chiefs will hate them. And it is also alleged that if a man lodges an appeal according to law his Chief will hate him . . . According to Sesuto customs if a chief goes astray and does not act according to law his councillor must force him to the law, and if the Chief does not listen to them it is their duty to report the matter to the higher Chief, and according

to the same custom if the Chief is found to be in the wrong usually the Councillors are fined and they are asked what they have been watching. Now that this custom is dying out, the Chiefs have no councillors to advise them.[154]

Chief Theko Makhaola's philosophical, and otherwise non-committal, approach to the solution of the problem was more directly tackled by other chiefs, who were less trammelled by blood relations and sentiments to the *Moreno e Moholo* than himself. The most direct of these was Chief Lengolo Monyake of Taung – not from Moshoeshoe's royal lineage – who stated:

> The Chief and the people are equal, if the Chief goes one way and the people go in the opposite direction there must be a collision somewhere. There are some Councillors who seem to think that in order to remain Councillors they must keep on saying the Paramount Chief is good: how long are we going to be hood-winked! Our position is becoming insecure. You want us to play with matters until we are pushed over the precipice . . . You should listen to the cry of the nation: the people are crying to you, Chief of the Basuto, they want you to stand up on your feet to support yourself and the people will stand by you to the end . . . When the people say a certain thing is bad do you think they are playing with matters? The people who say they will protect you will be the first to run away.[155]

So a motion for reforms raised at that Session yielded fruit at last. The motion came from Labane Chokobane of the BPA. Essentially it was a motion to accept J. C. R. Sturrock's Draft Regulations of 1929, with a few changes, mostly in form. The Reforms, promulgated by Sir W. H. Clark as the High Commissioner, on 15 December 1938, came in the form of two proclamations. Proclamation No. 61, the Native Administration Proclamation[156] provided that the High Commissioner, following a consultation with the *Morena e Moholo*, could declare any person to be principal chief, ward chief, chief or headman in the Territory. Section 3 of the Proclamation specifically gave the High Commissioner the powers to revoke or vary the appointments of chiefs. The functions of the chieftaincy were specifically defined and its powers reduced. Chiefs were brought fully under the machinery of the colonial administration and their numbers cut down from about 2500 to 1340. In the District of Maseru, for instance, where, under the jurisdictions of four chiefs –

Sekhonyana, Seeiso, Maama, Khoabane and the *Morena e Moholo* – there were 108 sub-chiefs and 597 headmen in 1928, the colonial administration had proposed a reduction to 27 sub-chiefs and 87 headmen. In Mokhotlong, the smallest District in Lesotho, the total number of chiefs and headmen was reduced from 128 to 74 in 1938.[157] Proclamation No. 62, the Native Courts Proclamation, provided for the 'recognition, constitution, powers and jurisdiction of Native Courts and generally for the administration of justice within' the Territory. Section 2 of the Proclamation specifically gave the Resident Commissioner powers 'to suspend, cancel or vary any warrant recognising or establishing a Native Court or defining the jurisdiction of any such Court or the limits within which such jurisdiction may be exercised'.[158]

In consequence of the proclamation of the Reforms, it became necessary to classify *The Laws of Lerotholi* into three parts. Part 1, being basically the Laws as passed in 1903, including additions and amendments, was called 'Declaration of Basuto Law and Custom'. Part 2 consisted of 'Rules' by the *Morena e Moholo*, for the making of which he was empowered by Proclamation No. 61, Section 8: these rules provided for the peace, good order and welfare of his people; Part 2 also included some aspect of Section 1. Part 3 consisted of the 'Orders' of the *Morena e Moholo*, for which his powers derived from Proclamation No. 61, Section 15.[159]

The Reforms of 1938 had a shattering impact on the structure of the chieftaincy, but especially at the lower end of the hierarchy – on the headmen and sub-chiefs. As most of them were not recognised in their former offices, they lost authority in society; and losing their courts, they lost their primary source of income. The experience was traumatic.

Because the Reforms were introduced in such a sudden fashion and had such a devastating effect, they have attracted a lot of attention from scholars, although none of these scholars have studied their causes as systematically as has been done in this chapter. Having thus not done so, these studies have invariably made the simplistic generalisation that the impetus for the Reforms came from externally, that is from the colonial administration, and that the Reforms were ostensibly the brain-child of Sir Alan Pim. The leading proponent of this interpretation, Richard Frederick Weisfelder states, in his otherwise illuminating study of 'The Roots of Factionalism in

The British colonial administration had accepted and rapidly sought to implement Sir Alan Pim's dubious conclusion that social ills in Basutoland could be remedied solely by major restructuring of chiefly administration and courts . . . Confronted with this sudden determination to impose reform 'from above', the aging Paramount Chief, Griffith, sought to temporize and soften the blow, by giving his consent to the proposed measures only when he had secured concessions delaying their full implementation.[160]

The length of this chapter, and the weight of evidence and quotations in it, have all been in the effort to give a conclusive reappraisal on this debate, and they point to the contrary. The impetus for the Reforms came from within; it came from the educated commoners. The principal chiefs themselves became abundantly aware that they needed some type of reform: they gave in to the Reforms in 1937 not merely because they had been overpowered but because they had come to accept the fact that their own efforts to reform the indigenous government through *The Laws of Lerotholi* had failed. The phrase 'to impose reform from above', in the circumstances, is quite off the mark. Further, evidence shows clearly that by the time of Sir Alan Pim's arrival in 1934–5, agitation for reform had achieved its first climax in 1921. Sir Alan Pim may have given the colonial administration and the *bahlalefi* moral support, but he was not the prime mover.

On the whole, this chapter has attempted to establish the fact that the first four decades of the twentieth century saw the emergence of two major commoners' movements – the Basutoland Progressive Association, comprising the educated élite (the *bahlalefi*) and the *Lekhotla la Bafo* (an assortment of agrarian-based, migrant labour commoners and small businessmen.) The aims and activities of the former were already sufficiently ambitious, and the numbers large enough, to suggest that the chieftaincy had a new type of leadership to contend with. This type of leadership was committed more to parliamentary institutions than it was to executive monarchy. Their wishes to this end would soon coincide with those of colonial administration in the next two decades.

5 The Regency and the Reforms

The Reforms of 1938 went a long way toward paving the way for parliamentary institutions: (a) they cut down the ponderous number of chiefs in the land and streamlined their responsibilities; (b) they restored a fair measure of accountability and justice in the indigenous court system. The general consequences of these results were: (1) the colonial administration assumed a greater degree of control over the chieftaincy and took up the initiative for constitutional advancement; (2) while the *bahlalefi* – the educated élite – emboldened by the political victory over the chiefs, in the form of the Reforms, doubled their efforts to gain more representation in the National Council and to turn it into a Legislative Council. The 1940s and 1950s would thus be characterised by rapid constitutional developments.

There was another factor, however, aside from that of the Reforms, which facilitated the rapid constitutional development. That factor was the problem of succession to the office of *Morena e Moholo* – a problem that will have been seen as a sustained theme up to this juncture, and one which, following Griffith Lerotholi's death, would become critical and would have to be resolved with an appointment of a female Regent.

THE PROBLEM OF SUCCESSION

Polygamy and Succession: Griffith's Puzzle to Select an Heir, and His Abdication of Authority to the Colonial Administration

Morena e Moholo Griffith Lerotholi's marriage arrangements were, as with those of his predecessors, complex and convoluted. It was clear that they might lead to a bitterly contested succession after his death. Hence, for his peace of mind, he attempted in 1926, just when the pressure for reforms escalated, to select an heir and present him to the colonial administration for recognition. His persistence notwithstanding, the colonial administration found itself so befuddled by complications surrounding the selection that after several efforts of attempting to determine the legitimacy of the heir-select and the counter-claimant, it decided, for better or for worse, to await Griffith's death before it could make its final decision.

The facts of Griffith's marriages and the legitimacy of his heirs-presumptive were as follows. Of his 28 wives, the first, Chieftainess 'Ma-Batho, was without a male child. She had allegedly died of grief about 1912 when she discovered that her husband, having then resolved to convert to the Catholic Church, and under pressure from his priests to divorce all his wives except one, could not decide between herself and another woman named 'Ma-Bereng, whom Griffith recognised as his second wife.[1] Although her death had released her husband's heart for 'Ma-Bereng, and his soul for the Catholic Church, it had done nothing to simplify the succession problem. For 'Ma-Bereng's rank, as the then wife number one, was being contested by her own full sister, 'Ma-Seeiso. Both were the daughters of Chief Nkoebe, the Principal Chief of Qacha'a Nek. Both had sons, Bereng and Seeiso, respectively.

Of the two contending Chieftainesses, as a matter of fact, 'Ma-Seeiso had been the first to get married; her *bohali* cattle had duly been exchanged and the concluding custom of *tlhabiso* (the slaughtering of a beast to conclude marriage) had been performed long before 'Ma-Bereng's marriage was mooted. No sooner than 'Ma-Seeiso had been married, however, she herself had deserted Griffith and returned to her own father, Chief Nkoebe. The couple's parents, *Morena e Moholo* Lerotholi and Chief Nkoebe, were obviously unable to get them to reconcile their differences. At the same time, the two were not formally divorced, that is, *bohali* cattle given by *Morena e Moholo* Lerotholi to Chief Nkoebe for 'Ma-Seeiso were not returned. Instead Chief Nkoebe caused two more of his daughters to be sent to Griffith. Of these, Tsebo had her own *bohali* cattle paid, there being no confusion as to the fact that she would take a junior rank as the last in the hierarchy of Griffith's wifes, while 'Ma-Bereng was specifically said to be taking the place of the deserted 'Ma-Seeiso and, accordingly therefore, no *bohali* cattle were given to legitimise her marriage. So far things seemed straight forward: 'Ma-Seeiso remained at her father's place as if she was no longer Griffith's wife. She conceived a daughter named Aa, whilst at her father's place, whom Chief Nkoebe recognised as his own daughter, in keeping with the custom that the child of an unwed woman becomes its own mother's sibling.[2] She was baptised without reference either to Griffith or *Morena e Moholo* Lerotholi, her would-have-been father-in-law; and, contrary to the *hlonepha* custom (whereby it is taboo to call a father-in-law by name), she began to call Lerotholi freely by name – as a symbolic indication of her admission that she no longer considered herself as wife to his son.[3]

Nonetheless the seeming divorce was shortlived. Although it is difficult to establish dates, it would appear that shortly after her father's death in 1903, and not more than three years after 'Ma-Bereng purportedly went to take her place, 'Ma-Seeiso returned to Griffith. It is at this point that marriage and succession were both confounded: quite clearly, 'Ma-Seeiso was aware when she got to Griffith's homestead, then at Phamong (in the District of Mafeteng) that she had lost her original rank. As it was worded in a subsequent judgment of the Royal Court in 1926, 'she found the talk that 'Ma-Bereng was before her', but she did not challenge the 'talk' and she did not seek formal clarification of her rank.[4] She was, as a result, assumed to have accepted a new rank of number three, with Chieftainess 'Ma-Batho as number one and Chieftainess 'Ma-Bereng as number two. By the time of that return, 'Ma-Bereng already had her son, Bereng. Shortly after her own arrival, 'Ma-Seeiso also had her son, Seeiso. The question then arose: who, between Bereng and Seeiso was the heir?

Several times subsequent to 'Ma-Seeiso's return and the birth of her son, Seeiso, *Morena e Moholo* Griffith wished his courtiers to take note of the fact that 'Ma-Bereng was his second wife and therefore her son Bereng was his heir. According to Chief Makhaola, the *Morena e Moholo* had once, about 1917, called to Chief Sekhon-yana Bereng in an apparently small, informal, family gathering, stating: 'I have called you because you are my younger brother Bereng today, and not my son, so that you may be a witness, this child [Bereng] is he who is heir, even though I should die you should witness this statement of mine, no change must be made.' Still living in 1926, Chief Sekhonyana agreed with the evidence.[5] At least by 1917, when some issue (now unknown to us) must have occasioned clarification of Chieftainess 'Ma-Seeiso's rank, she herself had agreed, in the presence of her own brothers, Chiefs Sempe and Tšepo, Chief Makhaola, and *Morena e Moholo* Griffith, her husband, that 'Ma-Bereng had been sent in her place and therefore had assumed her rank, and in this she was supported by her other sister and fellow wife, Tsebo.[6]

Subsequently, however, apparently when her son Seeiso grew anxious about his political future, Chieftainess 'Ma-Seeiso had a change of heart and wished to be recognised in her original position as wife number two. In so doing, as it turned out, circumstances favoured her: the swapping of roles between herself and 'Ma-Bereng could be seen as purely a result of mutual 'understanding' between her father Chief Nkoebe and Griffith's father *Morena e Moholo* Lerotholi. Beyond that it was only tenuously, if at all, supported by Sesotho law and custom.

Anxious about the development, Griffith then decided to settle the question of succession before his death by involving the colonial administration in his decision: without telling Seeiso his purpose and intention, one day, on 15 March 1926, he instructed his courtiers, headed by Chief Leloko Lerotholi, to take both Seeiso and his half-brother Bereng to appear before the Resident Commissioner at the colonial capital at Maseru, whereupon, to Seeiso's surprise, Bereng was presented as Griffith's senior son and heir.[7]

Seeiso challenged the selection and asked the Resident Commissioner to hold Bereng's recognition in abeyance until he had consulted his father. Meantime, he requested a council of his uncles and the sons of Moshoeshoe in general to decide the question of seniority between himself and his brother Bereng. Following much bickering within the royal family, in the course of which Seeiso was sent to the Resident Commissioner for a second time with the same purpose and result, the sons of Moshoeshoe sat on 12 November 1926 as a Court of Princes.

Chief Makhaola was the President of the Court, and Chief Sekhonyana was his 'right hand'. Both Chiefs had been involved in all the previous stages of the question and they stood by their previous understanding that Bereng was the heir. As Chief Makhola stated, 'I was bound to go by this same judgment. . . . For this reason I have no two tongues.'[8] Chief Sekhonyana, who was instructed by the President to pronounce the judgment, told the claimant Seeiso that 'the Court has found for itself good strong evidence' that his mother's original rank had duly been forfeited and therefore his father's decision 'is reasonable and the Court confirms this explanation of your father that Bereng is your Senior'.[9]

Seventy chiefs and courtiers were in attendance. The majority of those who cared to be counted were supportive of Griffith's decision, although it was noted that a significant number preferred to abstain from the final decision. The vote was 23 in support of Bereng and ten in support of Seeiso. Of those who stood to be counted, Bereng's supporters included one of Chief Jonathan's senior sons, Chief Motsarapane Jonathan, and Chief Mosiuoa 'Mota in the North; Chief

Masopha L. Masopha in the District of Berea; Goliath Mahale in Mafeteng in the South; and Councillor Josiaa Mopeli and Chief Leloko Lerotholi in Matsieng: these were all highly influential men in the royal family. Having them on his side, the *Morena e Moholo* must have felt convinced that the case was closed. It was not to be so, however. Seeiso appealed the decision to the colonial administration. While stating, as in the words of the Imperial Secretary, B. E. H. Clifford, that 'as far as the Government is concerned there is little to choose between Seeiso and Bereng',[10] the colonial administration was not convinced that the decision had been decisive. It was worried by the abstentions of certain of the principal chiefs at the Matsieng Court of Princes. Following exchanges of letters and a caucus of officers up through September 1927, B. E. H. Clifford summarised the view of the colonial administration that 'the Chiefs who actually voted in favour of Bereng were, for the most part, personal adherents of Griffith'. Further, Clifford was informed that 'in Leribe and the North there is overwhelming opinion in favour of Seeiso and that even in the South the majority favour him as the next heir'.[11] Otherwise, the Legal Adviser, Patrick Duncan, had given the opinion on 30 December 1926 that if it was in keeping with Sesotho custom that the heir should be selected in his father's lifetime, it would be judicious not to frustrate Griffith in his wish to settle the matter. That way, impending trouble after his death might be averted.[12]

When B. E. H. Clifford perused the High Commission's records, he confirmed that it had virtually become the practice in Southern Africa for African monarchs under British colonial administrations to present their successor to the High Commissioner for recognition in their lifetime. In that number were the Motswana monarch Khama, who had introduced his son Sekhoma to the High Commissioner as his successor. Sekhoma in turn had presented his brother Tshekedi as Prospective Regent during the minority of his infant son Seretse. The Lozi *Lethunga* Lewanika had followed the same procedure in regard to the reigning *Lethunga* Yeta.

The procedure was therefore approved for Lesotho which, strictly speaking, had not followed it. As Clifford was informed, 'the sons of the Paramount Chief were referred to as the "Children of the Grave" because the successor to the Paramountcy was usually selected at the grave of the Paramount Chief by the "Sons of Moshoeshoe" assembled there so as to avoid disputes and conspiracies during the lifetime of the Paramount Chief'.[13]

The method that the colonial administration chose as the best to get a decisive selection from the Sons of Moshoeshoe was a secret ballot. Additionally it stipulated that the *Morena e Moholo* should draw up a list of the Sons of Moshoeshoe entitled to vote on the matter, and that the list should be approved by the National Council.[14] The Resident Commissioner wished the *Morena e Moholo* to be cognisant of the fact that, while 'the question is primarily a matter to be decided by Basutho themselves, presumably in accordance with Law 1' of *The Laws of Lerotholi*, Seeiso's appeal would have to be satisfied, by the colonial administration if necessary, 'and then we shall be able to have that peace and quiet in the nation which you have told me you desire and which is equally desired by me'.[15]

Griffith was embittered by this allusion. First he did not understand how Seeiso could possibly be given an appeal on the matter, especially as 'Seeiso himself states that he asked for the House of Moshesh', the highest body with jurisdiction on his complaint, 'to whom he also stated that he trusted that from them he would get justice', and justice had been given to him. 'I wish to know', he asked, 'whether the good Government of His Majesty can grant an appeal in this case which was decided by all the Basuto, by all the Courts of the House of Moshesh. Under what customs or laws would those to whom it would go judge it?' Second he wished to be allowed to see the High Commissioner on the matter.[16]

Griffith had wished, when and if the request were granted, to see the High Commissioner in the company of his rival uncle, Chief Jonathan, whose knowledge on Sesotho custom and law was then presumed to be unrivalled; but the old man found the entire idea of going to see a white 'Chief' on matters of Sesotho custom and law absurd. As he told the Assistant Commissioner of Leribe, who had been instructed to relay the message to him.

> Chief, my reply is that I am not going and I am not sending a representative on the following grounds:- This is not matter for the High Commissioner. We have our own ways and customs which we fully understand and which His Excellency the High Commissioner does not know and understand. . . . We, the Basuto, do not elect whom we like for the Chief; the Chieftainship belongs to the first-born son whose mother was married by the parents of his father after consultation . . . is it not a fact that the mother of the boy who is in the mountain [Seeiso] is the one who is married by Lerotholi before any other wife of Griffith?[17]

Although he had not succeeded in enlisting Jonathan in his company,

Griffith did go ahead with his audience with the High Commissioner. He was accompanied by other chiefs and courtiers, including, of course, his principal supporters – Makhaola, Sekhonyana and Masopha L. Masopha. At the audience, held on 24 November 1927, with the Resident Commissioner, J. C. R. Sturrock, and the Imperial Secretary, B. E. H. Clifford, Griffith essentially registered his protest that the colonial administration should not intrude in the selection of his heir, as 'this matter is one of national custom of birthright'.

The High Commissioner, on his part, acknowledged the principle that 'The nomination and appointment of the Paramount Chief is entirely a State matter': it should not be settled in the law courts. Nevertheless he was not satisfied that the Sons of Moshoeshoe had decided 'beyond doubt in favour of Bereng'. He insisted on a secret ballot. Griffith observed that 'the ballot was not a Basuto custom'. The High Commissioner rebutted that, while it was not the custom of Basotho to seek the approval of the Secretary of State before the appointment of their monarch, 'nevertheless his approval had to be obtained'. The audience ended with the High Commissioner tossing the ball in Griffith's court with the words:

> If you accept this advice [of the secret ballot] the Government will formally approve the heir selected when you present him to the Resident Commissioner. But if you do not wish to hold such a ballot I can do no more than note of your own opinion that Bereng is your rightful heir. If no ballot is held I fear the Government would not at the present moment be able formally to recognise Bereng as your successor.[18]

At that point the colonial administration had become partial to one claimant to the throne, namely Seeiso. Significantly the High Commissioner's written brief for his audience with the *Morena e Moholo* clearly stated: 'Of the two sons it would appear that Seeiso has more character and would be likely to make the better ruler.'[19]

The *Morena e Moholo* probably sensed that feeling when he was interviewed; or perhaps he was merely aware that Seeiso was more popular than Bereng (or had become popular as a result of his contest for succession). Perhaps both considerations weighed heavily on his mind, and he dreaded losing both the case as well as his integrity by pushing the question of succession further. He dropped the entire affair and left it to be dealt with after his death. The total effect of his initial effort, however, was that: (a) he had made himself extremely vulnerable to the colonial administration – he was almost like a political hostage; (b) he had, for all intents and purposes, surrendered the prerogative of the Sons of Moshoeshoe to select the heir to the colonial administration.

The Colonial Administration Takes Full Management of the Procedure for Selecting the Heir: Seeiso Is Made the *Morena e Moholo* of Basotho

Griffith died in 1939, a year after the Reforms that overhauled his government, leaving the question of his succession unresolved. The colonial administration seized the opportunity created by circumstances to set the machinery of selecting his heir in motion. The Resident Commissioner convened a meeting of the Sons of Moshoeshoe in the Chamber of the National Council on 3 August that year to discuss the succession. Bereng and Seeiso were present.

The Sons of Moshoeshoe this time stayed clear of the technicalities of the alleged swapping of ranks by the chieftainesses. They also stayed clear of an allegation of illegitimacy, with which the late *Morena e Moholo* had belatedly saddled Seeiso. They stuck strictly to the Sesotho interpretation that offspring derive their legitimacy from the validity of their mother's marriage: *Ngoana ke oa likhomo* (a child belongs to the *bohali* cattle). They followed closely the principle of succession embodied in Law 1 of *The Laws of Lerotholi* (Part 1[20]). The decision was in favour of Seeiso. For one who had fought so hard for the high office and who in the end enjoyed such popularity, it is sad that *Morena e Moholo* Seeiso Griffith was fated to live but a few months. He died on 26 December 1940.

Not much had happened during that brief period, and hence he had left little for posterity to judge him by. One dramatic episode, however, is worth mentioning. Thrown into ecstasy by a gift from the Imperial Government of the King's Medal for African Chiefs, on 19 October 1940, at the 35th Session of the National Council, he had reacted with extraordinary compassion to the war cause: he prevailed over the National Council to donate £100 000, from a surplus of £223 000, to the British Government. The Council later proposed that the money be used to buy aeroplanes.[21]

Seeiso Griffith was heavily indebted to the colonial administration for his claim to the high office and this episode may serve to illustrate that sense of indebtedness. At the same time the measure of support that he had received from the nation at large, his striking personality, and the sense of duty to preserve the vigour of his office might have made him a powerful *Morena e Moholo*, under whom tendencies toward constitutional monarchy might have been stayed; but then there is not much that can be built on this type of speculation.

The Regency that Was Determined by a European Court:
Chieftainess *'Mantšebo* Comes to Power and the House of Letsie
II Is Emasculated

With *Morena e Moholo* Seeiso Griffith's death, the semblance of cohesion in the chieftaincy that had precariously been maintained from the times of Letsie II just about ended. No chief through the full breadth of the country would be available to serve as a rallying point. The powerful chief of Leribe, Chief Jonathan, who might have seized the opportunity, and in the absence of a male head in Matsieng wielded power creditably, had died in 1929. His successor, Chief Motsoene Josefa Molapo Moshoeshoe, Senate Letsie's son, had succeeded to office amidst a dispute, involving two other claimants.[22] At the end of the succession trials he was enervated and suspicious of intrigues. He was mentally imbalanced. He was no model for leadership.

Seeiso's eldest son and heir, *Khosana* Constantine Bereng Seeiso, by his second wife, was only four years of age. The uncle with the most immediate claim to the Regency was none other than Chief Bereng Griffith, who had disputed the high office with Seeiso since 1926 and, despite his own father's wishes, lost out in the contest. Bereng Griffith was understandably a bitter man. Understandably, also, both the royal house of Lesotho as well as the colonial administration were apprehensive that if he was made Regent, the coincidence of the sudden death of Letsie II's infant son Tau in 1913, while Griffith's Regency was being discussed, might be repeated. To use the words of Lord Harlech, the South African High Commissioner at the time, it was feared that Chief Bereng might resort to 'The Princes in the Tower methods of removing the two obstacles between him and the substantive Paramountcy.'[23] To use a contemporary Sesotho metaphor: 'A cat cannot nurse the children of a mouse.' In the circumstances, a decision was made to select a woman as Regent.

Shortly before Seeiso's death, when he was already critically ill, he had instructed his principal counsellor, Chief Gabashane Masopha (a great-grandson of Masopha, the third son of Moshoeshoe by his great wife), to be the Acting *Morena e Moholo* until he was well enough to resume his duties. In the event of his death at the hospital in Maseru, Chief Gabashane summoned a council of 'the Sons of Letsie' – some two hundred in number[24] – to convene in Maseru to consider the question of the Regency during the minority of the heir. Discord arising from the venue, the method used to convene the meeting, and the list of the principal chiefs invited to attend, wrecked the meeting in progress. The next meeting would be held at Matsieng on 31 December 1940.

Meantime Chief Gabashane, who was not one of the 'Sons of Letsie', had already taken full custody of the deceased's estate and had begun freely to slaughter his cattle and to enjoy the free use of his two motor cars. Chief Bereng Griffith, the deceased's brother and claimant to the Regency objected, not only to this apparent misuse of the estate, but also, and principally, to Gabashane's authority to convene the family council. Presumably, as it was revealed, had he had his way, Bereng Griffith would have convened a meeting of only 'the Sons of Lerotholi' who, according to him, numbered 'ten or more in number', but according to his uncle Chief Theko Makhaola were only six. The Sons of Lerotholi were well disposed to him and they might easily have appointed him as the rightful Regent and Acting *Morena e Moholo*.[25]

The meeting of 31 December in Matsieng also ended in disarray and almost degenerated to open violence. It was sharply divided between two candidates: one was Chief Bereng Griffith; the other was Chieftainess 'Matsaba, officially known as *'Mantšebo*, the late Seeiso's first wife, who had not been blessed with a male child. Matters of logistics were once more in the fore: principal chiefs could not agree on which body had the right to make a selection, 'the Sons of Letsie', or the umbrella body – 'the Sons of Moshoeshoe'. Having failed to resolve the impasse, the leaders of both candidates, accompanied by their followers, decided to return to the colonial capital Maseru, this time to present their respective cases to the colonial authorities.

Having initially listened to their case the Government Secretary, on the instruction of the Resident Commissioner, set the date of 28 January 1941 for both parties to meet under the umbrella body – the Sons of Moshoeshoe. Meantime he authorised Chief Gabashane to continue as the Acting *Morena e Moholo*.

On 10 January Chief Bereng Griffith submitted a petition to the High Commissioner through his lawyers setting forth his conditions. He requested that Chief Gabashane be set aside while the question of the Regency is being resolved and he himself appointed in his place; and he urged that the selection be left in the hands of the Sons of Letsie. In his personal letter of 16 January to the District Commissioner of Mohale's Hoek (his jurisdiction), which referred to the proposed meeting of the Sons of Moshoeshoe, he wrote:

> I humbly request you please to change this your intention and according to precedents and customs of the Basuto will you kindly leave these affairs in my hands as the successor and the present head of the Sons of Letsie to arrange the matters with them after which we shall have arranged what is to be done, call all the Sons of Moshoeshoe and the nation and present before you our arrangement for the inheritance of the Basutoland Paramountcy. Chief, I make this request because I notice that to-day procedure is very much against Laws, customs and our precedents.[26]

Chief Bereng Griffith's protest notwithstanding, the meeting of the Sons of Moshoeshoe went ahead on 28 January, with the Government Secretary Mr How chairing the meeting. 44 chiefs spoke in favour of Chieftainess *'Mantšebo*, as against 23 in favour of Chief Bereng. With the exception of Chief Theko Makhaola, who had supported Bereng Griffith since 1926, all the principal chiefs had supported the Chieftainess. *'Mantšebo*'s selection was formally approved by the then Secretary of State for the Colonies, Lord Moyne, on 10 May 1941.[27]

Late in 1941 Chief Bereng threatened through his lawyer to appeal the case to the courts. As his claim would not have been justifiable in the 'European courts' (courts of general jurisdiction), however, he set about to commit a legally actionable offence to attain his objective: in an act of provocation to *Mofumahali* (Queen) *'Mantšebo* and a challenge to her authority, he imposed a financial levy in his own ward on the grounds that he needed the money to appeal the case to the High Commissioner. (In this move, significantly, he was supported by Josiel Lefela's *Lekhotla la Bafo*.) *Mofumahali 'Mantšebo* had his instructions quashed. He disobeyed her. She had him fined, and the fine was upheld by the Court of the District Commissioner in Maseru. Chief Bereng then decided to appeal to 'European Courts', using the fine as a cause.[28] The Resident Commissioner's Court had recently, through Proclamation 57 of 1938, been substituted, and it was now called the High Court of Basutoland.[29] The case of *Chief Bereng Griffith (v) 'Mantšebo Seeiso*, famously known as the Regency Case, came before this Court in

October 1942, under Mr Justice Lansdown, from the Union of South Africa. It was a *cause célèbre*.

The Regency Case was significant in three major respects, the first two of which embodied Chief Bereng's primary claims. First Chief Bereng claimed that under Sesotho law and custom a woman has no *locus standi in judicio*: she cannot function as a chief, and even if styled chieftainess, law and custom force her to rely on her husband or male guardian. Second he claimed that as his late brother's wife, *Mofumahali 'Mantŝebo* was his wife by the levirate custom, whereby he was entitled to raise seed for the deceased. Alternatively, in the event that she held no affection for him, she was at least his ward. As such – that is, as she was either his wife or ward – the Regency devolved on him and not on her. The third issue of significance was that it was a test case of the validity to *The Laws of Lerotholi*, Law 1 of which made specific mention of succession through a male heir and did not envisage a female ruler.

In tackling Chief Bereng's contention that a woman cannot function as a chief, Mr Justice Lansdown had a fairly easy task to perform. He was able on the strength of evidence given by key witnesses, to establish that a number of chieftainesses in the land held their late husband's chieftaincies in their own right. Nonetheless to apply the rule to the case at hand could not satisfactorily be done without resorting to statutory law: while mindful of the fact that in so far as the office of *Morena e Moholo* was concerned, there was no precedent for a woman ruler, he argued, basing himself on Proclamation No. 61 of 1938 (as amended by Proclamation No. 35 of 1941), as well as on the General Interpretation Proclamation No. 12 of 1942, that 'the Acting Paramount Chief who may be recognised as such by the High Commissioner, need not have any precedent claim or qualification as such'; and, as such, his interpretation 'puts an end to the plaintiff's contentions as to the legal qualifications of the defendant to hold her present office'.[30] So that, without prejudice to Chief Bereng's claim that *Mofumahali 'Mantŝebo* was his wife or ward, by statutory law the High Commissioner chose whom he pleased to be Regent.

In order not to raise the issue of the conflict of legal systems by implication and then leave it unresolved, Mr Justice Lansdown then addressed himself to the question of the legal status of *The Laws of Lerotholi*, which he styled 'the Lerotholi Code'. He stated:

No legislative authority or official recognition has been extended to this code; nevertheless it is helpful, though not conclusive, on any question as to the existence or extent of any customary practice amongst the Basuto people . . . [it] is in no sense written law. Its provisions though reduced to print, do not emanate from any lawgiver.[31]

Thus the High Court decision formally supported the several confidentially-expressed views within the colonial administration, dating from 1903, that although the indigenous government of Lesotho was allowed to view itself as making laws, and notwithstanding the fact that those laws applied in the indigenous courts, they were not recognised as part of the general law. Of additional significance, the decision underscored the dilemma of the colonial administration that the application of indirect rule in Lesotho had led to an unforeseen political mutation: it had informally led to parallel government.

Mr Justice Lansdown's judgment was therefore received with jubilation in some quarters of the colonial administration. It seemed to have brought under control a situation that had gone out of hand. As Lord Harlech, the High Commissioner, observed:

Judge Lansdown's judgment in the Bereng case . . . strikes me as a masterly document of far-reaching importance in relation to the political and social evolution of Basutoland and Chiefdom questions in Africa generally. . . . The main conclusion I draw is that while we may have to take ancient native law and custom into 'consideration' we must never admit that we are bound by it hand and foot, and that native law and custom must evolve and alter under the impact of civilizing influences and our rule. If Lansdown's judgment is upset by the Privy Council on appeal there will be the devil to pay.[32]

Fortunately for Lord Harlech the case did not reach the Privy Council. Chief Bereng lost heart and dropped it.

THE *LAWS OF LEROTHOLI* AND THE CONSTITUTIONAL STATUS OF THE NATIONAL COUNCIL ARE REVISITED

The National Council's Reaction to Lansdown's Judgment

As it might have been expected, Mr Justice Lansdown's ruling on the legal status of *The Laws of Lerotholi* came as a rude shock to the National Council. The National Council was left to conclude that once Lesotho became a British dependency in 1868, at which time the Basotho believed that their country was merely being given protection, Sesotho customary law had ceased to be law. Further, the National Council was left in a daze as to what function it was deemed to have exercised when it reduced the Laws to writing, as well as when it made amendments and additions to them. In the final analysis it was left in a state of confusion regarding the applicability of those Laws in both the indigenous as well as the 'European courts'.

In November 1943 when the National Council met at its 37th Session, councillors were quick to show their discomfort regarding the outcome of the judgment on the legal status of customary law. From the general discussion on the subject, two proposals followed. One of these, by Councillor Thabo Lechesa, was from the chieftaincy of Matsieng, the immediate jurisdiction of *Mofumahali 'Mantšebo*. Councillor Thabo Lechesa reported that at their *pitso* held in preparation for the National Council, the people of Matsieng had charged him with the responsibility of expressing their wish that *Matalenyane* – that is, 'The Little Green Book' of *The Laws of Lerotholi* – should be recognised, and if need be, its recognition should be done in the same manner as *Khubelu* – meaning 'The Red Book' of the Reforms of 1938.

He stated:

They say as they understand that this book of theirs (Laws of Lerotholi) is not protected and they fear that anybody may alter it at any time, they request that it be protected by being included in a Proclamation signed by the High Commissioner like all other new laws which have been issued for their guidance. They make this request in view of the decision recently given by Mr. Justice Lansdown in which he states . . . that this is a mere code of Lerotholi and not law.[33]

The other councillor who had brought a specific proposal from his chieftaincy was Chief Goliath Malebanye, from the District of Mafeteng. Goliath Malebanye was basically supportive of the Matsieng proposal. In the main, however, his speech was aimed at accusing the colonial administration of having made a nonsense of the legal system of Lesotho. He intoned:

We have nowhere to turn: When we are in Basuto courts we are tried under the little Green Book, and if you win the case and the other party appeals the case goes to European Courts. When you get to European courts you are tried under Proclamations. We have nowhere to escape. . . . But *since we were not consulted* about this Red Book (Proclamations) as a Council to advise our Chief we ask you to guide us. We request you to confirm this little Green Book, chief. You have agreed that this book should be used. You should uphold it so that the laws in it may not be looked upon merely as advice but as laws. . . . Lead us to the winning post, Your Honour. [My italic][34]

The strange remark that 'we were not consulted' about the Proclamation of 1938 was a separate but equally contentious subject that had been before the National Council since 1939. It will be examined independently later in the chapter.

The discussions of the 37th Session were inconclusive. However, as there were several other critical issues, mostly relating to major constitutional changes in the structure of the National Council, a standing committee composed of five outstanding chiefs was established for the purpose of working out composite proposals, hopefully to be realistically drafted, for the consideration of the Council. Most of these would be tabled at the same Session. Of the remaining ones, which were tabled at the 38th Session in 1944 was one on *The Laws of Lerotholi.*

As a last, and apparently desperate move to get *The Laws of Lerotholi* to be recognised, the Standing Committee tabled a proposal at that Session changing the title of Part 1 of the 'Laws'. The title, given in accordance with the Native Administration Proclamation No. 61 of 1938, was 'Basuto Law and Custom'. The Standing Committee proposed the change to 'Basuto Law'. Chief Khosimotse Ntaote, a member of the Standing Committee, said: 'We have altered that to read "Natural Laws of the Basuto" because these do not include custom.' Chief Moiphepi Letsie, one of the majority who supported the proposal gave his reason as 'because customs cannot bind anybody . . . I suggest "melao" (laws) to be put in and not "meetlo" (customs) . . . we have so many rites and customs'.[35] When a member of the Progressive Association, the writer Zakea Mangoaela, demanded to know the need for the change, Chief Gabashane Masopha, the late Seeiso Griffith's principal counsellor and also a member of the Standing Committee, replied:

I think the speaker will remember we had one big case here in

Basutoland in which the Judge referred to the Laws of Lerotholi as a code of customs. I do not think there can be a nation which has no laws but only customs. The Judge spoke about this code of laws as if it is a thing which cannot have effect in European Courts. Therefore the Committee has found it fit, in the name of the Council, to have these declared laws, and we have made this draft which we submit to the Council and ask the Council to accept.[36]

Chief Khosimotse Ntaote, in his characteristic clarity of mind, underscored Goliath Malebanye's statement in the form of an intriguing query, which went to the core of the puzzle about the Laws.

Before Chief Moshesh asked for protection from Queen Victoria he had laws with which he governed his country, but now we have no laws because I understand that Basuto law can only become law if it is published by the High Commissioner. . . . My view is that before Moshesh was taken under the protection of the Queen he had laws, and I do not know when these laws were repealed.[37]

Chief Ntaote's query, it appears, was not based on the ignorance of what happens when one country, such as his own, loses its independence to another, such as Britain: that is, that when it loses its sovereignty its laws are set aside, or else require recognition from the new, foreign ruler. Rather it seemed to stem from his understanding, generally held by the Basotho, that the original pact between Lesotho's founding father Moshoeshoe, and Queen Victoria, was one of alliance, whereby Lesotho had only become a junior partner to Britain. In short that Lesotho had not lost its independence. There were two governments in the Territory, the one headed by the Resident Commissioner, the other headed by the *Morena e Moholo*. The Resident Commissioner and the *Morena e Moholo* were depicted as 'the two oxen under the same yoke'.

The Colonial Administration Is Confounded by the Problem

As it turned out, when Lord Harlech, the then High Commissioner, stated in April 1943 that Mr Justice Lansdown's judgment was a 'masterly document of far-reaching importance' and that 'we must never admit that we are bound by [customary law] hand and foot', he had gloated too soon. When his staff of officers attempted to reconcile the judgment with the National Council's general view that

The Laws of Lerotholi should be protected with the High Commissioner's Proclamation, it discovered that the task was not as simple as it had seemed on the surface.

The then Resident Commissioner, Lieutenant-Colonel C. N. Arden-Clarke, initially advised the High Commissioner on 1 December 1943 that it was 'essential' that there should be some reasonably authoritative compilation of native law and custom and of the many rules and orders issued by the Paramount Chief to act as a guide to the Native Courts. He found it 'essential', equally, to provide some means 'to enable amendments to native customary law to be raised and discussed and, once agreed upon, to be made known and become effective in the Courts'. Finally the Resident Commissioner felt that, subject to the opinion of the High Commissioner's Legal Adviser, the National Council's concern that customary law be 'protected', could be achieved by having the expanded *Laws of Lerotholi* issued by the *Mofumahali* under the authority granted to her office by Sections 8 and 15 of the Native Administration Proclamation No. 61 of 1938, that is, the authority to issue 'orders' and 'rules'.[38]

The High Commissioner's Office sought and received two legal opinions on the question, one from Sir Walter Huggard, the Legal Adviser, and the other from Major E. R. Roper, the Attorney-General for South Africa. Sir Walter was significantly uncomfortable with the National Council's Resolution that when approved by itself, *The Laws of Lerotholi* should be 'printed and recognised as an authoritative statement of Sesotho law and custom in all the Courts of Basutoland'. This appeared, particularly when read in conjunction with Arden-Clarke's letter of December, to mean that 'these so-called "laws", when approved, would form part of the general laws of the Territory and thus be binding on the Courts'. If that was the ultimate intention of the colonial administration, he thought that that 'proposal is open to serious objection, as it would have the effect of placing these "laws" in the same category as legislation promulgated by the High Commissioner'. He saw no objection to publishing the revised version of *The Laws of Lerotholi*, yet he did not think that the Laws should 'be given anything in the nature of "legislative sanction" ', as it appeared to have been suggested. He was in favour, in the final analysis, of adhering to the non-committal position adopted by the colonial administration in 1922.[39]

In 1922, it may be recalled, the Legal Adviser, Mr Feetman, had given the colonial administration the opinion that:

[T]he National Council has tended to assume the functions of a legislature in making from time to time additions and amendments to these native laws. This informal expansion of the Council may serve a very useful purpose in securing the gradual revision and development of native law and custom, so that it may be adapted from time to time to the changing needs of the Territory[40]

The result of Mr Feetman's opinion then had been that the High Commissioner had given his permission for the amplified Laws to be printed and circulated, yet with the following cautionary remark:

[B]ut my permission to print and circulate these Laws of Lerotholi must not be taken as implying approval of provisions which conflict with the general laws of the Territory made under the authority of His Majesty the King, or which might be construed as interfering with or encroaching on the High Commissioner's Authority or the Authority of the Resident Commissioner or the other officers of the Government.[41]

In short, the status of the Laws had been left vague: first they were not to be seen as the High Commissioner's piece of legislation: second the National Council was allowed to think, if it was disposed, that its work had the force of law; third nonetheless the Council was still to understand that it was only an advisory body – it had no legislative powers.

Major E. A. Roper, the Attorney-General, prefaced his own opinion with a lucid and, in hindsight, instructive statement on the peculiarity of the legal system currently obtaining in the Territory. Having held discussions with the witnesses in the Regency Case and otherwise quite conversant with the judicial problems of the Territory, he was in no doubt whatsoever that Basotho chiefs, headmen and counsellors, who were in charge of the indigenous courts, considered *The Laws of Lerotholi* as having the force of law. 'Whatever their theoretical status may be', he stated, 'in practice they are treated by the members of the Native Courts as binding upon those Courts'. Further, he pointed out, when a case involving Basotho litigants was taken on appeal to a subordinate court (it being a European Court) the District Commissioner generally sat with a Mosotho assessor (under Section 30 of Proclamation No. 62 of 1938). More often than not the District Commissioner himself had 'a somewhat sketchy knowledge' of Sesotho law and custom, 'and is dependent upon the native assessor for information as to what the law is upon any point involved'. The assessor, who regarded *The Laws of Lerotholi* as 'authoritative', advised the District Commissioner accordingly. 'The result is that the Laws of Lerotholi are not merely in effect binding upon the native courts, but are followed in the Subordinate Courts as well, in so far as the latter administer native law.' The position in the High Court was not dissimilar. There too, a judge was necessarily dependent for his knowledge of Sesotho law and custom on a Mosotho assessor, 'who in turn regards the Laws of Lerotholi as having the force of law'.[42]

Major Roper's considered opinion in the circumstances, therefore, was that, first *The Laws of Lerotholi* should be accepted as having the force of law in all the courts in the land. Second that, in passing amendments and making additions to them, the National Council ought to be deemed as exercising a legislative function. To put it in his own words:

> Any additions to, or amendments of, the Laws of Lerotholi which may be made in future will, in my opinion, inevitably be regarded in the same way as the existing edition of those laws. It would be well therefore to realise that whatever reservations the Government may make as to the extent of its recognition of amendments which may be adopted in the future by the Basuto National Council, as soon as those amendments became generally known (whether by printing or otherwise) to the members of the Native Courts, they will in practice have the force of law in those Courts. This again will mean that the European Courts when administering Native law must recognise them, because otherwise there will be two conflicting bodies of native law administered respectively by the Native Courts an the European Courts – an obviously impossible situation. . . . *All this means that in effect, and notwithstanding any reservations by the Government, if the Basuto National Council devotes itself to considering and passing amendments and additions to the Laws of Lerotholi, or amendments of Native Custom generally, it wil be exercising legislative powers.* [My emphasis]

Major Roper offered two suggestions for rendering the current situation more satisfactory, in the event that his opinion were accepted. First he suggested that the National Council should be given expert guidance in the formulation and drafting of its recommendations, and that its results should be controlled by adopting the rule that no resolution should have the force of law 'unless approved by the Government'. By the phrase, 'unless approved', Major Roper seemed clearly not to be suggesting that the Council's resolutions should be promulgated by the High Commissioner. Rather he seemed merely to be suggesting that there should be a mechanism for influencing the results. He reasoned (in Sir Henry Sumner Maine's familiar view) that the Basotho were at that juncture 'in a stage of transition from a primitive state of society, where rights are mainly regulated by status, to a more civilised and complex state, where rights will be increasingly governed by contract'. He thought that it was important that amendments and additions to Sesotho Law 'should not be dealt with at haphazard [sic] and without consideration of their possible effect upon the body of native law, as a whole, and possibilities of its future development' – along the lines favoured by the colonial administration.

Following upon the first, his second suggestion was that there was a need in Lesotho for 'some written statement of the principles of the whole body of Basuto law', such as Professor I. Schapera had recently undertaken with regard to *Tswana Law and Custom* (1938). He, in fact, specifically recommended that Professor Schapera should be induced to come to Lesotho to undertake the study.

The Resident Commissioner agreed with Major Roper's description of the peculiar status of *The Laws of Lerotholi* in the legal system of Lesotho. Beyond that, however, he found both Huggard's and Roper's opinions 'somewhat conflicting and confusing'; and, having made the observation, he went on to reveal his own confusion. As he understood it, in so far as Proclamation No. 61 of 1938 had empowered the office of *Morena e Moholo* to make 'rules' and to issue 'orders', it had thereby conferred legislative functions on that office. On the basis of that understanding he stated his own views on the legal status of *The Laws of Lerotholi* as follows:

The so-called 'Laws of Lerotholi' appear to me to be no more than orders and rules issued by the Paramount Chief. The Basutoland Council or its Standing Committee advises the Paramount Chief regarding the issue or amendment of orders and rules. I have never been very clear in my mind as to when an edict or a Native Authority should be an order or when it should be a rule, but it is obviously desirable that in every case the prior approval of Government should be obtained to ensure that the edict complies with the proviso in the law that it does not conflict with any proclamation or other law for the time being in force and to make sure that the Resident Commissioner or High Commissioner, as the case may be, will not exercise his powers of revocation.[43]

Just as he had never been clear as to the distinction between an 'order' and a 'rule', in terms of Proclamation No. 61 of 1938, the Resident Commissioner confessed that he was at a loss as to how the new and amplified 1943 edition of *The Laws of Lerotholi* was to be categorised: was it to be regarded as 'orders and rules' issued by the *Mofumahali*? If so, he thought, then it required the approval of the High Commissioner in terms of Section 15 of Proclamation No. 61 of 1938. If it did not fall under orders and rules in that sense, he thought, then perhaps Major Roper's proposal of adopting the vague formula followed in 1922 was unavoidable. The end result of the latter course of action, as Major Roper had pointed out, would be that, regardless of whether or not the colonial administration was willing to recognise the edition, it would 'in practice have the force of law' throughout the Territory's court system.

The Resident Commissioner was in agreement with Major Roper that there was a need for a written statement of the principles of the whole body of Sesotho law similar to Professor Schapera's *Tswana Law and Custom*. He thought that such an undertaking would be valuable and helpful and he had no objection in principle to the proposal that Professor Schapera could be invited for the task. He feared, however, that currently the *Mofumahali* and her chiefs, 'many of whom are already suspicious and hostile to the reforms we are undertaking', would get agitated: 'I think it would be more politic to leave the Standing Committee to do the work of compiling and revising the customary laws of the Basuto to the best of its ability under the guidance of the Judicial Commissioner, as the Council has proposed, even though better results could be achieved with the aid of a trained anthropologist.'

Sir Walter Huggard in the end had the last word. Having previously consulted with the Attorney-General, Major E. R. Roper, and having enlisted his support, on 29 January 1944 he submitted the following views to the High Commissioner's Office. First, while agreeing with the Attorney-General's original view that *The Laws of Lerotholi* were recognised and normally followed, in cases where they might be relevant, in the Subordinate Courts of District Commissioners as well as in the High Court, he would not go as far as to suggest that therefore the Laws were binding on those Courts. Rather he suggested that those Courts normally accepted *The Laws of Lerotholi* as correctly representing the native law or custom on a particular issue, and *not* because those Laws are in any way binding on the Courts.

Secondly he did not agree with the Resident Commissioner's view that Proclamation No. 61 of 1938 had conferred legislative powers on the office of *Morena e Moholo*. His interpretation was that the relevant Sections – 8 and 15 – of the Proclamation had only given 'certain limited powers to issue orders and make rules, but those orders and rules are not "legislation" in its ordinarily accepted meaning'. They were orders and rules 'of an administrative or executive nature', and they were 'of limited and not of general application'. In the final analysis they could be questioned in courts 'as to whether or not they are *intra vires*'. Consequently he did not think, as suggested by the Resident Commissioner, that the position in regard to *The Laws of Lerotholi* had been in any way altered by the enactment of Proclamation No. 61 of 1938.

Thirdly Sir Walter did not think that the revised edition of *The Laws of Lerotholi* could appropriately be issued as 'orders' and 'rules'. (Nor did he, for the benefit of the Resident Commissioner, attempt to draw the distinction between the two terms.) His view in this regard was that if the Laws were issued as 'orders' and 'rules' under Proclamation No. 61 of 1938, they would become the High Commissioner's legislation; and in that case, logically, it would be a misnomer to continue to call them *The Laws of Lerotholi*. On the other hand, if, as he believed, the desire was to produce a revised version of *The Laws of Lerotholi*, under that title, as a compilation of Sesotho law and custom, 'then I again suggest that they should be "for the guidance of the Native Courts" '. If the revised edition were issued in that manner, he pointed out, 'it will not form part of the statutory law of the country and will not be formally binding upon the European courts, which will consequently have the power, as they have at present, of declaring that any particular law does not correctly set out Basutho law and custom, or is not in harmony with the principles thereof, or that it is *ultra vires*.'[44]

The Final Outcome on The *Laws of Lerotholi*

Sir Walter Huggard's last opinion was the one in the end that was followed. By accepting that opinion, however, the far-reaching plan of action devised by the National Council was frustrated. The opportunity to resolve, or at least minimise, the conflict of legal systems, which was to continue to bedevil judges in the Territory, was lost. Of the resolutions that the Standing Committee eventually tabled before the National Council in 1944, only one was implemented. The 'rules' and 'orders' issued by the *Mofumahali*, together with the various amendments and additions which had been from time to time recommended by the National Council since 1922, were incorporated in the new edition of *The Laws of Lerotholi*. Two resolutions of far-reaching importance were not implemented. The two read:

(1) *The Laws of Lerotholi* as revised and amplified by the Committee should be submitted for the consideration of Council and of the Paramount Chief and Resident Commissioner and when approved should be printed and recognised as an authoritative statement of Basotho law and custom in all the Courts of Basutoland.

(2) The Council recommends that every year thereafter a printed volume incorporating all the amendments and additions to the Laws of Lerotholi recommended by Council and approved by the Paramount Chief, all new rules and orders issued by the Paramount Chief and all decisions of the High Court affecting these laws should be issued in the same way as is done in the case of Proclamations and notices issued each year by the High Commissioner.[45]

Also neutralised by the colonial administration was the Standing Committee's resolution, tabled at the 39th Session in 1944, that the title to Part 1 *The Laws of Lerotholi* (as provided under Proclamation No. 61 of 1938) be changed from 'Declaration of Basuto Law and Custom' To 'Declaration of Basuto Law'. As earlier alluded to, the Standing Committee had hoped that by removing the term 'custom' from the title, and retaining the term 'law', it would have conferred the legal validity on Sesotho law which Lansdown had questioned. The apparent reasoning behind this recommended change was that the white judge and the white colonial administration had erred in their non-recognition of Sesotho law as a consequence of a language problem: that they were not aware that Basotho did make a distinction between 'law' as a command backed by a sanction from a political authority, and is therefore binding, and 'custom', which, as Chief Moiphepi Letsie had pointed out, 'cannot bind anybody'. The President of the National Council, however, disabused the Standing Committee of its view. He pointed out:

Altering the title as suggested will make no difference at all to the validity of this in a Court of law. . . . If the Resident Commissioner finds himself unable to issue such Proclamation, then it will make no difference to the validity of these declarations in a Court of law whether you call them Basuto laws or customs. The words 'law and custom' are used in the Proclamation and in my mind it is purely (sic) academic point whether you use the term 'law' or 'Basuto law and custom.'[46]

General Observations on the Stand of the Colonial Administration

As it has been shown, the colonial administration was remarkably confused in its general policy of governing Lesotho. In consequence it was unclear as to what functions the National Council should be permitted to undertake and confused as to what status to accord Sesotho customary law. The confusion surrounding the status of Sesotho customary law necessarily made the rationalisation of the Territory's judicial system difficult. That being the case, it retarded an early separation of the judiciary from the executive functions of government, which the Basutoland Progressive Association had proposed as early as 1919, and to which the colonial administration itself was committed.

There is of course something to be said for Sir Walter Huggard's view that if Sesotho customary law were kept from forming a part of statutory law, the European courts would reserve the authority to dictate what does and what does not correctly set out customary law. Viewed from the point of view of the colonial administration, the advantage could be said to be the one that Sesotho customary law would be allowed to grow, and not be petrified under statutes. For, as the substantial amendments and additions of 1922 and 1943 illustrated, it was still in the process of development: discussions of 'Laws' in the National Council during both of these periods reflected uncertainties as to which was and which was not law. Viewed sceptically, however, from the point of view of the contemporary Basotho, two disadvantages could readily be anticipated. One was that the non-recognition of Sesotho law was done not so much on the grounds of legal theory – that is, in this case, the nurturing of customary law – as it was on political grounds. To wit, Lord Harlech, the High Commissioner, was excited by Mr Justice Lansdown's decision because it afforded the colonial administration the opportunity to 'never admit that we are bound hand and foot' by 'native law and custom'. The second, which would have been more distasteful to chiefs in general than to the educated élite, was that customary law would be allowed to grow provided it was along the lines favoured by the British staff of officers who presided over the Subordinate Courts, and by the South African judges, who generally presided over the High Court of Lesotho. As again, Lord Harlech had said on this point, his wish was 'that native law and custom must evolve and alter under the impact of civilising influences and our rule'. The *bahlalefi* – the educated élite – on the other hand, were generally infatuated with Western civilisation. They associated customary law with backwardness. Hence they would have echoed Lord Harlech's view.

A brief look at some other parts of the African continent under British rule suggests, however, that the colonial administration of Lesotho did have a more constructive alternative to the resolution of the problem of Sesotho customary law than the one that it took. In the Gold Coast, for instance, and at a much earlier period, in 1927, an effort was made to give customary law legal force without arresting its growth with a statute. The approach taken was at least to define, albeit imprecisely, what customary law should be regarded to be. The Gold Coast Native Administration Ordinance 1927, S. 2, in a quotation that was earlier but partially cited (in Chapter 2), defined customary law as follows:

> 'Native customary law' means a rule or a body of rules regulating rights and imposing correlative duties, being a rule or a body of rules which obtains and is fortified by established native usage and which is appropriate and applicable to any particular cause, action, suit, matter, dispute, issue, or question, and includes also any customary law recorded as such in a statement which shall have been declared under section 123 to be a true and accurate statement of such native customary law.[47]

As Anthony Allott, who cites this Ordinance, points out, this definition neither defined what was included in nor what was excluded from the law, and therefore, to that extent, it could be problematic.[48] On the other hand, it is here being argued that for that very reason, legislation of that type in the Lesotho context might have eased the conflict between the colonial administration and the indigenous government in their cherished but divergent aims – the former, to influence the growth of customary law through court judgments, and the latter to enjoy the assurance that it administered a generally recognised and respectable body of 'Laws'.

It is indeed significant that even Bechuanaland, Lesotho's neighbour under the same High Commission – a territory that was far more heterogeneous in its political organisation than Lesotho, and far less politically assertive – did similarly have its customary law recognised by means of this technique. Its own was, of course, as Allott describes it, a 'very unilluminating definition'. Nonetheless it was probably still more satisfactory to the Batswana than the contemporary Basotho who were themselves in a predicament. Coined in 1942 (a year before the National Council of Lesotho sought to resolve its own dilemma), under the Native Courts Proclamation, S. 1(2), the definition stated:

'Native law and custom', 'Native law or custom' and 'Native custom' mean in relation to a particular tribe or in relation to any native community outside any tribal area the general law or custom of such tribe or community except so far as the same may be incompatible with the due exercise of His Majesty's power and jurisdiction or repugnant to morality, humanity, or natural justice[49]

In both the Gold Coast and Bechuanaland the relevant Ordinance and Proclamation, respectively, which defined customary law and thus formally recognised its application in the courts, where relevant, had been preceded by studies which the colonial administrations had accepted as authoritative. In the Gold Coast John Mensah Sarbah, a barrister, had written *Fanti Customary Laws: A Brief Introduction to the Principles of the Native Laws and Customs of the Fanti and Akan Sections of the Gold Coast*, in 1897.[50] In Bechuanaland I. Schapera, a legal anthropologist, had written *A Handbook of Tswana Law and Custom*, in 1938.[51] It is likely that these studies influenced the trend in these two British dependencies toward the kind of recognition of customary law referred to.

All the same it is argued here that in Lesotho there was little justification, aside from that of lack of clarity in policy, buttressed with an unexamined view that Sesotho customary law needed to be guided by 'the impact of civilising influences and our rule', for the impasse on *The Laws of Lerotholi* following Lansdown's judgment. The absence of 'authoritative' studies on the principles of Sesotho customary law appears to have been only marginally, if at all, a determinant factor of the general outcome.

THE AFTERMATH OF THE REFORMS OF 1938: THE CHIEFTAINCY LOSES PRESTIGE AND RESORTS TO RITUAL MURDERS

The Abortive Attempt to Have the Reforms Repealed

The late Stimela Jason Jingoes, the grandson of Ngolozani – a headman and ironmonger (*mothula-tsepe*) under Chief Ramanehella Lesaoana (Moshoeshoe's favourite nephew) – has left us the following comment on the Reforms of 1938:

> [The British] acted in good faith. Reform was wanted and needed at that time; wanted by the people and the Chiefs alike and needed because of the conditions in some Chieftainships. I do not quarrel with that. What I do quarrel with is that the reforms came too suddenly, and altered, before we were ready for it, the customs of trust and reciprocity between Chiefs and people.[52]

From his position as a counsellor in Chief Boshoane's court at Mapoteng (or *Matśekheng*), in the District of Berea, Stimela Jason Jingoes smelled trouble: 'Many Principal Chiefs saw to it that their favourites were gazetted', he said, 'while many efficient and respected men went unrecognised'. Jingoes recalled that at a local *pitso* convened at Mapoteng, shortly after the promulgation of the Reforms, Chief Boshoane pointed out, ominously:

> We are not gazetting everyone who is a Chief or headman ruling a large village. We are gazetting only people who have proved their worth, men who can set a good example to others. Having many tax-payers is not an automatic qualification for being gazetted.[53]

Criteria for screening 'people who have proved their worth, men who can set a good example to others' were not anywhere written except in the chief's chest. While, as a principal chief, Boshoane was not subject to the screening process, he had little or nothing to lose from the implementation of the Reforms. Subordinate chiefs and headmen, people like Jingoes himself, stood to lose position, prestige and money. They felt insecure. They were scared. They were bitter. The same situation prevailed throughout the Territory.

Mapoteng, however, was distinctive in one respect of immense political significance: it was the seed-bed of the *Lekhotla la Bafo*, its headquarters, and the residence of its charismatic and irrepressible leader founder, Josiel Lefela. The politics of this organisation in regard to the chieftaincy – its harsh criticisms of chiefly abuses and its contradictory tendency of allying with chiefs against reforms in opposition to the plans of the Progressive Association – has already been told. It would be one of *Lekhotla la Bafo*'s startling perform-ances, and an indication of Josiel Lefela's political genius, that when the principal chiefs in the land had thus accepted the implementation of the Reforms, it succeeded in mobilising them in favour of having those Reforms repealed.

Stimela Jingoes informs us that at the conclusion of Chief Boshoane's *pitso*, the Mapoteng commoners under the Chief elected a committee 'on the spot' to draft a letter to *Morena e Moholo* Grifith Lerotholi. A deputation was duly appointed and having secured the approval of Chief Boshoane, as required by protocol, it proceeded to Matsieng to deliver the letter to the *Morena e Moholo*. Josiel Lefela had drafted the letter.[54] Stimela Jingoes was in the deputation. The purpose of the mission was to appeal on the *Morena e Moholo* to reverse the decision of the National Council on the Reforms.

According to the Russian-trained journalist and editor of *Umse-benzi*, Edwin Mofutsanyana (now 90 years of age) – Josiel Lefela's staunch supporter and confidant, who monitored this development – Josiel Lefela had been actuated by the conviction that the monarch, Griffith Lerotholi, was 'deliberately throwing the chieftaincy over the precipice, as a usurper to the throne who had failed to get the full support of the Nation, and as a tool of the white man, the first *Morena e Moholo* to sell his soul to a white priest'. Moreover, says Edwin Mofutsanyana, Lefela held the view that although the National Council had already agreed to the Reforms, Griffith should be able to reverse its decisions, in the same way as he had done in 1919, when the Council then had agreed that part of his mission to London should be to request Britain to restore Lesotho's 'conquered territory'. Then Griffith, in collusion with the colonial adminis-tration, had unilaterally and arbitrarily deleted the critical clause of the London Petition.[55] (The significance of that particular episode was related in the previous chapter.)

Griffith Lerotholi's initial reaction to the deputation was negative and hostile: ' "I can blow you out!" he said. "I can have you expelled from Lesotho NOW!" ' He demanded to know: ' "Is it your inten-tion to alter what I have done, I am the Government?" ' Jingoes, the author of these details, was told that later, when the deputation had scurried away from the royal brow-beating, Griffith had remarked to his courtiers:

> Among all the Chiefs in Lesotho, there is not Chief who has as hard a time in his administration as Chief Boshoane. His people are all politicians. I do not know how these people of Matse'ekheng [Mapoteng] became so spoiled![56]

The Matsieng set-back notwithstanding, *Lekhotla la Bafo* eventually succeeded in rallying a substantial number of principal chiefs to its point of view. Chief Boshoane's disaffected sub-chiefs and headmen deputed two members of the National Council, Josiel Lefela and Matseketseke 'Neko, the latter being also a member of *Lekhotla la Bafo*, to lobby fellow commoners in the National Council against the Reforms and it was coached:

> Do not appeal to commoners alone, either: try to gain the ear of the Chiefs on the Council as well, and warn them that they are also in danger. As we see these matters; this will not end among headmen only; at last we might find that there are no more sub-chiefs; even Chiefs themselves might disappear as a result of these laws. So plead before the Council as strongly as you can that these two Proclamations be abolished. They are an ulcer on the body of the Basotho nation.[57]

One of those principal chiefs that Lefela and 'Neko enlisted to their cause was the vocal Chief Goliath Malebanye of Mohales' Hoek. The other was Chief Gabashane Masopha of the Berea District.

When the 33rd Session of the National Council met in 1939, these chiefs had agreed on a strategy, probably suggested by Josiel Lefela, that the Proclamations of 1938, by then signed by the *Morena e Moholo* and promulgated by the High Commissioner, should be rejected on the grounds of procedure. The chiefs built their arguments around the principle of 'consultation', putting the case to the President of the Council that legislation of the type so binding on the entire indigenous government should have been tabled before the National Council in the form of a draft before being proclaimed, and that Griffith Lerotholi had had no just cause to sign the chiefs' rights away without the final approval of the National Council. More to the point, the reneging chiefs complained that the Proclamations served only to affect Sesotho customary law, and they claimed that all that the country needed to resolve the current problems of the indigenous government was to amend *The Laws of Lerotholi*.[58]

The general strategy did not work. The President of the Council was on solid ground in pointing out that, following a long history of intransigence on the part of the chiefs, agreement had finally been reached to introduce the reforms embodied in the two Proclamations: 'The Paramount Chief worked for many months on this proclamation with his advisers and the Government, and this is the result.' He denied the allegation that *The Laws of Lerotholi* were thereby adversely affected. Not anticipating Lansdown's decision, he pointed out that: 'Actually all through this book [the red book of the two Proclamations] it tends to uphold Native Law and Custom.'[59]

The President of the National Council was, of course, not alone in defending the implementation of the Reforms. There were a few other principal chiefs who stood solidly behind him. Of these, the most forceful was Chief Bolokoe Potsane, who stated:

I am grateful for these proclamations. We always say that our people do not obey us. Should we say the people do not obey us while we have no full power over them? Today we have full power and we have been joined up with Government Courts to show that our courts are looked upon as true courts. Therefore, Your Honour, I say you listened to our cry because with those who do not respect us you will help us with your authority.[60]

Chief Bolokoe Potsane's statement tacitly underscored one crucial point on the chieftaincy's view of the Proclamations: principal chiefs, uninfluenced by the politics of the *Lekhotla la Bafo*, saw themselves as the primary benefactors of the Reforms. The pruning of the chieftaincy, as the principal chiefs saw it, could only lead to a permanent preservation of their positions, a consolidation of their authority, and the enhancement of their material well-being. As a corollary to that development, the sub-chiefs and headmen stood to lose power, to be subjected to a greater degree of control from their superior, and, worst, to be levelled to the status of commoners.

Be that as it may, the campaign to repeal the Proclamations was conducted for five years, until 1943, when the principal chiefs who were sympathetic to it finally abandoned it; but this was not until a motion had been brought forward at the Session for that year of the National Council, by Chief Harebatho Letsie, purportedly as coming from 'the people' of Likhoele, in the Mafeteng District, that the Proclamations should be repealed. As Chief Harebatho Letsie put it:

The people of Likhoele ask that the two Proclamations of 1938 should cease to function. The first reason is, they say they have their own little Green Book of laws, the Laws of Lerotholi. They say that book was made and accepted by the Basutoland Council and the Basutoland Government, that that book has been used for many years by previous Chiefs, and that the book was amended and endorsed by the late Paramount Chief Nathanael Griffith in 1922. This was done by agreement with the National Council. . . . Further they say this Red Book contains Proclamations which hurt the Nation. It is clear that the people do not like the book, they have been talking about it from 1939 until today. It is because there is no foundation about it. For that reason the people ask that the book be abolished.[61]

That the motion came from Mafeteng is not surprising. The District of Mafeteng was the *Lekhotla la Bafo*'s second stronghold in the country, second only to Mapoteng. Josiel Lefela had nurtured the roots of the organisation there between 1919 and 1922, at the time that he still relied on the Mafeteng-published *Naledi ea Lesotho* to disseminate his views. The proprietors and publishers of *Naledi* were members of the Basutoland Progressive Association. Later, after 1922, when he had fallen out with the Basutoland Progressive Association, he had left an active branch there, which served the useful purpose of counteracting the influence of the BPA. There is, therefore, a strong possibility that that branch was behind Chief Harebatho Letsie's motion, although the personal interests of the chiefs cannot be discounted.

C. N. Arden-Clarke, the new Resident Commissioner of Lesotho since 1942, was completely nonplussed by the bold volte-face of the chiefs in general, who associated themselves with the motion at that Session of the National Council. He expressed his reaction as follows:

I think I should explain the position as I see it to the Council. Apparently [the] motion is that these laws, the Red Book, should be abolished because this Council was not consulted. Now, these laws were made in 1938 and there was very full and detailed consultation between the then Resident Commissioner and the then Paramount Chief. Now five years later you come to a new Resident Commissioner and a new Paramount Chief and ask them to repeal a law which their predecessors made, on the ground that their predecessors did not consult this Council. I do not know what decided the Paramount Chief, Chief Griffith at that time, and the then Resident Commissioner not to put this before the Council. The fact remains that they did so decide. You cannot ask their successors on this ground to repeal the Proclamations. . . . The Red Book is protecting this Green Book. That is the legal position.[62]

Councillor Labane Chokobane, who had moved the motion for the Reforms in 1937, was the Resident Commissioner's strongest supporter on that occasion. Essentially he was amazed by the amnesia, as it were, of the proponents of the new motion calling for the repeal of the Reforms. As he pointed out, the 'little Green Book' has been tried and abandoned because 'it served no useful purpose'; it had been made 'by these Chiefs here'. The people liked it; but the chiefs did not. Because of the outcry of the people, 'there was a little yellow book made by the late Sir John Sturrock', – the Draft Reforms of 1929. The people accepted the 'little yellow book'; 'but the Chiefs rejected it'. Finally, he said, the nation had come under the Red Book:

The Chiefs made use of the Red Book as soon as it was used and they have been punishing people under its provisions. Now today because they find that they also must be punished according to the provisions of that book, they say the book should be abandoned and we should revert to the little Green Book which they despised. Therefore I say, if we keep following the Chiefs, how are our people going to live? I do not think that nowadays the little Green Book would be of any help. That would mean this Council has been constituted for the mere purpose of rejecting good laws, and not for keeping and maintaining the laws of the Nation.[63]

Councillor Chokobane, quite clearly, was going beyond the constitutional issue at hand, that is, the question as to whether the Proclamations of 1938 had been promulgated in agreement and consultation with the National Council – which presumption was arguable. He was going further to advance the politics of BPA – his organisation. In doing so, he was revealing the organisation's cherished set of values: the belief that the leadership of the chieftaincy had become questionable and presumably, the *bahlalefi* (the educated élite) ought to take over that leadership; the conviction that customary law is backward and that it had fallen into disuse; the general feeling of closeness with the colonial administration, which was the major cause of conflict with the *Lekhotla la Bafo*.

Efforts to repeal the Reforms of 1938 ended with the 37th Session of the National Council in 1943; and with it went the semblance of solidarity between the principal chiefs, at one extreme, and the headmen and sub-chiefs, at the other. As it has been shown, the solidarity had never been genuine. In the main it was the brain-child of the *Lekhotla la Bafo*. Beyond that, in 1943 at any rate, the reaction of the principal chiefs was to a great extent influenced by Lansdown's decision.

Yet the break between the principal chiefs and the headmen and sub-chiefs had catastrophic effects on both rungs of the chieftaincy. Principal chiefs were polarised. Each began to fight for his own economic welfare and political fate. As already alluded to, the headmen and sub-chiefs felt further and further alienated. In the final analysis both rungs of the chieftaincy would become equally insecure; and they would resort to a desperate common solution – ritual murders.

The Establishment of the National Treasury: Its Constitutional Significance; and Its Net Effects on the Chieftaincy

The single most devastating event on the chieftaincy of Lesotho during the Regency was the establishment, in 1946, of an institution called the Basuto National Treasury, more popularly known as the National Treasury. The idea had been conceived by the colonial administration, and it was supposed to be beneficial to the chieftaincy. In the final analysis, however, instead of strengthening the chieftaincy, it actually crippled it.

The idea of establishing the National Treasury was first introduced in the National Council by C. N. Arden-Clarke, the Resident Commissioner, on 20 October 1942. His introductory speech was long but significant. Purporting to be fulfilling a long-standing wish of the Basotho, Arden-Clarke referred the National Council to that part of the Lesotho Petition to London in 1919 which read:

> That in Your Majesty's own good time Your Majesty will extend still further steps in the direction of self-government to the Chiefs, Headmen and people of the Basuto Nation, in terms of the expressed wish of the late Chief Moshesh when he sought the protection of the Government of Great Britain.[64]

Arden-Clarke drew a connection between that part of the Petition, made 23 years back, with his own current proposal: he wished the Council to note that it was about to consider 'a most important step forward in the direction of that self-government, for which the Basuto National then prayed – that is the establishment of a Basuto National Treasury'.

The Resident Commissioner then went on to make a quaint classification of the functions of government, within the context of which the National Treasury was to be established: 'Every government has three sets of functions to fulfil and needs to be given by law the powers necessary to fulfil them.' The first, he pointed out, was the executive, 'which includes the making of laws, regulations or rules and the issuing of orders which people are compelled to obey.' In Lesotho, as he saw it, 'powers to carry out certain of these functions have been delegated by the Central Government to the Native Administration, i.e. to the Paramount Chiefs, Chiefs, Sub-Chiefs and Headmen, 'by the Native Administration Proclamation of 1938.

The second function, he pointed out, was the judicial: 'to ensure the peaceable and just settlement of disputes and the punishment after fair trial of those who have offended against law or rules or disobeyed lawful orders'. Here powers to carry out those functions 'have been delegated to the Native Courts established and working under the Native Proclamation of 1938'.

Finally the third function was financial, and it included 'the imposition and collection of taxes, fees and levies and the wise and proper expenditure of the revenue so collected'. To date, he pointed out, 'practically no powers' had been delegated to the 'Basuto Native Administration' in this regard. Practically all the functions related to finance had been undertaken by the 'central Government and its Treasury'.

To drive his message home, the Resident Commissioner spun the following metaphor:

The structure of any government, whether it be of the central Government or of a local government body like a Native Administration, may well be compared to a three legged stool. The Basuto stool of self-government has got two legs, the executive and judicial, but it lacks the third, the financial, and a three legged stool with one leg missing cannot stand by itself: it is high time we fitted your stool with its own third leg instead of using the Treasury of the central Government as a prop to keep it upright.[65]

C. N. A. Arden-Clarke, quite clearly, believed that the establishment of the National Treasury would be a crucial constitutional development. It was his view that: 'Probably the best form of education in the art and practice of government is in the exercise of financial responsibility.' He wished the National Council to believe that the British Government was interested in promoting self-government throughout its dependencies, Lesotho included. As he put it: 'It is the policy of His Majesty's Government to develop and improve the institutions of self-government among all the people of the Empire, to teach them to stand on their own feet.' This was the first explicit and unequivocal statement from the colonial administration on the existence of a policy for preparing Lesotho for self-government.

Anticipating as he did some opposition from the National Council on the idea, C. N. A. Arden-Clarke had thought it would be tactically useful to illustrate his point by reference to specific countries. Shining examples in Africa were Nigeria, Tanzania and Uganda. Close by, in the Bechuanaland Protectorate, a Native Treasury system was also in operation. (In fact, a few weeks back, before the opening of the current Session of the National Council, a delegation of Basotho chiefs had visited Bechuanaland on a fact-finding mission on the system, a report on which had been submitted to *Mofumahali* 'Mantšebo and Arden-Clarke himself.)⁶⁶ Arden-Clarke should, perhaps, have stopped with the mention of these four examples. Quite unwisely, however, he went on to include some European settler colonies, even the detested and feared Union of South Africa, whose model 'Bantu-stan', the Transkei, was regarded by the colonial administration of Lesotho as a success story in 'Native Government'.

Initially a few prominent chiefs were suspicious of the idea of a National Treasury. In the main they could not understand the need in one and the same Territory for two treasuries. Chief Thabatšoeu Lebona – a sub-chief in the Mohale's Hoek District, for instance, did not think that Arden-Clarke had built a convincing argument by citing countries under the British Empire such as Australia to support the notion of a dual treasury system in Lesotho.⁶⁷ Chief Leloko Lerotholi, the controversial Matsieng courtier, an otherwise insecure sub-chief, provided the strongest opposition to him: 'His Honour has told us of a petition made by our father', he said, 'but they did not ask for a 'division of the country's money. Why this division now? Is the money going to desert us?' Chief Leloko argued that what was needed was not a dual treasury system, but rather that

Basotho children should be sent overseas for higher education so that they could come back and fully man the Central Treasury. When Arden-Clarke suggested that such education of Basotho children as might be needed for the purpose could be gained through the on-the-job training within the Civil Service in Lesotho, Chief Leloko protested the hidden premise that the Resident Commissioner was 'our schoolmaster'. He felt that a better option in that event was 'that we should have universities in Basutoland where we could have our children trained'.

Finally, in so far as Arden-Clarke had used the Union of South Africa as an example, Chief Lerotholi maintained 'that the example quoted by His Honour is entirely wrong'. It was wrong 'because in this case it is inferred that there is colour bar in this matter'. 'To whom will this other money belong if it is taken away from us? I would ask his Honour to teach us, train us and then let us have all our money.'[68]

The majority of the members of the Council, however, were completely in favour of the establishment of the National Treasury. To principal chiefs it meant an assurance for their positions and prestige. They were anxious to be seen as being of the same mind as Arden-Clarke.[69] Chief Goliath Malebanye, for instance, stated:

If we do a thing let us do it at once. Give us this thing: give us the Treasury. . . . You and the Paramount Chief are oxen under the same yoke, and what becomes you will become him. . . . Let us have the Treasury, Your Honour, and you should be with us and watch so that you can reduce the work if it appears to be too heavy for us. We love you, and may God keep His Majesty and maintain Him through all difficulties.

Although he was not one of the twenty odd members of the royal house whom the Sons of Moshoeshoe had specifically named as 'principal chiefs' when they amended *The Laws of Lerotholi* in 1922,[70] Goliath Malebanye's position under Bereng Griffith, the Principal Chief of Mohale's Hoek, was quite secure. Bereng Griffith trusted him, and with just cause. He had been one of those chiefs who had supported his candidacy for the Regency in 1941.[71]

Chief Theko Makhaola, the capable Principal Chief of Qacha's Nek, went even further to express anxiety that the Basotho (actually principal chiefs) should be given great powers of control over the National Treasury, once it could be established.

I want to state that this Basuto Treasury should be entirely in the hands of Basuto and the people administering it must be Basuto, leaving the supervision and inspection to our Chief, the Resident Commissioner, for if the Treasury is for the Nation it would be a difficult and unworkable thing to have Europeans in it.[72]

The *bahlalefi* councillors were for the most part also supportive, although, of course, from the point of view of their own interests. It was their sons who were going to man the professional aspect of the running of the National Treasury. A number of them had already gained useful education in Natal and in the Cape Province in the Union of South Africa by this time, and some of them had even become teachers of commercial subjects in the same country.[73] The *bahlalefi* councillors were very blunt in their expressions of anxiety in this regard. The Reverend Leonard Polisa, who summarised their view in the boldest and rudest fashion, stated:[74]

More than this [general utility of the National Treasury to the Nation], for many years now this Council has been asking to be given more responsibility for the services of this country. They have always said that the bread for their children is taken away and given to dogs: by that they meant certain Europeans from the Union who were employed in the service of Basutoland. They say that such posts, held by such Europeans, could adequately be filled by their sons in Basutoland. Now the answer to the request of the Paramount Chief and the Council has arrived, that we should have our own Treasury where we should be able to employ our own sons.

Even before the National Council met in 1942, a meeting had already taken place between *Mofumahali* 'Mantŝebo and the Resident Commissioner (and their respective advisers and staff officers) to discuss the idea of the National Treasury, and a Committee had been set up to draft appropriate proposals to implement it. The Resident Commissioner had appointed his Government Secretary, the Financial Secretary, two District Commissioners, and an Assistant District Commissioner – who would serve as Secretary to the Committee. The *Mofumahali* had nominated eight chiefs – Letsie Motsoene, Gabashane Masopha, Soko Letsie, Lerotholi Mojela, Mahabe Makhaola, Khosimotse Ntaote, Maama Lechesa, and Leloko Lerotholi. (As pointed out, Leloko Lerotholi attempted to undermine the idea when it came before the National Council.)

After some bickering, in which some councillors challenged the procedure of setting up the Committee and nominating its members without proper consultations, the National Council added to this number Chiefs Theko Makhaola, Makhobalo Theko, Mopeli Jonathan, and Councillor Z. D. Mangoaela. Starting in January 1943, the Committee began to meet, under the Chairmanship of the Resident Commissioner, to discuss proposals. And on 23 June 1944, it submitted its report to the National Council, signed by *Mofumahali* 'Mantšebo Seeiso.

The Committee's proposals, as finally accepted, were briefly as follows: the National Treasury would be established at Matsieng, under the control of the Regent, who would be advised and assisted by a Finance Committee representative of all the districts and sub-districts of Lesotho. Its work would be facilitated by a Treasurer with a staff of officials and clerks at Matsieng, with a sub-accountant and a number of other clerks in each district. The Treasury would be responsible for all expenditure involved in the acquittal of its duties and responsibilities which had been delegated to the 'Basuto Native Administration' – which meant the executive and administrative work formerly undertaken by the chieftainship, including the work of the Basotho courts. In addition it would take over from the 'Central Government' (that is, the colonial administration) the responsibility for collecting 'Native Tax' (that is, 'hut tax'), the maintenance of anti-soil-erosion works, village tree-planting, the construction of bridle-paths, eradication of burr-weed (which destroyed the quality of wool, one of Lesotho's main exports at the time), and the payment of allowances and rations to members of the National Council. 'Other duties', it was stated, 'could be assumed as the Native Administration proved its capacity to take them over from Government'.[75]

The paragraphs of the Report most injurious to the welfare of the chiefs in general, and lesser chiefs and headmen in particular, were the following three.[76] Paragraph 28: the Committee felt that the existing system, whereby the chieftaincy was 'fed' by 'eating' fines imposed by the indigenous courts, and 'eating' the proceeds of the sale of stray stock, was pernicious. Under this type of system the numerous chiefs, sub-chiefs and headmen who had been 'placed', as well as, correspondingly, the number of indigenous courts in existence, were 'far in excess of the numbers required by the Nation in the interests of efficient administration and of Justice'. The Committee believed that the time had come when the Nation should associate itself with the practice in other countries by paying 'allowances of salaries to those engaged on the work of the Basuto Native Administration' and ensuring that 'all public money collected by its public servants are [sic] brought properly to account and paid into the revenues of the Native Administration'.

Accordingly the Committee recommended, in Paragraph 29, that allowances should be paid to the Regent and to 24 principal chiefs, who were to be re-styled 'ward chiefs', and that provision should be made for the remuneration of those other chiefs, sub-chiefs and headmen 'whose work and responsibilities justify' financial reward. Following the implementation of the new system as recommended, no chief, sub-chief or headman would be recognised as such 'until he has received a Certificate of Appointment setting out his duties, powers and jurisdiction as an executive and administrative official of the Native administration'.

Paragraph 30, on the number of indigenous courts in the Territory, expressed the critical view that the existing 1340 'Basuto Courts were grossly excessive'. The Committee recommended a reduction of these courts to 117, 'which would be sufficient for the administration of justice and would adequately meet the needs of the people'.

As the number of courts corresponded to the number of chiefs and headmen in the Territory, it in essence meant that these officials should be scaled down from 1340, where the number stood as at 1938, to 117. The victims would be exclusively in the categories of headmen and sub-chiefs.

In the final analysis, however, when the National Treasury began to function in 1946, warrants were issued to 121 Basotho courts. Yet still that number would be further reduced to 106 in 1949. The rest of the courts in excess of the ones recognised were allowed to function as 'courts of arbitration': their decisions could not be reinforced; and those who presided over them got no financial recognition.

The Committee recommended that the holder of the office of *Morena e Moholo* should receive 'an allowance commensurate with the dignity and standing of the Head of the Basuto Nation and the responsibility of his office'. That meant, in essence, the doubling of the net income of £1800 per annum that the *Mofumahali* was receiving from the 'Central Government' to £3600. This was a substantial sum of money as the *Mofumahali*, unlike her predecessors in the office, did not have several wives to support. Some 22 surviving widows of former monarchs were to get their own allowances as a personal right.

The 24 principal chiefs recommended for annual allowances were to be paid on the basis of a combination of two factors: (a) the status of the chief; (b) the work and responsibilities of the chief as measured by the number of taxpayers in his ward. The highest-paid chiefs according to this formula would be Bereng Griffith, at Mohale's Hoek, at £1700. His emolument included a 'special allowance' of £152 in lieu of being 'the senior Chief in Basutoland next to the Paramount Chief'. (This was, no doubt, an appeasement measure for his loss of the Regency.) Letsie Motšoene, the then head of the District of Leribe received £1680. Gabashane Masopha, the head of the District of Berea (Teyateyaneng), received £1548. Theko Makhaola, more because of the small number of his taxpayers than because of his status, received £1296; and Qefate Sempe of Quthing got £1308.[77]

In contrast such sub-chiefs and headmen as qualified for certificates of appointment would be paid only 5 per cent of the Hut Tax (Native Tax) collected in respect of each 'ward', after deducting the salaries of Tax Collectors employed in the 'ward'. On the average such allowances were in the region of £50 per annum. Sub-chiefs and headmen with not more than 350 taxpayers under them were not 'normally' to be paid allowances.

The disparity in allowances between ward chiefs, on the one hand, and sub-chiefs and headmen with certificates of appointment, on the other hand, was wide, and it led to intense jealousies from below. Those who lost out altogether in the formulae for allowances were bitter.

The revenues of the National Treasury from court fines and fees and stray stock would not be that much, initially. They were estimated at £22 000 per annum. The expenditure recommended by the Committee was £85 000. The 'Central Government', therefore, would be making a grant of £85 000 per annum to the National Treasury to enable it to meet its expenditure.

The Basuto National Treasury began its operations on 1 January 1946, under Mr Thabiso Mohapeloa, the Reverend John Mohapeloa's son, as Treasurer, at a salary of £480 per annum. By 1960, when it would up, it had had two successive Treasurers, the last one being Mr R. Sefatsa Lesenyeho.[78]

The Outbreak of Ritual Murders: The Consequence of Reforms of 1938 and the Establishment of the National Treasury

Both Hugh Ashton and Gwilym I. Jones, who published their anthropological studies on Basotho in 1952 and 1951, respectively, offer convincing evidence that there was a cause and effect relationship between the spate of ritual murders that broke out in Lesotho in the 1940s and the Reforms of 1938, and, to use Arden-Clarke's terminology, the 'third leg' – the National Treasury. Completed in 1949 (although published in 1952), Hugh Ashton's *The Basuto* was a comprehensive anthropological study of the Basotho but it devoted a chapter to 'Medicine, Magic and Sorcery' with a focus on the problem of ritual murders. G. I. Jones, on the other hand, a Cambridge anthropologist, was specifically commissioned in 1949 to do a study of the causes of ritual murders. Hence his official report, *Basutoland Medicine Murder; A Report on the Recent Outbreak of 'diretlo' Murders* was to be regarded as an authoritative statement on the basis of which that social malady could be treated.

To facilitate an understanding of the problem, a brief statement on the meaning of a ritual murder, and its place in Basotho society, is necessary. On the term 'ritual murder' Jones writes:

> This term 'ritual', which implies the taking of a human life for religious purposes or in accordance with a religious or magic rite, is not a particularly happy one for there is no such element of human sacrifice in these Basutoland murders. They are not committed from any religious motives but for the purely material objective of cutting from the body of the victim strips of flesh or portions of particular organs, called by the general term *diretlo* . . . and used in the making of certain magical compounds usually called 'protective medicines'.[79]

The origins of *diretlo* or *liretlo* – in the current Sesotho orthography, are uncertain; but both Ashton and Jones gave two explanations based on their research. The first and commonly accepted view was that *liretlo* was not an ancient but borrowed Basotho practice: it was a phenomenon introduced by the AmaZulu doctors. The flesh used originally in the *manaka* (medicine horns) was procured from animals, usually associated with ferocity or strength to which human flesh, normally that of an enemy slain in battle, was added. The second view was that Basotho had always used human flesh in the *manaka*, but that invariably it was the flesh from an enemy slain in battle. When, after the turn of the century, Basotho became more settled, they ran out of battle-felled enemies. Consequently those who felt an acute need for 'protective medicine' were advised by their traditional doctors – the experts on these matters – to secure human ingredients for their *manaka* from any person in the community whom the doctors described as 'a suitable' quarry. 'The truth' says Jones, 'appears to lie between these two extremes': in settled times the *manaka* came to be undoubtedly 'fortified' with parts of a human body of 'a definite person who is thought to possess specific attributes considered essential for the particular medicine being made. Such a person is usually a member of the same community and is frequently a relative of some of the killers. He is killed specifically for this *diretlo* which has to be cut from his body while he is still alive.'[80]

It is nonetheless significant that the total number of suspected *liretlo* for the entire period of colonial Lesotho before 1938 was only 23. Yet between 1938 and 1949, the period of the great Reforms and the establishment of the National Treasury, the number was 81. This suggests that there was a relationship between the increase of *liretlo* and the Reforms.

The colonial administration reacted to the spate of these ritual murders aggressively. Cases were brought before the courts, and those who were found guilty of the crime were generally hanged. In the course of these trials it was found that in the majority of cases the general causes of the ritual murders were the 'placing' and the official recognition of headmen and sub-chiefs.

In this regard it is indeed instructive that when the Committee for the establishment of the National Treasury wrote its Report in 1944, it had noted that one ward, namely Chief Gabashane's ward in the District of Berea, was densely staffed with sub-chiefs and headmen: it had 14 sub-chiefs and 147 headmen, for a population of 15 660 taxpayers, while, by comparison, one ward in Leribe, Chief Mathealira Jonathan's ward, which was slightly larger, with 16 214 taxpayers, had nine sub-chiefs and 14 headmen. This imbalance of the sub-chiefs and headmen is the factor that inclined the Committee toward a fixed percentage of the Native Tax.[82] The result was that Chief Gabashane's ward was hit hard, and probably the hardest, by the 1946 cuts. A corollary to these cuts was that the ward sustained the highest number of ritual murders in the Territory: of the 70 suspected ritual murders reported in the Territory during the critical period – 1948 to 1949 – 20 took place in the Chief's District of Berea.[83]

Chief Bereng Griffith's ward in the District of Mohale's Hoek is another good example of the effects of the Reforms and the establishment of the National Treasury on the chieftaincy. As told by the High Commissioner, Sir Evelyn Baring in a report of his visit to Lesotho in November 1943, Chief Bereng Griffith's ward had 'no less than one hundred and fifty-one sub-ordinate courts'[84] (serving 15 342 taxpayers).[85] According to Sir Evelyn, Chief Bereng Griffith had himself proposed that the number be reduced to eight. (In the final analysis it was reduced to 16.)[86] Sir Evelyn was aware, at the same time, that the suggested reduction was provoking recrimination from some quarters. As he said: 'It is perhaps inevitable that the Sub-Chiefs and Headmen oppose such reductions as involving for them both loss of income and of prestige.'[87] What the High Commissioner could not have been aware of at the time, however, was that Chief Bereng Griffith's ward would soon be one of the vortexes of ritual murders in the Territory, and that the Chief would himself be found guilty of the crime and have to be hanged for it.

At least by 1948 it had become clear to the colonial administration that chiefs were largely responsible for ritual murders in Lesotho. That social sickness held the entire nation in a grip of fear, and it was an embarrassment to the staff of officers in charge of the administration. The High Commissioner, Sir Evelyn Baring, for his part, made it clear to the National Council at its 44th Session in 1948 that 'the increase of this evil and degrading practice' which had become 'a curse' in the Territory had to be stamped out. In his boldest ever attack on the chieftaincy, Sir Evelyn stated:

I thought the time had arrived when I should come in person to speak in the plainest possible terms to the Council, whose members represent the Nation. The Council is composed principally of chiefs who are, or should be, leaders of the people. And yet, *of the nineteen cases of ritual murder which the Police have taken to court since 1942, headmen or chiefs of one grade or another have been involved in every case but one. It is known too that they are involved in some cases still undergoing investigation or examination.* (My emphasis)[88]

The High Commissioner's concern stemmed only in part from his embarrassment that the Territory over which he was the chief executive manifested a predilection for this awkward device for securing personal power. It stemmed equally from the fear, remarkably, that ritual murders might tarnish the image of chiefs to the point of their destruction. As he said:

> If you Chiefs pause to think over this matter you will realise that if these crimes continue the chieftainship will be utterly discredited and undermined. People will cease to respect the Chiefs and the present system of indirect government through the Chiefs will break down entirely.[89]

This statement, it appears, was not made simply to produce salutary effects on the chiefs in the National Council, although, of course, that was its primary aim at the time. It stemmed from conviction. In a confidential memorandum made in January 1949, the High Commissioner would restate it with greater emphasis:

> The practice of ritual murder must be broken, but efforts must also be made to avoid breaking the chieftaincy in the process. Chiefs found guilty of murder should suffer as commoners have suffered. At the same time, the hand of the present Regent will be strengthened by three permanent councillors selected for her by the National Council.[90]

The High Commissioner still needed the chieftaincy to rule the country.

When Sir Evelyn Baring addressed the National Council on the subject of ritual murders – in September 1948 – the nation was already under a crisis. Two senior principal chiefs in the land had already been arraigned for the crime. These were Chiefs Gabashane Masopha and Bereng Griffith. Chiefs in the Council were nervous about the outcome of their trial, and so was the entire nation. In the circumstances it would appear, on hindsight, that it was politically unwise for Sir Evelyn to have threatened, as he did, to take collective action against chiefs if they did not assist him to eradicate the murders. The unfortunate words of desperation were:

> So determined am I that ritual murders must come to an end that I am already considering legislation to enable collective punishments to be imposed on the chiefs and people of areas in which these murders have occurred if prompt steps are not taken to furnish information to the Government which will enable the culprits to be brought to book. The measures contemplated are most drastic and I sincerely hope that it will prove unnecessary to impose them. I warn the Council most solemnly, however, that

the measures, drastic as they are, will be imposed if the murders continue.[91]

The statement left the impression in the minds of the chiefs and the nation that the colonial administration was out to destroy chieftaincy rule – the very opposite of the High Commissioner's intention. Additionally it is highly conceivable that police officers interpreted the statement to mean that they were licensed to extract evidence from witnesses and persons accused of these murders though unconventional means, including bribery and coaching Crown witnesses to give false evidence. In the end, at any rate, this was to be the campaign that the *Lekhotla la Bafo* waged against the colonial's administration. The most unremitting critic of the colonial administration along these lines would be Ntsu Mokhehle, a disciple of Josiel Lefela, who would later found the Basutoland African Congress in 1952. According to B. M. Khaketla, his political mate from the early 1950s: 'He spoke openly and vehemently against the murders which he regarded as a 'trick' intended to discredit the Chiefs and pave the way for the eventual incorporation of Lesotho into the Union of South Africa.'[92]

In November 1948 Chiefs Gabashane Masopha and Bereng Griffith were found guilty by the High Court of Lesotho of the ritual murder of a commoner named 'Meleke Ntai, and they were sentenced to death by hanging. The case was appealed to the Judicial Committee of the Privy Council; but on 25 July the Lords of the Judicial Committee dismissed it.[93] On 4 August 1949, Gabashane Masopha and Bereng Griffith were hanged.

The Scottish newspaper, *the Scotsman*, whose 'Special Correspondent' for South Africa gave a comprehensive and enlightening report of the hangings as well as the malady of ritual murders in Lesotho in general, revealed the fact that the colonial administration was aware that the ritual murders had something to do with its Reforms on the chieftaincy. First The *Scotsman* noted that there was no history of ritual murders in Lesotho, 'nor, in fact, in any of the Bantu' peoples of Southern Africa: 'Basutos are an intelligent, law abiding people. They have a tradition of independence and nationhood greater than any other native territory; there is far less external interference in their affairs.' Second, while acknowledging the existence of the 'ordinary, if increasingly acute economic and moral pressures to which all impoverished ignorant native races contiguous to civilisation are exposed', it dismissed this as the cause of the ritual murders. The cause, it pointed out, was to be found in the political sphere:

> The theory now bring put forward is that the growing inroads on their powers and influence are seriously preying on the minds of many of these small authoritarians [that is, chiefs and headmen]. In their ignorance and superstition, these men are apparently resorting to witchcraft doctors – conscious of their own diminishing influence – who deceive them with stories of how their medicine will bring about a return of their prestige. It is an indication of their desperation that they should resort to such extreme and dangerous methods as ritual murder.[94]

6 The Establishment of the Legislative Council

THE CONSTITUTIONAL AND POLITICAL DEVELOPMENTS LEADING TO THE ESTABLISHMENT OF A LEGISLATIVE COUNCIL

Discussions Leading to the Adoption of the Elective Principle

The first and most important constitutional development during the Regency was the introduction of the elective principle into the choice of the members of the National Council. The discussions leading to that development however, and the ones which evidently supplied the theoretical framework for it, had taken place at the 32nd Session of National Council, in 1937. Significantly, as it will be recalled, that was the Session at which the Reforms of 1938 were agreed to. Overwhelmed by the spirit of change that brought about those Reforms, the chiefs had come very close to accepting the several motions calling for an elective Council. The discussions of those motions reveal the councillors' insights on principles of government.

The first of these motions, submitted by Councillor Peete Molapo, was purported to be coming from 'the people of Leribe'. (More accurately, it came from a section of the District of Leribe represented by the Councillor.) Its formulation was striking:[1]

> Your people chief [President] propose that the members be elected by the nation, and the chiefs should not make the laws as they are judges. That is the request from the people of Leribe. They cry that the chiefs who rule the people are also the makers of the law through the council which may be called the chiefs' council. The people request that as the chiefs are judges who use the laws, it would be better if the makers of the law should be the National Council composed of commoners and not the chiefs. This will increase justice as the people will make laws for their own government and the chiefs will judge in accordance with the laws made by the people and there will be no complaints such as are caused by the laws of the chiefs. *The people request that the laws should*

be above everything and the chief should have no authority to do as he likes. (My emphasis)[1]

Over and above proposing the introduction of the elective principle, Councillor Peete Mølapo's motion was striking in three different respects. First it alluded to the doctrine of separation of powers: 'the chiefs should not make the laws as they are judges'. Second, as a logical outcome of the first, it emphasised the need for the National Council to be 'composed of commoners and not the chiefs'. In other words it underscored the view that laws made for 'the people' (commoners) ought to be made by 'the people'. Third it postulated, or rather restated, the doctrine of the Rule of Law: 'the laws should be *above everything* and the chief should have no authority to do as he likes.' (My emphasis)

Councillor Thabo Lechesa, representing the people of Matsieng, sponsored a motion along the same lines, but probably a bit more radical. His motion overlapped with that of Councillor Peete Molapo in so far as it proposed that 'members be elected by the people'; but then it went further. The people of Matsieng wished the National Council to be converted to a Legislative council, 'with authority to make laws for the people of Basutoland and the laws to be confirmed by the Paramount Chief and the Resident Commissioner, and these laws should rule this nation'. Additionally the people of Matsieng requested that the Legislative Council 'be divided into two chambers'. The first chamber would be composed of the chiefs, being fifty in number. The second chamber would be composed of 'ordinary people', also numbering fifty:

> They suggest that whatever motions are brought up for discussion they should first of all be discussed in the lower chamber, and then they should be passed in the chiefs' chamber, and the decision made by the chiefs' chamber will be regarded as final.[2]

Another motion worthy of attention was from Counsellor Labane Chokobane, representing the Basutoland Progressive Association. In comparison with the other two, the motion was not radical: but it was practical and politic. It was the BPA's version, in the final analysis, that the National Council would adopt six years later, during the Regency.

Counsellor Labane proposed that the National Council, being still an advisory body, 'should be divided into three parts'. The first 'part' would be nominated by the *Morena e Moholo* and it would represent the chiefs. The second 'part' would be nominated by 'the Government' and it would represent 'the Government'; and 'the third part should be elected by the people and should represent the people'. The BPA, on whose instructions Counsellor Labane acted, had 'thought it best that there should be smaller councils below the National Council and these should be established in every district and be presided over by the District Commissioners. Each district chief should be a member of such a council.' Two members would be nominated by the chief and the other two by 'the people', such that each District Council would consist of five members. Each District Council would 'investigate into matters pertaining to its district before the General Council meets'. Then, in preparation for the annual sessions of the 'General Council', the *Morena e Moholo* would 'nominate the chief of the district as well as the members' of the small councils, and some of the members nominated by the *Morena e Moholo* would 'have originally been elected by the people'. The motion did not stipulate the number to be chosen by the Resident Commissioner; nor did it stipulate the total number of the members of the 'General Council'; but it could be surmised that both were going to be small. The total number of the people's representatives and those of the *Morena e Moholo*, at any rate, would have been forty-five – calculated on the basis of the then nine districts in the Territory.

Although these motions generally received a warm reception in the National Council, almost on a par with the proposals for the Reforms of 1938, they suffered a defeat. In part this was so because the Resident Commissioner J. C. R. Sturrock, was not sympathetic to the idea of an elective council. He felt that 'the time has not yet arrived for any alteration in the constitution of the Council'. Additionally the number of chiefs and courtiers against the idea was still dominant. Afraid to lose their appointments and privileges, these chiefs and courtiers argued, in the words of Councillor Thompson Mothea – one of their number – that 'The Paramount Chief has been given these [present] counsellors by God in order that they should advise him in all matters.'[3] More substantially, Chief Tlhakanelo Moshoeshoe stated:[4]

At Matsieng the people who are appointed to the Council have been working since the time of the late Chief Lerotholi. I knew their fathers when they were working for the chiefs. Therefore I find they are the foals of those horses which used to run and they run like their fathers. If the Paramount Chief were to elect differ-ent people how could he tame such wild horses which do not know how to conduct cases? I fight against such a notion.[4]

This resistance notwithstanding, it remained quite clear that chiefs were not far from accepting the idea. The most significant indication for this came from the then leading member of the royal house, Chief Theko Makhaola. Theko Makhaola of course differed from those who said that chiefs should not be eligible as councillors. Other than that, however, he was fully in favour of the introduction of the elective principle. What was more, he felt that time was ripe for substituting the advisory National Council with a Legislative Council. His reasoning on this last point was that, after all, the National Council was already performing the function of legislation since its resolutions, 'if accepted, are usually made laws to govern this nation, that is, if accepted by the Chief Councillor and the Resident Com-missioner'.[5]

It is not surprising, therefore, that in 1942 when the National Council picked up the subject of introducing the elective principle once again, it was the chiefs themselves, more so than the commoners – or even the educated junior sons of chiefs, who led the discussion. Chiefs Tumane Matela – the Principal Chief of the Makhoakhoa – Theko Makhaola, Goliath Malebanye and his brother Bolokoe Malebanye, Nkoebe Mitchel of Berea, Khethisa Tau of Pitseng in the District of Leribe, and Talimo Joel – a descendent of the 'rebel' Chief Joel Molapo of the Gun War – all forcefully spoke in favour of the National Council being elective. As Chief Talimo Joel said, several years had passed since the National Council had first asked the High Commissioner, Lord Selborne, in 1910 that the Council should be 'elected by the nation'. It would hence be ludicrous for anyone to be still arguing, 33 years later, that the Nation was not ready for that constitutional development. He stated:

> This Council which has been likened to a child must have grown to be a man of ripe age, and no child will crawl for 33 years. I say now the time which was mentioned by our fathers has arrived. . . . I am in agreement with those Councillors who say that 100 per cent of the members should be elected by the nation.[6]

In that same session, as in 1937, Chief Theko Makhaola played the role of a statesman. He spoke as a disinterested leader who was hoping that his fellow chiefs could do likewise. As usual, his vision was clear. He was concise. His speech was historic:

> I know that the people are not satisfied. If therefore we do not satisfy the people, what are we ruling for? . . . We have our people who are not chiefs but agriculturists; they want to be protected and ask that they should have a voice in the Council. Say, for instance, they ask me to bring up their Matters in the Council and I am not an agriculturist, shall I be in a position to place their matters? We have traders and they can improve matters of trade because they must be arranged in this Council[.] [T]hough I [am] sometimes here . . . there is a Chamber of Commerce. Then we have another section of our people, teachers and ministers of religion and parents of school children, and they may give me messages to bring to Council, but I do not know much about school matters. As the nomination is left in the hands of the Chiefs, they choose as they like. There is no one who will deny that when we make our selections we select from those who are on our side. We must always remember that the people are looking to us, Chiefs, not to retard their progress, all I can say is that Basuto should march to catch time because time does not seem to come to them. I agree with the speaker who said that half of the members be nominated by the Chief. This is not a new thing; it is done all over the world. It is said that we should always liken ourselves to our British Government. . . . I speak from the bottom of my heart that the people must be given the right to express their views.[7]

It is quite clear from the discussion at that Session that a major constitutional advance might have been achieved. Besides being ready for the elective principle, the National Council might, with a little encouragement from the colonial administration, have been induced to accept the establishment of a Legislative Council. Further, it was not strenuously against bicameralism. Even the idea of having a full parliament as such attracted some discussion. Nonetheless the colonial administration was not at that point ready to concede a major constitutional development in the country.

In 1943 when the 38th Session of the National Council met to decide the fate of the previous year's motions, the Resident Commissioner brought his views into the open. 'It appears to me', he said, 'that the general feeling of the Council is not that it wishes to commit suicide and abolish itself altogether but that it wants to alter its constitution and its machinery so that it becomes more effective'. He admonished members of the Council 'not to try to go too fast or too far at once'. He was very doubtful of the wisdom, at that stage, of 'suggesting an alteration in the constitution or the method of government' of the country. Patronisingly, perhaps, he informed the councillors that 'in every dependency of the British Crown in Africa where there is a Legislative Council that Council has to this day still got an official majority', and yet those countries 'are further advanced politically than Basutoland is today'.[8] At the back of his mind, no doubt, were the Gold Coast, Nigeria and Uganda – Britain's political showpieces in Africa.

The councillors were left in no doubt as to the extent to which the colonial administration might permit a change in the constitution of the National Council. First there could be no Legislative council. Secondly the issue of a bicameral National Council was out of the question. Thirdly there could be no parity between the appointed and the elected members of the National Council.

These points having been made clear, a committee was set up on 26 October 1943 to reconsider the proposals and, in effect, present a version which the colonial administration might find fit to approve. The Committee was composed of the following influential chiefs: Leloko Lerotholi, Talimo Joel, Gabashane Masopha, Lerotholi Mojela, Goliath Malebanye, Solomon Nkoebe, and Matlere Lerotholi. The lone commoner included in the Committee was the Reverend L. Polisa.

The National Council Becomes Partially and Indirectly Elective. District Councils Are Established and Associations Are Formally Represented

The Committee submitted its report to the full Council on 3 November. The Committee recommended that the National Council should adopt the following resolutions. Resolution 1 stated that all proclamations 'closely affecting the administration of the Basuto Nation or the life and welfare of the people should not be enacted until both the Paramount Chief and the Basutoland Council have been consulted'. So as to enable the Council to be so consulted 'and to fulfil efficiently its functions of advising' the Paramountcy and the Resident Commissioner, Resolution 2 called for certain alterations in the constitution and procedure to be made. These alterations were:

(a) to bring Councillors into closer touch and to provide machinery to enable the people to make their wishes known to Councillors; (b) to make the Council more representative: (c) to provide means whereby the Council can be consulted when it is not in Session.[9]

Resolution 3 provided that, as regards (a) of Resolution 2 – 'to bring Councillors into closer touch and to provide machinery to enable the people to make their wishes known to Councillors – district councils should be established. It was recommended that these district councils should meet at least three months prior to the sitting of the annual Session of the National Council, at the headquarters of each of the nine districts, under the chairmanship of the District Commissioner. All principal chiefs (who would soon be reclassified as 'ward chiefs', with the establishment of the National Treasury in 1946) as well as members of the National Council from each district, would be members of their respective District Councils.

At the *lipitso* to be held in each ward, delegates would be nominated to attend the District Councils and represent the people of their wards. Details for establishing these District Councils were to be entrusted to the District Commissioner, 'in consultation with the district chiefs' (that is, the nine chiefs each of whom was in charge of a district, as opposed to the twenty-four ward chiefs) 'and submitted for the approval of the Paramount Chief and the Resident Commissioner'. In any event, the functions of the District Councils would be 'to prepare motions for consideration by the Basutoland Council and to elect one member from the district for nomination as a member of the Basutoland Council'.

As regard (b) of Resolution 2 – to make the National Council 'more representative' – the Committee recommended in its Resolution 4 'that the Paramount Chief nominate as a member of the Basutoland Council one person from each district who had been recommended for nomination by the District Council of each district'. This would mean, in effect, that of the 94 councillors nominated by the Paramountcy, nine would be elected by District Councils. The Committee further recommended that the *Mofumahali* and the Resident Commissioner would, 'by arrangement between them nominate as members' of the National Council 'one or more' representatives of the Agricultural Association, the School Teachers' Association, the Basuto Traders' Association, the Leper Settlement (based at Botšabelo in Maseru), after the War the Basuto Ex-servicemen's Association, and the Basutoland Progressive Association. The *Lekhotla la Bafo*, whose campaign against the establishment of the National Treasury was already evident during the session and which was launched promptly at its conclusion,[10] was not recognised even at this juncture.

There was some problem as to whether or not the leprosy-stricken patients ought to be represented in the National Council; but the problem was merely one of logistics impelled by the morbid fear that some councillors had of their unfortunate countrymen and women when it was not clear who was going to represent them – an independent spokesman or themselves. It would have been impractical not to have them represented. Having been interned for the first time in 1913, when the National Council decided to isolate them from society, and having once before mutinied (as they were being treated like prisoners) and several times after that broken out of their settlement, to the horror of the entire country, their militancy had left its record in the minds of councillors.[11] There was real fear that if they were not represented when other associations were, they might, one day, break out and descend on the National Council. Chief Bolokoe Malebanye may have had that fact in mind, more so than his manifest reason, when he said in their defence: 'I agree a thousand times that lepers should be represented. . . . They are our people who have been unfortunate, and if they are not to be represented we might as well close this council.'[12]

The councillors who opposed the representation of the leprosy-stricken patients did nevertheless also have a point. Cynically put by Chief Leloko Lerotholi, this point was that:

> There are people in Government hospitals who are not represented. And I have never heard that in any parliament there are representatives of lepers. Why should we do what is not done in other countries.[13]

This was the only aspect of the four Resolutions which in the end had to be put to vote, and it was decided in favour of the Leper Settlement: a representative would be a chief who enjoyed their esteem.

Arrangements were made to implement these Resolutions during the second half of 1944: but it was not until 1948 that they were promulgated into law – as Proclamation No. 48 of that year.[14] By then the National Council had made further recommendations to the arrangement: the members of the National Council to be elected by the District Councils had been increased to two for each district. By 1950 this number had been increased to four,[15] thus making for a total of 36 councillors returned by the District Councils. The composition of the National Council by 1958 was as follows: (a) the Resident Commissioner was still there as the President; (b) the Regent remained as the Chief Adviser; (c) there were still five members nominated by the Resident Commissioner; (d) of the 94 members nominated by the Regent, however, 36 were indirectly elected by District Councils. Six were elected by the six recognised associations – formally known as the Basutoland Agricultural Union, the Basutoland Progressive Association, the Basuto Traders' Association, the Basuto ex-servicemen, the Basutoland Teachers' Association, and the Basuto Leper Settlement, whose representative was chosen by the Regent.

Within a short span of time developments had moved more rapidly on the question of broadening representation than they had in the previous decades since the establishment of the National Council; but, until 1958 when in principle the establishment of a legislative council was accepted, the colonial administration was still most reluctant to move any further. The existing legislation by 1958, in fact, still gave the Resident Commissioner a wide latitude in the appointment of the members of District Councils. Section 19 of Proclamation No 48 provided that:

> The District Council of each district shall consist of the following members who shall be appointed as such by the Resident Commissioner: (a) as many as may be decided by the Resident Commissioner after consultation with the Paramount Chief. Such members shall be nominated by the Paramount Chief to the Resident Commissioner for his approval; (b) one representative nominated to the Administrative Office in charge of the District by each of the bodies enumerated [viz., the six Associations] as are, in the opinion of the Resident Commissioner, of such standing in the District as to warrant representation in the District Councils; (c) as many elected representatives of the residents of the district as may be decided by the Resident Commissioner after consultation with the Paramount Chief.[16]

The practice followed for appointments in the District Councils by 1958 was as follows. One member was elected by secret ballot to approximately one thousand taxpayers. For purposes of illustration this meant, for instance, that Mokhotlong – the smallest district in the territory – might have about nine members, while Maseru, the largest district might have about thirty-nine members. Ward chiefs in each district, as well as members of the National Council nominated from time to time, and such other members of the National Council as the Regent might nominate, were also members of District Councils. There were always about four representatives from associations. The District Commissioner was Chairman, although a Mosotho acted as Chairman for the major part of a District Council meeting.[17]

The Regent is Brought Firmly under the Control of the National Council. The High Commissioner is Asked to Declare a Policy of Consulting the Regent and the Council

The National Council's ad hoc Committee on constitutional reforms established at the 38th Session in 1943 prepared two other resolutions of far-reaching importance. Their effect, generally, was to bring the office of *Morena e Moholo* under the control of the National Council. Once begun, that trend would further be buttressed by other arrangements between 1949 and 1958. The net effect was to lay down the formal groundwork for the establishment of a constitutional monarchy.

This trend began with the establishment, based on Resolution 5, of the Standing Committee of the National Council. The Standing Committee was supposedly to satisfy point (c) of Resolution 2, namely, to provide means whereby the Council could be consulted when it was not in session. It was composed of five members elected by the Council, of whom three constituted a quorum. The Standing Committee met at least once every two months, and more often if necessary to transact its business of advising the Regent and the Resident Commissioner on any issues that did not require the decision of the full Council. It presented its report at each session. Its life was one year, but its members were eligible for re-election. As it was alluded to earlier, it was dominated by chiefs.

At least one logical outcome of the establishment of the Standing Committee was that it encroached on the sphere of the Matsieng courtiers. It overshadowed them in the name of the National Council. In turn, during the periods that it sat, it became important for the Regent to extend her influence over it. Very early upon its establishment, however, the Standing Committee felt it had to assert its own independence and make it clear to the powers that be that it would not be manipulated. The opportunity presented itself late in 1944 when the Standing Committee sat to screen a representative of the Teachers' Association to the National Council. Present through her own representative in the Standing Committee, the Regent threw in her weight with the minority, thus making the appointment quite awkward. On 22 November 1944, the Standing Committee felt compelled to write a letter to the Resident Commissioner to point out that: 'This is an indication that if the Paramount Chief can be present such acts as these can often occur.' Its general stand in the final analysis was as follows:

> We, the Standing Committee, to-day (22.11.44) humbly but with firm feelings request that our Paramount Chief who is the head of the nation, would not be acting with Justice if she attended meetings of the Standing Committee, because she has her senior advisers who are the House of Moshesh and the other Basuto who have such right have been so recognised. . . . Chief, we are the offspring of a nation which is accustomed to speak and express its views in freedom.[18]

The signatories to the letter, ironically, Chiefs Leloko Lerotholi, Gabashane Masopha, Matlere Lerotholi, Talimo Joel and Khosimotse Ntaote, were themselves all the Sons of Moshoeshoe. The first two, it will be noticed, had been intimate courtiers with previous Monarchs – Leloko Lerotholi with Griffith Lerotholi, and Gabashane Masopha with Seeiso Griffith. Matlere Lerotholi would dominate the 1950s as the senior uncle to the royal house. In the circumstances it appeared as if senior chiefs were doing as much to maintain the independence of the Standing Committee as further to divest the Regent of the old style of exercising authority, while they themselves shifted their allegiance to the National Council. In short the conflict between the indigenous royal court at Matsieng and the colonial National Council was being resolved at the cost of emasculating the office of *Morena e Moholo*.

Resolution 7 of the ad hoc Committee on constitutional reforms sought, explicitly, to bring both the Regent as well as the High Commissioner under the control of the National Council. As regards the latter, it stated that:

> The Council . . . asks for a declaration by the High Commissioner on behalf of His Majesty's Government that it is the policy of His Majesty's Government to consult the Paramount Chief and the

Basutoland Council before Proclamations closely affecting the administration of the country and the life and welfare of the people are enacted until the time comes for Basutoland to have its own Legislative Council.[19]

As regards the former, it stated

Council also asked for a declaration by the Paramount Chief that it is the policy of the Paramountcy to consult the Council before issuing orders or making rules closely affecting the administration of the country and the life and welfare of the Basuto Nation.

The Resident Commissioner, it is significant to point out, was generally pleased with the entire package of the 1943 Resolutions, including Resolution 7, its tacit challenge to the High Commissioner's powers notwithstanding. The Resolutions had not been radical, yet they had gone in a direction envisaged by the colonial administration. As he put it, in a letter to the High Commissioner, dated 13 May 1944:

In my opinion these resolutions, if implemented will be an important step to the gradual conversion of the Paramountcy from an autocracy to a constitutional monarchy and will tend to place the Basuto Native Administration on a more representative and democratic basis and better suited to modern conditions.[20]

In the same letter, the Resident Commissioner advised the High Commissioner on a suitable response to the part of Resolution 7 in so far as it affected him. Having secured approval on his own advice, he read it back to the National Council at its 39th Session, on 1 June 1944, as the High Commissioner's response:

I can assure Council that it is the policy of his Majesty's Government to consult the Paramount Chief and the Basutoland Council before proclamations closely affecting the domestic affairs and welfare of the Basuto native administration are enacted. To avoid misunderstanding I must make it clear that there are proclamations dealing with matters which do not fall within this definition, such, for example, as proclamations imposing income or other taxes on Europeans only, or making changes in customs and excise duties in accordance with the customs agreement with the Union Government, or dealing with the conditions of service of officials, or with certain technical and legal matters, and that in the case of such proclamations it is left to the discretion of the Resident Commissioner as President of the Council whether Council is consulted or not.[21]

In one sense, the statement was a clear and concise exposition of the High Commissioner's role in Lesotho's dual government. In another sense, it was a clear play on words: essentially, while the evolved style of government impelled the colonial administration to 'consult' the Regent and the National Council, the discretion for consultation was left exclusively to the High Commissioner and the Resident Commissioner. Most of the time they consulted; but when it suited them, they claimed that they were not obliged to do so. So the National Council had not made any *real* gains in this direction; the Order-in-Council of 1884, on which the powers of the High Commissioner and the Resident Commissioner vested, was not formally amended.

The Regent's own response to Resolution 7, addressed to the President of the National Council (10 May 1944), was as follows:

> Chief, regarding these recommendations which were made and approved by Council I beg to state that with reference to resolution 7 asking for a declaration by the Paramount Chief I request His Honour the Resident Commissioner as President of the Basutoland Council to inform the Council that I, as Paramount Chief of the Basuto nation, confirm that it is the policy of the Paramountcy to consult the Basutoland Council before issuing orders or making rules especially affecting the life or welfare of the Basuto people and the administration of the Basuto.[22]

Although, as in the case above (involving the High Commissioner), no proclamation was promulgated to establish this policy of consultation vouched for by the Regent, the National Council's authority on her powers as stipulated was effective. It may be said in constitutional terms that a *convention* in this regard had been established. From the point of view of the National Council, however, it was probably construed as the result of a legislative exercise – in the same way as *The Laws of Lerotholi* continued to be regarded, official advice notwithstanding.

In 1948 the National Council made a 'suggestion' to the Regent 'that three advisers should be chosen by her from a panel elected by Council', composed of twelve councillors. A delegation, interestingly headed by Chief Lerotholi – a former Matsieng courtier – was sent to put the 'suggestion' to the Regent. Although the Regent was reported to have 'fallen in with Council's suggestion', it was unmistakable that the question of power was wrapped in the apparently simple language. Proof of this was manifested in the Regent's own suggestions. First she suggested that the panel from which she was to choose her advisers should be expanded to eighteen. Her suggestion was granted, but only following an impasse which, in the end, was resolved by voting. Second, as if to say she was not alone going to be subjected to the Council's influence and control, she suggested that 'a similar provision should be made for the ward Chiefs'; 'their advisers should also be nominated by Council'. That suggestion too was granted.[23]

Two years later, in 1950, the National Council took yet another step in the direction of bringing the Regent under its control. It succeeded in ensuring that no local rate or levy imposed by her office under the Native Administration Proclamation of 1938 should be deemed valid unless the Council concurred.[24]

The 49th Session of the National Council, in 1953, can be viewed as the peak in the trend during the Regency for the Matsieng house to be subjugated under the National Council. This was signified by two related developments. One was that, quite significantly, the Regent, in consultation with, and at the instigation of, the Resident Commissioner, E. P. Arrowsmith, requested the National Council to aid her with a fourth Adviser. The other was that, arising from a motion from the District of Mohale's hoek, something akin to a 'cabinet' was formalised at Matsieng: each of the four Advisers was given a portfolio, so to speak, responsibilities being divided into Administration, Judicial Matters, Finance, and Agriculture. Before that, as Chief Kelebone Nkoebe observed:

> The Position has been that these Advisers of the Paramount Chief were merely put there and it was not decided what particular work each of them would be responsible for. At the present time they only know themselves as the Paramount Chief's Advisers but they do not know what work each one is responsible for.[25]

With the formalisation of the functions of these Advisers, the indigenous Royal Court of Matsieng was, for all intents and purposes, dead. For the subsequent period, until 1960, when the Legislative Council sat for the first time, and when Prince Bereng Seeiso was given the sceptre, Matsieng was dominated by five chiefs. These were, Chief Matlere Lerotholi, the late Griffith Lerotholi's half-brother, who was the *de facto* Acting Regent whenever *Mofumahali*

'Mantšebo could not, for one reason or another, fulfil the responsibilities of her office. Matlere Lerotholi, it may be added, had been one staunch supporter for an additional Adviser as well as for the division of the Advisers' responsibilities at the 49th Session in 1953. The other four were the Regent's Advisers: Chiefs Nkoebe Mitchel, Leabua Jonathan (a junior son of the late Jonathan of Leribe), Leshoboro Majara, and Patrick 'Mota. All the five Chiefs fell under that ill-defined banner termed the Sons of Moshoeshoe. In the case of Nkoebe Mitchel, he was the descendent of Makhabane, the more famous of Moshoeshoe's two full brothers. Leabua Jonathan and Leshoboro Majara were the descendents of Molapo and Majara, Moshoeshoe's second and fourth sons, respectively, by his great wife 'Mamohato. Patrick 'Mota was a descendent of Moshoeshoe by his second house, under the charge of 'Manneko. All the four Advisers were from the North. None of the five Chiefs owed their allegiance to Matsieng: they derived their authority either from the National Council or from their individual caretakings or wards. In other words, the office of *Morena e Moholo* had become ceremonial.

The Question of Lesotho's Constitutional Status under the British Government Becomes an Issue

Beginning in 1947, with the 43rd Session of the National Council, both the Council as well as the Regent began to raise and to assert the point that Lesotho was not a crown colony, that it was a protectorate, and as such it was constitutionally anomalous that the colonial administration was exercising so much power over it. Motion No. 2, from the Mafeteng District Council, represented by Councillor MacDonald Phasumane, on the question, had to be postponed to the 44th Session in 1944, to give the Resident Commissioner, A. D. Forsyth Thompson, the opportunity to undertake research and enlighten the Council accordingly.

In his introduction of the motion – 'that Basutoland should be declared to be a Protectorate and not a Colony' – Councillor Phasumane expressed the Mafeteng District Council's wish to know 'whether Basutoland is a Colony or whether it is a Protectorate'. In the view of the District Council, it was the latter.[26]

The motion had the maximum support of the Council. Best expressed by Chief Leloko Lerotholi, the view of the Council was that 'Chief Moshesh, the founder of this Nation, thought we were a Protectorate'. The National Council, Chief Leloko Lerotholi revealed, had only recently been made anxious when the Resident Commissioner, A. D. Forsyth Thompson, kept throwing the suggestion when he was giving war veterans medals, to the effect 'that this was a Crown Colony', although in the same breath 'he stated, publicly, that in 1868 when Basutoland was accepted it was taken as a Protectorate'. (The Resident Commissioner interjected that on the second point he was being misinterpreted.)[27] Further, the Chief disclosed, 'recently' one of the officers in the colonial administration, a man named MacKenzie, had written a pamphlet 'that really roused our feelings' in which he stated that 'Basutoland is a Crown Colony; it is a King's possession'.[28] 'Nobody had ever told us before then', Chief Leloko said, 'that we were taken under the British Crown in any other manner than being protected from the Boers'.[29]

An immediate issue at stake at that point, which stood to be affected by Lesotho being a crown colony, as opposed to being a protectorate, was land. Europeans, for the most part the colonial officers, were concentrated in each of the nine administrative centres in the districts, styled 'Camps'. With time these camps had come to be associated with European authority. They were expanding, and as they expanded, more by usage than by law the colonial administration was beginning to define them as 'Government Reserves'. The Basotho were being forbidden to encroach into them – either for grazing, building, or agricultural purposes. The end result was that animosity between the Basotho in general and the colonial officers was building up. This issue had been the subject of debate at the 44th Session of the Council, where the Resident Commissioner had alleged that 'the Government' had been given sites on the reserves by Moshoeshoe and his successors. Besides the query, as Chief Leloko also indicated, that 'the country did not belong' to any Mosotho monarch to give,[30] there was the natural fear that if, as Mackenzie was said to have stated, Lesotho was 'a King's possession', those reserves might be lost for ever, and possibly the entire country together with them. Chief Leloko, in step with other councillors and quite discerning at that session, insisted that it was about time the President of the Council distinguished the English terms 'Crown Colony', 'Protectorate', and 'Territory'.[31]

From the lengthy and heavily-documented exposition that the President of the National Council gave in response to the motion, it was clear that he had made effective use of the Government Archives in Maseru over the past year. His speech traced Lesotho's relations with the British Government from the 1840s to the present. It was beaded with appropriate quotations. Yet it was not convincing. He admitted at the outset that it was 'not altogether an easy question to understand'. There was, he admitted, 'considerable confusion in the minds of many people, both the Europeans and the Africans, as to what the status is of the three High Commission Territories' – Lesotho, Bechuanaland and Swaziland – 'even when people know what the difference is, for convenience they continue to use the word "Protectorate"'. He confessed his own lack of confidence in attempting to settle the question; he would deal with it only 'in so far as my limited abilities allow'. Those abilities, it had to be concluded at the end, did not encompass the knowledge to distinguish the terms 'Crown Colony', 'Protectorate', and 'Territory', which was at the centre of the discussion. He did not even attempt it.[32]

In a nutshell, his explanation was the following:

Basutoland was in a peculiar position. In 1862 Moshesh asked that the Queen should rule his people through him. 'The man whom I ask from the Queen to live with me will guide and direct me' he said. That is why, that is to say he stipulated that there should not be direct administration by the Government but that the country should be ruled through him. That was before Basutoland was annexed to the Crown. But in spite of annexation the British Government has ever since administered the country through the Paramount Chief, and has tried as much as possible to draw the people into the process of administration. In other words it has paid constant attention to Moshesh's request made before the Territory was annexed. . . . The important thing to remember is that the system of indirect rule which has of recent years received recognition in Africa has been in force for many years in Basutoland. That is to say the Government does not normally give its orders direct to the people and enforce them; it leaves that to the Paramount Chief and his Chiefs. But it does give constant encouragement and guidance to the Chiefs and people to adapt themselves to changing conditions and to learn to govern themselves on modern lines.

The National Council quite clearly did not think that the Resident Commissioner had said anything of value. The mover of the motion, MacDonald Phasumane, asked that all correspondence cited in the speech should be made available to the Council. Beyond that he was very cynical:

> I say we should not be in the Government of Pharaoh(.) [W]ho knows Joseph? Because it may happen that hereafter there will be another Pharaoh who will not know Joseph.[33]

In other words, as Councillor Phasumane saw it, the only thing that the Resident Commissioner had convinced the Council of was that the answer to the question was as elusive as finding the Biblical Joseph, who could only be found by those who knew the colour of his blanket – in this case, His Majesty King George VI's officers. Chief Malebanye also reacted in the same vein:

> [W]e have been told a very long story, an important story, but if you listened very carefully you will find that some letters say there is really nothing in this matter, and others say there is really something. Now Chiefs, look lest the water has grown very much behind your hut, and the water is now percolating into your houses, and let us scrape away the dirt from behind our huts. Everything will not be visible.[34]

The statement, it appears, meant that the Resident Commissioner's exposition had served only to camouflage the truth, and if the Council was still interested in it, it had to do the assignment for itself.

The assignment was, of course, never done; but the issue was not dropped. It was picked up again with rigour early in 1951. When the colonial administration had continued to assert its authority on the administrative 'Camps', the Sons of Moshoeshoe and the Advisers to the Regent held a meeting at Matsieng on the 3rd, 4th and 5th of January 1951, in which they decided that the Resident Commissioner, being still Mr Forsyth Thompson, should be put in his place. Consequent upon that meeting, *Mofumahali* addressed a bold letter to the Resident Commissioner reminding him that he was only 'His Majesty's Representative who has come to work and to advise one another with the Paramount Chief who is herself the caretaker of this country in administrative matters concerning this Nation, to bring about its advancement and to see to the prosperity of the country'. She expressed the kernel of her message as follows:

> Your Honour, the undistinguished action pursued in general by the Government Officers in Basutoland indicates that Government authorities on reasons known to themselves alone have taken

upon themselves powers which are not laid down in the Covenant between Queen Victoria the Good and Moshesh the Wise, Chief of the Basuto, and that it is attempting to separate administration of the Basuto living out of the Reserve. . . . Basutoland as a whole is an integrated State inhabited by Basuto ruled by the Paramount Chief of Basutoland and the Basuto Chiefs under him. . . . May the Government please hold in abeyance any action which might tend to indicate the taking upon itself powers which are not included in the Covenant of the alliance and protection between the late Moshesh the Wise and Victoria the Good.[35]

Forsyth Thompson was infuriated by the tone and content of the letter; and in his venomous response he did much to confirm the suspicions of the likes of Councillor MacDonald Phasumane who had tacitly suggested in 1948 that perhaps he (Forsyth Thompson) could discover Joseph's body because he seemed to know the colour of his blanket. He lashed out:

I was placed here to govern this country and I mean just that. The fact that Her Majesty, Queen Victoria, in her greatness of heart consented to govern through the Paramount Chief and Chiefs, and that her successors have done so, and will probably continue to do so, appears to have blinded you to the fact that His Majesty can rule His Basuto subjects exactly as he pleases. You have forgotten that Moshesh was at his [last] gasp, he was on the point of being overwhelmed by the Boers, and with a last despairing cry he begged the Queen to save him. She did so but without terms. Drowning men are in no position to dictate terms. . . . And the result? Not gratitude, as you might expect, but growing arrogance on the part of the Sons of Moshesh.[36]

Forsyth Thompson might have thought that he had put the Regent and the Sons of Moshoeshoe in their place; but he did not succeed in removing the subject of their letter from the nation's political agenda. It would resurface under E. P. Arrowsmith, his successor, in 1953. At the 49th Session of the National Council, held that year, the District of Mokhotlong presented a motion (Motion No. 34) to the effect that the Order-in-Council of 1884, which Forsyth Thompson had previously, in 1948, said was the one that had made Lesotho a crown colony, should be amended: 'before his Excellency the High Commissioner can make a Proclamation he should consult the Paramount Chief or the Basutoland National Council or the Standing

Committee'. Speaking to the motion, Councillor Joshua Khali, the District Council representative from Mokhotlong, reiterated the national view on the constitutional status of the country:

> This is by no means new; in fact it is the foundation on which we have founded Basutoland. When Moshoeshoe placed himself under her Majesty the Queen amongst other things he made a request that her Majesty might be pleased in making laws; when these laws are made he himself should be consulted and he in turn would send word to Her Majesty to say that my Council is in agreement with this proposed law. . . . It was only around 1871 that matters changed. . . . The Paramount Chief of Basutoland was forgotten and as a whole the Nation of the Basuto were forgotten. *The wishes of the Nation also became forgotten in that the Nation should be satisfied they should be governed to their own wishes.*[37] [My emphasis]

The Establishment of the Basutoland African Congress; Its Objectives and Its Agitation for Self-government 'Now'

The agitation for constitutional advance in the 1950s which culminated in the establishment of a Legislative Council by 1959 owed a great deal of its drive to the founding in 1952 of the Basutoland African Congress. A great deal of the vision and the vitality of the BAC was itself owing to its founder, Clement Ntsu Sejabanana Mokhehle. He was the son of Cicerone Mokhehle, one of the early Basotho Inspectors of Schools, or more accurately, Supervisors of Schools, as the former title was reserved for European counterparts.

Ntsu Mokhehle had been awarded a Bachelor of Science degree and a Masters in Science in Zoology at Fort Hare, submitting a thesis entitled 'Parasitology of Birds', for which he got a distinction, in the mid-1940s. Already, whilst he was at Fort Hare, in the company of Oliver Tambo, he had taken an active interest in politics. In South Africa he was a member of the Youth League of the South African National Congress (ANC). On the home front, in Lesotho, he later became one of Josiel Lefela's disciples in the Lekhotla la Bafo. His efforts to start an early teaching career in his own country were frustrated by race prejudice and fear of his radicalism at Lesotho High School (founded in 1939) where he was not allowed to teach his subject, science, and so for a while he took a teaching job in the Union of South Africa. Later he came home to become the

Headmaster of the Higher Primary School in Maseru. He joined the Basutoland African National Teachers' Association (BANTA), of which he soon became the President, before founding the BAC in 1952.[38]

The BAC's Manifesto, published on 7 October 1952, emphasised three general objectives. First 'that the incorporation of Basutoland within the Union of South Africa would both be impolitic and repugnant to the best wishes of every Mosotho'. The BAC believed 'that Basutoland must never, at any time in the present, in future, as it has not been in the past, be incorporated within the Union of South Africa, except by consent of two thirds majority of the Basotho'. Second it declared that 'Discrimination Must Quit Basutoland'. It called for the total removal of 'all discriminatory laws' and practices in the Territory, which had come into vogue with almost the same virulence as in the Union of South Africa, and it demanded that any European who practised colour discrimination should 'be caused to leave the country'. Third it stated, 'We want Self-Government for the Basotho in Basutoland NOW.' The substance of this objective is worth quoting:

> Whereas Basutoland is sometimes referred to as a democracy, we of the Basutoland African Congress hold that there is no democracy in Basutoland – the High Commissioner in Pretoria and the High Commissioner at Matsieng, rule this territory with such powers as amount to open dictatorship, in practice though not by law. The Basotho, who in fact own the land have, through the National Council, been reduced to mere advisors on vital matters that fundamentally affect their own political, social, economic and educational matters. . . . We of the Basutoland African Congress, therefore, without a desire to create any impression whatsover that Basotho desire or have intentions of any sort to break away from the British Government, do demand self-government in Basutoland by the Basotho NOW.[39]

The BAC's reluctance to demand full independence can, no doubt, be attributed to the fear, even in the unlikely event that such independence might be granted, of incorporation into the Union of South Africa.

Consequent upon the founding of the BAC, all resistance to the attainment of self-government was forced to give way. Agitation intensified both in and outside the National Council. In the latter arena the agitation was sharpened by the founding of the press organ

Mohlabani (The Warrior) in September 1954. As pledged in the Editor's letter announcing the first issue of *Mohlabani*, it was meant to be 'an independent fearless paper, which is not tied to the apron strings of capitalists' or a political party. Its aim was to 'give praise where it is due, and expose inequity and unfair treatment where they exist'. *Mohlabani*'s editor pledged that it would not 'turn into a spineless appeaser, sacrificing its principles for fear of offending those who deserve the sharp lash of its whip'. And indeed the paper lived up to its founder's mark.[40]

At the time, in 1954, that Bennet Khaketla joined Lesotho politics, he was not yet a member of Mokhehle's BAC. He would join later. However, as with many other educated Basotho of the breed with university degrees such as, for instance, Dr Maile Emsley Maema (a medical doctor who had made a financial contribution toward the founding of *Mohlabani*, but was otherwise a member of the Progressive Association), he simply felt that the pernicious aspects of colonial administration must be brought to an end. The Basotho must take full charge of the internal affairs of Lesotho, *under British protection* (from the Union of South Africa). Racial discrimination must come to an end. Basotho who qualified for employment in the public service must be employed in positions commensurate with their qualifications and be paid the salaries that their European counterparts were getting.

This new breed of the educated élite was a healthy political hybrid between the Progressive Association and the *Lekhotla la Bafo*: it had all of the *Lekhotla la Bafo*'s sentiments of nationalism, but none of its scattered sense of purpose. It had all of the BPA's sense of focus, but none of its compromising spirit with the colonial administration. Above all else, it was quite clear that this breed was interested not so much in participating in the political sphere of its country as in controlling its destiny.

The BAC's attitude toward the chieftaincy was basically that 'the nation could progress very well without Chiefs'.[41] As B. M. Khaketla stated it in *Mohlabani* in 1957, if the chieftaincy continued to be unresponsive to the needs of the nation, it would be 'superseded and sent to join the mesozoic reptiles upon the evolutionary scrap-heap of discarded political experiments'.[42] His own interpretation of the role of the chieftaincy was basically as follows:

> In Sesotho we have a saying that a Chief is a Chief because of the people. In other words it means that he remains Chief so long as

he protects the interests of his people, and rules them according to their wishes and not his own whims and idiosyncracies. This saying expresses a very great fundamental truth, and explains the nature of Chieftainship in a manner that is accepted by all democratic countries the world over. It means that Chieftainship is the product of the wills, the desires, the sympathies and the thoughts of men over which it rules. It is constituted by comradeship in work, by fellowship in purpose and in hope, by a general desire for and a general willingness to submit to constituted authority that will be the protector of the interests of the ruled and not of a privileged section. Take away this desire, this willingness, this sympathy, and there is no Chieftainship.[43]

B. M. Khaketla was of course aware of the fact that the type of constitution he was so ably describing was a thing of the past. As a reality it had waned and virtually ceased to exist. His statement was a virtual epitaph on its grave. The chieftaincy continued, but with neither a respect for the old principles of government, nor a commitment to the novel parliamentary institutions. Whichever direction it went – to the past or to the future – it went for convenience or for survival.

Concurrent with these developments – the founding of the BAC and the launching of the explicitly political *Mohlabani* – was a concerted effort in the National Council for an immediate constitutional advance. In two successive years, 1952 – a month before the BAC would publish its Manifesto in September – and 1953, motions had been introduced which had a bearing on legislative and executive powers. On the second occasion, at the 49th Session, two such motions, by Councillor Kaizer Jubilee of Butha Buthe and Councillor N. M. Tlale, had been passionately presented. N. M. Tlale, whose Motion No. 83, sponsored by the Progressive Association, was the better argued, read:

In short what could only be emphasized is that this country should be given the right of Legislating in regard to matters which affect the country. The laws which were made by Lerotholi and used to great benefit in this country have been so done for the last fifty years. The Courts whenever they make their decisions refer to this law. It is strange that we are not recognised as a legislative council. What we now request is that this working should be approved and confirmed by law that this is a legislative council. . . . I would like to point out the rights which we are now claiming are not strange.

Other African races in Africa have already been given the right to make laws, it should be remembered that some of these countries are those which fell under the British Government after Basutoland, although by progress and education they are behind the Basuto.[44]

Against this background, the High Commissioner authorised the establishment in April 1954 of the Administrative Reforms Committee, chaired by Sir Henry Moore, for the purpose of examining 'the structure of Native Administration . . . and to make recommendations regarding the lines of its future development'. Particular reference was made to the following areas: '(1) Existing system of Native Authority. (2) The need for more effective instruments of Local Government at the district level. (3) The relationship of the local government structure which they recommend with the Central Government and its offices, and (4) the financial implications of their recommendations.'[45]

The great expectation of all the predominantly commoner led organisations – the Progressive Association, the *Lekhotla la Bafo*, but mostly the BAC, was that the establishment of a legislative council would be at the centre of Sir Henry Moore's Committee considerations; but in this they would be sorely disappointed, the Progressive Association much less than the other two. Sir Henry totally excluded the question as falling outside his mandate. In its Memorandum to the Secretary for Commonwealth Relations, Lord Swinton – dated 20 June 1954 – the BAC expressed its disappointment as follows:

> The Basutoland National Council had, on behalf of the nation requested that the High Commissioner enter into reforms to effect the establishment of a legislative council; hence the nation was surprised when Sir Henry Moore baulked the recommendations in this respect. If the Basutoland people had known that the commission's terms of reference number three did not cover the legislative council they would not have accepted the commission – for without that the 4 terms of reference are made to establish an administrative machinery that has been telescoped in our administrative development and we have long passed that stage.[46]

A number of influential chiefs, however, were supportive of Sir Henry Moore's exclusion of a legislative council in his Report. This, Weisfelder correctly points out, was owing to 'their fears that the more far reaching demands for self-government under a legislative council would ultimately lead to the subordination and destruction of the chieftainship by an elected majority'.[47] However, the time when chiefs alone could forestall constitutional developments in the country had passed. Political leadership was shifting to the side of the more radical educated commoners represented by Ntsu Mokhehle and Bennet Khaketla. The colonial administration could not ignore their existence and their demands.

Report on Constitutional Reform and Chieftainship Affairs: A Legislative Council is Established

In 1955, only a year following the controversial Moore Report, the question of a Legislative Council was back on the agenda of the National Council. This time virtually all the chiefs fell in line hoping, perhaps, to avoid the *Mohlabani*'s indictment that their reluctance to fight against the Moore Report stemmed from their desire to establish 'an oligarchy of autocratic chiefs;'[48] but mostly because they were losing the leadership.

On 21 September 1955, the National Council passed Motion 90, which requested 'that the Basutoland Council be given power to make laws in all internal matters, such laws to be confirmed by the Paramount Chief'. Further, the motion proposed that the Resident Commissioner and departmental heads of his staff of officers should guide and advise the Council in policy. It concluded by stating that 'the Resident Commissioner, Heads of Departments and District Commissioners should deal with external affairs on behalf of Her Majesty's Government'. The motion proved acceptable to the colonial administration, and on 5 May 1956, the Secretary of State replied:

I am prepared to consider proposals whereby the Basutoland Council should be given power to make laws in regard to internal matters affecting the Basuto alone, but not in regard to matters affecting people other than the Basuto or countries other than Basutoland. But before the Basutoland Council are given powers to pass laws, however, they will have to think how they should go about law-making, and who is going to put the laws they pass into effect. . . . the Basutoland Council must, therefore, submit its considered recommendations on these matters at the same time as it submits detailed proposals with regard to the scope of its law-making powers.[49]

In terms of Motion 90, nine councillors were appointed to form what came to be known as the Constitutional Reform Committee. Of these nine, only two were commoners, and these were Councillors Gabriel C. Manyeli of Roma and Edwin Leanya of Mafeteng. Of the chiefs, Leabua Jonathan was an Adviser to the Regent, destined in a few years time to be Prime Minister of an Independent Lesotho. Chief George Bereng, who had attempted a bachelor's degree at the University of South Africa, was made Chairman of the Committee. The Government Secretary, Gordon M. Hector, was the Secretary; and D. V. Cowen, a Professor of Comparative Law at the University of Cape Town, was invited to be the Committee's Constitutional Adviser.

The Committee's recommendations were brought for discussions in London, where the Delegations of Lesotho and the United Kingdom sat in November and December 1958 to agree on a constitution for a Legislative Council. Two developments at those discussions would be of interest for the purpose of this study. First, as it was minuted on November 21.

> Professor Cowen said that the Basutoland Delegation were agreed that the Paramount Chief should not be a member of the Executive Council. But if she was not to be a member, she would need advice in exercising their (sic) functions – and not least in connection with recommendations of the Executive Council. The Paramount Chief had herself said that she wished to be a constitutional ruler and to act in accordance with the wishes of the Nation. . . . The Delegation did not suggest removing her right to consult anyone whom she pleased but wished to protect her position by providing that she must consult the Resident Commissioner, the member of the Executive Council nominated by the Paramount Chief.[50]

The significance of this statement, besides its indication for the establishment of an Executive Council at the same time as the Legislative Council was beign established, is that the Regent, on the counsel of her Advisers, had agreed to be a constitutional monarch. That meant that when Prince Bereng Seeiso would succeed to Office in 1960, he would find himself already bound by that decision.

Second it is significant to note that those discussions almost broke down completely on one contentious issue – the issue of whether

Lesotho was a protectorate or a crown colony. The constitutional point that had sparked the issue was that the UK Delegation had insisted, basing itself on the British colonial experience, that the High Commissioner would be a member of the Executive Council with the power of veto over it, exercised on his behalf by the Resident Commissioner. Holding the contrary view, the Lesotho Delegation insisted that the High Commissioner ought not to be a member of the Executive Council at all. Challenging the UK Delegation,

> Professor Cowen said that the United Kingdom's proposals in regard to the Executive Council rested on their assumption that they were the only proposals compatible with Basutoland having the status of an ordinary colony. The Basutoland Delegation might however wish to challenge both the assumption that Basutoland was in fact a colony and the assertion that an Executive Council of this kind which the United Kingdom were proposing was the only one consistent with the contention that Basutoland was a Crown colony.[51]

Sir Kenneth Roberts-Wray, on whose authority (together with Berriedale Keith) 'Basutoland' is accepted in Commonwealth constitutional law as a crown colony, was a member of the UK Delegation.[52]

The issue of whether Lesotho was a protectorate or a crown colony was, in the final analysis, not faced up to. Purely in the interests of sportsmanship, following a recess necessitated by rising tempers, and because it was close to Christmas – of which the Lesotho Delegation was subtly reminded that Christmas might be allowed to interrupt discussions indefinitely – the UK formula was followed.

REPRESENTATIVE GOVERNMENT IS ESTABLISHED

In 1958 Lesotho received a constitution giving it a legislative council and an executive council.[53] The Constitution necessarily bore the heavy print of Professor Cowen, who, although as the National Council's own invitee he enjoyed its confidence, had nevertheless his own convictions on the making of constitutions. Professor Cowen was then developing his views for *The Foundations of Freedom* (1961), on the conditions under which 'true democracy is to survive'. He believed in parliamentary institutions. He generally subscribed to the British model of government. The Lesotho situation, difficult as it was to fit within Western historical development of political institutions, presented a special challenge for him to test his stock in trade.[54]

Under his guiding hand, the Constitutional Reform Committee of 1958 had provided a theoretical background for the new Constitution which it had described in the following words:

> It has been said that constitutional progress in the British dependencies lies broadly in the direction of giving the peoples of the territories (i) a more *representative* share in government; and (ii) a more *responsible* share in government. This is a useful distinction; though the two ideas are related and cannot be kept entirely separate. . . . In speaking of responsible government we have in mind, primarily, the relationship between the executive arm and the legislative arm. There are varying degrees of responsible government; but full responsible government may be said to exist when the executive is entirely drawn from the legislature and is collectively responsible or accountable to the legislature, and through the legislature to the people. Looking at the matter from a slightly different point of view, full responsible government may be said to involve the transfer of the ultimate power of decision in all matters of government from the British authorities to the territorial electorate.[55]

Viewing Lesotho against this theoretical background, the Constitutional Reform Committee had recognised that 'it might take years before the idea of responsible government' could be implemented in Lesotho, even if it meant only that matters should fall within the competence of the National Council. The question before it, it felt, was 'how to associate the Basuto more closely with the legislative (law-making) and executive (policy-making and administrative) side of government in a satisfactory way'. In that regard the Committee accepted the fact that 'during the immediate future the control of policy-making will have to rest primarily in the hands of the British authorities'. At the same time, 'Africanisation of the public service' would be 'allowed to develop as much as possible'. Members of the National Council 'capable of exercising administrative responsibility' in high positions of the colonial administration would be encouraged 'to develop their talents'.

The Committee had then given the following specific constitutional framework for the Lesotho situation:

We have . . . sought to find a technique of government which, on the one hand, will make official control at the executive level both effective and acceptable during the immediately forseeable future, and, on the other hand, will provide sufficient scope for the exercise and development of the political energies of a people imbued with ideas of self-government. . . . If one had to put a descriptive label on the kind of constitutional machinery which we have devised, it could appropriately be called a form of 'representative government'; that is to say, we are recommending a legislative assembly of whom one half are to be elected by the inhabitants . . . , and an executive body which will not be 'responsible' to the legislature. . . . Now this is a system which may be said to confer power without 'responsibility'. It is probably an inevitable stage in the progress of a British dependency towards self-government; and it has its own familiar difficulties. . . . The situation which gives rise to these difficulties has been described in a familiar metaphor: 'We have made the fire but we have stopped the chimney'. The smoke, which cannot escape up the chimney is, of course, the feeling which is engendered when a legislature containing an unofficial majority is able to pass or reject legislation and to refuse supplies, but is not able to control or dismiss the executive.[56]

The special feature of the 1959 Constitution was that it was a diarchy of representative government, with a unicameral legislative council consisting of 80 members, half of whom were elected. The 40 elected members were to be 'elected from among the members of predominantly elected District Council, by the District Councils' which would serve as electoral colleges. These District Councils would also become the main instruments of local government. Of the 40 non-elected members 22 were ex-officio principal chiefs, fourteen were nominated by the Regent/*Morena e Moholo*. And there were four 'official' members – the Government Secretary, the Financial Secretary, the Legal Secretary and the Commissioner for Local Government.

The reason why the Legislative Council was unicameral, instead of being bicameral, as some councillors had demanded, was noteworthy. The Constitutional Reform Committee, quite simply, had reasoned that: 'A single chamber . . . is what the Basuto are used to.' The Committee had felt that 'the interaction of thought between chiefs and commoners in a single body is in consonance with national traditions which long antedate the establishment of Basutoland

Council'. While recognising the usefulness of a second chamber, the Committee felt that in the case of Lesotho:

> The main function of a second chamber, which is to serve as a check on hasty legislation, may be carried out in a dignified and, it is hoped, efficient way by according certain powers of delay to the Paramount Chief.[57]

This type of rationale, of course, no longer accorded with the realities of a modern Lesotho. Over a period of over fifty years since the establishment of the National Council, during which the political bond between the educated commoners and the chiefs had worn very thin, the divergent interests of the two had sharpened. (Indeed in just three years from the first sitting of the Legislative Council it would seem judicious, in the light of recent experience, and in preparation for Independence, to opt for bicameralism. A bicameral legislature seemed to have been recognised as the better-suited, to keep at least the principal chiefs separate from commoners.)

The Basutoland National Council, as the legislature would continue to be officially called, would legislate for all persons in the Territory on all matters except on external affairs and defence, internal security, currency, public loans, customs and excise, posts and telegraphs, broadcasting, public service, copyright, trade marks, patents and designs. These subjects remained the responsibility of the High Commissioner, although the Council had the right to discuss all matters which fell in the High Commissioner's field. The rest of the powers, the most important being the financial powers, remained with the Legislative Council and the Executive Council, the latter being closely associated with the Resident Commissioner and loosely associated with the office of *Morena e Moholo*.

The Constitution provided for an Executive Council with four official members – the Resident Commissioner, who was the Chairman and who had a casting vote, the Government Secretary, the Financial Secretary and the Assistant Attorney General. In addition it had four 'unofficial' (that is, Basotho) members three of whom were elected by the Legislative Council and one was to be nominated by the *Morena e Moholo* from amongst the members of the Legislative Council. The official members were to hold office on the Executive Council at the High Commissioner's pleasure. The seat of an unofficial member could become vacant if the High Commissioner terminated his appointment, on the recommendation of the *Morena e Moholo*; if he accepted permanent appointment in the public service; if he resigned from the Executive Council; when his member-ship in the Legislative Council ceased (except, on the dissolution of the Legislative Council he might remain in office until a new Execu-tive Council was formed, when he would be eligible for re-appoint-ment if his membership in the Legislative Council continued).

Broadly speaking, the qualifications of elected members were to be similar to the qualifications for being a voter. The qualifications were to be: (a) membership of the Basotho Nation; (b) a minimum age of 21; (c) literacy in Sesotho (which was not a requirement for a voter); (d) residence in the Territory for a minimum period of six months immediately preceding election; (e) payment of tax (for men); and (f) all persons qualified, without prejudice on the grounds of race, religion or sex.

Strictly speaking, the 1959 Constitution did not address the ques-tion of the Judiciary. This question had been dealt with separately and with a different purpose for the most part from that for which the Constitutional Reform Committee of 1958 had been charged. Consequently it had been considered by a special Committee of the National Council, namely the Court Reforms Committee.

Nonetheless, in so far as the Constitutional Reform Committee had found it relevant to relate the question of the judiciary to its proposals (which would be the way in the final analysis in which it would be understood under the Constitution of 1959), it had treated it loosely as follows:

> In regard to judicial appointments and promotion we are clear that the Judiciary must be safeguarded against political influence and controversy; and see no reason, at present, to recommend any change in the existing system. In regard, however, to the jurisdiction of courts, which may well be regulated by the legislat-ive action, we are anxious to avoid a diversion of the field of competence in a way which involves discrimination between white persons and non-white persons; or in a way which implies that different systems of law must necessarily continue to be adminis-tered in two different sets of Courts. We have not found this an easy problem to solve, but believe that the best solution lies in giving the High Commissioner and the Basutoland Council concur-rent legislative powers in this field with a repugnancy test in favour of the High Commissioner.[58]

The National Treasury, which had become a symbol of Indirect Rule was abolished. No longer essential to the colonial administration as an instrument for ruling the Territory, but for the most part still essential to retain, in particular for purposes of local government, the chieftaincy was recognised by establishing a College of Chiefs. The college was concerned with the recognition of chiefs, settling disputes concerning succession, and generally for the settlement of all cases in the Territory which did not fall under courts of general jurisdiction. The College of Chiefs was designed to adapt the chieftaincy 'to fit more comfortably into the emerging pattern of modern Basuto society'.[59]

The first meeting and the First Session of the Legislative Council was held from 11 March to 6 June 1960. *Khosana* Constantine Bereng Seeiso had interrupted his studies at Oxford, obviously anxious that too many crucial decisions had already been taken in his minority which affected the office of *Morena e Moholo*, and he had been installed on his father's stool early in February 1960, with the new title of *Motlotlehi*.

Thus the old National Council ran its course. Having begun as a body of chiefs in 1903, it had gradually undergone change. It had infused principles and practices of a parliamentary government in the process, adjusted the political views of the chiefs, and challenged commoners to join politics, in spite of its originally conservative aims. In the end there was no doubt that the path toward a parliamentary form of government which Lesotho had taken was the one in which the leaders of an independent Lesotho, chiefs and commoners alike, generally believed was the correct one for their country. The role of the colonial administration in charting the path was of course evident. At the same time, the Basotho leaders were not passive.

7   The Placing of the Westminster Model

THE YOUNG PRINCE AND THE WAR OF THE ROYAL WIDOWS

Following the confirmation of *Mofumahali* 'Mantŝebo Seeiso as the Regent of Lesotho after her husband's untimely death in 1940, Prince Constantine Bereng, the late King's son by his second wife 'Mabereng (Sekhothali) Seeiso, began a bitter childhood. Promptly after the court case that confirmed her, the Regent desired that the Prince should be under her immediate care as the legal guardian. This, the natural mother and her supportive members of the royal house, Chiefs Theko Makhaola, Thabo Mojela (the Prince's future father-in-law), Kelebone Nkoebe, *Mofumahali* 'Mamathe G. Masopha, and Khethisa Tau, among others, could not allow. There was the fear that the Regent and her own supporters of royalty would deftly precipitate his demise, as indeed it apparently had happened before with the young Tau, Letsie II's son in 1913. That story has already been told. As the popular saying went: 'You cannot entrust a cat to raise the progeny of a mouse.'[1]

Whilst the Regent remained as his legal guardian, from the age of four the Prince was secretly placed under the care of a number of chiefs in succession – away from the potential dangers of Matsieng, by his mother's supporters. First he was placed in the North of the country, in the ward of Pitseng, under the care of Chief Khethisa Tau. Next he was placed under Chief Gabashane Masopha in Berea. Finally, in 1942, he was moved to Mokhotlong, far in the mountain gorges of Lesotho, under Chief Matlere Lerotholi, where he settled until 1948 when he was ready to begin his Standard IV studies in the lowlands.

During this period tensions between the rival cliques of the royal lineage were at their fever pitch and the future King of Lesotho absorbed the full effects of the horror stories and political intrigues surrounding his right to high office. These included one acute episode, on an occasion when it had seemed propitious for him to be in Matsieng, when it was put into circulation that he was going to be garrotted. He and his elder sister, Princess 'Mampoi, had to be hidden in a cave for some two days.[2]

Another decision seems to have been made in 1942, apparently in consultation with the Regent, that Prince Bereng should be raised in the company of another high-ranking youth of the royal house. Thus Prince Raphael Leshoboro, Seeiso's second son, born to his third wife Debora 'Maleshoboro, was also shorn from his own mother at Likhoele in the Mafeteng District to be raised by Chief Matlere in Mokhotlong.

In part for security reasons, and in part because the nearest school belonged to the PEMS, and the Regent, a staunch adherent of the Roman Catholic Church, did not favour it, the Princes received their education under private tutorship. Initially there seems to have been a high turn-over of these private tutors. From 1942 to 1945 there had been four of them at different times, namely, Mofana Morojele of the PEMS; C. Makoro, Eli Mohapi and Zacharia Mokhali of the Roman Catholic Church. Mofana Morojele seems to have been dropped because of the Regent's Church sensitivities. Although Makoro and Mohapi were dropped on the grounds of incomplete qualifications,[3] they were also not zealous Church adherents and that might have strengthened the Regent's hand in getting rid of them. The reasons for terminating Mokhali's services have been difficult to establish. All four tutors were Chief Matlere's own appointments and had not been initiated by Matsieng.

The fifth and lasting tutor was Francis J. Lekoatsa. His appointment was initiated by the Regent personally.[4] He was indeed a well-qualified and experienced teacher. On appointment he was teaching at the Government Intermediate School at Matsieng and hence he was well-known to the Regent. He was a zealous adherent of the Roman Catholic Church.

The significance of the issue of religion here is that, as *Mofumahali* 'Mantŝebo was a staunch Roman Catholic, so was *Mofumahali* 'Mabereng a staunch adherent of the PEMS. The two royal widows loathed each other thoroughly. Hence, viewed in this context, 'Mantŝebo's manoeuvre to induct Bereng into the Roman Catholic faith was a disagreeable move to 'Mabereng, which might sooner or later culminate in an active conflict of interests.

Francis Lekoatsa took to his work on 16 January 1945 with energy and drive and he was generally pleased with the academic performance of his royal pupils. When he set his first examination in March 1945 he arranged for them to sit with their counterparts in the nearby school. Constantine Bereng came out number 3 out of thirteen pupils in Standard I, while Raphael Leshoboro came out number 1 in Standard III out of five pupils. (Leshoboro, although junior in status, was three years older than the Crown Prince.)[5] However, there were also times when the tutor got frustrated. In September 1946 Constantine Bereng performed below par, getting an aggregate of 117 out of 200 marks. This courted the remark from Francis Lekoatsa that: 'Bereng is surely still a baby (seven years) hence you notice some weaknesses in his work, however, . . . he promises much for the future.' While Raphael Leshoboro, who had an aggregate of 220 out of 300 marks had his conduct described as 'fair, lazy, obstinate'; while he was otherwise 'naturally intelligent'.[6] Francis Lekoatsa's general frustration was that his pupils, in particular Leshoboro, 'would do better if only he was not stationed within so uneducative an environment as this'.[7]

The private tutorship was deemed to have come to an end in December 1947 when Bereng passed his Standard III and Leshoboro his Standard VI. A decision had then to be made as to which school they should be sent to. In any course, Francis Lekoatsa was to accompany them as *in loco parentis.*

Following her own conscience as the legal guardian, *Mofumahali* 'Mantŝebo decided that the royal pupils should go to Roma College, a Roman Catholic School, otherwise with good academic standards. Then, an incredible row erupted. The National Council voiced its strong view at its Session held in December that, as a future king who would be responsible for subjects of all religious denominations, Bereng should be sent to a non-denominational school. The same argument was advanced in respect of his brother Leshoboro. *Mofuahali* 'Mantŝebo dug in her heels, pointing out that religion comes first in the education of a child. In an effort to contain the situation, the Resident Commissioner intervened with a letter to 'Mantsebo which summarised the view of the National Council, appealed for calm, and pointed to the negative role of religion in the nation. He stated:

The Paramount Chief must rule people of all sects, and that, I presume, is why the nation wishes the boys to attend a non-sectarian school, where, however, they would receive religious instructions from a member of the Church to which they belong. I would suggest that you ponder this matter deeply before you make any decision. *I have noticed with regret in Basutoland that often the people are divided on public issues according to the Church to which they profess adherence. This is a great pity and it does not make for harmony.* [My italic][8]

The Regent did ot change her point of view, however; and it can fairly be surmised that she was receiving active counsel from her priests. In the last resort, on 23 January 1948 the Sons of Moshoeshoe met in Maseru to resolve the impasse. Fourteen of the most powerful chiefs in the land convened,[9] with the Resident Commissioner and the Government Secretary in attendance. Chief Matlere was significantly absent. Somewhat surprising, in that some of them were great supporters of *Mofumahali* 'Mabereng, whose firm position in favour of a non-denominational school could be assumed, the chiefs unanimously gave the Regent her wish, reasoning that:

Religion comes first, and later the children can be sent wherever the parent lives. There is nothing to discuss. Education is a matter for the parents. The children should go to a school of their religion and faith. When they are grown they can go on (sic) debate.[10]

As could have been expected, when *Mofumahali* 'Mabereng received the news, she was furious. Right away she let her views known directly to the Regent. She objected 'to the sending of Bereng Seeiso' to Roma College and wanted him to be sent instead to the Government Intermediate School at Maseru.[11]

'Mantŝebo disregarded her objection. She duly put the Princes on board a train at Underberg, the nearest station in the Union of South Africa to Mokhotlong, and prepared to have them met at the Maseru railway station. 'Mabereng, in turn, supported by her own relatives, principal among them being her eldest brother, Jacob N. Lebopo and her maternal cousin, Rampoi Ntlibi Matete, hatched a plot to abduct the Crown Prince before he got to his destination. A fearless member of the Progressive Association and its former Chairman, Ramaria Tlale undertook to be the family's instrument. Accompanied by Princess 'Mampoi, Bereng's eldest sister, he abducted him at the penultimate railway station of Marseilles, leaving Leshoboro and Francis Lekoatsa to finish the course by themselves.

The abduction ended Bereng's isolation from his mother. Through the Resident Commissioner's persuasion *Mofumahali* 'Mabereng allowed him to go to Roma as decided; but the incident unleashed a full-scale war between the royal widows, in which *Mofumahali* 'Mantšebo had the upper hand.

Mofumahali 'Mantšebo unceremoniously routed Jacob Lebopo from Matsieng, where he worked at the National Treasury, not allowing him to pack his clothes. He was fleeced of £105.10d in hard cash in the process and the police investigation appears never to have recovered it.[12] *Mofumahali* 'Mantšebo told him and the Resident Commissioner that '[Jacob Lebopo's family] should return my husband's [lobola] cattle and take their children', and that Jacob 'should take his sister, and not persist on entering my family raiding children in this fashion'.[13] For the first few months the Regent gave instructions to Francis Lekoatsa and Brother Jules, the Director of Roma College, not to permit *Mofumahali* 'Mabereng access to the Crown Prince.[14]

Feeling quite persecuted, 'Mabereng appealed to the Resident Commissioner to 'be given real and adequate protection for my life, the life of the people on my side, as well as the life of my own brothers and even that of my brother-in-law', George Lerotholi, who had had a finger in the Marseilles affair. Further, quite significantly, 'Mabereng revealed her real fears for her son, which might have been the primary cause behind the abduction, namely that:

At the school at Roma there is another child who is under the guardianship of Chieftainess 'Mantšebo and I do not consider this a good thing because anyone may go there at any time and may have *access* to my child, for it is rumoured that the child of Chieftainess Debora Seeiso, Leshoboro, might be considered for Bereng Seeiso's position. (My emphasis)[15]

The word 'access' in 'Mabereng's statement appeared to carry the meaning that her son was going to be killed.

The Resident Commissioner seemed to be out of his resources for containing the war any further. The only response that he could give to 'Mabereng, which he made worse by communicating directly to her adversary, the Regent, was 'that if she was in fear of her life there was nothing to prevent her from moving and living elsewhere with her relatives'.[16]

The last stage of the Prince's youth in Lesotho ended in 1953 when he completed his 'Junior Certificate' (JC), that is, junior secondary-school education at Roma College (later Christ the King) and proceeded first to Ampleforth (Yorkshire) in 1954 and later, in 1957, to Corpus Christi, Oxford. It had been a truly unpleasant upbringing, even not considering that he was a Prince. A large account of his woes under the Regent was his parentage: his mother, *Mofumahali* 'Mabereng, a Motlokoa woman, was not born of the ruling royal lineage of Moshoeshoe, as had both *Mofumahali* 'Mantŝebo and *Mofumahali* Maleshoboro. Her marriage was therefore viewed as morganatic. That may explain why a *mohalitso* (fellow-wife), namely 'Mantŝebo, could so boldly declare that her people might just as well 'return *my husband's* [lobola] cattle and take their children' (My italic) together with their mother.

The Installation of Prince Bereng Sows Further Seeds of Discord

The future King of Lesotho was thus at Oxford when the Constitution for the Legislative Council was formed. Both himself as well as the chiefs and commoners who were either sympathetic to his cause or their own felt strongly that he should interrupt his studies so as to be closer to home and influence the constitutional developments that were potentially to affect his future status as a king. Early in 1960 a decision was taken. At 10 a.m. on Wednesday 3 February that year some one thousand people assembled at the site of the Legislative Council Chamber to listen to the Sons of Moshoeshoe's deliberations on the fate of the Prince. The precise nature of the point to be decided was however illusive: it was not clear as to whether the point was one of when or of whether the Prince should be installed. To the Regent, *Mofumahali* 'Mantsebo and her supporters, particularly her official Advisers, it appeared to be one or the other. Their contention on the issue of installation had always been two-pronged. First they insisted he should complete his studies at Oxford. Secondly they insisted that he should get married. To the Prince's supporters and the general gathering, on the other hand, the purpose of the meeting was a straightforward one of proclaiming that the Prince be installed. The Chairman of the meeting was Chief Matlere Lerotholi of Mokhotlong. Gordon M. Hector, Government Secretary, was the 'official' observer. Prince Bereng was present, and so, significantly, was his half-brother Prince Leshoboro, the silent pretender to the throne.[17]

The Regent, flanked by four of her Advisers, the most notable being Chief Leabua Jonathan, rose to present in a few words the essence of the subject. The substance of her address was vaguely that the purpose of the meeting was to discuss 'issues' surrounding *ts'usumetso* (instigation) from some members of the royal house who said that Prince Bereng be installed. This *ts'usumetso*, she pointed out, had caused 'confusion' in the country and it was time that something was done about it.

Action began immediately thereafter, when Chief Letsie K. Mots'oene, a supporter to Bereng's cause, challenged the Chairman to read a letter convening the meeting. A flurry of paperwork followed, but the letter could not be found, and the Chairman was left to muster an oral presentation, to the effect that the purpose was to 'advise' the Regent regarding the 'placing' of the Prince. Then, from under his sleeve Chief Letsie pulled out a telegram that he had received which specifically said the purpose was to 'install' the Prince. The statement was loudly applauded by the house. At the same time the Regent and her Advisers and supporters reacted with looks of consternation and musings of betrayal. The telegram clearly emanated from the Royal Office in Matsieng, but the Regent and her Advisers and supporters were astounded by the inclusion in the telegram of the crucial word 'install'. They did not know who at Matsieng had inserted the fatal word.

Despite the Regent's protest, which resulted in a brief midday adjournment for private consultations with the Resident Commissioner, the house, led by an observer named Herbert Taka, began to shout that Bereng should be installed. That started the first of several loud applauses in favour of the Prince. Up to eighteen letters were subsequently read out, including one signed just that morning by eighteen chiefs led by Chief David Theko Makhaola, all of which buttressed the cry for installation. For the duration of the day, up to 6 p.m., only three feeble anti-Bereng speeches were attempted by Chief Seeiso Tumo, Chief Matete Majara, and Mr Stephen Motlamelle. All three were shouted down.

The day was won in favour of the Prince;[18] but that was not before *Mofumahali* 'Mamathe Masopha, a Bereng supporter, had angrily accused the Regent of having infiltrated her entourage from her district of Berea with two detractors from her own cause. These were Mr Stephen Motlamelle of the Basutoland Congress Party, who held strong views against the chieftaincy in general, and Mr Cicerone Mokhehle, a former school inspector and father of Mr Ntsu Mokhehle, the leader of the BCP.[19]

The matter of Bereng's installation was effectively sealed by Chief David Theko Makhaola, even then still the most influential member of the royal house of Matsieng and certainly very close to *Mofumahali* 'MaBareng. As an eye witness recalls it:

[F]ortified not a little by his potations over the lunch hour, [Theko Makhaola] spoke with skill and indeed with dramatic effect which reached its climax when he pointed to *Khosana* Bereng on the dais and asked him to stand up as the Son of Seeiso whom the Sons of Moshesh had decided should be placed.[20]

There was loud and prolonged applause. At the end of it Chief Reentseng S. Makhaola presented the letter from the Sons of Moshoeshoe dated 3 February – caucused the day of the meeting – demanding that the Prince be installed immediately. The letter was signed by the following chiefs:

(1) David Theko Makhaola
(2) Mohlalefi Bereng
(3) Letsie K. Theko
(4) 'Mamathe G. Masopha
(5) Letsie Mots'oene
(6) Kopano C. Selomo
(7) Molapo Qhobela
(8) Thabo Lerotholi Mojela
(9) J. Moholobela
(10) Makhabane Peete
(11) Mots'ohlo Sekonyela
(12) Mohale Seeiso Maama
(13) Goliath L. S. Moshoeshoe
(14) Ts'epo Q. Sempe
(15) Ts'itso Griffith
(16) Monare Moeketsi
(17) Sempe Mahaba Mokhaola
(18) Reentseng G. Lerotholi (for the Chief of Phamong)[21]

The Regent's Advisers were quite clearly unhappy about the outcome of the meeting and several times in the afternoon they had attempted to prevail on the Chairman to postpone the meeting, protesting that the audience had become too noisy. The following day, at 2.30 p.m., the meeting reconvened. Chief Matlere 'tersely and briefly announced to the gathering that the Paramount Chief [Regent] thanked them for their advice, she accepted, she agreed that Bereng should be placed immediately and that on the following morning she would discuss with His Honour, the Resident Commissioner, the exact details and formalities to effect the placing'.[22] 'There were wild outbursts of cheering.'[23]

On 12 March 1960, Prince Bereng Seeiso was installed. In a splendid Roman Catholic wedding held at the Cathedral in Maseru, on 23 August 1962, he married Princess Tabitha 'Masentle Mojela, the daughter of Thabo Lerotholi Mojela. Born in 1902, *Mofumahali* 'Mantŝebo did not live long after the installation. She died in 1964, an evidently depressed and broken-hearted lady.

For the first time in the history of the country, the new monarch was installed under a new title. Both the colonial title of Paramount Chief and the precolonial Sesotho title of *Morena e Moholo* were replaced by *Motlotlehi*, while the monarch was renamed Moshoeshoe II. From the point of view of the British Government and those Basotho who accepted its argument that *Morena e Moholo* was conceptually an inferior political title to 'King', the term *Motlotlehi* connoted an advance in constitutional development toward the title of king. For that section of Basotho who obviously viewed the once honourable title of *Morena e Moholo* as merely having been politically debased, *Motlotlehi* seems to have been accepted as simply a redemptive title for an old office. The majority of Basotho were clearly confused by the new title. The official, but not literal, translation of the term into English before Independence was 'His Highness'. The literal translation is 'The Honourable', while the Independence translation is 'His Majesty'.

The controversy surrounding the installation of Constantine Bereng Seeiso was significant in five respects. First it revived and intensified the cleavages and rivalries within the royal house of Matsieng, which had broken out when Regent 'Mantŝebo Seeiso came to power. Thereby an opportunity was created for the northern aristocracy of the House of Molapo to take advantage of the confusion thus created. Second Chief Leabua's undisguised disenchantment with the success of the installation appears to have fuelled strength in him to seek his place and power through other means. So unhappy was the Chief that shortly after the decision of 4 February he unceremoniously relinquished his portfolio of Adviser in Matsieng, perhaps understandably fearing potential humiliation from *Motlotlehi* in the event that the latter might dismiss him. Chief Matete Majara's association with Leabua obviously brought the two of them closer than ever before. Matete was in Leabau's first Cabinet when he became the Prime Minister of Lesotho as the leader of the BNP; but in the main, Chief Leabua appears to have been equally the political head of the House of Molapo, fighting the old historical battles of the House with Matsieng, as he was the leader of the BNP.

Third, unwittingly perhaps, the BCP reaffirmed its own cold sentiments toward the chieftaincy in general, and *Motlotlehi* in particular. Stephen Motlamelle's stand toward the Prince on 4 February, and *Mofumahali* 'Mamathe's strategic uncovering of the unwelcomed presence in her entourage of the father of the BCP leader, Mr Cicerone Mokhehle, forced the conflict between the Party and *Motlotlehi* into the open. Needless to say, the young monarch could not ignore that. Fourth, potentially alienated from the two major parties, the BCP and the BNP, the new King of Lesotho was left politically more or less alone and lonely.

As at 1960 *Motlotlehi*'s main supporter in the political area was Chief Samuel Seepheephe Matete. An influential member of the Legislative Council and member of the BCP, S. S. Matete had resigned from his post as Adviser to the Regent just before the establishment of the Legislative Council. Supposedly he resigned in protest against the Regent's 'suffocating influence on initiative', fostered by the 'self-seeking "yes-men" drawn from a narrow and unrepresentative section of the chieftaincy' – her Advisers.[24] Seepheephe quit the BCP and formed his own party called the Marema Tlou Party (MTP) and using it as an instrument threw himself fully behind the cause of installing Prince Bereng into office. According to one source he had formerly attempted to woo the BCP to join forces with him in this cause but Ntsu Mokhehle rebuffed him: '[Mokhehle] had come to believe that the whole question of Chieftaincy was irrelevant to the Country's political future'.[25] After 1962, when Marema Tlou Party merged with B. M. Khaketla's newly-formed Basutoland Freedom Party (BFP) to form the Marematlou Freedom Party (MFP), B. M. Khaketla became *Motlotlehi*'s unfailing and loyal supporter.

The fifth lesson to be drawn from the question of the installation is that the controversy gave rise to a new burning issue in the constitutional development of the Territory, the issue of *Motlotlehi*'s status – his powers in the Independence Constitution. In short, political activity began to focus grimly on the question: is the independent Lesotho to be a constitutional monarchy or an executive monarchy? This was the main issue to be decided between 1960 and 1966, the year of Independence.

A Bull Without Horns: Motlotlehi's Stand on the Status of His Office

What was *Motlotlehi*'s own view on the issue? At the time of his installation, Constantine Bereng Seeiso had never been involved in the public affairs of his country. He had never publicly had to make statements that might help reveal his thinking on constitutional or, for that matter, any national issues of the country. It is difficult therefore to extract his views from his past at that juncture. It is difficult to say what were his own thoughts on the future nature of the Basotho monarchy and the status of its king.

In the light of developments as presented up to this point, however, it is conceivable that he did harbour 'dreams' of being an executive monarch, as was the case with his great-grandfather and namesake, Moshoeshoe I. At the minimum, it is reasonable to suppose that, like his predecessors in the colonial era, up to his own father, who still wielded real power within the indigenous structure, he desired the same for himself. He would then quite understandably have felt cheated by the constitutional developments contrary to his wishes that had taken place under the Regent to date. Hence Richard Weisfelder's view would stand correct, where he says: 'The 1959 Basutoland Constitution embodied a triumph for the National Council over royal power and proved to be a difficult, if not insuperable obstacle to Moshoeshoe's dreams of playing a consequential executive role.'[26]

Tenable though this point may seem, the monarch's own extant official statement on the subject may be said to cast him in a refractory light. Addressing the subject for the first time, at the opening of the Legislative Council on 11 September 1961, he stated:

It is evident from public statements that there is a general desire for the introduction of Responsible Government . . . AND ALSO OTHER DEVELOPMENTS WHICH ARE THE PILLAR OF ANY POLITICAL ADVANCE. I desire to make it very clear – perhaps publicly here for the first time – that if Responsible Government and all that it involves, BUT *at the same time preserving our good, old traditions true and characteristic of Basotho Nation – is the wish of my people*, I will not only WELCOME it, but will use my position as Paramount Chief of Basutoland to see that the people's desires are accomplished. . . . The whole administration of the country – the Government of Basutoland – would fall under *Motlotlehi* Moshoeshoe II as Head of State, and would be carried out in his name and on his behalf. The laws of Basutoland would be enacted by him with the advice and consent of this Parliament. . . . And I, as Head of State, would wish the desires of my people. . . . *Our internal institutions of Government would develop in a natural way, true to the Basotho Nation and tradition.*[27] (My emphasis)

B. M. Khaketla, in his *Lesotho 1970*, cites this statement to support the view that 'it has never been the King's desire' to be given 'extraordinary executive powers'.[28] My own interpretation rather derives from Sesotho idioms: the Basotho say, 'You grab a bull by the horns and a man by his words'; then they say, 'A *morena* is a bull without horns' – that is, you can never (or should not be able to) pin him down on his words. The least that it seems can be said of *Motlotlehi*'s statement of 11 September 1961 is that he very royally presented himself to the Legislative Council as a bull without horns: he was non-committal. He shed no light on his 'dreams'.

THE PUBLIC STATES ITS VIEWS ON THE CONSTITUTION

On 11 September 1961, a motion of self-government was put before the Legislative Council. It was moved by B. M. Khaketla, then still the Deputy Leader of BCP, and seconded by Chief S. S. Matete, the founder and leader of the Marema Tlou Party (MTP). Following a brief discussion, the motion was adopted unanimously.[29] Subsequently *Motlotlehi* Moshoeshoe II set up a commission to collect evidence from the people concerning the form of the Constitution that they wanted. Comprehensively the Commission was to seek the views of the public on eight main points:

(1) the status of the Basotho king
(2) the status of chiefs
(3) the status of the country
(4) the relationship between Britain and Lesotho
(5) the process of elections, direct or indirect
(6) the franchise
(7) the form of the parliament
(8) the future of the Basotho courts

It was evident from the beginning, however, that the crucial point was number one – the status of the king. In fact that is how the public generally responded to the Commission.

The results were remarkable, if disappointing. For a study of the verbatim report of the Commission reveals abounding conflict and confusion in the public's grasp of concepts. To illustrate the point I shall give a brief review of responses from the district of Mokhotlong in the mountain areas in the Ward of Tlokoeng. The interview took place on 5 September 1962.

The Chief of the Ward, Chief M. K. Sekonyela, opened his response with an impressive statement which in tone seemed to speak in favour of Moshoeshoe II being given executive authority. The Chief stated:

> The Paramount Chief [then already *Motlotlehi*] is the backbone of the country. If he is not there then there could be no life in the country; he is there for (sic) the pillar around which the whole nation is built. He should be given the higher title than he has at present. *He should* therefore *be the ruler* of Basutoland; *he should be the Resident Commissioner of Basutoland*. It will be understood, then, that if he is Resident Commissioner he will be understood, [the] whole of the administration under him, and he will have under him all the various departments of Government. *His power will be undisputed.* . . . Parliament will be stable under him if he is put in the position in which I propose he should be placed. [My italic][30]

While the first and sixth sentences of the response suggested that Chief Sekonyela advocated executive monarchy, especially his reference to *Motlotlehi*'s *power* being '*undisputed*', the third and fourth sentences suggested a special although understandable lack of understanding of the concept of executive monarchy. First, stemming from the first sentence, that 'Paramount Chief' should be raised to a higher title, the Chief appears to have been reacting to colonial jargon, instead of adding to constitutional debate. As the colonial jargon had cheated the Sesotho word *Morena e Moholo* of its precolonial meaning of king, by merely translating it to 'Paramount Chief', M. K. Sekonyela had come to accept the colonial view that '*Morena e Moholo*' was in fact not the equivalent of its pre-colonial prototype. Second, being even more mystified by colonial titles and their holders, he revealed in his fourth sentence that to him the *ruler*, or 'Chief of Chiefs', so to speak, in Lesotho, was in fact the Resident Commissioner. The term 'King' (or Queen) totally escaped his mind in this context. In this logic he was obviously guided by the fact that a Resident Commissioner in colonial Lesotho had never provided any insight into the context of the constitutional monarchy of Great Britain. There had not been anything about a Resident Commissioner that inspired the nation toward the parliamentary democracy that was then in 1962, being advocated for a self-governing Lesotho. His power in the Territory was 'undisputed'. He was for all intents and purposes an executive monarch; and of course he had more power than the 'Paramount Chief'.

Then, put under questioning, Chief Sekonyela revealed another difficulty. He was asked the question by Ntsu Mokhehle, a member of the Commission:

> In your understanding a ruler is one who is in charge of the administration, who makes laws; is that your understanding?

The Chief responded: 'There will be [a] difference when we come to the law, because the law will be made by Parliament.'[31]

The questions that one needs to ask oneself here are: what was the political basis of the Chief's distinction between the law-maker and the executive; was it the pre-colonial Basotho government, which seemed to be implied in the opening words of his first sentence?; was it the Westminster model, which was in gestation in the Territory at that historical juncture?; did the Chief envision a new type of Constitution in which a monarch with executive authority was nonetheless not directly involved when a law-making body sat for that purpose? From the interview it appears as though the Chief could no longer make a distinction between the British Constitution and his own traditional form of government; and he had not a sufficient appreciation of the political forces that were shaping the future of his country.

Several other persons who followed Chief M. K. Sekonyela manifested similar difficulties of conceptualisation. One A. Sekonyela, for instance, a teacher for that matter, gave the following response:

> The status of the Paramount Chief: I liken unto a pillar in this country, the status of the Paramount Chief, which should not be interfered with in any way. *He should be like the Resident Commissioner.* By that I mean he should confirm everything without any fear, through advisors who shall have been elected by the people. They should be elected by the people only. That means that the Paramount Chief should have the *right to make a final decision* in Basutoland on every matter. That will be *in accordance*

with the tradition of our people, because *the Paramount Chief has been created by God, more than any other Chief.* (My emphasis)[32]

To a lesser or greater degree people throughout the country manifested the same kind of difficulties. Yet there was one significant variation provided by one segment of the populace. According to B. M. Khaketla, also a member of the Commission, in advance of the Commission's country-wide interviews, the BCP had sent a circular to all its members instructing them on how to respond to questions. On this particular question of the status of *Motlotlehi*, they had been instructed to advocate constitutional monarchy.[33] A close scrutiny of the Verbatim Report does indeed reveal that there was a remarkable uniformity of responses on questions from the members of that Party. To illustrate the point I shall quote two of these, remarkably both being peasants. M. Sebehela, a peasant from Tlokoeng stated:

The Paramount Chief should be the *Head of State like the Queen of England.* He should sign all laws. But *the Head of the Administration should be a Prime Minister* supported by Ministers elected by the nation. *The Paramount Chief should not take part in politics. He should work strictly according to the law under Parliament.* Even if the Paramount Chief has a say in matters concerning land, he should have nothing to do with disputes regarding land. There should be no nominated members in the Legislative Council. It should be entirely of elected members. (My emphasis)[34]

J. Nkalai, another peasant from Tlokoeng spoke briefly but clearly in the same vein. He stated:

The Paramount Chief should have the same status as the Queen of England. That is why he should be titled the King, and he should administer through the wishes of the people because he alone would not be in a position to know what the wishes of the people are.[35]

To a constitutional historian a strategy, such as the one adopted by the BCP leadership in 1962, of conditioning people's responses to questions, is frustrating. It makes it difficult to determine with any degree of certainty the extent to which a response to a constitutional issue is genuine. It renders it problematic to establish what the development of a political culture – a national perspective – actually is.

Moreover, to the extent that those who influence responses may have an immediate personal or party gain in mind, overlooking what might otherwise be desirable constitutional developments, the strategy can also have an inhibiting effect on the target group. To illustrate the point, it seemed desirable and timely in 1962 that the handicap placed on women's right to vote be lifted and adult suffrage be truly universal; but as Ntsu Mokhehle obviously feared that the change might give Chief Jonathan an advantage over him (which point will be elaborated on below), the Leader of the BCP instructed his followers in anticipation of the Commission to argue against it. Fortunately in this case his instructions backfired, quite embarrassingly. In one crucial case, at the Sekake Branch in the district of Quthing, where the no-nonsense Robert Matji was Party Leader, he got a severe rebuke. Robert Matji wrote him a trenchant letter stating:

> National unity without the support of women of our country is worthless. It becomes a phrase reminiscent of the days of slavery when some bestial men considered themselves overlords over other human beings. Are we not emulating these same overlords when, perhaps for tactical (and bad tactics) reasons we arrogate to ourselves the right to deny our women the fundamental right to participate in the Government of the country. This is a betrayal of declared policy of universal franchise, stated by us both inside and outside the country. For us today to exclude the full participation of women in the management and running of the country is, to say the least, the height of hypocrisy and dishonesty. This line is being adopted without reference to the organisation, nor to the nation as a whole.[36]

On those grounds Robert Matji defied the order; and the one good thing about it is that his bold stand had a sobering effect on Ntsu Mokhehle, who subsequently lay low on the issue.

The lack of understanding, or downright confusion, among the politically untutored masses of Lesotho regarding the constitution for self-government was nevertheless not a product of stupidity, nor was it owing to lack of intellectual acumen. It was a consequence of the paralysing nature of colonial rule on the development of political thought, more so as the masses generally felt its impact, without appreciating how the colonial functionaries were themselves governed in Britain.

MAJOR POLITICAL PARTIES AND THEIR LEADERSHIP
BEFORE INDEPENDENCE

Defining the nature of the monarchy, and therefore of the role of
its king, was a fundamental constitutional issue of the early 1960s
which every political party viewed with keen interest. Hence, in
order to get a better appreciation of political party stands in the
resolution of the final constitutional framework, and in particular of
the nature of the monarchy, it should be useful at this juncture to
give a brief appraisal of the country's three major political parties,
their policies and their leadership.

The Basutoland Congress Party (BCP)

The origins of the BCP, the earliest of Lesotho's political parties,
were established in the previous chapter. Only a few more salient
features will be provided to complete the picture.

It is worth noting at the outset that as the BCP (originally BAC)
grew in power and numbers in the 1950s the monarchy was losing
power, and the Regent was getting subjected to the will of the then
advisory National Council. Further, beginning in 1952 when the
BAC was formed, issues to which it committed itself were those that
had a strong appeal to the majority of the people – the issues of
non-incorporation into the Union of South Africa, eradication of
colour discrimination, a call for self-government. On these issues the
Party stood on firm ground.

Alongside these were three other issues that increasingly had a
negative impact on the Party: one was the Party's relationship with
the Roman Catholic Church; another was the Party's stance on the
monarchy; a third was the white power structure.

Both the chieftaincy as well as organised religion had always come
under criticism in Lesotho. They were, as it should be recalled, two
of Josiel Lefela's pet subjects. The BCP stance on these issues by
1960 was however significantly different from that of its political
antecedent, *Lekhotla la Bafo*. Ntsu Mokhehle rather pointedly indicated both as enemies of his Party and of the people. He rather
impolitically courted a direct confrontation with all the three powerful forces (including the white colonial administration) at the same
time. Witness the following statement that he made in 1961 before
the United Nations.

The British officials have organised Chiefs, the white businessman, the white missionaries, and all these are set against us. They have also formed, with the help of the missionaries and Chiefs, small political gangs – erroneously financed and morally supported by the white people both in Basutoland and in the Union of South Africa. Our policy is non-violence, but the British officials, using Chiefs, the white traders, the white missionaries and their political gangsters, are set on provoking trouble and creating confusion in our peaceful but effective struggle for freedom.[37]

Speeches of this type, whether made outside or inside Lesotho, strengthened the resolve of some religious groups, ostensibly the Roman Catholic Church, to declare a political war on the Party. (In so far as that is concerned, however, the Roman Catholic Church had at the same time as Mokhehle's barbed criticisms revealed its anxieties to control the future of the country as such, by dictating to their following what political party to join and which not to join.) In like manner, these speeches got the chiefs nervous and so drove more and more of them into Mokhehle's so-called 'political gangs' – the BNP and MFP; and thus early most of the chiefs, especially senior chiefs, were forced to view the Leader of the BCP as a budding dictator who had no place for their lot in the future scheme of things.

Ntsu Mokhehle was a staunch Pan-Africanist. He was good friends with President Kwame Nkrumah of Ghana and Abdel Nasser of Egypt. He was on good terms with Peking. He was no friend of the Republic of South Africa. Of all the political leaders in the country he was probably the most widely travelled. He had been to Ghana, Guinea, China, Russia, Yugoslavia and the United States of America, among other places. In the course of these travels, where he met a number of leaders from other Third World countries, he had developed strong views of the type of government that his country needed. Such a type of government was a parliamentary democracy, but with a specific bent. As he put it to Denis Cowen in the summer of 1963:

Limited government is a bit of a luxury. It presupposes a substantial degree of economic affluence and is all very well in the rich countries of the West. But we in Africa, in common with many of our fellow men in the Far East and in Latin America, are economically frightfully poor. In addition, we are scourged with ill health, malnutrition, and lack of education. What we need is emphasis upon what government should do, positively to remove these evils.

It should not be forgotten that, because of long exploitation and neglect, we in Africa are attempting to crowd in a few years what the countries of the West have taken hundreds of years to achieve. . . . *If anything, therefore, the presumption should be in favour of the exercise of State power. Perhaps Ayub Khan is right: and what we need in Africa is benevolent autocracy rather than limited government.* (My emphasis)[38]

The image that the Roman Catholic Church attempted to present to its following, however, that the BCP and its leadership were communists, was greatly exaggerated. By 1960 there were a handful of men in the BCP who held strongly to Marxist-Leninist views. The most notable of these were Robert Matji and Jack Mosiane. Both were affiliates of the South African Communist Party (SACP) and the ANC. As a teacher at the Basutoland High School in Maseru, Ntsu Mokhehle, who was sufficiently well read in Marxist thought, had begun in 1958 to encourage some students to be familiar with Marxist views before rejecting or accepting them; but he was not a Marxist. By 1960 he was making bold statements to the effect that the SACP was aimed at crippling African nationalism. Finally, Ntsu Mokhehle's power and confidence rested to a large degree on the Secretary-General of the Party, Godfrey Kolisang, and his Deputy, Gerard Ramoreboli, both remarkably conservative. At that, Gerard Ramoreboli was a member of the Roman Catholic Church.

There was no doubt in the minds of most people in 1960 that the BCP was the party that would lead Lesotho to independence, with Ntsu Mokhehle as the first Prime Minister. The Party's greatest setback, however, was its inability to accommodate the ambitions of all its élitist top leadership. It has variously been suggested that the main reason for the breakaway of the top leadership, who either started new parties or joined others, was Ntsu Mokhehle's inflexibility and intolerance of criticism.[39] A more accurate account of the problem however, seems to be the one that 'The B.C.P. [not merely because of Mokhehle] became embroiled in an enervating series of internal ideological and power struggles.'[40] In other words, the list of men and women who left the Party – before and shortly after Independence – were themselves forceful personalities who needed greater political space in which to breathe. The most significant of these included S. S. Matete, Ellen 'Maposholi Molapo, B. M. Khaketla, Robert Matji and C. D. Mofeli.

Indeed Mokhehle manifested strong signs of intolerance of criticism; but then too, the period in which his Party got politically enervated, between 1960 and 1966, was one when there was a general lack of tolerance for differences of opinion in the country's leadership which probably exceeded any other period. One's political opposite tended to be viewed as one's natural enemy. The spirit of democracy which had typified in Lesotho's pre-colonial monarchy had vanished.

The Basotho National Party (BNP)

The BNP had four distinctive characteristics. First it was highly patronised by chiefs; and this was partly because Jonathan, its Leader, was himself a chief; but what had mainly triggered their enrolment was Ntsu Mokhehle's hostility toward them, which forced them to seek sanctuary either in the BNP or MPT and the MFP, after the MPF-MFP merger in December 1962.

Secondly, increasingly as the Party prepared for the elections of 1965, the BNP had taken a bold move to establish friendship with the Republic of South Africa (a Republic as from 1960). The Republic of South Africa was anxious to get some control of the future of the Territory, and the Party presented itself as the efficient instrument. While Chief Jonathan sought to develop a policy of 'dialogue' with the internationally unpopular Apartheid State. The height of the relations between the two was in 1965 when, shortly after Jonathan lost elections in his constituency, the Republic of South Africa sought to bolster his chances of winning a by-election with a gift of 100 000 bags of maize. The gift was generally denounced by the BCP, and B. M. Khaketla called it 'a cheap political trick intended to buy support for Chief Leabua Jonathan and his National Party'.[41]

Third the BNP was basically a party of women. One reason for the Party's appeal in this regard was that the 1959 Constitution had, by making taxation one of the qualifications for voting, excluded women from the franchise, and Chief Jonathan had taken advantage of that fact. While the BCP, mainly, insisted on the propriety of the position, Jonathan had come up strongly as a champion for women's franchise and women's rights generally. Thus during the country tour of the 1962 Constitutional Commission the Chief had consistently and positively asked more questions on this issue than any of the other commissioners with him.[42] The main reason, however, was that the Party's most powerful backing in the country came from the Roman Catholic Church; and as the majority of followers in the Church were women, their numbers greatly boosted the Party's membership.

Fourthly, then, one of the main characteristics of the BNP was that it enjoyed the official support of the Roman Catholic Church. Actually, the year before the launching of the National Party the Church had attempted to found its own party, named the Christian Democratic Party (CDP), and a South African Roman Catholic lawyer named Vyeira, of Johannesburg, had been charged with the responsibility of drawing up its manifesto. The programme of the Party was to 'fight against Communism under whatever name it may present itself in Basutoland';[43] but then, in the nick of time, Patrick Duncan, the former Judicial Commissioner to Lesotho, advised Chief Jonathan, who had served as an assessor under him, to form a party. The CDP Manifesto was then handed over to him, albeit with some amendments, as a basis for forming the BNP.[44]

The views of the Roman Catholic Church leadership following the founding of the BNP were paraphrased by the Bloemfontein *Friend* early in 1959 as follows:

> Members of the Roman Catholic Church in Basutoland should take part in the political development of their country, said the Bishop, the Right Rev. J. D. Des Rosiers, of Maseru, in an interview with the *Southern Cross*, official organ of the Church. The Bishop said that as the population was mainly Christian, it would be the natural thing for them to belong to parties which subscribed to Christian Principles, and were led by Christians. Unfortunately, up to the present, the majority of political leaders had been left-wing and anti-religious. He did not think it proper for a Catholic party to be formed in Basutoland. All Christians should join in the fight against communism.[45]

The charges of 'left-wing', 'communist' leaders, and parties, were of course levelled at Ntsu Mokhehle and the BCP; and as it has been shown, they were greatly exaggerated.

A more specific exhortation to members of the Church was made in a joint pastoral letter by two local bishops. Entitled 'The Church and Politics – Duties and Responsibilities of Catholics in Basutoland' (published by the Catholic Centre Mazenod in 1959), the pastoral letter cited papal authority to remind Church followers to be 'good candidates, candidates who are acquainted with the laws of God and of His Church and capable and desirous of having them respected'. The Church followers were instructed to vote for candidates who were organised 'in justice and liberty, in love and in peace' and they were counselled in favour of 'a government which believes in God and accepts His Holy law with love and submission'. Roman Catholics who failed to vote according to Church counsel would be deemed to have committed 'a mortal sin'.[46]

Chief Leabua Jonathan, the Leader of the Party, had a rather inconspicuous background before he joined politics. He came from quite low among the several wives of his father, the late Chief Jonathan Molapo. His mother *Mofumahali* 'Masekalakati was married well after ten wives were already married. Born and raised of a Roman Catholic mother, he nevertheless attended PEMS schools. He had to terminate his studies at Standard VI: his father's death in 1929, leaving his mother with constrained financial resources, forced him to go to Johannesburg where he began working in the gold mines. Following that experience he had become a headman of Kolonyama, a small village in the Leribe District. He served as an assessor to the Judicial Commissioner. His last employment before going into politics was as an Adviser to the Regent *Mofumahali* 'Mantŝebo. Coincidental with this Matsieng career, the Chief became a staunch member of the Roman Catholic Church.

Chief Jonathan had begun briefly as a member of the BCP, although he never became active in it. He joined politics with all the signs of someone who was being manipulated into starting a party while he himself had no formulated views of his own and no striking political traits. As late as 1966 the Bloemfontein *Friend* still described him as 'a curious novelty'. It said 'His best claim to leadership appeared to be as a *Senior* Chief and a prominent Catholic in a Party which drew its main support from tribal and religious loyalties'. It even appeared that some of his supporters 'found his image embarrassing' and 'would have liked to have seen the more voluble Charles Dube Molapo, lawyer and General Secretary of the party, in his place'.[47] This, at least, is the general impression that Jonathan seemed to present to political observers at that stage. It would later come to the surface, however, that behind the apparently dull outward appearance was a cunning, devastating politician.

The Maramatlou (MTP) and the Marematlou Freedom Party

As earlier pointed out, Chief S. S. Matete left his post as Adviser to the Regent, *Mofumahali* 'Mantšebo, and the BCP, to found the Marematlu (MTP). The constitutional discussions of the years 1954 to 1958 which culminated in the 1959 Constitution had convinced the Chief of the need at Matsieng for a 'fresh, clear and diligent brain . . . at a time when many great and painful changes are taking place'.[48] The MTP's major commitment was hence to ensure that that 'fresh, clear and diligent brain', in the person of Prince Constantine Bereng Seeiso, got installed and got his due as a monarch with executive power. Mainly because of shared policies and a common political outlook, S. S. Matete merged his party with B. M. Khaketla's BFP in December 1962 to form the MFP.

Although Khaketla had worked closely with Ntsu Mokhehle, from the time that he founded *Mohlabani* in 1954, it was not until 1958 that he joined the Party and got elected as the Deputy Leader at the December Conference of that year. The delay in joining the Party might have been caused by the anxiety to give *Mohlabani* an independent, non-partisan outlook. In the 1960 election for members of the Executive Council Khaketla got sufficient votes and thus became Member of the Executive Council, with a portfolio in Health and Education. His victory drew disaffection from both Mokhehle and Ramoreboli, who had made a bid for the Executive Council and lost.

Then too, either because of the discomfort caused by the BCP's sharpening ideological squabbles, or because the secrecy oath that he had signed when he took office potentially denied the Party leadership 'inside' information, developments led to a confrontation. The Executive Committee of the Party instructed him not to accept his appointment in the Executive Council. Khaketla refused and instead convened a meeting at Fraser's Hall to justify his stand. The BCP Youth League, recently formed in 1960, assaulted him with eggs and tomatoes and generously heaped invectives on him.

Subsequently, at the Annual Conference of the Party in December 1960 Khaketla was re-elected Deputy Leader of the Party by 110 out of 182 votes; but so harassed he felt that two days later he resigned. He gave as his reason for the resignation the following diatribe from Ntsu Mokhehle which was clearly aimed at him:

In his final speech at the annual party conference on 27 December,

1960 the leader, Mr Mokhehle, made the following remarks:- That in 1961 there could be no compromise with the imperialists, and anyone who imagined he could get anything from imperialists by 'soft talk' was mistaken: 'There is no place for sweet reasonableness,' he said, and for being called a 'good Christian gentleman because of one's soft talk;'

That in 1961 all members of the National Executive Committee must go out and address meetings in the villages and that those who felt they wished to pray must say their prayers along the road to the villages; That the imperialists must not imagine they can buy the nation with their cars;

That any leader who would say he had any imperialist secrets he could not disclose to the nation should not be regarded as a leader but a sell-out and 'must be called a sell-out.'[49]

Indeed the Leader of the BCP had subjected his Deputy to a philippic treat. He could take no more.

In April 1961 Khaketla launched the Basutoland Freedom Party. The BFP was moderate in its aims. It did not wish early independence. It advocated executive authority for the newly installed *Motlotlehi* Moshoeshoe II.

On 5 September 1962 the Leader of the BFP, B. M. Khaketla, and the Leader of the BNP Leabua Jonathan shared a room in Eliot Morojele's Hotel at Mokhotlong. The Constitutional Commission of 1962 was visiting that area to collect evidence toward the drafting of a new Constitution for self-government. Upon their nightly discussions, which centred on the common view that the BCP was so powerful in the mountain areas that it needed neutralising, they agreed on an early meeting of their Executive Committees in Maseru to prepare a merger of their parties.[50]

A joint meeting of the Executive Committees of the two parties did duly meet. Chief Jonathan was absent. In his place was the Secretary-General of the BNP, Gabriel Manyeli. Otherwise, on that occasion Chief S. S. Matete, Leader of the Marematlou Party (MFP), who had heard of the development, 'expressed his desire to join the merger'. Thus at the next meeting the Executive Committees of all three parties met. 'The joint meeting unanimously accepted the principle of amalgamation'. A small sub-committee composed of representatives of the parties was charged with the responsibility 'to suggest a new name for the new Party, draw up a constitution and a programme of principles'. The sub-committee subsequently submitted the name of the new Party as the Basutoland Independence Party (BIP). 'The recommendations were accepted unanimously'.[51]

There was to be no tripartite merger, however. When there was to be a final meeting in December 1962, the BNP defaulted participation. Subsequently Seepheephe and Khaketla went ahead to form the Morematlou Freedom Party, leaving the name Basutoland Independence Party to be used when Jonathan might make up his mind. He never did. Instead Chief Jonathan and his party Executive issued a scathing report, to the dismay of the other two, to the effect that the BNP was 'not willing to amalgamate with fragments of the BCP'.[52]

In the ensuing formation of the MFP, Chief S. S. Matete was elected the President. B. M. Khaketla became the Vice President; and Dr Seth Makotoko, a medical doctor in the civil service, quit his employment to become the Secretary-General of the party. Weisfelder's description of the MFP was accurate when he stated:

> Generally, the MFP position could be described as middle of the road and non-dogmatic, if only because this stance approximated the centre of the wide political spectrum contained in the party. The MFP has been more cosmopolitan than the BNP yet more restrictive in the sense of nationhood than the BCP. It has sought to walk the middle road between cooperation with and hostility towards South Africa. The one unifying principle of the Freedom Party was the belief that the Basotho national interest could be most effectively represented by the living symbol of national identity, the King.[53]

The MFP had run into two major difficulties before Independence, one internal to the Party, the other external to it, which damaged both its morale as well as its credibility. The internal one was of the nature of a power struggle: Chief S. S. Matete was out of the country on official business in London in 1964 when the Executive Committee met and among other things agreed to call a National Conference to renew the Executive Committee. Time was actually due for such a renewal. On his arrival back from the UK S. S. Matete was informed of the decision; but he did not agree with it. According to Khaketla, who bore the responsibility of briefing him, 'he said he was not ready'.[54]

The Executive Committee was the highest decision-making body and the President had no powers of veto over it. So the National

Conference was called. S. S. Matete boycotted it. It chose Dr Seth Makotoko as President. Chief Matete then broke away and revived his MTP. That dampened the morale of the MFP and weakened it in numbers.

The external factor was the more unfortunate, if not tragic. Ntsu Mokhehle was outside the country on official business when, on 18 October 1964, the Deputy Leader of the Party, Gerard Ramoreboli led a BCP motor procession, armed with knobkerries, to Rothe, to the South of the country. (The knobkerrie was a standard article of identity within the Party). Rothe was Chief Mohlalefi Bereng's Ward. He expected that he should, in keeping with tradition, be officially forewarned of the meeting; but Gerard Ramoreboli did not feel the need to do so. Chief Mohlalefi, a staunch monarchist and member of the MFP, supposedly acting in his capacity as a chief, gave warning that the BCP should not come to his Ward. The Chief may, among other things, either have been incensed or threatened by the BCP song that was composed for that particular occasion, the words of which were to the effect of bringing 'Mohlalefi's head on a platter'.[55] His royal pride was certainly punctured by this dirge.

The end result was that Chief Mohlalefi had the procession ambushed. A nasty stone-throwing, knobkerrie-bashing and gun-firing ensued. In the wake of it four people were dead, and Ramore-boli was wounded.

Chief Mohlalefi got a two-year jail sentence for instigating the fatal ambush; but then, any explanation that he was acting as a chief and not as a member of the MFP did not stick. The ambush was fully exploited by the other two parties which pointed out that the MFP was a party of violence and murder. The Chamber of Commerce, an all white body, withdrew its support. Members left the Party in large numbers. In at least one constituency, the entire local committee and followers defected to other parties. That was the MFP's biggest setback. And it cost it dearly in the upcoming 1965 general elections.

ON THE GENERAL STRUCTURE OF THE NEW CONSTITUTION

When the Constitutional Commission of 1962 had completed the exercise of gathering information throughout the Territory, it sat down to prepare its Report and essentially to draft a revised, new

Constitution designed for an independent national status; and for legal assistance, Professor Denis V. Cowen, who had served as the Constitutional Advisor in 1958, was invited to give the Commission his professional guidance. Thus he spent the summer of 1963 in Lesotho working with the men whose personalities and views he had become familiar with, having worked with all of them in the preparation of the 1959 Constitution.

As Denis Cowen stated at the conclusion of the drafting of the new Constitution:

> The basic plan of the proposed governmental structure is to pro- vide Basutoland with a bicameral legislature, a British-style execu- tive responsible to a democratically elected legislature, a Bill of Human Rights, and an independent judiciary charged with the duty of enforcing the constitution.[56]

The Commission, Denis Cowen further pointed out, was fully aware of 'the dangers of instability' in contemporary Africa that were inherent in a parliamentary executive model. Just the same, for reasons of 'acquired habit and familiarity' which weighed on the Fathers of the Constitution – the members of the Commission – the Cabinet system, with only minor adjustments, was decided upon.[57]

Against the background of constitutional developments traced thus far, it appears that not much meaning can be attached to Basotho's 'acquired habit and familiarity' with the Cabinet system. The facts that a legislative council had been established only three years back, and that as late as 1962 there was still a general view in the masses of the Territory that a Resident Commissioner and an executive monarch were analogous, are sufficient points to support the contention.

Nevertheless it is quite clear that to the members of the Com- mission, to no less a degree than to Denis Cowen, there was a belief (or perhaps wishful thinking) that the 'seeds [of a Cabinet System] had already been planted in their country and had begun to sprout'.[58] If so, it should perhaps not strike one as surprising that there was such a faith, or wish. For only two years before in Nigeria, in circumstances not far removed, the Nigerian jurist, O. T. Elias (now a judge in the International Court of Justice at the Hague), had found a similar decision just as justifiable. So he stated:

> Both the African and the British Systems should . . . be able to accommodate each other in the emergent parliaments of post-war

British Africa. There is no *a priori* reason of political expediency why the African should not be able to operate the modern institutions of constitutional government, given the will to succeed.[59]

Such was the faith in former British possessions in Africa, that Africans should be able to operate Anglo-Saxon political institutions.

Basotho Views of a Bill of Human Rights

In discussing a Bill of Human Rights for adoption in the revised new Constitution, both Professor Denis Cowen and the Constitutional Commission seem to have been one in the view that the notion was already familiar to Basotho and hence their task was essentially one of pouring old wine into new bottles. 'The general idea of constitutionalism', said Cowen, 'of limited government, has long been familiar to the Basotho'. He was impressed with the fact that 'long before the arrival of the white man, the Basotho had developed the art of government by discussion, coupled with a remarkable tolerance of individual opinion'. His understanding of the Basotho *pitso*, seen through the eyes of Lord Bryce on his visit to Lesotho in the late nineteenth century, was that of 'the acute rationality and the freedom of discussion which marked the indigenous Basotho assemblies', 'whose proceedings reminded [Bryce] of the Greek agora'. Bryce had been impressed by the Basotho traditional maxim 'that no man shall be punished for what he says in a *pitso*' and thought that the custom put one 'in mind of the parliamentary freedom of debate so familiar in Britain'.[60]

The discussion of a Bill of Human Rights had been preceded by extensive readings of materials that the Constitutional Advisor had sent to the Commission on comparative constitutionalism. Some members were of course ahead of others, by dint of their higher education, in their academic knowledge of the subject. (The record of their deliberations shows, for instance, that Bennet Khaketla, a student of politics, lavishly displayed his familiarity with Aristotle, Montesquieu, Diderot, Rousseau, Burke, and Dicey.) Professor Cowen found the Commissioners 'well prepared'. Discussions were academically mature and highly sophisticated.

The Nigerian Bill of Rights served as the main basis for framing the Lesotho version of a Bill of Rights; and it seems that the discussion of Section 24 of the Nigerian model served efficiently to reveal the key concerns of the Commission. Section 24 pertained to guarantees of freedom of expression, especially the first subsection, which provided that 'every person shall be entitled to freedom of expression, including freedom to hold opinions, and to receive and impart ideas and information without interference'. Two individuals dominated the discussion, each representing a discrete point of view.

Ntsu Mokhehle first raised the following question: 'Does Section 24 bind private persons and groups as well as state organs?' Further elaborating on the question, he pointed out that he was aware that an American style Bill of Rights was aimed at placing limits upon what organs of government might do; but, at the current stage of constitutional development in Lesotho, he did not think there was a primary need for protection against organs of government. He rather saw the need as one of 'protection against powerful private interests'.[61]

His illustration of 'private interests' was indicative of the immediate problems that the BCP was facing, and it was forthright:

> After all, it is possible that I may be the government quite soon, and I am not likely to hurt anybody. The real trouble here is that the Churches have too much power, and so, too, do the Chiefs, and so do the white traders. What I would like to know is whether we will be able to rely on the Bill of Rights if a white trader tries to keep Africans out of his restaurant or his bar. Again, can we use the Bill of Rights when the Roman Catholics preach in their sermons that voters should not vote for the Congress Party? Can we use the Bill of Rights when the Chiefs refuse permission to people to hold political meetings?[62]

The last question was clearly an allusion to Chief Mohlalefi Bereng and the Rothe affair.

The Leader of the BCP had misgivings about the utility of a Bill of Rights. Basically he felt that 'limited government is a bit of a luxury' for Third World countries. It presupposed 'a substantial degree of economic affluence', which was 'all very well in the rich countries of the West'. What Africa and the rest of the Third World needed was 'more emphasis upon what government should do, more emphasis on planning, and less on noninterference with private enterprise'.[63] It was on that occasion that he articulated his own view of a suitable government for Lesotho, earlier quoted, whereupon he said: 'What we need in Africa is benevolent autocracy rather than limited government.'

Commissioners generally felt that there should be no exaggeration in favour of extremes either way – in favour of 'benevolent autocracy' or unguarded 'eighteenth and nineteenth century notions of constitutionalism'. Giving a counter-balancing view to the Leader of the BCP, B. M. Khaketla said: 'Life itself is difficult and facts are variable. It does not follow that the same principle, applied in different countries to different situations, would lead to the same conclusion.' Yet, in any event, instead of abandoning the fundamental principle which is in any case that government should be made to justify all *prima facie* cases of infringements of human rights, it was preferable to uphold the principle, while at the same time admitting that 'it should be easier for an African government, in present circumstances, to justify curtailments of private rights in the interests of economic security than it should be for a government operating in an affluent society'.[64]

B. M. Khaketla's view represented the general outlook of the Basotho Fathers of the Constitution; but then Ntsu Mokhehle too, in the end, conceded the prudence of a Bill of Rights, and he did it in a statesmanlike fashion. Turning to Denis Cowen he said:

> [P]erhaps the real value of entrenching a Bill of Rights in our Constitution is that it may stimulate us to place an ultimate value on human education and our need to discover ourselves.[65]

REPORT OF THE CONSTITUTIONAL COMMISSION OF 1962

The Report of the Constitutional Commission of 1962 completed, it was brought before the Legislative Council, where it was debated from 25 November 1963 to 11 February 1964. The debate was interrupted by only a short Christmas break. The general framework of the Constitution was accepted in principle. However there were two main issues of great concern to the Legislative Council and which were not to be glossed over. One was an amendment in favour of allowing women to vote. The other was an amendment giving the Basotho king extraordinary powers, as a variation from the British model.

Voting Rights for Women

As earlier alluded to, women had not been able to vote in the first general elections of 1960. This was the case because, although the

1959 Constitutional Handbook emphasised universal adult suffrage, it was with the qualifications that: (a) a voter should be a British Subject or a British Protected Person; (b) should have passed 'his' 21st birthday on the day of his application for registration as an elector; (c) should have 'paid tax at any time during the five years immediately preceding *his* registration as an elector' (my emphasis); and (d) should have been resident in the Territory for a continuous period of six months immediately before registration as an elector, absences for a short period being disregarded. So, first, the language itself, in the use of the pronoun 'his', excluded women. Secondly, and more substantively, the requirement of the payment of tax, to which reference was to 'hut tax', excluded women, who could not pay tax since they were minors under customary law and common law.

In the main there seemed to have been no reason why the nation did not deem it timely for women to be accorded the right to vote, except that some politicians saw women as a potentially formidable political instrument in the hands of their rivals which needed to be controlled. In that respect Chief S. H. Mapheleba, a member of the MFP, put his finger on the problem when he stated early in the debate:

> Mr President, Sir, I have misgivings about the whole thing because in the beginning the Marema-Tlou-Freedom Party and the B.C.P. were reluctant that women should vote, more especially the B.C.P. The voting of women was especially advocated by Chief Leabua who was misled by the words that women will be entitled to vote, and he overlooked the electoral rules which operated since 1960.[66]

The point has already been made that Chief Jonathan stood a lot to gain from women's votes because the Roman Catholic Church had handed members of its faith, most of whom were women, over to him. Such of women's votes as he might not get would be of those whose political convictions in favour of other parties overrode their fear of Church sanctions; and of those there were a few.

The amendment received a strong support from the Legislative Council. Chief Jonathan, apparently satisfied that his general campaign had finally aroused the House to a higher moral ground, refrained from speaking. B. M. Khaketla spoke to the motion positively and technically, emphasising the obvious: 'It is because under the present constitution which governs the franchise in Basutoland the women have been disenfranchised.' 'Those women who ran business concerns and qualified for the payment of income tax qualified for the vote, but the bulk of our women folk who were not engaged in trade were therefore disqualified from exercising the vote'; and so forth and so on.[67] In the end the motion was carried.

Should the King Be the Head of the Armed Forces?

When the debate came to the issue of the powers that ought to be reserved to His Highness, *Motlotlehi* Moshoeshoe II on the attainment of self-government, tempers began to rise. Those who had been significantly quiet rose to their feet.

There were actually three aspects to the issue: recommendations for His Highness '(a) to assent to Bills; (b) to be Head of the Armed Forces of Lesotho; and (c) to exercise the prerogative of mercy on the advice of the Privy Council provided such advice will not bind him in any way'. The first and the third presented no problem. They were agreed to without passion and rancour. The second however, reserving to His Highness the power 'to be Head of the Armed Forces of Lesotho', the point that tinkered with the issue of whether Lesotho would become a constitutional monarchy or an executive monarchy, created great discomfort to one political party.

The strongest view of the MFP came from B. M. Khaketla. It was brief, presented as a matter of course, and strong: 'In the first place', he stated, '[the subsection of the motion in question] deals with the position of *Motlotlehi* which thing must be entrenched.'[68] As if to suggest that the point was self-evident, he did not care to argue the case.

Arguments came from chiefs in the Council. Coming from Chief Mohlalefi Bereng, a staunch supporter of the MFP, was the most salient of them:

> The tribal custom of the Basotho has the Chief as the pivot and the Commander-in-General of the State Army. During the Basotho wars, which are even mentioned in the Report, the Paramount Chief has always been leading the armies. I have my fears that if any man, besides the Paramount Chief is appointed to take up this responsibility, the tribal institutions will disintegrate.[69]

Speaking in this same vein, Chief Nqhae Selabalo, a close supporter of *Motlotlehi*'s causes, said, 'we would like to see *Motlotlehi* acting in the name and on behalf of Her Majesty, carrying out instructions as the Head of the Army'.[70] These views, according to the MFP and sympathetic chiefs, had been supported by the people.

The arguments provoked a grim rebuttal from Ntsu Mokhehle, who commenced to give a speech which lasted for almost two days, from early Thursday, 30 January to 6 p.m. on Friday, 31 January, with some interruptions and official recesses. His performance was impressive, and on the surface he was convincing.

To show the extent of his provocation and the strength of his convictions, he opened his speech by pointing out that 'we [the BCP] had intended not to participate in the debate before the House'; and indeed the BCP had been uncomfortably reticent up to that point; 'But when it is constantly stated in this House that, the people say this or that', he said, 'then we thought we would not like to be committed with these statements.' He then presented an exhaustive statistical analysis of all the gatherings throughout the country which the Commission had interviewed; 'The challenge being to those that say that any *radical changes* that may be made in this report are the views of the people; *especially matters continued (sic) in this amendment'*. (My emphasis)[71]

Ntsu Mokhehle's statistical analysis implicitly supported the view that the majority of the people interviewed were not in favour of *Motlotlehi* being given control of the armed forces of Lesotho. Indeed, elsewhere, in a letter to Harold Macmillan dated 10 May 1963, the Leader of the BCP had indicated that '1916 persons gave written or oral evidence. Of these 1390 witnesses took the Basutoland Congress Party views that the Paramount Chief should be a constitutional Monarch';[72] except, from what has already been shown, those who favoured that view were for the most part members of the BCP, who had been instructed on how to respond to questions. That, therefore, weakened his argument.

As Ntsu Mokhehle had been quiet when that issue was being discussed, so had Chief Leabua Jonathan, the Leader of the BNP. On his part, however, when he took the opportunity to speak, it was in support of the MFP and the chiefs. He simply stated:

I similarly cannot agree that the Head of the Armed Forces should be the Prime Minister. In the memorandum of our Party we have specifically stated that this power should be vested in the Head of State.[73]

THE LAST LAP TOWARD INDEPENDENCE

The First Round of Discussions in London

In April 1964 a Delegation composed of the representatives of the three major parties and the chieftainship was in London to present the Secretary of State, Duncan Sandys, with a Resolution arising from the Constitutional Report of 1963. The Resolution, presented in pursuance of Motion No. 62 of 19 September 1961, was as an acceptable basis for negotiations with Her British Majesty's Government for the improvement of the 1959 Constitution. Professor Denis V. Cowen, constitutional Adviser, was a member of the Delegation. So were Walter Standford, President of the Legislative Council since 1961, and Brian O'Leary, who served as Chairman of the Delegation. His Highness *Motlotlehi* Moshoeshoe II was also present yet not as a member of the Delegation. It had been thought convenient and proper that he be invited to accompany the Delegation in case it became necessary that he be consulted.

The Resolution had four Sections, with Section 2 containing eighteen amendments to the 1959 Constitution. To mention a few of these, they were: (a) 'that the duration of parliament is five years, unless it is sooner dissolved by *Motlotlehi*'; (b) 'that in the first place elections to the new Parliament universal adult suffrage' be extended to include women; (e) 'that the Head of State should have further powers as follows: (i) to assent to Bills; (ii) to be Head of the Armed Forces of Lesotho, and (iii) to exercise the prerogative of mercy on the advice of Privy Council'; (l) 'that a Judiciary should be established which is free and independent from the Executive and the Legislative, and that its position should be entrenched; (p) 'that the number of persons who compose the Lower House shall be sixty'.

All the other amendments were discussed amicably and agreement was reached with little or no difficulty; but when the discussion moved on to the amendment on increasing the *Motlotlehi*'s powers, the Secretary of State dug in his heels. According to B. M. Khaketla, who was present in the debates and took a keen interest on the amendment, (in as much as the motion had been moved by the MFP), Duncan Sandys informed the Delegation that as Lesotho was being granted internal self-government, and not sovereign independence, the British Government could not agree to the transfer of powers suggested by amendment 2 (e) at that juncture. The Secretary of State, Khaketla recalls, said, 'they [those powers] should remain with the British Government for the period of internal self-rule, which we agreed should be one year; the appropriate moment to say on whom they should devolve was when we came back for our final round of talks, and not before'.[74]

The Lesotho Delegation was made to feel that if it did not compromise, it might come back home empty-handed. So, anxious to return home with a Constitution, the Delegation compromised and deferred to Duncan Sandys' argument; but in the process, Khaketla states on hindsight: 'We did not insist that Duncan Sandys' assurance about the powers of the King should be recorded in our daily minutes.' Khaketla realised only after damage had been done that 'it would have been the wisest thing to have insisted'.[75] The Agreement having been reached, Lesotho was granted self-government.

The New Constitution and the General Elections

When the new Constitution came into force, on 30 April 1965, His Highness *Motlotlehi* was to perform his functions under the Constitution on behalf of Her Majesty the Queen. After the elections, *Motlotlehi* was to appoint as Prime Minister the Leader of the Party, or coalition of Parties, that had the support of the majority of the members of the National Assembly. Acting on the advice of the Prime Minister, *Motlotlehi* was to appoint the other Ministers from among the members of the National Assembly or from the Senators. They were to be the Cabinet, and that was to be *Motlotlehi*'s Government.

The Constitution established the post of British Government Representative, who was to be responsible for External Affairs, Defence and Internal Security. The British Government Representative was also responsible for ensuring proper financial administration and for protecting the terms of service of public officers, until a date to be fixed later.

Parliament was to consist of Her Majesty the Queen, the Senate and the National Assembly. The Senate was to be composed of 22 Principal or Ward Chiefs and eleven other members appointed by *Motlotlehi*. Parliament, unless dissolved, was to continue for five years. A modality for the dissolution of Parliament was in keeping with the Westminster conventions.

There was to be a Privy Council to assist *Motlotlehi* in the discharge of his functions. It was to consist of the British Government Representative, the Prime Minister, and one other person nominated by

Motlotlehi. One of the most important functions of the Privy Council was to facilitate consultations and the exchange of information between the Government of the United Kingdom and *Motlotlehi*'s Government in respect of external affairs, defence, internal security and schemes of the retirement from the Public Service of expatriate officers in order to make way for local candidates.

Not earlier than one year from the holding of the general elections, the people of Lesotho, by resolutions of both the National Assembly and the Senate, might ask for full independence. In the event of a dispute between the National Assembly and the Senate, the matter was to be settled by a referendum. Independence was to be granted if conditions of law and order existed in the country.

General elections commenced on 29 April 1965. The BNP won 31 seats in the National Assembly, the BCP got 25 seats and the MFP four seats. Altogether the BNP had polled 108 140 votes, followed by the BCP with 102 068, and MFP with 40 414. Still in the race, the Marematlou of S. S. Matete had poled 5697. In Maseru, the BCP candidate, Shakhane Mokhehle, brother to the Party Leader, had beaten B. M. Khaketla 4699 to 876. Both the Leaders of the BNP, Chief Jonathan, and of the MFP, Dr Seth Makotoko lost elections in their respective constituencies.[76]

Because Chief Jonathan had lost elections, Chief Sekhonyana 'Maseribane, Deputy Leader of the BNP, also a Roman Catholic by faith, became Prime Minister. Meantime Chief Jonathan awaited a by-election.

Several members of the BNP with seats in the National Assembly offered to resign in favour of the Leader of their Party in lieu of a by-election. His Highness *Motlotlehi* Moshoeshoe II had conveniently effected only ten of the eleven appointments to the Senate to which the Constitution entitled him, and so there was the faith on the part of each member who offered their resignation that they would be appointed to the eleventh vacant seat.[77] In the event, Chief Jonathan accepted the offer from John Mothepu, of the constituency of Mpharane, where the BNP had scored its highest majority. And duly John Mothepu was appointed to the Senate.

The by-election was on 1 July. On 9 June an announcement was made to the effect that the Republic of South Africa had offered Chief Jonathan a 'personal gift' of 100 000 bags of maize-meal valued at R315 000, as aid to the 'starving masses of the Basotho'. This was the gift which B. M. Khaketla denounced as 'a cheap political trick intended to buy support for Chief Leabua Jonathan and his National

Party'.[78] It is doubtful that the Leader of the BNP actually needed this gift to win the by-election. Nonetheless it did have some effect in boosting the morale of its immediate peasant benefactors. Above all, it tightened the bonds between the BNP and the South African Government.

Chief Jonathan won the by-election and accordingly replaced Chief 'Maseribane as Prime Minister. Chief 'Maseribane then became the Deputy Prime Minister and Minister of Home Affairs. Of the other important losers in the political game, His Highness had already appointed S. S. Matete, Leader of the MTP and Seth Makotoko, Leader of the MFP to the Senate; B. M. Khaketla got the plum – His Highness appointed him to the Privy Council.

The BNP was a minority government, with an overall majority of only two seats. That position was not made easy by the fact that the BCP successfully petitioned against the results of two constituencies, that of 'Masemousu and the other of Qaqatu. Following a High Court hearing the BNP member of 'Masemousu was unseated, lowering the Party's seats in the National Assembly to 30. Before the second High Court hearing concerning Qaqatu took place, Chief Jonathan, evidently fearful that he would lose that one as well, adjourned the National Assembly *sine die*. Indeed the Qaqatu case was also lost and the BNP candidate was unseated, creating an unsettling situation whereby the BNP remained with 29 seats and the BCP-MFP with 29 seats in the National Assembly.

Some politicians, chief among whom was Ntsu Mokhehle, felt strongly that *Motlotlehi* should declare that therefore there was no government and dissolve Parliament; but with the National Assembly not in session, rendering it impossible to table and debate a motion of no confidence, *Motlotlehi* apparently found himself in a quandary and so declined to act. In the end the BNP won the by-elections both at 'Masemousu as well as Qaqatu; and so at last an ugly situation was saved.[79] It had been a bitter and traumatising general election. The smell of advancing Independence was becoming disagreeable.

Independence Turns Bitter

Once the elections were over and the BNP was in power, the issue of the *Motlotlehi*'s authority was back on the agenda. This time it was almost to abort the nation's bid for Independence.

On 4 May 1965, when Chief Jonathan gave his first press conference since the elections, he made what seemed like either a protectionist move or a veiled threat toward the monarchy. He stated:

> The dignity of the Chieftainship which has been brought to a low level by the political manoeuvre of the Marema Tlou Freedom Party will be restored.[80]

The meaning of this statement remained unclear for some time.

A year later, at the fourth meeting, First Session of the National Assembly, the Chief rose to propose a motion 'that Her Majesty's Government . . . grant Independence to Lesotho in terms of the Agreement reached in London in 1964'.[81] The House was looking forward to the motion, and so there was nothing surprising about that as such.

What startled the opposition parties, however, was when Chief Jonathan began to refer to 'What may be described as a contract between the Basotho and Her Majesty's Government'. By that, as he further elaborated, he meant that the 1964 London talks had (a) produced a solemn agreement on the nature of the Constitution, (b) that the only issues that were agreed upon were those that went on record and (c) that the issue of increasing the powers of His Highness was not among them.[82] So he said:

> But let us be under no illusion about *Motlotlehi*'s position. It was agreed by the 1963 Constitutional Commission, and it was endorsed by the Secretary of State, and by those present at the London Conference – including *Motlotlehi* – that *Motlotlehi* should exercise his powers as Head of State in accordance with the provisions of the Constitution. *Motlotlehi*'s position, in short, is that of a Constitutional ruler. And from this there can be no departure.[83]

To those in the National Assembly who had painted an image of Chief Jonathan as a tyro and a simpleton in politics – as earlier surmised by *The Friend* of Bloemfontein – it must have come as a rude shock when he made a perfect *volte-face*. Employing Ntsu Mokhehle's original argument to turn on his heels, Jonathan stated:

> I would . . . like to remind this House that the very people who are now advocating an increase of *Motlotlehi*'s powers are the same people whose views on the subject were decisively rejected by the nation when the Constitutional Commission went around the country gathering views in 1963.[84]

The opposition parties, including the BCP, were confounded by these pronouncements. It in essence meant that the question of *Motlotlehi*'s control over the Armed Forces of the country was a dead issue. And the last blow came from a chief.

Equally confounding, Ntsu Mokhehle had changed his own position of 1963–64 on the monarchy. Having lost the premiership, he no longer wished that the Armed Forces be controlled by the Prime Minister. In essence he feared that Jonathan might use this power against him and so he now preferred that the Armed Forces be under *Motlotlehi*. He and Jonathan had swapped positions.

The only hope of the opposition parties was that the issue would be brought back to life when the Independence Conference took place in London on 8 June 1966. At the Independence Conference the Secretary of State, Fred Lee was, however, fully on the side of the BNP. If anything, the British Government was amenable to the confirmation of a BNP-sponsored section in the Independence Constitution which gave the Prime Minister fuller control over *Motlotlehi*. Section 78 – (4) (5) of *The Lesotho Independence Order*, defining the exercise of the king's functions read:

> 76, (4) Where the King is required by the Constitution to do any act in accordance with the advice of any person or authority and the Prime Minister is satisfied that the King has neglected or declined to do so, the Prime Minister may inform the King that it is the intention of the Prime Minister to do that act himself after the expiration of a period to be specified by the Prime Minister, and if at the expiration of that period the King has not done that act the Prime Minister may do that act himself and shall, at the earliest opportunity thereafter, report the matter to the Parliament; and any act so done by the Prime Minister shall be deemed to have been done by the King and to be his act.
>
> (5) No act of the King shall be valid to the extent that it is inconsistent with an act deemed to be his act by virtue of Sub-Section (4) of this Section.[85]

The most unfortunate thing for the nation at that juncture was that the entire leadership of the country was acting either from fear or from suspicion. Trust had broken; and there was no one to pull the pieces together. The most powerful Church in the country, the Roman Catholic Church, had made itself party to political strife, thus goading other religious denominations to take sides. The BCP-MFP Representatives of the Lesotho Delegation to London were bitter with the British Government for having not made any concession to their pleas in support of giving the monarch executive authority; and so, on 15 June the three – Ntsu Mokhehle, Gerard Ramoreboli, and Edwin Leanya (MFP) (Khaketla having not gone to London on that occasion) – withdrew from the Conference and made a joint declaration before the press. In part the address read:

> The role we have been allocated in this Conference is that of puppets in a carefully rehearsed pantomime. We are, therefore, forced to protest in the only way immediately open to us by disassociating ourselves completely from this travesty.[86]

That statement, buttressed by the action to persuade the United Nations to intervene against the granting of independence, had the general effect of galvanising hostility and mutual mistrust in the nation.

His Highness *Motlotlehi* too had reached the full extent of his capacity for tolerance. He obviously felt chained by the Independence Constitution, and seems further to have concluded that grumblings to the effect that Chief Jonathan was poised to depose him were born of truth. The latest of these grumblings had been heard at the London Conference in June, where, in the presence of the Secretary of State for Colonies, Chief Jonathan had made a threat to the effect 'that His Highness would find himself in the same position as the Kabaka of Buganda who was deposed by his Prime Minister'.[87] At the time this statement was made, the Kabaka of Buganda was on his way to exile in London.

The *Motlotlehi*'s fears and frustration seem to have come clearly to the surface on 25 September 1966, when he addressed a crowd at Matsieng of about 30 000 people and told the crowd (as paraphrased by *Mohlabani*) that:

> [T]he British Government, together with the so-called Government of *Motlotlehi*, conspired to change the London agreement, and therefore the Constitution which has resulted from it, to fulfil Chief Kaizer Leabua's desire so oft-repeated that His Highness should abdicate in favour of someone who has not been named.[88]

Consequently upon the address, much ado was made by *Mohlabani* of an irreverent remark from a Roman Catholic priest who was heard to shock the waves in the course of the royal address, saying: 'I have never heard so much rot in all my life!'[89]

Lesotho celebrated her Independence from Britain on 4 October 1966 and *Motlotlehi* was officially granted the title of King. The

Westminster model, with very minor adjustments, was in place; yet not in substance, but in form. That change marked an official line of divide between the old executive monarchy and its vital institutions such as the *pitso*, and the new constitutional monarchy with its ceremonial king; but while the old lingered on a romantic plane, no longer amenable to efficient use, the new and attractive form of government exacted no commitment from those who had to operate it. In all this, the masses became a factor for exploitation by those whose immediate objective became power, and all that power could bring for their personal gratification. Thus the New Monarchy began in strife, resting on an untenable constitution, with no agreed locus of power, and no universal recognition for appointed authority.

Notes and References

CHAPTER 1

1. The term 'Bantu', shorn of its racialist overtones (since the Boer element of the white settler community of South Africa began calling itself African – Afrikaner – and calling Africans the Bantu) owes its academic origins as a term of linguistic classification to the philologist W. H. I. Bleek (1827–75) and, within the context of South Africa, as a political entity, and Botswana, Lesotho and Swaziland it recognises two major linguistic groups: (a) the 'Sotho' who are divided further into the Batswana, Bapedi, Basotho (in and outside the country Lesotho); (b) the 'Nguni' (Abakuni or Bakone), who are further divided into the AmaXhosa (including AmaMpondo, AmaMpondomise, AbaThembu), AmaZulu (Zulu) and AmaSwati (AmaSwazi). See C. M. Doke, *The Southern Bantu Languages* (London, 1967) pp. 11–13; and S. M. Molema, *The Bantu: The Past and Present* (Cape Town, 1963) p. 35. On the problem of Bantu migrations see J. Vansina, 'Bantu in the crystal ball', *History in Africa,* VI (1979) and VII (1980); and ibid., 'Western Bantu Expansion', *Journal of African History,* XXV (1984) 2.
2. J. D. Omer-Cooper, *The Zulu Aftermath: A Nineteenth-Century Revolution in Bantu Africa* (Essex, 1966) p. 15. Omer-Cooper acknowledges his dependence on I. Schapera, *Government and Politics in Tribal Societies* (London, 1956, reprint, 1963).
3. T. Arbousset, *Narrative of an Exploratory Tour to the North-East of the Colony of the Cape of Good Hope* (Cape Town, 1846) p. 401.
4. Peter Sanders, *Moshoeshoe, Chief of the Sotho,* (London, 1975); Leonard Thompson, *Survival in Two Worlds, Moshoeshoe of Lesotho, 1786–1870* (London,1975).
5. E. Sidney Hartland, *Primitive Law* (London, 1924) introductory paragraph to ch. II: 'Constitutional Law', p. 10.
6. Omer-Cooper, *The Zulu Aftermath*, p. 173.
7. Eugene Casalis, *The Basutos, or Twenty-Three Years in South Africa* (London, 1861) p. 209.
8. Arbousset, *Narrative of an Exploratory Tour*, p. 373.
9. 'About the beginning of the last [that is, the seventeenth] century, a band of refugees calling themselves Bamaru, or People of the Clouds, migrated from Zululand to the south of Basutoland. These people adopted Basuto customs and intermarried with the followers of Monaheng, by whom they were termed Maphetla, or the pioneers'; Germond, R. C., *Chronicles of Basutoland* (Morija, Lesotho, 1967), p. 330.
10. D. F. Ellenberger, and J. C. MacGregor, *History of the Basuto, Ancient and Modern* (London, 1912) p. 263. See also Arbousset, *Narrative of an Exploratory Tour*, p. 373.

307

11. Ellenberger and MacGregor, *History of the Basuto*, p. 303.
12. Arbousset, *Narrative of an Exploratory Tour*, p. 373.
13. Casalis, *The Basutos*, p. 214. Although Ian Hamnet takes issue with Casalis on this point, for being 'unduly swayed by sentiment' (a criticism with which I do not agree), in his own translation he writes: 'The verb *ho rena* means "to be rich not to work; to be a chief." ' This translation is not functionally different from Casalis'. Ian Hamnet, *Chieftainship and Legitimacy: An Anthropological Study of Executive Law in Lesotho* (London, 1975) pp. 86, 151.
14. On the view that *Morena e Moholo* is analogous to King see also Hamnet, *Chieftainship and Legitimacy*, p. 86. Leonard Thompson also writes 'By 1833 [Moshoeshoe] was recognised not merely as a *Morena e Moholo* (a chief) but as the *Morena e Moholo* (the Great Chief: the King).' Thompson, *Survival in Two Worlds*, p. 64.
15. Arbousset, *Narrative of an Exploratory Tour*, pp. 378, 385.
16. For a comprehensive modern historical appraisal of Mohlomi see L. B. B. J. Machobane, 'Mohlomi: Doctor, Traveller and Sage', *Mohlomi, Journal of Southern African Historical Studies*, vol. II (National University of Lesotho, 1976) pp. 5–23. On Ratlali see Ellenberger and MacGregor, *History of the Basuto*, p. 83. Even after Mohlomi's death, according to the self-trained Mosotho historian Azariel Sekese, 'Maliepollo maintained interest in Lesotho. She is said to have sent a messenger named Thamanamane to Moshoeshoe, from Grahamstown where she had retreated since *lifaqane*, in 1833, advising him to get white missionaries to help him to maintain his kingdom. Sekese, *Leselinyana*, 1 April 1892, p. 1.
17. Arbousset, *Narrative of an Exploratory Tour* p. 380.
18. Indeed when Casalis published his first work on Basotho in 1861 even the territory of Basotho was already styled 'Lesotho'. Casalis, *The Basutos*, p. 319.
19. According to Thompson, Moshoeshoe can be assumed to have taken over effectively from his father at the start of *lifaqane*, on the occasion of Sekonyela's pending attack of Mokhachane's chiefdom (1823); but this is speculation, albeit plausible. Thompson *Survival in Two Worlds*, p. 41.
20. 'Bohali for the first wife of the chief', writes Rolland, 'was paid for by the community, usually before he came to power'. Emile Rolland, *Journal des Missions Evangeliques* (hereafter JME) 18 Dec. 1844, p. 212, cited in Judy Kimble, 'Towards an Understanding of the Political Economy of Lesotho: The Origins of Commodity Production and Migrant Labour, 1830–c.1885' (M A thesis, National University of Lesotho, 1978) p. 74.
21. Hugh Ashton, *The Basuto*, (London, 1952), p. 193.
22. F. Laydevant, OMI, 'Le Sceptre Des Chefs Basuto', *Africa: Journal of the International African Institute*, vol. 18 (1948) no. 1, p. 41. Translated for me by Miss H. M. Ewan (M A (Hon.) French, Edinburgh University).
23. Thebeamang Masopha, who had what was probably Masopha's

(Moshoeshoe's third and valorous son's) rhinoceros club, and Batho Hlalele, who had led me to the former. 6 March 1979.

24. Laydevant, 'Le Sceptre Des Chefs Basuto', p. 41.
25. Ibid.
26. Ibid, p. 42.
27. Casalis, *The Basutos*, p. 220.
28. Ashton, *The Basuto*, p. 204.
29. Schapera, *Government and Politics in Tribal Societies*, pp. 137–43.
30. Ibid., p. 137, cited from Soga (1932), p. 31.
31. Machobane, 'Mohlomi', pp. 18–21.
32. N. S. Luthango, *Umohlomi* (Pietermaritzburg, 1938) p. 146.
33. Arbousset, *Narrative of an Exploratory Tour*, p. 278.
34. George Tlali (Moshoeshoe), 'Litaba tsa Basotho', pt. 1, edited and translated with an introduction and notes by M. Damane and P. B. Sanders, sect. 20, in *Mohlomi Journal*, vol. II (CapeTown, 1858) p. 133.
35. Ellenberger and MacGregor, *History of the Basuto*, p. 106.
36. Jacques Heurgon, *The Rise of Rome to 264 B.C.*, translated by James Willis (London, 1st Eng. edn, 1973) p. 113.
37. Jonathan Molapo, 'Minutes of Meeting held by the Chief Letsie at Thaba Bosigo, on the 3rd July 1880, in order that the deputation sent by him to Cape Town might make known to the people the result of their mission', in *British Parliamentary Paper*, LXVI (C. 2755), 1881, Frere to Kimberly, no. 22, 2 August 1880, Enclosure 2 in No. 22, p. 52.
38. Ibid. p. 54.
39. Ellenberger and MacGregor, *History of the Basuto*, p. 292.
40. Casalis, *The Basutos*, p. 206.
41. Casalis, Morija, May 1834, in Robert C. Germond, *Chronicles of Basutoland* (Lesotho: Morija, 1967) p. 517.
42. Casalis narrates yet another incident when he was interrupted in the middle of a very rewarding conversation with the King. Moshoeshoe tried in vain to chase the man away: 'Begone! my white man is with me, pray leave him in peace!'; but the man retorted: 'No, it is now three days that I have been waiting for you to judge my case; judge it at once; my wife and children are alone at home, I wish to return to them.' The King was only able to get rid of his subject, temporarily, by sending him to one of his wives to 'tell her on my behalf to give you a shoulder of mutton which I left anon'. Ibid. p. 516.
43. See Schapera, *Government and Politics in Tribal Societies*, pp. 69–74.
44. Casalis, Thaba Bosiu, September 1838, in Germond, *Chronicles of Basutoland*, p. 540.
45. Ellenberger and MacGregor, *History of the Basuto*, p. 266.
46. Chief Jobo, *Commission on Laws and Customs of the Basutos 1873* (Cape Town, 1873, reprinted by Morija, Lesotho) p. 50.
47. According to Reverend F. Coillard, Basotho observed the rule that 'the person of an ambassador is sacred, whatever his message'. C. W. Mackintosh, *Coillard of the Zambesi*, pp. 54–5. By way of comparison, it is interesting to note that in the neighbouring AmaMpondomise

polity, according to its authorities, even an insult to a ruler's messenger was 'a great crime' for which punishment was 'to take up the "Tiger Tail"', which means that he would have to pay one head of cattle'. Evidence of Gangalizwe, Nyanga, Sangoni, Mpiti, Xelo, Sila Pantshwa, Nqayi, Cutalele, Dinase, Umgendiki, Umsengi, and twelve others, *Report of the Commission on Native Laws and Customs* (Cape Town, 1881) Minutes of Evidence, p. 442.

48. For this part of the paragraph see Casalis, *The Basutos*, p. 224.
49. *Morena e Moholo* Letsie, recalling his role in the Langalibalele affair to Colonel Griffith. 'Report of Proceedings of Meeting in School room of the Morija Mission Station on 22nd June, 1881, in *Cape of Good Hope Report of the Honourable the Secretary for Natives Affairs on His Visit to Basutoland*, June 1881, (G. 26–82) p. 27.
50. Casalis, *The Basutos*, pp. 261–6; Ellenberger and MacGregor, *History of the Basuto*, pp. 280–9.
51. Casalis, *Mes Souvenirs*, 1833. Cited in Germond, *Chronicles*, p. 516.
52. Schapera, *Government and Politics in Tribal Societies*, pp. 13–15.
53. Hartland, *Primitive Law*, p. 15.
54. Reverend Mr Mackenzie, 'Minutes of Evidence', *Report of the Commission on Native Laws and Customs*, p. 495.
55. Gangelizwe, Nyanga, Sangoni *et al.*, ibid, p. 443.
56. Cited by J. M. Mohapeloa, 'Tentative British Imperialism in Lesotho, 1884–1910: A Study in Basotho-colonial Office Interaction and South Africa's Influence on it', (M. Phil. thesis, Sussex, 1982) p. 14.
57. Schapera, *Government and Politics in Tribal Societies*, pp. 14–15.
58. For Maine's elaboration on territorial sovereignty see Sir Henry Sumner Maine, *Ancient Law: Its Connection with the Early History of Society and Its Relation to Modern Ideas* (London, 1861; the 'Cheap' edition, 1905; p. 90 of the 10th Edition, 1884). (The notion of territorial sovereignty aside, it is mainly to Maine that scholars of the non-literate modern studies owe the formulation distinguishing between primitive and civilised societies, at least until recently. For a review of Maine's impact in this respect see Schapera, *Government and Politics in Tribal Societies*, pp. 3–21). Modern scholarship on the notion of territorial sovereignty has only been slightly qualified. Starke, for instance, writes: 'Occupation consists in establishing sovereignty over territory not under the authority of any other state whether newly discovered, or – an unlikely use – abandoned by the state formerly in control. Classically, the subject-matter of an occupation is *terra nullius*, and territory inhabited by tribes of peoples having a social and political organisation cannot be of the nature of *terra nullius*. Where land is inhabited by organised tribes of peoples, territorial sovereignty is acquired by local agreements with the rulers or representatives of the tribes or peoples.' Needless to say, this test of 'agreements' is inadequate, unless 'agreement' is broadly defined to include 'mutual recognition' of territorial limits between contiguous political communities. J. G. Starke, *Introduction to International Law* (London, 1984) p. 155.
59. Maine, *Ancient Law*, p. 93.

60. Casalis, *The Basutos*, p. 222. Arbousset, *Narrative of an Exploratory Tour*, p. 374.
61. For a section on Basotho counsellors see Thompson, *Survival in Two Worlds*, pp. 204–13.
62. Ibid.
63. Ibid.
64. Sanders, *Moshoeshoe*, p. 47. Pule Phoofolo, thesis draft on 'Rinderpest Epizootic', (Northwestern University, 1981). p. 19. Phoofolo listed Makoanyane in the 'House of Moreneng', great house, Thiberi as 'general and councillor of the House of Mahebeng', Thafeng as councillor of the House of Tlokotsing; but he did not give his source of information; at least not as of then.
65. For details on Mokolokolo's career see Thompson, *Survival in Two Worlds*, pp. 204–5.
66. Casalis, *The Basutos*, p. 222.
67. Ibid. Peter Sanders also observes (on the same authority): 'Moshoeshoe at least made it a practice to appoint a particular messenger for each of the chiefs with whom he was in contact.' The statement as it stands may give effect to the view that this specialisation was Moshoeshoe's own innovation; whereas the view that Casalis had clearly meant to portray was that the specialisation was a pre-Moshoeshoe development. See Sanders, *Moshoeshoe*, p. 141. In so far as he writes on Moshoeshoe, in any event, Sanders adds, on Arbousset's authority: 'he was in regular contact with many other chiefs too'. Arbousset, *Relation d'un voyage d'exploration au nord-est de la Colonie du Cap de Bonne-Espérance* (Paris, 1842) p. 336.
68. Letsie, 'Minutes of meeting at Morija, 26 March, 1883', B P P 1883, xlviii (C. 3708) p. 82.
69. See Chapter 3: The Boundary Question.
70. See Ntho's recall of High Commissioner Sir Philip Wodehouse. Sir Walter Currie, 'Moshoeshoe negotiations in 1868', in 'Minutes of meeting' at Morija, 26 March, 1883', B P P 1883, xlviii (C. 3708), pp. 77–8.
71. Thompson, *Survival in Two Worlds*, p. 103.
72. On that occasion Moshoeshoe even gave his AmaZulu ambassadors a present of horses to his overlord, Mpande, among other things. 'Minutes of Conference held at Thaba Bosigo (sic), from 11th February, 1962, to the 21st, between the Chief Moshesh on the one part, and Messieurs Burnet and Orpen, Commissioners appointed by His Excellency, for the purpose of ascertaining the chief's views and Government', in Theal, *B R*, vol. iii(a), p. 141.
73. Enclosure 3 in No. 2 Memorandum by Sect. for Native Affairs on Letter from Moshesh, dated July 15, 1866, B P P 1868–69 (4140) vol. xlii, pp. 84–5.
74. Theal, *B R*, vol. ii, p. 58.
75. Sanders, *Moshoeshoe*, p. 137.
76. Casalis to Rolland, 14 Feb. 1848, *B R* iii. 99
77. For his major *lipitso* see in Sanders, Moshoeshoe's joint *pitso* during the pre-*lifaqane* period, p. 30; *pitso* to grant Moroka, ruler of

Barolong to settle at Thaba Nchu in 1833, p. 64; *Morena* Mojakisane's re-admission into the kingdom in 1837, p. 70; settlement of the Basotho-Boer boundary in August 1845, p. 93; *pitso* to decide on the Napier treaty in 1843, p. 103; *pitso* to explain the new relationship of the Queens MaSekhonyana and MaMosebetsi to the King subject to their conversion to Christianity, p. 129.

78. Casalis, *The Basutos*, pp. 233–6.
79. Casalis, Morija, May 1934, in Germond, *Chronicles*, p. 517.
80. The term 'Kafir' was first employed by Heinrich Lichtenstein (1808) to refer to people whom Bleek later referred to as the Bantu. See Doke, *The Southern Bantu Languages*, p. 12. In time, however, the term came to be used, at first to refer to the various AmaXhoza political communities, after which the White settlers of South Africa used it synonymously with Black, and ultimately it has become an unqualified term of opprobrium similar in its racial overtones to 'nigger', and so it is no longer used in contemporary Africanist scholarship.
81. *Report of the Commission on Native Laws and Customs*, 1881 s. 121, p. 45.
82. See in particular the following two works as proof of the existence of Basotho customary law: Poulter, Sebastian, *Family Law and Litigation* (Oxford, 1976). I. Hamnet, *Chieftainship and Legitimacy: An Anthropological Study of Executive Law in Lesotho* (London, 1975).
83. Antony Allot, *New Essays in African Law* (London: 1970), p. 145.
84. *Report of the Commission on Native Laws and Customs*, 1881, p. 433.
85. *Commission on Laws and Customs of the Basutos*, 1973, p. 58.
86. Schapera, *Government and Politics in Tribal Societies*, pp. 69–70.
87. *Report of the Commission on Native Laws and Customs*, 1881, s. 31, pp. 20–1.
88. Casalis, 15 July 1843, *JME*, xix (1844) p. 124–5, cited by Thompson, *Survival in Two Worlds*, p. 95.
89. Theal, *BR*, vol. ii, p. 152, cited by G. Tylden, *The Rise of The Basuto* (Cape Town, 1950) p. 68. Tylden's assertion that the law was passed 'after a long sitting of a tribal council' is not revealed in the source as cited (and as his footnote comes just before the statement: perhaps it was not meant to give that impression). We therefore have to assume that the information on the 'long sitting of a tribal council' is derived from a different, undisclosed, source.
90. Cited by Ashton, *The Basuto*, p. 250.
91. Theal, *BR*, vol. ii, pp. 152–3.
92. Thompson, *Survival in Two Worlds*, p. 182.
93. Arbousset, Thaba Bosiu, 27 August 1855, in Theal, *B R*, vol. ii, p. 153.

CHAPTER 2

1. George McCall Theal, *Basutoland Records* (hereafter *BR*) (Cape Town, 1883) vol. I, pp. 55–6.
2. Ibid., p. 89.
3. *British Parliamentary Papers* (hereafter *BPP*) 1851 (1360) XXXVII, pp. 95–6. Despatch No. 7 from Earl Grey to Governor Sir H. G. Smith, November 28, 1850, enclosure in no. 7, Jos. John Freeman, London Missionary Society, London, to the Right Hon. Earl Grey, Her Majesty's Secretary of State for the Colonies, August 20, 1850.
4. *BPP*, 1847–8, (969) XLIII, p. 5. Commission under the Royal Sign Manual, appointing Major-General the Right Hon. Sir Henry Pottinger, High Commissioner.
5. Ibid., pp. 62–3. Smith to Grey, no. 16, February 3, 1848, enclosure no. 2, Agreement between Moshesh and Smith on the creation of the Orange River Sovereignty, January, 2, 1848.
6. G. Tylden, *The Rise of the Basotho*, (Cape Town, 1950), pp. 30–1.
7. *BPP*, No. 16, 3 February, 1948.
8. *BR*, vol. I, pp. 158–9.
9. Ibid.
10. It is indeed an established principle of British Constitutional Law that the King 'cannot change the laws of himself without the consent of Parliament.' See *Campbell* v. *Hall* (1874), 1 Cowp. 204, King's Bench, Lord Mansfield. C. J. in D. L. Keir and F. H. Lawson, *Cases in Constitutional Law*, (Oxford, 1954), p. 491.
11. Paris Editorial (n.d., *c.* 1850, in Robert C. Germond, *Chronicles of Basutoland* (Morija, Lesotho, 1967) p. 233.
12. John Allen Benyon, 'Basutoland and the High Commission with Particular Reference to the Years 1868–1884: The Changing Nature of the Imperial Government's "Special Responsibility" for the Territory' (Ph.D. thesis, University of Oxford, 1968) pp. 197–8.
13. *BR*, vol. II, p. 99.
14. Thanks to Eugene Casalis, we are able to establish the fact that this historic letter was in content not only an expression of the thoughts of Moshoeshoe and his councillors but even the wording (presumably in Sesotho in its original form) was original. So writes Casalis: 'Moshoeshoe sent me two of his confidential agents to acquaint me with those thoughts of his and his son Nehemia Sekhonyana wrote the following letter in my presence.' In Germond, *Chronicles*, pp. 207–8. See also *BPP* 1852 (1646) LXVI, p. 102. Despatch from C Cathcart to The Right Honourable Sir John S. Pakingson Bart., January 13, 1853, no. 21; Moshesh to Cathcart, December 20, enclosure to no. 21.
15. Cited by J. M. Orpen., *History of the Basutos of South Africa*, reprinted from the Cape Argus in 1857 (Mazenod, Lesotho, 1979) p. 118.
16. Sir Arnold Duncan McNair, *The Law of Treaties: British Practice and Opinions* (Oxford, 1938) p. 525.
17. Germond, *Chronicles*, pp. 259–62.

18. *Ibid.*
19. *Ibid.*
20. *BPP*, 1868–9 (4140) vol. XLIII, p. 2. Cape of Good Hope and Natal Despatches from the Governor of the Cape of Good Hope and the Lieut.-Governor of Natal on the Subject of the Recognition of Moshesh, Chief of the Basutos, and of His Tribe, as British Subjects. Moshesh to Prince Alfred, Aliwal North, August 18, 1860.
21. *Ibid.*, pp. 3–7, Wodehouse to Newcastle, February 1, 1862, no. 9, Enclosure 1 in no. 2, Moshesh to High Commissioner, December 6, 1861.
22. *Ibid.*
23. It has to be assumed here that in Moshoeshoe's original version in Sesotho the designation of 'Lesotho' had been used and that 'Basutoland' was the High Commission designation . Although this is not to suggest that Basotho, especially when they wrote in English, did not, as a matter of influence use 'Basutoland' as well.
24. *Ibid.*; *BR*, vol. III, pp. 143, 145.
25. *BR* vol. III, p. 163, Wodehouse to Secretary of State, April 19, 1862.
26. *BPP*, 1868–69 (4140) vol. XLII, *Ibid.*, p. 9. Despatch from Wodehouse to Cardwell, M.P. October 13, 1865.
27. *Ibid.*, pp. 11–12, Brand to Moshesh. Enclosure in no. 4.
28. *Ibid.*, pp. 9–10. Moshesh to Wodehouse, August 29, 1865. Enclosure in no. 4. Also *BR*, vol. III, pp. 457–8.
29. *Ibid.*, pp. 12–13. Wodehouse to Moshesh (reply to Moshesh letter of August 29).
30. *Ibid.*, p. 9. Despatch from Wodehouse to Cardwell, M.P. October 13, 1865. Also *BR*, vol. III, pp. 493–4.
31. *Ibid.*, pp. 13–15. Despatch from Wodehouse to Cardwell, January 13, 1866, no. 6.
32. *Ibid.*, pp. 18–19. Robert W. Keate to Wodehouse, September 9, 1867. Enclosure 1 in no. 8. Despatch Wodehouse to Buckingham and Chandos, September 17, 1867.
33. Benyon, 'Basutoland and the High Commission', p. 149.
34. *BPP*, 1868–69 (4140) vol. XLII, ibid., pp. 18–19. Robert W. Keate to Wodehouse, September 9, 1867.
35. Benyon, 'Basutoland and the High Commission', p. 163.
36. *BR*, vol. III, pp. 596–9, Wodehouse to Secretary of State, January 13, 1866. *BPP*, Ibid., pp. 13–15. Despatch from Governor Wodehouse to Cardwell, January 13, 1866, no. 6.
37. *Ibid.*
38. *Ibid.*, p. 9. Wodehouse to Cardwell, October 13, 1865.
39. *BR*, vol. III, Wodehouse to Secretary of State, January 13, 1866, no. 42.
40. *BPP*, Ibid., pp. 84–5. Cardwell to Wodehouse, March 9, 1866, no. 21.
41. *Ibid.*, p. 103. Enclosure 3 in no. 2, Memorandum by Secretary for Native Affairs on letter from Moshesh, dated July 15, 1866.
42. *Ibid.*, p. 17. Statement of Makotoko, Confidential Messenger, from

Chief Moshesh and Letsea (sic), August 19, 1867. Enclosure 1 in no. 8. Despatch from Wodehouse to Buckingham. (No. 88)
43. The word 'Basutos' here is obviously an official translation. It is linguistically incorrect. It should be Basotho, or, at least for the nineteenth century orthography, 'Basuto'.
44. *BPP*, Ibid., p. 15. Despatch Wodehouse to His Grace the Duke of Buckingham and Chandos, May 3, 1867.
45. Ibid., pp. 86–7. Buckingham to Wodehouse, December 9, 1867. No. 78. Also in *BR*, vol. ii, pp. 834–6.
46. Ibid., *BPP*, p. 25. Wodehouse to Moshesh, January 13, 1868; *BR*, p. 12.
47. Ibid., *BPP*, p. 24. Wodehouse to President of Free State. January 13, 1868. Enclosure 1 in no. 9, 1868. Despatch Wodehouse to Buckingham, January 14, 1868.
48. The Bloemfontein *Friend*, 31 January 1868. Cited by Gordon Haliburton, 'The First British Annexation of Lesotho', (1977, unpublished) p. 13.
49. *BPP*, ibid., pp. 26–7. Brand to Wodehouse, January 31, 1868, Enclosure in No. 10, Despatch Wodehouse to Buckingham and Chandos, February 18, 1868. No. 15.
50. Ibid., pp. 38–9. Wodehouse to Brand, March 10, 1968, in enclosure in no. 11 of Despatch from Governor Wodehouse to Buckingham, 18 March 1868. No. 24.
51. Proclamation No. 14, 12 March 1868.
52. Public Record Office (hereafter PRO) CO, 48/441, no. 32, Moshoeshoe to Wodehouse, April 21, 1868, p. 69.
53. PRO, CO 48/494, no. 67, Memorandum by Wodehouse, (n.d. *c.* May 1880), under 'Disposal of Quthing District', March 15, 1885. I am indebted to Benyon, 'Basutoland and the High Commission', p. 403, for both the reference as well as the dating of this crucial memorandum. For the quotation, however, of which Benyon has quoted only the phrase: 'such was the very thing to the attainment of which all my efforts were directed'. I have consulted the source personally.
54. *Despatches on the Subject of the Recognition of Moshesh Chief of the Basutos and his Tribe, as British Subjects*, 2319 (1869), p. 190.
55. *Hansard*, 3rd Series, cclvii, June 14, 1883, Col. 524, Derby's Speech.
56. G. M. Hector Papers (by special permission), Rhodes House, Oxford, MSS Brit. Emp. s. 381, box 2, no. 6 of 6, 'Mantsebo Seeiso to Forsyth Thompson, January 8, 1951. Letter no. 24/8, pp. 15–16.
57. *Cape of Good Hope Report of the Honourable the Secretary for Native Affairs* on His Visit to Basutoland in June, 1881, (G. 26-'82), p. 25. Report of Proceedings of Meeting in School Room of the Morija Mission Station on the 23rd June, 1881. Letsie's speech.
58. *Basutoland Miscellaneous Blue Books* (1867–1909), 1881 (C.–2821) (Rhodes House, Oxford) p. 71.
59. Benyon 'Basutoland and the High Commission', p. 205, quote from Government House Records, File GH 14/7: A. Davies (Mohales Hoek to Bowker, June 6, 1869).

60. BR, vol. v, (unpublished), p. 118. Buchanan to Moshesh, March 16, 1869.
61. Ibid., p. 119. Moshesh to Buchanan, March 17, 1869.
62. Ibid.
63. Ibid., p. 135. High Commissioner to Bowker, April 13, 1869.
64. Ibid., p. 157. Moshesh and Some of his Sons to the High Commissioner's Agent. (n.d. *c.* April 14, 1869).
65. Ibid.
66. Ibid., p. 158. George and Letsie Moshesh to High Commissioner's Agent, April 14, 1869. Bowker to High Commissioner (*c.* April 14–15) p. 133.
67. PRO 48/445, Wodehouse to Granville, no. 21, April 23; also, Wodehouse to Granville, no. 22, April 30, 1869.
68. Benyon, 'Basutoland and the Commission', p. 196. Quoted from CO 48/445: Wodehouse to Granville, no. 13, April 14, 1869, Minute by Rogers.
69. Ibid., pp. 197–8.
70. PRO, London, CO 48/441: Wodehouse to Buckingham, no. 31, May 2, 1868.
71. Benyon, 'Basutoland and the High Commission', p. 208.
72. Ibid., p. 233.
73. Ibid., p. 203.
74. Ibid., p. 224.
75. *Hansard*, 3rd Series, vol ccix, March 8, 1872, Col. 1626. Speech by Salisbury.
76. Benyon, 'Basutoland and the High Commission', p. 225. Quote from CO 48/455: Barkly to Kimberley, no. 53, May 31, 1871, Minute by Herbert, July 14.
77. Ibid., p. 244. Quote from CO 48/455: Barkly to Kimberley, no. 49, May 18, 1891.
78. Ibid., pp. 148–59.
79. Ibid., pp. 251.
80. Joseph Orpen, *The Native Question in Connection with the South African Bill or Constitutional Act 1909* (Rhodes House, Oxford). p. 25.
81. *Basutoland and Miscellaneous Blue Books*, 1881 (C. 2821) p. 71.
82. *BPP*, 1881, lxvi (32754). Kimberley to Robinson, December 30, 1880, paragraph 17.
83. Joseph Orpen, *Some Principles of Native Government and the Petitions of the Basuto Tribe to the Cape Parliament* (Cape Town, 1880), Rhodes House, Oxford – 620. 121 p. 13.
84. Ibid., p. 52.
85. *Blue Book on Native Affairs* (G. 21 '75 1875) p. 26.
86. Ibid., p. 27. Governor's Agent to Paramount Chief Letsie, December 19, 1872.
87. Ibid., pp. 14–15. Governor's Agent's Speech, Pitso held Maseru, October 2, 1874.
88. Benyon, 'Basutoland and the High Commission', pp. 320–1.
89. Ibid.

90. Moorosi had a jurisdiction in Lesotho which was always difficult to classify: Moshoeshoe had conquered his father, *Nkosi* (Sephuthi title meaning *Morena*) Mokuoane in 1825. Either in recognition of what may be termed a peace treaty or, with an equal weight of possibility, a simple payment of tribute, *Nkosi* Mokuoane had given Moshoeshoe 'a famous yellow ox of immense size with horns artificially trained to meet over the nose'. (See Germond, *Chronicles*, p. 330.) When Mokuoane succeeded his father as the Baphuthi *Nkosi*, Moshoeshoe styled him in the conventional manner that he styled the rest of his territorial chiefs – as one of his 'great men' – and Moorosi acquiesced to that title and status to the extent, significantly, of undertaking errands for the Basotho King. (See Casalis, 1837, in Theal, *BR*, p. 17.) All that notwithstanding, in the 1840s Moorosi manifested discomfort at being regarded as Moshoeshoe's 'great man' or territorial chief and attempted to migrate out of his overlord's immediate reach. His disposition was countermanded: Moshoeshoe moved on him, in a show of force, called a *pitso* in his province, and rebuked him for lack of gratitude and 'vomiting the food' (protection and comfort) that he had received within the Kingdom. (Thompson, *Survival in Two Worlds*, pp. 55–6.) His status under Moshoeshoe thereafter remained confused.
91. Tylden, *The Rise of the Basuto* (Cape Town, 1950) pp. 128, 144.
92. *BPP*, LXVI (C. 2755), Frere to Kimberley, no. 25, August 10, 1880, pp. 67–8. The Petition of the Basuto Chiefs and People, enclosure in no. 25, to Frere, Her Majesty's HC. and Governor of the Cape Colony, January 21, 1880.
93. *BPP* 1883, XIVIII (C. 3708) p. 83. Minutes of Meeting at Morija, 26 March, 1883, Response by Letsie to Cape Premier. Ntho Mokeke was one of those roving ambassadors under the *Morena e Moholo* Letsie who ranked at the same level as Nathanael Makotoko. As Letsie said of him on one occasion: 'I rather wanted to keep Ntho here, close to me, because he is like my own book, and knows about everything belonging to me, and he has always been a man I trusted and sent anywhere to the white people or to others'.
94. *BPP*, LXVI (C. 2755) op. cit.
95. Ibid., pp. 17–26. Frere to Kimberley, no. 12, July 9, 1880, enclosure in no. 12, 'Cape Argus', July 1, 1880. House of Assembly (Wednesday, June 30, 1880). Joseph Orpen's speech on the question of the alienation of Quthing.
96. Ibid., p. 19. The Attorney General's Speech.
97. Ibid., p. 18.
98. *BPP*, LXVI (C. 2755) op. cit., p. 23.
99. Ibid., p. 10. Letsie's petition on Disarmament.
100. Ibid., p. 24. The Colonial Secretary's report.
101. Ibid.
102. Ibid., p. 24, Sol Solmon's speech.
103. Ibid., p. 30. Frere to Kimberley, July 20, 1880. Pitso minutes.
104. Ibid.
105. *BPP*, 1883, XLVIII (C. 3708) Report of Proceedings of Meeting in

School room of the Morija Mission station on June 22, 1881, pp. 25–27. Letsie's speech.

106. Ibid.
107. Ibid., p. 20. Ramabilikoe's speech.
108. *BPP*, 1884, LVI (C. 3855) p. 47. Smyth to Derby, telegram, received December 12, 1883.
109. *BPP*, 1883, XLVIII (C. 3493) pp. 21–2. Proposed Convention between the Colony and the Basuto people by Gordon, July 1982.
110. Ibid.
111. Ibid.
112. *BPP*, 1883, XLVIII (C. 3708) pp. 121–2. 'Draft Constitution: Proposed Terms for the Future Government of Basutoland.'
113. Ibid., p. 121. Speech by Secretary for Native Affairs.
114. Ibid., p. 26. Makotoko's speech.
115. Ibid.
116. Ibid., p. 105. Proceedings of Morija meeting, Wednesday, March 28, 1883.
117. *BPP*, 1883, XLVIII (C. 3708) op. cit., p. 25, 'Draft Constitution', Rampa's speech.
118. *BPP*, 1883, XLVIII (C. 3493) p. 22. Reverend M. P. D. Keck to Gordon, in reply to his own of May 31, to Masopha. Also see Benyon, *Basutoland and the High Commission*, p. 534.
119. Benyon, op. cit., p. 612. Quote from Merriman Papers, no. 276 of 1883, Scanlen to Merriman, December 20, 1883.
120. *Hansard*, Third Series, CCLVII, June 14, 1883, col. 520. Lord Emily's speech.
121. Ibid., col. 521. Lord Derby's speech.
122. Ibid.
123. Ibid.
124. *BPP*, 1883, XLVIII (C. 3493), op. cit., p. 125. Blyth's speech.
125. Letter Received from Miscellaneous Persons, 1884. Lesotho Archives, S7/7/1. Copy of the Proceedings of the National *Pitso* held at Peter Mokolokolo's village on November 29, 1883, pp. 16–21.
126. Sandra Burman, *Chiefdom Politics and Alien Laws* (London, 1981) p. 179.
127. For an extended study of the imposition of alien laws in Lesotho during the Cape Colony rule see Burman, *Chiefdom Politics*. See also a recast of the same material as a study of the 'reception' of Roman-Dutch law in Lesotho in her article, 'How the Roman-Dutch Law Became the Common Law of Lesotho', *Lesotho Law Journal, A Journal of Law and Development* (Faculty of Law, National University of Lesotho, 1985) vol. I, no. 1, pp. 25–43.
128. Burman, *Chiefdom Politics*, p. 46.
129. Lesotho National Archives *LNA*, Theal, *BR* (unpublished), vol. IV, pt 1, 1868, pp. 125–50. Emile Samuel Rolland, 'The Basuto Tribe'.
130. Rolland, 'The Basuto Tribe', p. 125.
131. Ibid., p. 136.
132. Ibid., p. 128.
133. Rolland's use of the term 'sale' here is essentially wrong, and that not

because he did not understand the concept of *bohali*, to which he was making reference. The distinction between the two is as follows:

> The Basutos make use of the word 'reka' when they say buy a horse, & c., but the cattle given in marriage are called *'bohali'*, and a man does not say he is going to 'reka', or buy a wife, but he says he is going to 'nyala' a wife, or marry. If a woman is ill-treated by her husband she can go and complain to the chief, and if the husband is found to be in fault, the chief will fine him, and the fine will be sent to her parents. If after this decision of the chief, the husband continues his ill-treatment, then the wife can leave him and go to her relatives and divorce her husband. . . . If the woman refuses to live with her husband, there is no law to compel her to do so.

As given by one of Moshoeshoe's sons, Sofonia Moshoeshoe, in 1872. In the Cape of Good Hope *Report and Evidence of Commission on Native Laws and Customs of the Basutos*, (Cape Town, 1873) p. 43.

134. Rolland, 'The Basuto Tribe', p. 130.
135. Rolland, 'The Basuto Tribe', p. 132.
136. Ibid., pp. 126–38.
137. Ibid., p. 147.
138. Burman, *Chiefdom Politics*, p. 43.
139. *Almanaka ea Ba-Sotho* (Morija, 1907) p. 16.
140. D. F. Ellenberger, and J. C. MacGregor, *History of the Basuto, Ancient and Modern* (London, 1912) p. 269.
141. The preceding two paragraphs are based on Sandra Burman, *Chiefdom Politics*, pp. 43–6, with additional comments and qualifications derived from a personal scrutiny of the primary sources.
142. *Lesotho National Archives* (LNA) no. 5, Civil Note Book. From August 1876 to May 1879, pp. 107–14. *Motseko v. Adriaan Maphathe and 'Makubutu*, heard before the Assistant Magistrate of Mafeteng, Emile Samuel Rolland, November 8, 1876.
143. Cape of Good Hope. *Correspondence Respecting the Affairs of Basutoland and the Proposals of the Cape Government with Respect to its Future Administration*. 1883 (C. 3708), Appendix, p. 59. George Tlali Moshoeshoe's response to the Cape Premier, T. C. Scanlen, on the question of Bigamy. Meeting held in Maseru, March 20, 1883.
144. Proclaimed in the Schedule to the Proclamation No. 75a, March 18, 1884.
145. Cape of Good Hope. *Correspondence Respecting the Affairs of Basutoland*, 1883 (C. 3708) op. cit., p. 65.
146. PRO, CO 48/510, January 2, 1884. Sir Hercules Robinson's draft. Also see R. M. Cassidy, 'Britain and Basutoland: A Study of Men and Policies from the Gun War to the Anglo-Boer War' (Ph.D. dissertation, 1967) p. 44.
147. Estimate of Revenue and Expenses, July, 1884 – June 30, 1885, submitted May 15, 1884. Basutoland Report c. 4263, pp. 71–2. Cassidy, 'Britain and Basutoland', p. 56.

148. Clarke, Report on Basutoland, July 2, 1885. (C. 4644) p. 26. Ibid., p. 65.
149. Granville to Robinson, February 25, 1886. (C. 4838) p. 3. Ibid., p. 65.
150. PRO, CO 417/54, Confidential, no. 380. Speech by Robinson, Cape Town, April 27, 1889. See also ibid., p. 74.
151. Ibid., 417/248, Minute by Just, July 31, on Milner to Chamberlain, May 25, 1898. Cited by Cassidy, op. cit., p. 91. For Milner's strong statement to 'clear out bag and baggage', see Lagden, vol. II, pp. 595–6.
152. For a full treatment of the breakdown of the indigenous government in Lesotho at this period, pointing to political, economic and social factors, see L. B. B. J. Machobane, 'The Political Dilemma of the Chieftaincy in Colonial Lesotho, with Reference to the Administrative and Courts Reforms of 1938', (revised paper presented as Occasional paper no. 1, Institute of Southern African Studies, National University of Lesotho, September 24, 1985), for publication in the *Review of Southern African Studies* N.U.L. 1986, pp. 6–16.
153. See L. B. B. J. Machobane, 'Succession to Chieftainship in Lesotho: Management and Exploitation by the Colonial Government', seminar paper presented at the Centre of African Studies, University of Edinburgh, November 4, 1985.
154. Machobane, 'The Political Dilemma of the Chieftaincy', p. 7.
155. PRO, C.O. 417/565, no. 336. Minute to Mr Just, 'Remission of Sentence on Joel Molapo, April 6, 1903. Cited op. cit., p. 8.
156. Machobane, 'The Political Dilemma of the Chieftaincy', pp. 10–11.
157. *BPP*, 1883, XLIII (C. 3708) p. 44. Appendix. Official Report of Interviews between the Premier and the Secretary for Native Affairs and Certain Basuto Chiefs, Counsellors, and Headmen. March 16 to April 2, 1883.
158. *BPP*, XLVII (C. 3493) 1883, p. 22. Reverend M. P. D. Keck to Gordon, writing on behalf of the Paris Evangelical Missionary Society, May 31. Cited op. cit., 12.

CHAPTER 3

1. South Africa. *Further Correspondence Respecting the Colony and Adjacent Territories*, 1884–85, LVI (Cmd. 4263) pp. 81–5.
2. Ibid. In this connection, J. M. Mohapeloa makes the misleading statement: 'The only merit the proposed council had was that although it was a repetition of a Cape idea, this was a "new" Cape.' This statement is difficult to infer from this source. See Mohapeloa, 'Tentative British Imperialism in Lesotho, 1884–1910: A Study in Basotho-Colonial Office Interaction and South Africa's Influence on it', (M.Phil. thesis, Sussex, 1983) p. 103.
3. J. M. Mohapeloa's statement that 'the Paramount Chief . . . made

no response', suggesting that he had been asked, is not based on any cited evidence and is suspect. Ibid., p. 104.

4. Basutoland Annual Report. 'Further Correspondence Respecting the Affairs of Basutoland'. In (Continuation of Cmd. 4838, June 1886) p. 17.

5. Public Record Office (hereafter PRO), CO 417/14, High Commissioner, Robinson, Despatch 165, Basutoland National Pitso held at Motseki's Klein Caledon, April 6, 1887, p. 453. The letter is alluded to in the discussions.

6. Ibid.

7. Ibid., p. 461

8. Ibid., p. 467

9. Ibid., p. 465

10. Ibid., pp. 463–4.

11. His significant omission of this source led J. M. Mohapeloa incorrectly to conclude that it was 'Letsie's coolness toward the proposed Council' that delayed the talks on its establishment before 1889. Mohapeloa, 'Tentative British Imperialism', p. 108.

12. G.M. Hector Papers, Mss. Brit. Emp. s.381, box 2, item 4, p. 89. Clarke's private letter to Letsie, (n.d.).

13. Ibid., pp. 90–91. Letsie to Clarke, December 25, 1889. Evidently J. M. Mohapeloa erred when he stated that Letsie had 'suddenly', on his own initiative, submitted a proposal on this occasion. Mohapeloa, 'Tentative British Imperialism', p. 108.

14. Ibid., pp. 92–3. Resident Commissioner to High Commissioner, Sir Henry Lock, April 30, 1890.

15. Ibid., p. 92. See, in particular, paragraph 7.

16. G. M. Hector Papers, op. cit., p. 94.

17. Cited and translated by J. M. Mohapeloa, 'Tentative British Imperialism', p. 110.

18. Basutoland Annual Report, 1900 (Cmd. 3–11) LIV, 135, pp. 5–6. G. Y. Lagden to High Commissioner, August 1899.

19. Basutoland Annual Report, 1900–1901 (Cd. 788–13) p. 6. Assistant Resident Commissioner, H. C. Sloley, to High Commissioner, September 1901.

20. Basutoland Annual Report, 1901–1902 (Cd 1388–4) p. 12. Resident Commissioner, H. C. Sloley, to High Commissioner, Viscount Milner, September 30, 1902.

21. See L. B. B. J. Machobane, 'The Political Dilemma of Chieftaincy in Colonial Lesotho, with Reference to the Administrative and Courts Reforms of 1938', *Occasional Paper No. 1*, Institute of Southern African Studies (ISAS), NUL, Lesotho, 1986, p. 17.

22. PRO, CO 417/468. Secret. 'Memorandum on Scheme for Employment of Imperial Troops in Basutoland in Event of Trouble' by Methuen, General, Commanding the Forces in South Africa, Army Headquarters, Pretoria, May 17, 1909.

23. PRO CO 417/375, no. 515, 'Proposed Native Council'. See 'Proposed Regulations for Constitution of Basutoland Native Council', 1903.

24. My count is based on the names that appear in the national *lipitso* of

this period, and it is confined to those chiefs who normally attached their names to official documents as principal chiefs, for example, on Lerotholi's nomination as heir in 1891, and Letsie II in 1905. The names include Letsie II, Theko, Sekhonyana (Nehemiah), Maama, Jonathan, Motŝoene, Joele, Masopha II, Seeiso Maama, Api, Griffith, Sempe, Makhaola, Sekake, Ramabilikoe, Lelingoana (Chief of Batlokoa), Rafolatsane, Bereng, Malebanye (Goliath), Moletsane, Matela (Thaabe), Mokhele, Hlalele.

25. Ibid., Regulation 9.
26. Ibid. 'Suggested Regulations for Conduct of Council'.
27. V. Ellenberger, *A Century of Mission Work in Basutoland' 1883–1933* (Morija, 1938) p. 260.
28. PRO, CO 646/1, 'Basutoland Proceedings of National Council, 1903–1912. See 1903. High Commissioner, Milner, to Resident Commissioner, Sloley, June 27, 1903. The message was just three paragraphs long. See also CO 417/375, no. 660.
29. Ibid., The President's Address, July 6, 1903, pp. 8–14.
30. Ibid., p. 11.
31. *South African Native Affairs Commission: 1903–4* vol. LV, Appendix C, p. 384. Chief Jonathan's response on Sesotho customary law, September 26, 1904.
32. Ibid., p. 15. The Paramount Chief's Speech.
33. Ibid., p. 19. Paramount Chief to Resident Commissioner, July 24, 103.
34. *British Parliamentary Papers*, 1906, (Cmd. 3094) LXXIX, p. 7. 'Reports by High Commissioner on His Visit to Basutoland and the Bechuanaland Protectorate in 1906', no. 1.
35. PRO CO 646/1 op. cit., p. 34.
36. PRO, CO 417/394, no. 896, 'Letters addressed to the High Commissioner by the Chief Jonathan Molapo', August 28, 1904.
37. Basutoland Annual Report, 1901–1902, (Cmd. 1388–4) p. 9.
38. PRO, CO 417/394, no. 896, op. cit.
39. Ibid., Milner to Sloley, October 10, 1904.
40. The Resident Commissioner's appointees were the Reverends M. Mpiti, C. M. Sebeta and Tsepinare, Enock, and Dichaba Labane. See 'Report of Proceedings of the Basutoland National Council, 1908, and the Correspondence as to Affairs of Basutoland, 1908, (Cmd. 4196), LXXI, p. 11.
41. PRO, CO 417/394, no. 894, op. cit. pp. 42–7. Members of the Committee were Chiefs Theko, Peete, Joele, Nehemiah, Letlatsa, and Mpiti, and Councillors Mosehle, Abele, Namane, Khomoealeburu, 'Nena, B. Ntsie, Motlepu, J. Sefadi, Setha Matete, Raboroko, Lefi, Makhoathi, Malephane, Theofil, Mokhadinyane, Pchoatlella, Josias Mopedi and Jas. R. Makepe (Secretary ex officio).
42. Ibid., p. 56, July 16, 1903.
43. Ibid., pp. 21–90.
44. *BPP*, 1881, (Cmd. 2755,) LXVI, Frere to Kimberley, September 15, 1880, no. 42. Interview with the Colonial Secretary, Mr S. Sprigg, Morija, August 26, 1880, p. 156.

45. Despatch from Sir Hercules Robinson, with Report of the Resident Commissioner, Basutoland, 1887, (Cmd. 4907), p. 4.
46. PRO, CO 417/468, Secret, op. cit.
47. According to one of his counsellors, Lefi Nkhasi, his mentally demented brother, Josepha Molapo, and his own son, Jan Vick, were sick. *PRO*, CO 417/394, no. 896, op. cit., pp. 46, 49.
48. PRO, CO 646/1, 'Basutoland Proceedings of National Council, 1903–1912. See July 14, 1903, p. 49.
49. Ibid., pp. 58–63.
50. *South African Native Affairs Commission, 1903–4*, vol. IV, Appendix C, 'Minutes of Evidence taken in Rhodesia, Bechuanaland Protectorate, British Bechuanaland (Cape Colony), Orange River Colony, Basutoland, Transvaal Colony, and Again in the Cape Colony' (Cape Town, 1904).
51. Ibid., p. 397. Lerotholi. Philip Molise's response.
52. PRO, CO 417/375, no. 927, op. cit., Resident Commissioner to High Commissioner, August 31, 1903.
53. 1908, (Cmd. 4196), LXXI, p. 12. 'Report of Proceedings of the National Council, 1908 and Correspondence as to Affairs of Basutoland, Philip Molise's speech.
54. Ibid.
55. See the full version of the Proceedings, January 28, LNA, not numbered.
56. Ibid.
57. (Cmd. 4196), LXXI, op. cit., p. 12.
58. Ibid.
59. PRO, CO 417/485, no. 469. Proclamation No. 53 of 1910.
60. Ibid., 'Legal Advice by A. E. Balfour to Imperial Secretary, June 30, 1910'. Imperial Secretary's minute dated August 6, 1910.
61. Basutoland Annual Report 1898–99, 1900, (Cmd. 3–11), LIV, 135. Resident Commissioner, G. Y. Lagden to High Commissioner, August, 1899. Placed on May 8, under the colonial authority of J. W. Bowker, Assistant Commissioner, Mohale's Hoek, pp. 7, 41.
62. Ibid., p. 41. P. W. Bowker, Assistant Commissioner, Mohale's Hoek.
63. LNA, S11/6, 'Pitsos 9 May 1899–15', 'Notes of a Pitso held at Government Offices on 3rd, 4th and 5th April, 1902 for the Purpose of Enquiring into the Conduct of Mocheko Moorosi and Semenekane and other Baphuti (sic)'
64. Basutoland Annual Report 1900–1901, 1901, (Cmd. 788–13). Assistant Resident Commissioner, H. C. Sloley, to High Commissioner, September 1901.
65. Ibid., p. 73. Attending: Paramount Chief Lerotholi, Malebanye, Theko, Jonathan, Maama, Letsie Lerotholi, Nkoebe, Mojela, Griffith Lerotholi, Ntho Mokeke, Tsepinare Letsie, Thebe Masopha, Malefane, Moeketsi, Seshophe Mitchell, Letlatsa, Tau, Ntsane, Pchoatlella, Nahemiah, Joel, Mabilikoe, Mahao, Motlepu, Mahapela, Leshoboro, and others.
66. Ibid., pp. 90–4. Mocheko's defence.
67. Ibid., pp. 94–5.

68. Proclamation No. 46, 1907.
69. PRO, CO 417/545, no. 158, 'Case of Mocheko L. Moorosi', R. C. Sloley to High Commissioner, Gladstone, January 20, 1914.
70. Ibid., no. 284, 'Case of Mocheko L. Moorosi', Resident Commissioner to High Commissioner, March 20, 1914.
71. Basutoland Annual Report, 1904–1905, Cmd. 2684–25, LXXIII, Resident Commissioner to High Commissioner, June 30, 1905, pp. 8–9. Also PRO, CO 417/411, tel. no. 178, and no. 486, on Lerotholi's death and succession.
72. PRO, CO 417/411, no. 486, Resident Commissioner, Herbert Sloley, to High Commissioner, the Earl of Selborne, August 24, 1905.
73. *High Commission Territories Law Reports* (HCTLR) (1926–53) 50.
74. Cited from the unedited record of the case in PRO, CO 417/67, no. 808, p. 30.
75. Op. cit. Clarke, in response to Lerotholi's letter of November 26. The letter was not before the court, and I have not been able to locate it.
76. PRO, CO 417/67, no. 808, High Commissioner, Henry Lock to Resident Commissioner, Marshal Clarke, November 30, 1891.
77. PRO, CO 417/411, no. 934, tel. 196. The nomination was made and a telegram sent to the High Commissioner on August 28, 1905. The letter of request by the National Council was written on September 18, 1905. See no. 990.
78. PRO, CO 417/411, no. 1138. Resident Commissioner to High Commissioner, October 10, 1905.
79. Ibid.
80. Ibid.
81. PRO, CO 417/455, no. 67, 'Report on Griffith Attack on Chieftainess 'Masefabatho'. Resident Commissioner to High Commissioner, December 17, 1907.
82. Motsoene's weight is legendary. Since his death Basotho have had an idiom that goes: 'O itlama ka lebanta la Motsoene!' 'He is trying to fit himself into Motsoene's belt'. The idiom is used to suggest that a person is trying to take up responsibilities beyond his capacity. His weight, as cited, is based on Lord Selborne's estimation on his visit to Lesotho in 1906. *BPP* 1906, Cmd. 3094, LXXIX, p. 7.
83. Basutoland Annual Report, 1906–1907, Cmd. 3729–20, LXVII, p. 15. The village that he burned was under Chief Hlajoane, Chief Seshophe's son.
84. PRO, CO 417/501, no. 372. High Commissioner, Gladstone, to Secretary for Colonies, Rt. Hon. Lewis Harcourt, June 5, 1911.
85. Rhodes House, Oxford, 625, r. 41, Basutoland Council, Minutes of Proceedings, 1912, the Sesotho version, February 17, 1912, p. 14.
86. Ibid.,'Ha e le potso eo le tsoa e botsoa ea hore kajeno ho batleloa 'ng batho, athe ho no no ntse ho ahloloa linyeoe mehleng ea Moshoeshoe, ke re mehla e fetohile.'
87. Ibid., February 16, 1912, February 16, 1912, Chief Motŝoene's speech: U hlokomele setulo sena sa Moshoeshoe . . . Ha u sa tiise kobo ea

hao e mong o tla tŝoha a e hata, a e tabola . . . nke ke ka sebeletsa
Letsie le ha e le ho mo amoha borena ba hae.

88. PRO, CO 417/458, 'Union of South Africa: Position of Bastuoland', *Daily Mail*, 25 March 1909.
89. PRO, CO 417/528, no. 541, Basutoland Council Minutes.
90. PRO, CO 417/528, tel. 28, January, 1919. Announcing Letsie's death to the High Commissioner, no. 83 and no. 90 being reports of his burial. No. 95, 'Selection of Chief Griffith to act as Paramount Chief'.
91. PRO, CO 417/515, Confidential Memorandum from Acting Resident Commissioner, J. Wroughton to High Commissioner, January 8, 1911. The then Resident Commissioner, G. Y. Lagden was the official at the centre of things.
92. Ibid., Confidential, 'Relations of Letsie and his wife', tel. communication with High Commissioner, January 1912.
93. Ibid., PRO, CO 528, no. 95. Also, CO 417/501, no. 274. High Commissioner to Secretary of State. Co., Rt. Hon. Lewis Harcourt, April 23, 1913.
94. PRO, CO 417/468, 'Notes on Sloley's Memorandum on Chief Jonathan's Letter to the High Commissioner, dated October 1908'.
95. Ibid., PRO, CO 417/528, no. 541. Resident Commissioner to High Commissioner, July 14, 1913.
96. Ibid.
97. Op. cit., PRO, CO 417/501, no. 274, *Cape Times*, 12 April 1913.
98. PRO, CO 417/545 (1914), Confidential 7, 'Relations between Griffith and Chief Jonathan', High Commissioner to Colonial Office, March 14, 1914.
99. Ibid., no. 152, *Cape Times*, Tuesday, 17 February 1914.
100. Ibid.
101. PRO, CO 417/565 (1915), 'Leribe Disturbances'. Also, CO 417/607 (1918), no. 571, 'Dispute between Chiefs Jonathan and Joel'.
102. PRO, CO 417/565 (1915) no. 983, 'Leribe Disturbances'. Under Resident Commissioner to High Commissioner, November 17, 1915. For figures of Chiefs Masopha and Maama's cases see PRO, CO 417/580 (1916), no. 663, 'Payment of Paramount Chief of portion of fines'. Griffith's annual allowance in 1920 was calculated as follows: £1200 per annum as Paramount Chief; £480 per annum broken down to : (a) £300 as Chief of Maseru; (b) £120 as Chief of Mohale's Hoek (where he had left a headman when he took office); (c) £60 as Chief of Mafeteng (also under a headman). See PRO, CO 417/645, no. 362, 'Emolument of the Paramaount Chief'.
103. PRO, CO 417/465 (1915), 'Confidential' 'Attempt by Jonathan to smuggle rifles and ammunition into Basutoland', Resident Commissioner to High Commissioner, 29 September 1915.
104. PRO, CO 417/580 (1916), no. 198, 'The Petition of Jonathan Molapo Moshoeshoe, a chief of Leribe in the Protectorate of Lesotho'.
105. PRO, CO 417/645 (1920), no. 331, 'Native Affairs in the Leribe District', *Naledi ea Lesotho*, 19 March 1910. Under no. 481 see Paramount Chief to Resident Commissioner, May 10, 1910. *Leselinyana la Lesotho*, 12 March 1920.

106. Taped interviews, Chief 'Mako Moliboea and Mr J. J. Machobane.
107. *South African Native Affairs Commission*, 1904. J. G. Frazer's Response, September 21, p. 275.
108. Op. cit. J. G. Hobson, Merchant, Basutoland, 26 September 1904.
109. Basutoland Annual Report, 1903–4, Cmd. 2238, LI, Resident Commissioner to High Commissioner, June 1904. PRO, DO 25/4 (1929), *Basutoland Blue Book*, p. 107.
110. *Naledi*, vol. v., no. 113, 3 June 1908.
111. *Naledi*, ibid.
112. *Naledi*, vol. v, no. 114, 17 June 1908.
113. PRO, CO 417/455 (1908), no. 'Confidential' 'Federation, Inclusion of Native Territories', Letsie II to Resident Commissioner, May 20, 1908.
114. Ibid., Resident Commissioner to Paramount Chief, May 20, 1908.
115. Ibid., High Commissioner to Resident Commissioner, May 26, 1908.
116. Ibid., Minute by Just, June 24, 1908.
117. PRO, CO 417/468 (1909), no. tel. 2, 'Deputation of Basuto Chiefs to England', High Commissioner to Secretary of State for Colonies, January 11, 1905. See no. 25, 'Expulsion of Undesirables'.
118. Ibid. no. 25.
119. W. P. M. Kennedy and H. J. Schlosberg, *The Law of the South African Constitution*, (London: Oxford University Press, 1935) p. 59.
120. *Official Minutes of Proceedings of the South African National Convention* Durban, p. 1, cited by Kennedy and Schlosberg, *The Law of the South African Constitution*, p. 58.
121. Ibid., p. 62.
122. Section 147 of the South African Act, 1909. /A.B. 49-'34/
123. PRO, CO 417/468 (1909) no. 30, E. Jacottet, for PEMS Conference, January 29, 1909.
124. Ibid., High Commissioner to Colonial Office, February 15, 1909.
125. PRO, CO 417/468 (1909) no. 30, Resident Commissioner to High Commissioner, January 19, 1909.
126. Ibid., no. 25, High Commissioner to Secretary for Colonies, January 11, 1909.
127. PRO, CO 417/468 (1909) no. 30, op. cit.
128. Ibid., no. 81, E. Jacottet (PEMS) January 29, 1908. Also Archdeacon of Basutoland, Francis R. E. Balfour, January 20, 1908 – for the clergy of the English Church.
129. Ibid., Geo. R. Hobson, Chairman, Chamber of Commerce, to Resident Commissioner, January 29, 1909.
130. Ibid., no. 358, 'Union of S.A. Position of Basutoland', clipping from *Daily Mail*, 25 March 1909.
131. Ibid., National Council letter to High Commissioner, May 2, 1909.
132. Ibid., Secret, 'Memorandum on Scheme for Employment of Imperial Troops in Basutoland in event of trouble', by Bethuen, General Commanding the Forces in South Africa, Army Headquarters, Pretoria, May 17, 1909.
133. Ibid.

134. Proclamation No. 7 of 1910, Basutoland Annual Report, 1911, Cmd. 5582, LIII.
135. Schedule, S. 153, Article 14.
136. PRO, CO 417/515 (1912), no. 96, 'S. A. Native Congress Report by Philip Mochekoane and Josias Mopedi', Under Report, Resident Commissioner to High Commissioner, February 12, 1912.
137. Ibid.
138. *Basutoland, The Bechuanaland Protectorate and Swaziland. History of Discussions with the Union of South Africa 1909–1939*, Cmd. 8707. See letter with enclosed memorandum from General Botha to the Secretary of State (Lord Milner), July 2, 1919, p. 13.
139. PRO, CO 417/607 (1918) No. Confidential, Paramount Chief to Resident Commissioner, September 19, 1917.
140. Ibid., Conf. 2, 'Disturbing Rumours Circulated among Basuto by Native Thakampholo Masupha', Report by Inspector and Protector, Kimberley Mines to Director of Native Labour, Johannesburg, January 5, 1918.
141. PRO, CO 417/645 (1920) no. 77. The statement was quoted by *Mochochonono*, 14 January 1920.

CHAPTER 4

1. Public Record Office CO 417/375, No. 30, D. Fred. Ellenberger, President, and Louis Germond, Secretary, 'Conference of Paris Evangelical Missionary Society', to Resident Commissioner.
2. *Report on Education in Basutoland 1905 – 6*, cited by J. M. Mohapeloa, 'Tentative British Imperialism in Lesotho', p. 222.
3. *Leselinyana la Lesotho*, 15 January 1908.
4. Basutoland Annual Report, 1905–6, Cmd. 3285, LIII, p. 61.
5. PRO, CO 417/607 137, 'South African Native College. Lesotho Contribution', High Commissioner to Colonial Secretary, March 18, 1918.
6. PRO, DO 9/8 (1927) No., 'Individuals', Medical Report, July 18, 1927,
7. Op. cit., CO 417/375, no. 30.
8. PRO, CO 417/713 (1925) no. 105, Report by Director of Education.
9. PRO, DO 25/4, *Basutoland Blue Book*, p. 107.
10. PRO, CO 417/455 (1907) no. 67, Simon M. Phamotse, Editor, *Naledi ea Lesotho*, Naledi Office, Mafeteng, no. 16, 1907 to Resident Commissioner.
11. Of these interpreters, George Masiu was probably the earliest to serve the colonial administration. He was first employed in the Cape Colony, serving as a Constable at Cornet Spruit from 1 April 1873 to 31 December 1878. He began the service in Lesotho as an interpreter in Mafeteng on 1 January 1879 and after two transfers to Mohale's Hoek and Quthing, respectively, he retired on 30 April 1912. See PRO, CO 417/515 (1912) no. 534, 'Pension, G. Masiu, Native Interpreter, Quthing, Resident Commissioner to High Commissioner,

September 2, 1912. Jeroboam Modibeli was in the colonial service as an interpreter from 4 December 1884 to 2 January 1912. Ibid., no. 56, 'Pension, J. Modibeli, native Interpreter', High Commissioner to Secretary for Colonies, January 31, 1912. Abimael Tlale and Bernard S. Matete retired on 8 December 1908, and April 1910, respectively. See PRO, CO 417/501 (1911) no 187, 'Retirement of Interpreter B. S. Matete' (Refers to Abimael Tlale case), High Commissioner to Resident Commissioner, April 8, 1910. Manama Molapo joined the service on 1 August 1907 and resigned because of chronic illness on 31 May 1917. He is likely not to have been politically very active, thereafter. See PRO, Co 417/595, 'Gladstone. Feb. 1917', Resident Commissioner to High Commissioner, February 17, 1917. Simon Phamotse had retired at least by 1907, when he was appointed to the National Council.

12. The first Mosotho Inspector of Schools was Elias Letele, in 1909. As the Director of Education, Mr Dutton commented, with some satifaction over his performance in February 1910: 'I have to report that the experiment of employing a native inspector has been tried.' Dutton was happy with the way Elias Letele had acquitted himself; but he remarked that the missionaries were still suspicious of the appointment, for no other reason than that he was a Mosotho. See PRO, CO 417/485, no. 171, 'Education', Resident Commissioner to High Commissioner, February 3, 1910. F. Mapetla was for 31 years with Lerotholi Technical School, retiring on 31 May 1939. PRO, DO 92/6, Basutoland Departmental Reports, 1935–40, Index no. 11, Annual Report of the Director of Education for the year 1938, p.16.

13. When I first proposed this interpretation of Azariel Sekese's book to Professor Daniel Kunene (University of Wisconsin, December 1982), a short time after he had completed his research on *Leselinyana la Lesotho*, he pointed out to me that the theme of *pitso ea linonyana* had more than once been carried by *Leselinyana* before Sekese published his book and that it was not original with him. That view notwithstanding, I still maintain the interpretation that at least when he published the story as a book, following severe harassment by Chief Jonathan, Sekese had a political motive.

14. See Daniel Kunene's translation of the book.

15. This information was supplied to me by the writer, J. J. Machobane, author of the historical novel, *Senate: Shoeshoe 'a Mosheoshoe*, being a biography of Chief Motsoene's mother. J. J. Machobane did research on Basotho businessmen between 1937 and 1942, while employed as an editor at Morija Book Depot. The book that came out of the research, *Likoankoetla Tsa Khoebo* (The Vanguards of Business), was never submitted for publication.

16. For information on 'Willie' Mafoso, I am indebted to the writer, Dr Njabulo Ndebele, Senior Lecturer at the National University of Lesotho, who has been doing research on him for a book.

17. 'Opening Address on the Occasion of the 50th Anniversary of the Basutoland Progressive Association, 11th January, 1958' in *Some Speeches and Addresses by G. M. Hector*, p. 8. Gordon Hector was

the Government Secretary of Lesotho for ten years, from 1956 to 1966, when the Territory became independent.

18. PRO, CO 417/545 (1914) no. 592, BPA farewell letter to the High Commissioner, June 19, 1914.

19. PRO, CO 417/545 (1919) no. 591, Resident Commissioner, June 18, 1914.

20. For the BPA membership in 1914 see PRO, CO 417/545 (1914) no. 592, BPA farewell letter to the High Commissioner, June 19, 1914. For population census, 1911, see Basutoland Annual Report, 1910–11, Cmd. 6007–10, LVIII, pp. 11–12. For BPA membership in 1924 see PRO, CO 417/706 no. confidential, October 10, 1924, Visit of High Commissioner (Earl of Athlone) to Basutoland, BPA Address, Co. 417/683 (1922), confidential, *Cape Times*, 5 April, 1922: Notes that 35 Besotho women 'have applied to the Association lately'.

21. *Naledi*, 19 July 1904, vol I, no. 12, translated from Sesotho to English by myself. For complete text of Sesotho version see Appendix.

22. *Naledi* vol. IV, no. 85, 4 June 1907.

23. *Naledi*, vol. V, no. 114, Phupu 17 (July) 1908.

24. PRO, CO 417/515 (1912) no. 353, 'Basutoland Council and Free Speech', *Naledi*, 23 February 1912.

25. Ibid., Resident Commissioner to High Commissioner, May 22, 1912.

26. Eugene Casalis, Morija, May 1934. Cited by R. C. Germond, *Chronicles of Basutoland: A Running Commentary on the Events of the Years 1830–1902 by the French Protestant Missionaries in Southern Africa* (Morija, 1967) p. 517.

27. Edwin W. Smith, *The Mabilles of Basutoland* (London, 1939) p. 345.

28. PRO, CO 417/528 (1919) no. 541, 'Basutoland Council Minutes', Resident Commissioner to High Commissioner, July 14, 1913.

29. PRO, CO 417/545 (1914) no. 591, 'Proceedings of the National Council (10th Session), Resident Commissioner to High Commissioner, June 18, 1914. Discussion on Regulation No. 13: Payment of Councillors.

30. PRO, CO 417/580 (1916) no. 750, 'Minutes of Basutoland Council (11th Session)', held August 23 to September 2, 1916, Resident Commissioner to High Commissioner, October 24, 1916.

31. Ibid., no. 750, 'Minutes', Chief Motšoene's Speech.

32. PRO, DO 9/8 (1927) no. ? 'Individuals', Medical Reports, July 18, 1927.

33. PRO, DO 92/7, 'Basutoland Departmental Reports, 1941–50', p. 12.

34. Op. cit., CO 417/580 (1916) no. 750.

35. Basutoland Annual Report, 1902–3, Cmd. 1768–13' LVI, p. 7.

36. Basutoland Annual Report, 1919, Cmd. 1–20, xxxv, p. 2.

37. PRO, CO 417/593 (1917), Secret, Resident Commissioner, R. T, Coryndon, to High Commissioner, August 14, 1917.

38. Ibid.

39. PRO, CO 417/501 (1911) no. 372, 'High Commissioner's Visit to Basutoland, Mid-March, 1911', High Commissioner to Secretary for Colonies, June 5, 1911. *The Star*, 12 May 1911.

40. Op. cit. Co. O. 417/350 (1916) no. 750.

41. Ibid.
42. PRO, CO. 417/593 (1917) no. 404, 'Basutoland Council', March 26 to April 5. Labane Chokobane's Speech.
43. Ibid., CO 417/580 (1916) no. 715.
44. PRO, CO 417/624 (1919) no. 720, 'High Commissioner's visit to Basutoland. May 1919', 'Private Interview between His Excellency Lord Buxton and Paramount Chief Griffith' May 24, 1919.
45. Ibid., no. 499, Draft Petition to His Majesty the King, 1919.
46. For the only historical study of Lesotho's participation in World War I, see Robert Edgar, 'Lesotho and the First World War: Recruiting, Resistance and the South African Native Labour Contingent', Mohlomi: Journal of Southern African Historical Studies, combined vols. II/IV/V–1979/80/81 (NUL, Lesotho, 1981) pp. 94–108.
47. PRO, CO 417/624 (1919) no. 720.
48. Ibid., no. 499, 'Paramount Chief's Visit to England', Minutes of Council, May 28, 1919.
49. Ibid., May 30.
50. Ibid.
51. Ibid.
52. Ibid.
53. Ibid., Paramount Chief to Resident Commissioner, June 13, 1919.
54. Ibid., no. 683, Tel., Resident Commissioner to High Commissioner, September 12, 1919.
55. Ibid., Telegram, High Commissioner to Resident Commissioner, September 13, 1919.
56. Ibid., no. 939, 'Future of Basutoland. Tr. Copies of the "Mochochonono", a Native Newspaper Containing Articles in English on the Subject', Mochochonono, 26 November 1919.
57. Ibid., Mochochonono, 3 December 1919.
58. For the use of the expression see, in particular, the occasion of Prince Arthur Frederick's visit to Lesotho, May 1921, PRO, CO 417/645 (1920) no. 651,
59. Op. cit., CO 417/624 (1919) no. 828, 'Jurisdiction of Native Chiefs', The Times, 5 December 1919.
60. Ibid.
61. The Times, 19 December 1919.
62. Ibid.
63. PRO, CO 417/645 (1920) no. 9, 'Basutoland Council', Resident Commissioner, December 19, 1919. High Commissioner to Resident Commissioner, January 2, 1920.
64. Ibid., no. 77, 'Future of Basutoland. Fwds. Extracts from the Native Newspaper 'Mochochonono' of the 14 January Regarding the Basuto Petition to H. M. the King'.
65. PRO, CO 417/624 (1919) no. 505, 'Paramount Chief's Visit to England'. See Resident Commissioner's ultimate recommendation: 'It is the question of Confession and Sacraments. . . . Under these circumstances I am of the opinion that it would be advisable to allow him to take a priest with him, who should not be an enemy subject [i.e. German], and who should take the place of one of the Chiefs

for whom accommodation was asked.' Resident Commissioner to High Commissioner, June 30, 1919. High Commissioner to Resident Commissioner, July 9, 1919.

66. F. Laydevant, *Morena N. Griffith Lerotholi 1871–1939* (The Catholic Centre, Mazenod Institute, Basutoland, 1953) pp. 10–13.
67. PRO, CO 417/645 (1920) no. 277, 'Higher Education for the Sons of the Paramount Chief. Establishment of Government Secondary School', Paramount Chief to Resident Commissioner, February 6, 1920. Not in the records, the letter of 14 January is cited in the one of 6 February.
68. Ibid., Resident Commissioner to High Commissioner, March 17, and May 27, 1920.
69. PRO, CO 417/580 (1916) no. 750, 'Minutes of Basutoland Council (11th Session)', cited by Reverend Motsamai, 4th Day, August 30, p. 7.
70. Ibid., The President's Speech, 5th Day, August 31, 1916, p. 9.
71. Ibid., 5th Day, p. 11.
72. Ibid., p. 13.
73. Ibid., Labane Chokobane's Speech.
74. Ibid., Bernard Matete's Speech.
75. Ibid., p. 14, The President's Speech.
76. PRO, CO 417/593 (1917) no. 404, 'Basutoland Council', Abstract of the Minutes of 12th Session, held March 26 to April 5, 1917. Also A. C. Thompson, (ed.), *The Laws of Basutoland*, Revised Edition (Cape Times Limited, Cape Town, 1961) p. 806.
77. Robert Edgar, *Prophets With Honour: A Documentary History of Lekhotla La Bafo*, (Raven Press, Johannesburg) p. 7. Edgar's is a pioneering and most helpful documentary history of the Association.
78. PRO. CO 417/624 (1919) no. 499, Minutes of National Council, 1919. Josiel Lefela's Speech, p. 18.
79. Ibid., no. 939, 'Future of Basutoland. Tr. Copies of "Mochochonono". Re: Hostel for Native Women. Johannesburg. Sept. 3, 1920. Translated from Sesuto'.
80. Ibid., E. C. F. Garraway to Stanley, Imperial Secretary, September 6, 1920.
81. For the conduct of this meeting I am indebted to Robert Edgar, who consented to my reading his manuscript on the *Documentary History of Lekhotla la Bafo*, p. 103–4. The book was published by Longmans, London, 1986.
82. PRO, CO 417/624 (1919), no. 939. Stanley to Garraway, September 14, 1920.
83. Ibid., Legal Adviser, Feetman, Quoted by Imperial Secretary to Resident Commissioner, September 28, 1920.
84. Ibid., *Mochochonono*, 9 March 1921.
85. Ibid., no. 651, 'High Commissioner's Visit to Basutoland, May 1921', Z. Mangoaela, President, Basutoland Progressive Association, Address, May 18, 1921.
86. Ibid., High Commissioner's Response to Basutoland Progressive Association, May 18, 1921.

87. PRO, CO 417/665 (1920) no. 1060, 'Basutoland Council, 16th Session'. See discussion on 4th Day.
88. PRO, CO 417/665 (1921) no. Confidential, December 1921, 'Objectionable Articles and Letters in Native Newspaper "Naledi"'. See *Naledi*, 30 September 1921.
89. Ibid., *Naledi*, 18 November 1921.
90. Ibid., High Commissioner to Resident Commissioner, December 20, 1921.
91. Lesotho National Archives, S3/22/2/3, 'Supplement to Presidential Address Read at Matsieng, n.d., *c*. 1928.
92. PRO, CO 417/665 (1921) no. Confidential, December 1921, 'Objectionable Articles and Letter in Native Newspaper "Naledi" Sephatsi Marung', Ndabeni Location, Cape Town, *Naledi*, 25 November 1921.93. Ibid., Phalatse, Ndabeni Location, Cape Town.
94. PRO, CO 417./683 no. 53, 'Mosotho', 'Justice in Basutoland', *The Friend*, 2 December 1921.
95. Ibid., Simon Phamotse, 16 December 1921.
96. Ibid., *Naledi*, 24 February 1922,
97. Ibid., No. Confidential. Resident Commissioner to High Commissioner, January 27, 1922.
98. Ibid., Resident Commissioner to the High Commissioner (His Royal Highness), May 5, 1922, *The Friend*, 4 May 1922.
99. Ibid., Resident Commissioner to High Commissioner, 5 May 1922.
100. Lesotho National Archives, S3/16A/5/2, Secret Report by 'M.T.R.' to Government Secretary, 24 July 1928. See also 'A man of Mohales' Hoek'. Both were members of the Royal Court.
101. PRO, CO 417/683 No. Confidential, Resident Commissioner to Paramount Chief, n.d. *c*. 5 May 1922.
102. Ibid., *The Friend*, 3 May 1922, citing the current issue of *Naledi*.
103. Ibid., Resident Commissioner to High Commissioner, July 14 1922.
104. Ibid., Confidential 2, Criminal Investigation in Johannesburg to Officer Commanding Basutoland Police, July 7, 1921.
105. Ibid., no. 1196, 'Basutoland Council Minutes'. Session sat August 26 to September 16, 1922. Leloko Lerotholi's Speech, 13th Day, p.11.
106. Ibid., no. Confidential, July 25, 'Alleged Unrest in Basutoland', Resident Commissioner to High Commissioner, July 14, 1922.
107. Laydevant, *N. Griffith Lerotholi*, pp. 67–8.
108. PRO, CO 417/624 (1919), Telegram May 19, 'Visit of paramount Chief to Europe', High Commissioner to Secretary for Colonies, May 19.
109. PRO, CO 417/706 (1924), no. Confidential, October 10, 1924, 'Visit of High Commissioner to Basutoland' Address by J. Cenez, DD, OMI, RCM.
110. PRO, DO 25/4, *Basutoland Blue Book*, p. 107.
111. PRO, CO 417/683 (1922), no 53, January 19, 1922, 'Administration of Justice by Native Courts', Resident Commissioner, December 24, 1921, Memorandum.
112. Ibid., no. Confidentiazl, 'Administration of Justice by Native Courts', Resident Commissioner to High Commissioner, January 27, 1922.

113. Ibid.
114. Ibid., no. Confidential, April 20, Resident Commissioner to His Royal Highness, February 18, 1922.
115. PRO, CO 417/706 (1924), Confidential, October 10, 1924, Speech to Basutoland Progressive Assoiciation by the Earl of Athlone, High Commissioner for South Africa and Governor-General and Commander-in-Chief in and over the Union of South Africa, September 1924.
116. Ibid, High Commissioner to Secretary for Colonies, J. H. Thomas, October 6, 1924.
117. Ibid.
118. Ibid.
119. PRO, CO 417/683 (1922). no. 1196, 'Basutoland Council Minutes', Resident Commissioner to His Royal Highness, High Commissioner, October 30, 1922. For relevant speeches see Days 17th and 18th.
120. Ibid., Labane Chokobane's Speech, 18th Day, p. 1. Reverend Leshota's Speech, 14th Day. p. 7.
121. Ibid., Libopuoa Maama's Speech, 14th Day.
122. PRO, DO 35/1177, no. Confidential, Legal Adviser, Mr Feetman, November 28, 1922.
123. Sebastian Poulter, 'The Place of the Laws of Lerotholi in the Legal System of Lesotho', *African Affairs*, 1922, p. 154.
124. PRO, CO 417/683 (1922) No. 1120. The principal chiefs were listed as Griffith Lerotholi (*Morena e Moholo*), Makhaola, Api, Sekhonyana, Khoabane, Maama, Seeiso Letsie, Nkoebe, Mojela, Lepolesa, Mokhele (of the Bataung), Lelingoana (of the Batlokoa), Motŝoene, Joel (died in 1919), Matela, Masopha, Majara and Peete Lesaoana.
125. PRO, CO 417/696 (1923), 815, 'Native Courts Administration of Justice', Resident Commissioner to His Royal Highness, the High Commissioner, 13 July 1923. See report by *Naledi*, 22 June 1923, 'Paramount Chief's Court'.
126. Ibid., *Mochochonono* 27 June 1923.
127. PRO, DO 9/2, 'Basutoland National Council'. Met 31 August to 17 September 1925, p. 4.
128. PRO, DO 9/4, 'Individuals', Bloemfontein *The Friend*, 15 January 1926, 'Basutolander from Basutoland'.
129. PRO,DO 9/9, no. Secret, 'Future of High Commission Territories'. Copy of letter from Mr Amery to Mr Baldwin, October 4, enclosing Memorandum on the High Commission Territories.
130. Ibid.
131. Lesotho National Archives, S3/16A/5/2, Memorandum by Resident Commissioner, J. C, R. Sturrock, February 8, 1928.
132. Lesotho National Archives, S3/16A/1/1, Judicial Work of Resident Commissioner's Court. See Resident Commissioner to High Commissioner, July 7, 1928; but especially R. C. to H. C., February 2, 1929. Also John Tennent to Patrick Duncan, February 8, 1930.
133. Ibid. The office of Deputy Commissioner was established by Proclamation No. 24, 1916. The first appointment to the office was made on 3 July 1916.

134. Ibid., High Commissioner (Athlone) to Resident Commissioner, February 29, 1928. For Draft Proclamation establishing the office see High Commissioner to Resident Commissioner, April 28, 1928.
135. Ibid., Transport Problem. Appears in Schedule of Cases for Judicial Commissioner's Attention. Registrar, Resident Commissioner's Court to Patrick Duncan, Judicial Commissioner, August 17, 1928.
136. Ibid., Resident Commissioner to High Commissioner, May 28, 1928. Minute, apparently by Imperial Secretary.
137. Ibid., Duncan to B. E. H. Clifford, Imperial Secretary's Office, Pretoria, December 5, 1929.
138. Ibid., J. C. R. Sturrock to B. E. H. Clifford, April 2, 1930.
139. Ibid., Duncan to Clifford, December 5, 1929.
140. Surviving copies as published for reforms a second time, *New Native Court Regulations* (Morija Printing Works, 1935). Original Draft in PRO, DO 9/10, no. 353, High Commissioner to Resident Commissioner, December 8, 1927.
141. Ibid., DO 9/10, no. 353, Resident Commissioner to High Commissioner, June 1, 1928.
142. PRO, DO 9/13, no. 147, High Commissioner, February 28, 1929. Report by Interpreter D. Mochochoko.
143. A representative collection of these songs has been collected by Robert Edgar and is due to be published in his book on *Lekhotla la Bafo*.
144. PRO, CO 417/580 (1916), no. Confidential, R. T. Coryndon to High Commissioner, May 18, 1916. There were then 153 adult Indians in the Territory.
145. Lesotho National Archives, S3/22/2/1, Lefela's article on Indians, in *Naledi*, 25 November 1921.
146. With a Junior Secondary School Certificate (JC), Maphutšeng Lefela was the most educated member of the Association. He supplied researched information and generated a lot of correspondence and published editorials. See Edgar, *Prophets with Honour*, p. 7.
147. LNA, S3/22/2/4, *Lekhotla la Bafo* Presidential Address, Maseru, October 1929.
148. LNA, Proceedings of the National Council, October 16–19, pp. 35–95, and October 23, p. 98.
149. LNA S3/22/2/4, Presidential Address Thaba Bosiu, March 12, 1930.
150. Internal quotation is cited from the *Journal of the International Institute of African Languages and Culture*, vol. vii, no. 3.
151. Sir Alan Pim, *Financial and Economic Position of Basutoland*, Cmd. 407 (London: H.M.S.O., 1935).
152. LNA S3/22/2/1, BPA Interview with Sir Alan Pim.
153. PRO, DO 92/5, 'Basutoland Proceedings of 32nd Session, 1937', p. 9, Chief Leloko Lerotholi's Speech, pp. 12–13.
154. Ibid., pp. 17–18.
155. Ibid., Chief Lengolo Monyake's Speech, p. 4.
156. Proclamation No. 61. Basutoland Native Administration Proclamation, 1938, *Basutoland Proclamations and Notices. 1938*, p. 175, National University of Lesotho.

157. LNA S3/16A/5/2. Attachment to Resident Commissioner's Draft Regulations, 1928. (For purpose of the exercise, the Chief of Ha Marakabei, whose jurisdiction also fell within the District, was not included.) For Mokhotlong see Hugh Ashton, *The Basuto*, (London, 1952) p. 211.
158. Proclamation No. 62, Basutoland Native Courts Proclamations, 1938. *Basutoland Proclamations and Notices. 1938.*
159. See also Sebastian Poulter, *Family Law and Litigation in Basotho Society* (Oxford, 1976) p. 5.
160. Richard Frederick Weisfelder, 'Defining National Purpose: The Roots of Factionalism in Lesotho', (Ph.D. thesis, Department of Government, Harvard University, 1974) p. 160.

CHAPTER 5

1. F. Laydevant, *Morena N. Griffith Lerotholi 1874–1939*. (Basutoland, Mazenod , 1953) p. 49–53.
2. This fact surfaced before the Royal Court at Matsieng. it was cited by the President of the Royal Court, Chief Makhaola, who recalled that as late as in 1917 he had verified its correctness. See PRO, DO 9/5 (1926), no. 17, 'Paramount Chief's successor. Trs. Copy of correspondence with RC regarding Paramount Chief's nomination of his son, Bereng, as his Successor. Protest of another Son, Seeiso, against nomination', Chief Makhaolo's evidence, November 12, 1926.
3. Ibid., Chief Sekhonyana's announcement of the judgment, on the instruction of the President of the Royal Court, Chief Makhaola.
4. Ibid.
5. Ibid., Chief Makhaolo, President of the Royal Court at Matsieng, November 12, 1926.
6. Ibid.
7. Ibid., Statement by Seeiso Griffith before the Royal Court at Matsieng, September, 1926.
8. Ibid., Chief Makhaola, President of the Royal Court at Matsieng, November 12, 1926.
9. Ibid., Chief Sekhonyana's announcement of the judgment on the instruction of the President of the Royal Court, Chief Makhaola.
10. PRO, DO 9/7 (1927), no. 447, 'Succession to the Paramount Chieftainship', B. E. H. Clifford, Imperial Secretary, to J. C. R. Sturrock, September 1927.
11. Ibid.
12. PRO, DO 9/5 (1926), no. 17, Patrick Duncan to B. E. H. Clifford, Pretoria, December 20, 1926.
13. PRO, DO 9/7, no. 447, Clifford to Sturrock, September 12, 1927.
14. Ibid., Resident Commissioner to Paramount Chief, September 26, 1927.
15. Ibid.
16. Ibid., Griffith to Sturrock, October 7, 1927.

17. Ibid., Chief Jonathan to Assistant Commissioner, Leribe, November 17, 1927.
18. Ibid., 'Record of the Proceedings at an Interview Granted by His Excellency the High Commissioner to the Paramount Chief of Basutoland at Government House, Cape Town, on the 24th November, 1927'.
19. Ibid., Attachment to the Record of the Interview.
20. PRO, DO 35/1181/Y981/1 (1943). Facts adduced in the case of *Chief Bereng Griffith* v. *Mantšebo Seeiso*, pp. 34–41. Also my interviews of Chiefs 'Mako Moliboea and George Bereng, and Dr Mosebi Damane.
21. PRO, DO 92/11, 'Basutoland Proceedings of the National Council, 35th Session, 1940, Opening Day, Saturday, October 19, 1940'.
22. The claimants were Chief Motšoene, Chief Tau, and Chief Mathealira.
23. PRO, DO 35/1181/1 (1943), no. 5868, *Personal and Confidential* 'Appeal by Chief Bereng Against the Decision of the Paramount Chief', Harlech to Sir Eric Machting, March 29, 1943.
24. PRO, DO 35/1181/Y;981/1, *Bereng Griffith* v. *'Mantšebo Seeiso*, p. 39.
25. Ibid., p. 37.
26. Ibid., p. 41.
27. Ibid., p. 41–2. See also Harlech to Sir Eric Machting, March 27, 1943. *Personal and confidential* no. 5868.
28. PRO, DO 35/1181/Y981/1. Harlech to Machting, March 27, 1943.
29. The High Court Proclamation No. 57, 1938. It came into force January 1, 1939. *Laws of Basutoland*, p. 148.
30. PRO *Bereng Griffith* v. *'Mantšebo Seeiso*, pp. 47–9.
31. *High Commission Territories Law Reports*, p. 50, cited by Sebastian Poulter, in 'The Laws of Lerotholi', *African Affairs*, p. 155.
32. PRO, DO 35/1181/Y981/2. Extract from a personal letter from Lord Harlech to Sir Eric Machting, April, 1943.
33. 'Basutoland Proceedings of the National Council, November, 1943, 26th Day', p. 56. The National Library of Scotland.
34. Ibid., Goliath Malebanye's Speech, p. 57.
35. The National Library of Scotland, 'Basutoland Proceedings of the National Council, November, 1944, 9th Day', pp. 177–8.
36. Ibid., Chief Gabashane Masopha's Speech, p. 178.
37. Ibid., Chief Khosimotse Ntaote's Speech, p. 179.
38. PRO, DO 35/1177 (1943), Confidential, C. N. Arden-Clarke to Lord Harlech, December 1, 1943.
39. Ibid., Sir Walter Huggard, 'Notes on "Resolutions" Attached to (6) in 5192' enclosed in H. Lester Smith, High Commissioner's Office, to Lieutenant-Colonel C. N. Arden-Clarke, December 27, 1943.
40. Ibid., Confidential, Legal Adviser, Mr Feetman, November 28, 1922, cited by Sir Walter Huggard.
41. Ibid., cited by Sir Walter Huggard, December 9, 1943.
42. Ibid., Major E. R. Roper, December 22, 1943.
43. Ibid., C. N. Arden-Clarke to Priestman, High Commissioner's Office, January 13, 1944.

44. Ibid., W. C. Huggard to High Commissioner's Office, January 29, 1944.
45. PRO, DO 92/12 'Basutoland Proceedings of National Council, 38th Session, 1943'. See Report on the Standing Committee, 10th Day, November 3, 1943, pp. 161–3.
46. 'Basutoland Proceedings of the National Council, 39th Session, 1944', p. 179.
47. cited by Antony Allot, *New Essays in African Law* (London, 1970) p. 179.
48. Ibid.
49. Ibid., cited at p. 146.
50. John Mensah Sarbah, *Fanti Customary Laws: Brief Introduction to the Principles of the Native Laws and Customs of the Fanti and Akan Sections of the Gold Coast with a Selection of Cases Decided in the Law Courts*, (London 1897, 2nd edn, 1904).
51. I. Schapera, *A Handbook of Tswana Law and Custom*, 1938.
52. Stimela Jason Jingoes, A Chief is a Chief by the People (Oxford, 1975) p. 196.
53. Ibid., p. 185.
54. Ibid., p. 186. The information that the letter had been written by Josiel Lefela was provided by Mrs. J. Jingoes in a personal interview. Ha 'Mamathe, Teyateyaneng, September 8, 1985. Mrs. Jingoes was, in her own right, a member of the *Lekhotla la Bafo*.
55. Edwin Mofutsanyana, Personal interview, Nqechane, Leribe District, September 30, 1985.
56. Jingoes, *A Chief is a Chief by the People*, p. 186.
57. Ibid., p. 188.
58. PRO, DO 92/11, 'Basutoland Proceedings of the National Council, 34th Session, 1939', Speeches by Goliath Malebanye and Samuel Ntŝekhe (on behalf of Gabashane Masopha), pp. 149–51.
59. Ibid., The Resident Commissioner's Speech, p. 151.
60. Ibid., Chief Bolokoe Potsane's Speech, p. 152.
61. The National Library of Scotland, 'Basutoland Proceedings of the National Council, 1943', Under Heading: Proclamations Nos. 61 and 62 of 1938, Chief Harebatho Letsie, Item no. 6 on the Agenda, 'The People of Likhoele' (October 26, 1943) p. 55.
62. Ibid., The Resident Commissioner's Speech' p. 57.
63. Ibid., Councillor Labane Chokobane's Speech, p. 55.
64. PRO, DO 92/12, 'Basutoland Proceedings of the National Council, 37th Session, 1942', October 20, 1942, p. 4.
65. Ibid.
66. Ibid.
67. Ibid., Chief Thabatŝoeu Lebona's Speech, p. 6.
68. Ibid., Chief Leloko Lerotholi's Speech, p. 6.
69. Ibid., Chief Goliath Malebanye's Speech, p. 16.
70. PRO, CO 417/683 (1922), no. 1120, Under Draft: 'Basutoland Native Laws of Lerotholi (amended)', p. 7.
71. PRO, DO 35/1181/Y981/1 (1943), *Bereng Seeiso* v. *'Mantsebo Seeiso*.

See analysis of voters on the meetings of the Sons of Moshoeshoe held February 1941, pp 41–42.

72. PRO, DO 92/12, 'Basutoland Proceedings of the National Council, 37th Session, 1942, Chief Theko Makhaola's Speech, p. 13.
73. Ibid., The Point was specifically brought out in the National Council by Chief Khosimotse Ntaote. p. 11.
74. Ibid., Reverend Leonard Polisa's Speech, p. 16.
75. J. J. Machobane, Nqechane, Leribe, Personal Library, *Explanatory Memorandum: Basuto National Treasury* no. 1/47, ch. III, paras. 24–7.
76. Ibid., p. 8, 9, paras. 28–30.
77. Ibid., ch. VII, pp. 29–31. Also Appendix, p. 48.
78. Rubin Sefatsa Lesenyeho, Personal interview, Maseru, August 9, 1985.
79. G. I. Jones, *Basutoland Medicine Murder: A Report on the Recent Outbreak of 'diretlo' Murders in Basutoland*, (London: HMSO Cmd. no. 8209) p. 12.
80. Jones, *Basutoland Medicine Murder*, p. 14. Ashton, Hugh, *The Basuto*, pp. 305–310.
81. Jones, *Basutoland Medicine Murder*, p. 104.
82. *Explanatory Memorandum: Basuto National Treasury*, p. 31.
83. Jones, *Basutoland Medicine Murders*, p. 104.
84. PRO, DO 35/1172/Y701/1/5, Confidential 'Short Visit of Basutoland from November 23rd to 29th, 1943", Report dated December 29, 1943.
85. *Explanatory Memorandum: Basuto National Treasury*, p. 48.
86. PRO, DO 35/1172/Y701/1/5, 'Short Visit of Basutoland from November 23rd to 29th, 1943'.
87. Ibid.
88. 'Basutoland Proceedings of the National Council, 39th Session, 1944', High Commissioner's Speech, September 18, 1948, pp. 70–1. The National Library of Scotland.
89. Ibid.
90. PRO, DO 35/4025/Y2025/13, 'Notes by Sir E. Baring on the Political and Economic Position of the High Commission Territories', January, 1949.
91. 'Basutoland Proceedings of the National Council, 44th Session, 1948', p. 71. The National Library of Scotland.
92. B. M. Khaketla, *Lesotho 1970: An African Coup Under the Microscope*, (London, 1971) pp. 49–50.
93. PRO, DO 35/4025/Y2025/13, 'Appeals to the Privy Council Bereng Griffith and Other', Confidential, Privy Council Appeal no. 6 of 1949, 3rd proof. Having failed to persuade the authorities not to execute the Chiefs, at least pending G. I. Jones's Report, 'Mantšebo Seeiso and some 31 chiefs wrote a passionate letter to His Majesty 'the King of England' on September 5, protesting the way the case had been handled. Rhodes House, Mss. Afr. G1681, Box 219 (Africa Bureau Papers). Petition from 'Mantšebo Seeiso.
94. 'Seven Basutos Executed for Ritual Murders' in *The Scotsman*, 4 August 1949 The National Library of Scotland.

CHAPTER 6

1. PRO, DO 92/5 'Basutoland Proceedings of National Council, 32nd Session 1937, 'Motion by Councillor Peete Molapo, p. 1–2.
2. Ibid., Motion by Councillor Thabo Lechesa, p. 2.
3. Ibid., Councillor Thompson Mothea, Leribe, p. 6.
4. Ibid., Chief Tlhakanelo Moshoeshoe, p. 10–11.
5. Ibid., Chief Theko Makhaola, p.9.
6. PRO, DO 92/12, 'Basutoland Proceedings of the National Council, 37th Session, 1942', 'Chief Talimo Joel' p. 54. Chief Talimo was referring to a letter written on behalf of the National Council by *Morena e Moholo* Letsie II to Lord Selborne, 2 May 1910. Other chiefs who had signed the letter were Jonathan, Griffith, Makhaola, Sekhonyana, Theko, Maama, Sempe, Seeiso, Mojela, Motŝoane, Masopha, Joel, Leshoboro, and Peete. It was a request that in time the National Council should be 'elected by the Nation'.
7. Ibid., Chief Theko Makhaola, p. 43.
8. PRO, DO 92/12, 'Basutoland Proceedings of the National Council, 38th Session, 1943', Resident Commissioner's Speech, pp. 52, 55.
9. Ibid., Committee Report, p. 161–3.
10. Jingoes, *A Chief is a Chief by the People*, (Oxford, 175) pp. 187–95.
11. PRO, CO 417/545 (1914), 'Riot at Leper Settlement, May 20, 1914'. See also *Cape Times*, headline: 'Mutiny Amongst the Lepers', Thursday, 21 May 1914. There were, at the time, about 800 inmates at the Settlement.
12. PRO, DO 92/12, 'Basutoland Proceedings of the National Council, 38th Session, 1943', Chief Bolokoe Malebanye's Speech, p. 176.
13. Ibid., Chief Leloko Lerotholi's Speech, p. 175.
14. Proclamation No. 48 of 1948, A. C. Thompson, (ed.), *The Laws of Basutoland* (Cape Town, 1961).
15. As amended by Proclamation No. 39, 1950.
16. Proclamation No. 48 of 1948, Thompson, *Laws of Basutoland*. See also *Basutoland Council Report on Constitutional Reform and Chieftainship Affairs* (Maseru, Basutoland, 1958). Ibid., p. 43.
17. This paragraph is based on the *Basutoland Council Report on Constitutional Reform and Chieftaincy Affairs* (1958). Ibid., pp. 43–4.
18. 'Basutoland Proceedings of the National Council, 39th Session, 1944. Letter signed by Chiefs Leloko Lerotholi, Talimo Joel, Khosimotse Ntaote, Gabashane Masopha, Matlere Lerotholi, p. 232. The National Library of Scotland.
19. PRO, DO 92/12, 'Basutoland Proceedings of the National Council, 38th Session, 1943', Standing Committee Resolutions.
20. PRO, DO 35/1177/Y832/3, enclosure in no. Confidential, No. 2174, Arden-Clarke to Baring, May 13, 1944.
21. Ibid., The High Commissioner, Lord Harlech, June 1, 1944. See also G. M. Hector Papers, Box 6/6, p. 36, Rhodes House, Oxford. (This letter as cited in the *Basutoland Council Report on Constitutional*

Reform (1958), p. 45, has been inadvertently misdated January 1, 1944)

22. PRO, DO 35/1177/Y832/3, 'Mantŝebo to Clarke, May 10, 1944.
23. 'Basutoland Proceedings of the National Council, 44th Session, 1948', p. 120. National Library of Scotland.
24. Proclamation 9 of 1950, S. 3.
25. 'Basutoland Proceedings of the National Council, 49th Session, 1953', Chief Kelebone Nkoebe's Speech, p. 53. National Library of Scotland.
26. 'Basutoland Proceedings of the National Council, 44th Session, 1944', pt. xi, Miscellaneous: Motion No. 2, Councillor MacDonald Phasumane, p. 117. National Library of Scotland.
27. Ibid., Chief Leloko Lerotholi and the President, p. 117.
28. This pamphlet, possibly by W. F. Mackenzie, who later became the Resident Commissioner for Swaziland in 1953, has so far eluded my search.
29. 44th Session of the National Council, 1948, Chief Leloko Lerotholi, p. 117–18.
30. Ibid., p. 118.
31. Ibid., p. 119.
32. Ibid., The President's Speech, p. 120–6.
33. Ibid., Councillor MacDonald Phasumane, p. 127.
34. Ibid., Chief Goliath Malebanye, p. 126.
35. G. M. Hector Papers, Box 6/6. 'Mantŝebo Seeiso to Forsyth Thompson, January 8, 1951. Letter No. 24/8(S.328/1), p. 15–16. Rhodes House.
36. Ibid., Forsyth Thompson. See notes on Meeting with the Regent and the Sons of Moshoeshoe, February 1951.
37. Minutes of the Proceedings of the National Council, 49th Session, 1953. Motion 34 from Mokhotlong, presented by Councillor Joshua Khali, p. 250–1. National Library of Scotland.
38. This paragraph is based on Khaketla, *Lesotho 1970*, p. 34–41.
39. 'Basutoland African Congress Manifesto', October 7, 1952. Signed by N. M. Ntŝekhe, National Secretary, and N. C. Mokhehle, National President, Basutoland African Congress. Rhodes House, Mss. Afr. G1681, Box 219 (Africa Bureau Papers).
40. *Mohlabani*, vol. 1, no. 1 (September, 1954) p. 1–2.
41. Khaketla, *Lesotho 1970*, p. 41.
42. The Editor Speaks, *Mohlabani*, vol. 3, no. 6. (June, 1957) p. 4, cited by Richard Frederick Weisfelder, 'Defining National Purpose: The Roots of Factionalism in Lesotho' (Ph.D. thesis, Harvard University, Cambridge, Massachussetts, 1974) p. 186.
43. Ibid.
44. 'Basutoland Proceedings of the National Council, 49th Session, 1954', Councillor N. M. Tlale, pp. 454–6. National Library of Scotland.
45. Lesotho National Archives, *The Moore-Report of the Administrative Reforms Committee, 1954*, Terms of Reference included in the Introduction, p. 1.
46. G. M. Hector Papers. Box 2/4. Basutoland African Congress Memor-

andum to Lord Swinton, Secretary for Commonwealth Relations, June 20, 1954. Rhodes House.

47. Weisfelder, 'Defining National Purpose', p. 184.
48. The Editor Speaks, *Mohlabani*, vol. 3. no. 6 (June, 1957), p. 5. Cited by Weisfelder, 'Defining National Purpose,' p. 185.
49. *Basutoland Report on Constitutional Reform and Chieftainship Affairs* (Maseru, Basutoland, 1958) p. 9.
50. Prime Minister's Office, Maseru, Lesotho, *Basutoland Constitutional Discussions*, November-December, 1958, Minutes of Plenary Meetings (Printed for the Use of the Commonwealth Relations Office, 1959) p. 19.
51. Ibid., pp. 21–2.
52. Sir Kenneth Roberts-Wray, *Commonwealth and Colonial Law* (London, 1966) p. 45.
53. *Basutoland Report on Constitutional Discussion*, Cmd. 636, (London: HMSO, 1959).
54. D. V. Cowen, *The Foundations of Freedom* (Oxford, 1961). See also, resulting directly from his experiences as Lesotho's Constitutional Adviser, D. V. Cowen, 'Some Problems of Constitution-Making in Contemporary Africa' (University of Natal, 1962) and 'Human Rights in Contemporary Africa', *Natural Law Forum*, vol. 9, 1964, pp. 1–24.
55. *Report on Constitutional Reform and Chieftainship Affairs* (1958), p. 82.
56. Ibid., pp. 82–3.
57. Ibid., p. 151.
58. Ibid., p. 76.
59. Ibid., p. 51.

CHAPTER 7

1. The story of Prince Bereng's youth is based on interviews with Monnabatho Bereng, August 10, 1983; 'Mako Moliboea, October 10, 1979; 'Mampoi (Makhaola) Seeiso (the King's eldest sister), December 30, 1988.
2. Interview with *Mufumahali* 'Mampoi (Makhaola) Seeiso, 30 December, 1988
3. 'Bound Photocopy of Correspondence on Prince Bereng's Education, 1942–1948', Private Collection, Dr Mosebi Damane. For query on Makoro's qualifications see Resident Commissioner to *Morena e Moholo*, October 12, 1942. He was described as 'a teacher who was not well qualified'. For query on Eli Mohapi see Resident Commissioner to *Morena e Moholo*, April 28, 1944, based on 'A Confidential Report on Masaleng Private (Chief Matlere's house) School, by E. B. Ramaqabe, Supervisor of Schools, March 17, 1943. The Report indicated: 'Qualification of the teacher. E.V.1: has failed E.V.2'.
4. Ibid., Resident Commissioner Telex to Paramount Chief, August 17, 1944.

5. Ibid., Francis J. Lekoatsa School Report, March 25, 1943.
6. Ibid., Report for Quarter Ending September 1946.
7. Ibid., Report for Quarter Ending September 1945.
8. Ibid., Resident Commissioner to Paramount Chief, January 7, 1948.
9. The Chiefs were Bereng Griffith, Theko Makhaoala, Letsie Mots'o-ene, Gabashane Masupha, Lerotholi Mojela, Qefate Sempe, Joel Moholobela, Seeiso Maama, Jacottet Theko, Majara Theko, Leloko Lerotholi, Thabo Lerotholi, Molapo Maama, and Bofihla Seeiso. Ibid., 'Notes of a Meeting in the Office of the Resident Commissioner on Friday 23, 1948'.
10. Ibid. The statement was sponsored by Chief Leloko Lerotholi.
11. Ibid., 'Mabereng Seeiso to 'Mants'ebo Seeiso, January 27, 1948.
12. Ibid., Jacob N. Lebopo to District Commissioner, Maseru, n.d. (*c.* February 11, 1948). Resident Commissioner to Paramount Chief, February 14, 1948.
13. Ibid., Paramount Chief to Resident Commissioner, February 10, 1948.
14. Ibid., Paramount Chief to Director, Roma College, February 12, 1948. Also Paramount Chief to Francis Lekoatsa, February 31, 1948.
15. Ibid., 'Mabereng Seeiso to District Commissioner, Maseru, February 11, 1948.
16. Ibid., Resident Commissioner to Paramount Chief, February 14, 1948.
17. The details of this drama have been pieced together over the years from interviews with the following: Mr Herbert Taka, Maseru, December 4, 1975; Chief Letsie K. Theko, Lower Thamae Maseru, August 22, 1977; Gordon M. Hector, Edinburgh, November 25, 1985.
18. The argument in favour of the installation had actually been won within the first one hour of the meeting; but the Chairman decided to prolong the meeting until all potential opposition was heard.
19. Hector, Edinburgh, November 25, 1985.
20. Ibid.
21. Gordon M. Hector, MSS. Brit. Emp. S. 381, Box 2 3/3.
22. Ibid.
23. Ibid.
24. Bernard Leeman, *Lesotho and the Struggle for Azania*, vols. I and II (University of Azania, 1985) p. 86.
25. Ibid.
26. Richard Weisfelder, 'The Basotho Monarchy', ed. René Lemarchand, *African Kingdoms in Perspective* (Plymouth, USA 1977) p. 176
27. *Legislative Council Debates*, vol. A, week 11–15th September, 1961, Address by His Highness Moshoeshoe II.
28. B. M. Khaketla, *Lesotho 1979: An African Coup Under the Microscope* (Berkeley and Los Angeles, 1972) p. 4.
29. Ibid.
30. *Basutoland Constitutional Commission, Verbatim Record of Evidence Heard*, vol. 1, p. 168–9, Chief M. K. Sekonyela's Speech.
31. Ibid.
32. Ibid., p. 170, A. Sekonyela's Speech.
33. Honourable B. M. Khaketla, telephone conversation, Maseru, January 7, 1989.

34. *Basutoland Constitutional Commission*, vol. 1, pp. 176–7, M. Sebehela's Speech.
35. Ibid., p. 168, J. Nkalai's Speech.
36. Cited by Khaketla, *Lesotho 1979*, pp. 55–6.
37. *Verbatim Record of the 49th Session of Twenty-Four*, May 14 1962, A/Ac. 109/PV49, cited by Khaketla, *Lesotho 1970*, pp. 56–9.
38. Quotation in D. V. Cowen, *Natural Law Forum*, 9 (1964) pp. 5–6, cited by L. B. B. J. Machobane, 'Perceptions on the Constitutional Future for the Kingdom of Lesotho,' *The Journal of Commonwealth and Comparative Politics*, v xxvi no. 2 (July 1988) p. 186.
39. See for example Khaketla, *Lesotho 1970*, p. 51; Halpern, *South African Hostages*, p. 139.
40. Weisfelder, 'The Basotho Monarchy', p. 177.
41. *The Friend*, 11 June 1965. On Jonathan's relations with South Africa generally see L. B. B. J. Machobane, 'Perceptions on the Constitutional Future for the Kingdom of Lesotho', pp. 187, 200. Khaketla, *Lesotho 1970*, p. 30. Leeman, *Lesotho and the Struggle for Azania*, p. 125.
42. See *inter alia* the *Basutoland Constitutional Commission* 1962.
43. See Khaketla, *Lesotho 1970*, p. 18.
44. For a convincing evidence of this see Khaketla, *Lesotho 1970*, p. 18.
45. *The Friend*, 6 January 1959, cited by Khaketla, *Lesotho 1970*, p. 18.
46. *The Friend*, 6 January 1959, cited by Khaketla, *Lesotho 1970*, p. 18.
47. *The Friend*, 28 January 1966.
48. S. S. Matete, 'Why Did I Resign Counsellorship?', *Mohlabani*, vol. 2, no. 2 (March 1956) p. 16.
49. *The Friend*, 28 January 1966.
50. This account is based on B. M. Khaketla in *Mohlabani*, September 24, 1966, pp. 3–7. In a more recent conversation with him, Honourable B. M. Khaketla has added a few more credible points to it. Conversation of 9 January 1988.
51. Ibid., p. 3
52. Ibid.
53. Weisfelder, 'Defining National Purpose in Lesotho', International Studies Series No. 3 (Athens, Ohio, 1969) p. 26, cited by Leeman, *Lesotho and the Struggle for Azania*, vols. i and ii (1988) p. 114.
54. Conversation with Honourable B. M. Khaketla, 9 January 1989.
55. Ibid.
56. Cowen, 'Human Rights in Contemporary Africa, *Natural Law Forum, (3 November, 1963)*, p. 5.
57. Ibid.
58. Ibid., Reference to *Report of the Basutoland Constitutional Commission* (Maseru, 1963) p. 56.
59. Elias T. Olawale, *Government and Politics in Africa* (London, 1961) p. 20.
60. Cowen, 'Human Rights in Contemporary Africa', pp. 5–6. The way this article has been prepared makes its value as a source equatable with memoire, and I have tended to use it as such.
61. Ibid., pp. 7–8, Ntsu Mokhele. Denis Cowen's quotations do not carry

the names of those he quotes, and of course this suited the purpose of his publications. I have had to establish the names through both textual analysis as well as interviews with the surviving members of the Constitutional Commission.

62. Ibid., pp. 7–8, Ntsu Mokhehle.
63. Ibid., pp. 9–10, Ntsu Mokhehle.
64. Ibid., p. 11, B. M. Khaketla.
65. Ibid., p. 24, Ntsu Mokhehle.
66. *Legislative Council Debates*, Second meeting – Third Session of the Legislative Council, week, 24–31 January 1964, p. 783, Chief S. H. Mapheleba's Speech.
67. Ibid., p. 783, B. M. Khaketla's Speech.
68. Ibid., p. 760, B. M. Khaketla's Speech.
69. Ibid., pp. 840–1, Chief M. Bereng.
70. Ibid., p. 857, Ntsu Mokhehle's Speech.
71. Ibid., p. 859, Ntsu Mokhehle's Speech.
72. *Legislative Council Debates*, vol. ii, week 22–29 November 1963, p. 81, cited by Justice T. Mokotso.
73. *Legislative Council Debates*, Second Meeting – Third Session of the Legislative Council, week 3–11 February, 1964, p. 961.
74. Khaketla, *Lesotho 1970*, p. 10.
75. Ibid., pp. 10–11.
76. See *Lesotho Times*, vol. iii, no. 18, Friday, 7 May 1965.
77. The ten were: (1) Chief Goliath L. S. Moshoeshoe, (2) Chief Enoch Moliboea, (3) Mr S. M. Kolisang, (4) Dr S. P. Makotoko, (5) Mr C. D. Molapo, (6) Chief E. D. Letete, (9) Mr C. T. Chakela, and (10) Mrs E. M. Molapo. See *Lesotho Times*, vol. iii, no. 19, Friday, 14 May 1965.
78. *The Friend*, 11 June 1985.
79. For the 1965 General Elections see *Lesotho and the Struggle For Azania* (1985) pp. 122–6.
80. *Lesotho Times*, vol. iii, no. 18, 7 May 1965.
81. *Parliamentary Debates Hansard*, National Assembly Official Report, Fourth Meeting, First Session, 18 April 1966–11 May 1966, p. 7.
82. Ibid., p. 20.
83. Ibid., p. 23.
84. Ibid., p. 26.
85. *The Lesotho Independence Order 1966*, Supplement to Gazette No. 4, S. 76 (4) (5), p. 56.
86. B. C. P. Cairo, (1967), p. 27, cited by Leeman, *Lesotho and the Struggle for Azania* (1985), p. 129. For the full text of the statement see Khaketla, *Lesotho 1970*, pp. 100–103.86.
87. *Mohlabani*, vol. ii, no. 16, 4 September 1966.
88. Ibid.
89. Ibid.

Bibliography

(A) Articles

Burman, Sandra, 'How the Roman-Dutch Law Became the Common Law of Lesotho', *Lesotho Law Journal: A Journal of Law and Development* (1985) (Faculty of Law, National University of Lesotho)

Cowen, D. V., 'Human Rights in Contemporary Africa', *Natural Law Forum*, vol. 9 (1964).

Cowen, D. V., 'Some Problems of Constitution-Making in Contemporary Africa' (1962) (University of Natal).

Edgar, Robert, 'Lesotho and the First World War: Recruiting, Resistance and the South African Native Labour Contingent', *Mohlomi: Journal of Southern African Historical Studies*, combined vols iii/iv/v, 1979–81 (1981) (National University of Lesotho).

Hargreaves, John D., 'Toward the Transfer of Power in British West Africa', in Prosser Gifford and Wm. Roger Louis (eds), *The Transfer of Power in Africa: Decolonization, 1940–1960* (London 1982).

Laydevant, F., 'Le Sceptre Des Chefs Basuto', *Africa: Journal of the International African Institute*, vol. 18 (1948) no. 1.

Legassick, M., 'The Sotho-Tswana Peoples Before 1800', in Thompson, Leonard (eds), *African Societies in Southern Africa* (London 1969).

Lye, W. F., 'The Distribution of the Sotho Peoples after the Difaqane', in Thompson, Leonard (eds), *African Societies in Southern Africa* (London 1969).

Macartney, W. J. A., 'African Westminster? The Parliament of Lesotho', *Parliamentary Affairs*, vol. xxii (1970) no. 2 (Hansard Society for Parliamentary Government).

Machobane, L. B. B. J., 'Mohlomi: Doctor, Traveller and Sage', *Mohlomi: Journal of Southern African Historical Historical Studies*, vol. ii (1976) National University of Lesotho.

Machobane, L. B. B. J., 'Perceptions on the Constitutional Future of the Kingdom of Lesotho', *The Journal of Commonwealth and Comparative Politics*, vol. xxvi no. (1988) 2 (London).

Machobane, L. B. B. J., 'The Political Dilemma of the Chieftaincy in Lesotho, with Reference to the Administrative and Courts Reforms of 1938', Occasional Paper No. 1 (Institute of Southern African Studies, National University of Lesotho, 1985).

Machobane, L. B. B. J., 'Succession to Chieftainship in Lesotho: Management and Exploitation by the Colonial Government', Seminar Paper, (Centre of African Studies, University of Edinburgh 1985).

Madden, A. F., ' "Not For Export": The British Model of Government and British Colonial Practice', *The Journal of Imperial and Commonwealth History*, vol. viii (1979) no. 1).

Martin, Robert, 'Legislatures and Economic Development in Commonwealth Africa', *Public Law* (1977).

Mohapeloa, J. M., 'Indirect Rule and Progress Towards Self Rule and Independence: The Case of Lesotho', presented at the International Conference on Southern African History, National University of Lesotho, August 1977.

Motlamelle, Stephen, 'Considerations on the Constitutional Problems of Basutoland', *Voices of Africa* (1907).

Pearce, R. D., 'Governors, Nationalists, and Constitutions in Nigeria, 1935–51, *The Journal of Imperial and Commonwealth History*, vol. IX (1981) no. 3.

Poulter, Sebastian, 'The Place of the Laws of Lerotholi in the Legal System of Lesotho', *African Affairs* (1972).

Webber, P. E., 'The Church in Basutoland, 1833–84' (MA thesis, University of Southampton, 1966–7).

Vansina, J., 'Bantu in the Crystal Ball', *History in Africa*, VI (1979) and VII (1980).

Vansina, J., 'Western Bantu Expansion', *Journal of African History*, XXV (1984) 2.

(B) Theses

Benyon, John Allen, 'Basutoland and the High Commission, with Particular Reference to the Years 1868–1884: The Changing Nature of the Imperial Government's "Special Responsibility" for the Territory' (Ph.D thesis, University of Oxford, 1968).

Cassidy, R. M., 'Britain and Basutoland: A Study of Men and Policies from the Gun War to the Anglo-Boer War,' (Ph.D dissertation, University of California, Los Angeles, 1967).

Frank, Lawrence Peter, 'Khama and Jonathan: A Study of Authority and Leadership in Southern Africa' (Ph.D thesis, Columbia University, US, 1974).

Kimble, Judy, 'Towards an Understanding of the Political Economy of Lesotho: The Origins of Commodity Production and Migrant Labour, 1830-c.1885' (MA thesis, National University of Lesotho, 1978).

Mohapeloa, J. M., 'Tentative British Imperialism in Lesotho, 1884–1910: A Study in Basotho – Colonial Office Interaction and South Africa's Influence on It' (M.Phil. thesis, Sussex, 1982).

Weisfelder, Richard Frederick, 'Defining National Purpose: The Roots of Factionalism in Lesotho' (Ph.D thesis, Harvard University, Cambridge, Massachussetts, 1974).

(C) Books

Allot, Antony, *New Essays in African Law* (London, 1970).

Arbousset, T., *Narrative of an Exploratory Tour to the North-East of the Colony of the Cape of Good Hope* (Cape Town, 1846).

Ashton, Hugh, *The Basuto* (London, 1952).

Bennion, F. A. R., *The Constitutional Law of Ghana* (London, 1962).

Burman, Sandra, *Chiefdom Politics and Alien Law* (London, 1984).

Casalis, Eugene, *The Basutos, or Twenty Three Years in South Africa* (London, 1861).

Cowen, D. V., *The Foundations of Freedom* (Oxford, 1961).

Dale, Sir William, *The Modern Commonwealth* (London, 1983).

Doke, C. M., *The Southern Bantu Languages* (London, 1967).

De Smith, S. A., *The New Commonwealth and Its Constitutions* (London 1964).

Dicey, A. V., *An Introduction to the Study of the Constitution*, 10th edn, (London, 1959).

Duncan, Patrick, *Sotho Law and Customs* (Cape Town, 1960).

Edgar, Robert, *Prophets with Honour* (Johannesburg, 1988).

Elias, T. Olawale, *Ghana and Sierra Leone: The Development of their Laws and Constitutions* (London, 1962).

Elias, T. Olawale, *Government and Politics in Africa* (London, 1961).

Elias, T. Olawale, *Nigeria: The Development of its Laws and Constitution* (London, 1967).

Ellenberger, V., *A Century of Mission Work in Basutoland, 1833–1933* (Morija: Sesuto Book Depot, 1938).

Ellenberger, D. F., and J. C. MacGregor, *History of the Basuto, Ancient and Modern* (London, 1912).

Ghai, Y. P., and J. P. W. B. Mcauslan, *Public Law and Political Change in Kenya: A Study of the Legal Framework of Government from Colonial Times to the Present* (London, 1970).

Hailey, Lord W., *An African Survey*, revised 1956 (London, 1957).

Hailey, Lord, *The Republic of South Africa and the High Commission Territories* (London, 1963).

Hall, William Edward, *A Treaties on the Foreign Powers and Jurisdiction of the British Crown* (Oxford, 1894).

Halpern, Jack, *South Africa's Hostages* (Baltimore, 1965).

Hamnet, Ian, *Chieftainship and Legitimacy: An Anthropological Study of Executive Law in Lesotho* (London, 1975).

Harris, C. L., *The Laws and Customs of the Bapedi and Cognate Tribes including Native Administrative Act No. 38 of 1927* (Johannesburg, 1928).

Hartland, E. Sidney, *Primitive Law* (London, 1924).

Hector, G. M., *Some Speeches and Addresses by G. M. Hector* (Morija, Lesotho, n. d.).

Heurgon, Jacques, *The Rise of Rome to 264 B.C.*, c. tr. James Willis, (London, 1st Eng. edn, 1973).

Jingoes, Stimela Jason, *A Chief is a Chief by the People* (Oxford, 1975).

Johnson, Nevil, *In Search of the Constitution: Reflections on State and Society in Britain* (Oxford, 1977).

Kanyeihamba, G. W., *Constitutional Law and Government in Uganda* (Kampala, 1975).

Keir, C. J., and F. J. Lawson, *Cases in Constitutional Law* (Oxford, 1954).

Keith, Berridale (ed.) *Constitutional Law*, Seventh Edition of Ridge's Constitutional Law of England* (London, 1939).

Kennedy, W. P. M., and H. J. Schlosberg, *The Law of the South African Constitution* (London, 1935).

Khaketla, B. M., *Lesotho 1970: An African Coup Under the Microscope* (London, 1971).

Laydevant, F., *Morena N. Griffith Lerotholi 1871–1939* (Mazenod, Basutoland, 1953).

Luthango, N. S., *Umohlomi* (Pietermaritzburg, 1938).

McNair, Sir Arnold Duncan, *The Law of Treaties: British Practice and Opinions* (Oxford, 1938).

McNair, Sir Arnold Duncan, *Legal Effects of War* (Cambridge, England, 1948).

Maine, Sir Henry Sumner, *Ancient Law: Its Connection with the Early History of Society and Its Relation to Modern Ideas* (London, 1861, 10th edn, 1905).

Molema, S. A., *The Bantu: The Past and Present* (Cape Town, 1963).

Morris, H. F., and James S. Read, *Indirect Rule and the Search for Justice: Essays in East African Legal History* (London, 1972).

Morris, H. F., and James S. Read, *Uganda, The Development of its Laws and Constitution* (London, 1966).

Nwabueze, B. O., *Constitutionalism in the Emergent States* (London, 1973).

Omer-Cooper, J. D., *The Zulu Aftermath: A Nineteenth-Century Revolution in Bantu Africa* (Essex, England, 1966).

Orpen, J. M., *History of the Basutos of South Africa*, reprinted from the *Cape Argus* in 1857 (Mazenod, Lesotho, 1979).

Perham, Margery, *Colonial Sequence, 1930 to 1949* (London, 1967).

Poulter, Sebastian, *Family Law and Litigation* (Oxford, 1976).

Poulter, Sebastian, *Legal Dualism in Lesotho* (Marija, Lesotho, 1979).

Roberts-Wray, Sir Kenneth, *Commonwealth and Colonial Law* (London, 1966).

Roberts, Simon, *Order and Dispute* (Middlesex, England, 1979).

Sanders, Peter, *Moshoeshoe, Chief of the Sotho* (London, 1975).

Sarbah, John Mensah, *Fanti Customary Laws: Brief Introduction to the Principles of the Native Laws and Customs of the Fanti and Akan Sections of the Gold Coast with a Selection of Cases Decided in the Law Courts* (London, 1897, 2nd edn, 1904).

Schapera, I., *Government and Politics in Tribal Societies* (London, 1956, reprinted 1963).

Smith, Edwin W., *The Mabilles of Basutoland* (London, 1939).

Starke, J. G., *Introduction to International Law* (London, 1984).

Thompson, Leonard, *Survival in Two Worlds, Moshoeshoe to Lesotho, 1786–1870* (London, 1975).

Thompson, A. C., (ed), *The Laws of Basutoland*, revised edition (Cape Town, 1961).

Tylden, G., *The Rise of the Basuto* (Cape Town, 1950).

Wade, E. C. S., and A. W. Bradley, *Constitutional and Administrative Law*, 10th edn (London, 1986).

Wheare, Joan, *The Nigerian Legislative Council* (London, 1949).

Wight, Martin, *The Development of the Legislative Council 1606–1945* (London, 1945).

Wight, Martin, *The Gold Coast Legislative Council* (London, 1946).

Oral Evidence: Principal Sources

Bereng, George. Tapes. Interviewed at Maseru, 8 August 1985. 75 years old. Then Deputy Speaker of the House. Since President of the Senate, until January 1986 when the Government was overthrown. Veteran of World War II. Member of the National Council in 1954. Chairman of the Basutoland Council Constitutional Reforms Committee in 1958.

Bereng, Monnabatho. Notes and, mostly, correspondence. About 75 years old on 25 August, when last interviewed in Maseru. Regular correspondence was established with the Informant in 1980, which led to ten lengthy letters on Moshoeshoe's royal lineage, problems of succession, and the indigenous court system. Now retired, he began working with the indigenous court system after the establishment in 1946 of the National Treasury.

Damane, Mosebi. Notes. Interviewed at intervals since 1977. Last interviews held on 24 and 29 September 1985, at Maseru and Mafeteng, respectively. 68 years old. A historian with virtually unrivalled knowledge on oral traditions.

De Chazal, E. Charles. Notes. Interviewed in Edinburgh, 8 July 1986. Born 1918. Colonial Officer. He served in Tanganyika from 1940 to 1947. Resumed service in Lesotho in 1947 as District Commissioner. He became Financial Secretary and 'official' member of the Executive Council in 1963.

Fobo, Rock Fanana. Notes. Interviewed at Roma, 22 September 1985. 85 years old. A descendent of one of Moshoeshoe I's trusted warrior-counsellors. One of the early teachers of the Roman Catholic Schools. Expert informant on the political involvement of the Roman Catholic Church in the country's affairs since the 1950s.

Giles, Sir Alexander. Notes. Interviewed in Edinburgh on 8 July 1985. Born 1915. Colonial Officer. He served as District Officer in Tanganyika from 1946 to 1955, when he resumed the service in St Vincent (West Indies). He became Resident Commissioner in Lesotho from 1962 to 1966.

Hector, Gordon Matthew. Notes. Interviewed at intervals, at his home in Edinburgh, from October 1983 to 21 August 1986. Born 1918. Colonial Officer. He served as District Officer in Kenya until 1956, when he joined the service in Lesotho as Government Secretary. He supplied most of the research data on Lesotho's constitutional history to the Basutoland Council Constitutional Reforms Committee of 1958. Jointly with J. P. I. Hennessy, he was the Secretary of the Committee. He became the Leader of the House in the Legislative Council in 1960.

Hughes, Peter. Notes. Interviewed on 8 July 1986, in Edinburgh, and subsequently, 16 August, at Helensburgh (telephone conversation). Born 1912. Colonial Officer. He served in Swaziland from 1931 to 1934, when he joined the High Commission Staff in Cape Town as Private Secretary. He joined the service in Lesotho in 1936, serving as District Commissioner, until 1947, when he went to the Solomon Islands. He returned to Lesotho in 1955. In 1959 he became the first Commissioner of Local Government and 'official' member of the Legislative Council.

Jingoes, Mrs J. Tapes. Interviewed at Ha 'Mamathe, 8 September 1985.

About 65 years old. Wife of the late Stimela Jason Jingoes, author *A Chief is a Chief by the People*. She and her husband were members of *Lekhotla la Bafo*.

Jonathan, Leabua. Taped interview. Kolonyama, 24 August 1985. Then Prime Minister (until January 1986). 71 years old. Informant was involved in the judicial and constitutional developments of Lesotho since the 1940s.

Khaketla, Bennet Makalo. Notes. Interviewed at intervals since 1980. Last interviews on 28 January 1989. 75 years old. Novelist and politician. Editor and founder of the political paper *Mohlabani* (1954).

Kolisang, G. M. Notes. Interviewed at intervals since 1980. Last interviews held at Maseru on 30 August and 28 September 1985. Joined Lesotho politics in the 1950s. Former General Secretary of Basutoland Congress Party. He is a treasure chest of information on the party.

Leanya, Edwin. Notes. Interviewed at Kolo, Mafeteng, 7 July 1985. 70 years old. He is an ex-teacher and former Chairman of the Marema Tlou Freedom Party. His involvement in the politics of the country began in the 1950s.

Lesenyeho, Rubin Sefatsa. Tapes. Interviewed in Maseru on 9 August 1985. 71 years old. He was the second Treasurer of the Basutoland National Treasury and held the post until 1960 when the National Treasury was abolished.

Machobane, J. J. Tapes. Interviewed at intervals since 1975 until 6 July 1985, at Maseru. He is a historical novelist. Fellow of the Royal Anthropological Institute, and former employee of the Morija Sesuto Book Depot, from which he retired in 1944. Highly informed on the politics of Leribe District from the 1930s onward. Undertook an independent study into the causes of ritual murders in Lesotho in the late 1940s.

Appendix 1

Draft Constitution for Basutoland, 1883

'Proposed Terms for the Future Government of Basutoland'

I.   Basutoland as annexed to the Colony of the Cape of Good Hope by the Act No. 12, 1871, shall remain intact for the Basuto people. Basutoland, as described in the said Act, includes Quithing (sic).

II.   The Governor of the Cape of Good Hope will, from time to time, appoint a Resident Officer, to be styled the Governor's Agent, and such other officers as may be necessary for the administration of the affairs of Basutoland.

III.   The Governor's Agent, or any other person appointed by the Governor, shall have the sole cognizance of the following cases.

    1.   All civil cases wherein European, or persons not being Basutos, alone are parties.

    2.   All criminal cases wherein Europeans or persons not being Basutos are accused of the Commission of any crime or offence, except when the Governor shall order the trial of the offender before some competent Court in the Colony.

IV.   All civil cases wherein Europeans and Basutos are parties as plaintiffs or defendants shall be heard and determined by the Governor's Agent or by one of the other officers appointed by the Governor; advised or assisted by the principal chief of that part of Basutoland in which the Mosuto party shall reside, and by such other chief (,) headman or person as the Paramount Chief shall appoint for that purpose, if such principal Chief shall think fit to attend, or if the Paramount Chief shall think fit to appoint any person to attend, and any such Chiefs, Headmen, or others who shall attend, shall be at liberty to express their opinions upon the matters in dispute. The decision of the Court shall be the decision of the Governor's Agent or other officer presiding. The Paramount Chief engages for himself and on behalf of the tribe that the judgment in every case against any Mosuto shall be observed and satisfied in full, or to the extent that the dependent shall be possessed of property wherewith to satisfy the same.

V.   All cases of treason or sedition shall be tried before one of the Supreme Courts of the Colony.

VI.   All cases wherein any Mosuto shall be charged with murder or culpable homicide, or wherein any Mosuto shall be charged with the Commission of any crime against or in respect of any person not being a Mosuto, shall be tried before the Governor's Agent or one of the other officers appointed by the Governor, advised or assisted by two or more chiefs, nominated by the Paramount Chief, if they see fit to attend. The decision of the Court shall be the decision of the Governor's Agent or other officer presiding, but in

351

the case of murder or homicide, if the person killed shall not be a Mosuto, it shall be competent for the Governor to order the trial of the offender before a Superior Court of the Colony.

VII.   The Paramount Chief engages for himself and on behalf of the tribe that every possible effort will be made to prevent Basutos from committing thefts beyond the borders of Basutoland.

VIII.   The Paramont Chief promises, when thereto by the Governor's Agent, to cause to be arrested and handed over to justice any person within Basutoland against whom a warrant may be issued for the commission of any crime or offence for which such a person is liable to be tried.

IX.   When the spoor of any animal stolen beyond the boundaries of Basutoland is traced to any kraal or village within Basutoland, the Chief of that part of Basutoland, in which such kraal or village is situated, shall be responsible for delivery of the stolen animals or payment of the value thereof to the owner.

X.   A Council of Advice shall be constituted to consist of Chiefs and Headmen. The names of the Chiefs to be submitted by the Paramount Chief for consideration. The number of Headmen to be determined after the names of the Chiefs have been submitted and approved and when determined one-half of the number shall be nominated by the Paramount Chief and the other half by the Governor's Agent. Every Headman appointed to a seat in the Council shall hold office for three years, unless his seat shall become vacant by death or his removal from office by the joint act of the Governor's Agent and Paramount Chief.

XI.   A meeting of the Council shall be convened by the Governor's Agent at least once a year for the discussion of public business, and at every annual meeting an account shall be submitted showing the revenue and expenditure for the past financial year. The Paramount Chief promises to give notice to members of any meeting of Council whenever required to do so by the Governor's Agent.

XII.   It shall be competent, at any meeting of the Council duly convened at the request of the Governor's Agent, to adopt resolutions suggesting alterations in the laws of Basutoland. All such resolutions will be considered by the Governor of the Colony, and, if approved, the necessary proclamation will be issued for giving effect thereto.

XIII.   The revenue of Basutoland shall be expended exclusively for the government of the people.

XIV.   The term Mosuto or Basuto shall include persons of the other tribes, who not being Basutos are resident in Basutoland, and subject to the control of the Paramount Chief or any subordinate Chief.

XV.   Except in so far as may be necessary to amend the laws of Basutoland for the purpose of giving effect to the altered system of Government, such laws shall remain in force until repealed or amended.

XVI.   Except where otherwise provided, the Paramount Chief shall by himself and through his subordinate Chiefs have the management of the internal affairs of Basutoland. And the Paramount Chief promises that the laws of the country shall be observed, and nothing allowed to be done contrary to the principles of justice and humanity.

XVII. Appeals will be allowed from the decisions from the Chiefs in cases between Basutos, subject to conditions to be considered by the Council, and approved by the Governor.

XVIII. Hut-tax shall be paid for the purpose of defraying the expenses of the Government of Basutoland. Arrears at the present rate of one pound shall be paid up.

XIX.   The subjects of all persons in Basutoland shall be respected without distinction. No Mosuto shall be molested, dispossessed, or interfered with, merely on the ground that he took part on either side during the hostilities.

XX.   The Paramount Chief promises to inform the Governor's Agent promptly of all matters of importance which may transpire in the country, coming to his notice, and to report upon any matter upon which the Governor's Agent may require information.

British Parliamentary Papers, 1883, xlviii, (Cmnd. 3708) p. 122.

Appendix 2

[PROCLAMATION No. 7 of 1910]

PROCLAMATION BY HIS EXCELLENCY THE HIGH COMMISSIONER

Whereas in the year 1903 there was established in Basutoland under the authority of the High Commissioner a Council consisting of representatives of the inhabitants of the territory for the purpose of discussing the domestic affairs thereof:

And whereas the High Commissioner as from time to time issued instructions and regulations determining the constitution powers and procedure of the said Council:

And whereas it is expedient to revise such regulations and instructions and to embody the same in a Proclamation:

Now thereof under and by virtue of the powers in me vested I do hereby declare proclaim and make known as follows: —

1. There shall be in Basutoland a Council for the discussion of the domestic affairs of the territory to be styled the Basutoland Council consisting of a president and not more than one hundred members.

2. — (1) The Resident Commissioner or in his absence the officer performing the duties of Resident Commissioner shall be President of the Council.

(2) The Paramount Chief for the time being shall be a member of the Council.

(3) The Paramount Chief shall nominate to the Resident Commissioner not more than ninety-four persons belonging to the Basuto tribe and such persons shall if approved by the Resident Commissioner be appointed by him to be members of the Council.

(4) Such appointments shall include the principal persons exercising authority as chiefs of the Basuto tribe provided that such persons are not in the opinion of the Resident Commissioner for any reason unfitted for membership of the Council and shall further so far as practicable be representative of the different interests and opinons of the members of the tribe.

(5) The Resident Commissioner shall have power to appoint not more than five persons to be members of the Council.

3. — (1) Persons appointed under sub-sections (3) and (5) of the preceding section or under section four shall continue to be members of the Council until the thirty first day of December in the year in which they are appointed and shall after that day cease to be members but shall be eligible for reappointment.

(2) Appointments of members of the Council shall be made as soon as may be after the first day of January in each year.

(3) The President shall have power to suspend any member of the Council

for such period as he may determine and no member so suspended shall be permitted to attend any meeting of the Council during such period.

4. Where any casual vacancy occurs in the Council through the death or resignation of any member the Resident Commissioner may appoint a person to fill such vacancy provided that if such vacancy occurs among the members appointed by the Resident Commissioner on the nomination of the Paramount Chief the Resident Commissioner shall before appointing any person to fill such vacancy invite the Paramount Chief to nominate a person for such vacancy and if the Resident Commissioner approves such nomination he shall appoint the person so nominated.

5. It shall be lawful for the President to appoint an officer of the Government to be his deputy and to preside in his absence at sessions of the Council.

6. Sessions of the Council may be convened by the Resident Commissioner at such times and places as he may determine provided
   (a) that not less than one session shall be convened between the first day of January and the last day of December in each year;
   (b) that each session shall commence on being declared by the President to be open and continue until declared by him to be closed.

7. The Resident Commissioner shall in each year cause to be submitted to the Council an account showing under such heads as the Resident Commissioner may approve the amount of any revenue collected in and from Basutoland for the last preceding financial year and the manner in which such revenue has been expended.

8. It shall be lawful for the President to lay before the Council the draft of any proposed law affecting Basutoland and to invite the expression of the opinion of the Council upon such draft and any discussion or resolution of the Council thereon shall be recorded in the minutes of the Council's proceedings.

9. It shall be lawful for any member of the Council to discuss the provisions of any Proclamation of the High Commissioner affecting Basutoland and to suggest amendments to any such Proclamation and any dicussion or resolution of the Council on the subject of such Proclamation shall be recorded in the minutes of the Council's proceedings.

10. It shall not be lawful for the Council to discuss or to pass resolutions upon any matter which in the opinion of the President is not one of those domestic affairs of the territory for the purpose of discussing which the Council exists and any member of the Council who shall disregard the ruling of the President on this subject shall be liable to suspension under section three sub-section (3) of this Proclamation.

11. As soon as may be after the close of each session the Resident Commissioner shall forward to the High Commissioner the minutes of the Council's proceedings and any resolution passed by the Council with his report thereon.

12. The Resident Commissioner may from time to time make alter and revoke rules for regulating the proceedings of the Council and the payment of members and for fixing the quorum and preserving order at meetings of the Council provided that it shall be lawful for any member of the Council to discuss or suggest amendments in such rules and any discussion or resol-

ution of the Council on the subject of such rules shall be recorded in the minutes of the Council's proceedings.

13. It shall be lawful for the Resident Commissioner in consultation and co-operation with the Paramount Chief to bring before the Council or before such member of the Council as may be specially selected by him and the Paramount Chief and constituted for this purpose a committee of the Council any questions or disputes of a purely tribal character arising between natives and to invite the opinion of the Council or committee of the Council on such questions or disputes. It shall be the duty of the Resident Commissioner to communicate to the High Commissioner for his information the opinion of the Council or committee of the Council in reference to such questions or disputes.

14. All powers conferred by this Proclamation upon the Resident Commissioner shall be exercised by him subject to such instructions as he may from time to time receive from the High Commissioner.

15. This Proclamation may be cited for all purposes as The Basutoland Council Proclamation 1910 and shall have force and effect from the date of its publication in the Gazette.

GOD SAVE THE KING.

Given under my Hand and Seal at Johannesburg this Thirty-first day of March One thousand Nine hundred and Ten.

SELBORNE,

High Commissioner.

By Command of His Excellency the High Commissioner.

C. H. RODWELL,

Imperial Secretary

Basutoland Annual Report, 1911 III, (Cmnd. 5582).

Appendix 3

'Puso Ea Lesotho' by F. Seele
  Theang Lekhotla la Bafo
  Benghali puso ea Lesotho kea lekhotla la marena kea lumela, 'me ke tsoanelo. Ke se ke utloile hangata ba bang ba natse ba bua ka hore hoja le batho ba hlalefileng ba teng khotleng leo ke hona lekhotla le ne le tla tseba ho sebetsa litaba. Ba bang ba re esale le kena hang lea kena neng hape? 'Na ke re moo ho tsoa ho bona beng ba lona. *Khotla lena ke la marena ruri, ke bona ba le kopileng 'me ba ba ba le fuua 'me le tsoanetse ho kenoa ke bona feela le ho le tsamaisa. Haeba sechaba se rata hore se utloe tabeng tsa puso se tsoanetse ho kopa lekhotla le tla kenoa ke bana ho thoeng ke bahlalefi ba tla khethoa ke sechaba literekeng tsa Lesotha*, ba tla etsa liphutheho literekeng tseo ba li khethetsoeng ba amohele le mangolo a tsoang ho batho ba setereke sa hae ba hlahisang tseo ba ratang hore a tle a li hlahise lekhotleng la sechaba mohla le kopaneng, li tle li talingoe ke lekhotla la sechaba pele li ntano fetisetsoa khotleng la marena mohlang le kopaneng. Le bona le Engelane *moo re busoang ho na le lekhotla la marena le lekhotla la sechaba* a emeng ka ona mokhoa ona ke tsoang ho o bolela *e le hore le sechaba se be le puo tabeng ea puso* e tle e kholise sechaba e le hore taba e kang ea Russia e fele. *Sechaba se nahane tsa ho ntsetsa lefatse la sona pele.*
  Joale ke re na mohai kajeno o khutselitseng. Kopang lekhotla le joalo la sechaba hoba lekhotla le teng joale ke leo marena a ikopetseng lona. Taba tse kang tsena tsa mesebetsi e fuoang balichaba empa Basotho ba le teng ke tse tsoanetseng ho hlaisoa ke lekhotla la sechaba ha e le la marena ke batla ke sa bone hore na ho lona li ka hlaisoa ke mang ka ha e le marena feela bona ba sena pelaelo ena rona mafutsana re nang le eona. E ka khathatso kotleng leo (sic) ea motho a le mong ka hoba ha e hlahisoe ke lekhotla. Joale lona ba hlalefileng le sitoa keng ho etsa phutheho ea lona le bue ka tsa ho kopa lekhotla leo. Ha ho thuse letho ha le ntse le belaela empa pelaelo tsa lona li sa fihle tse beng tsa ba tsoanetseng ho le lokisetsa litaba. Joale ka ha le boletse hoba marena a lekhotla ke batho ba sa hlalefang le thusang ho bua 'Naleding' empa marena a sa tlo utlo. Kopang 'Musisi hore a le kopele ho Morena e Moholo le lekhotla la hae. Ha lekhotla la Morena e Moholo le lumela le tle le *laele* 'Musisi ho hlahisa taba tsa lona ho Leqosa le Phahameng la Morena Edward. Ho seng joalo re se ke ra 'na ra nyefola lekhotla la marena. Hoba taba tseo khotla la marena le tla li sebetsa ke life ha sechaba se sena lentsoe pusong ea lona.
  F. Seele. *Naledi.* Volume ɪᴠ, No. 85, Phuptjoane 4, 1907.
[The italic is mine and it coincides with my own translations in Chapter 5, reference 21.]

Index